THE ENCYCLOPAEDIA OF ISLAM
THREE

THE ENCYCLOPAEDIA OF ISLAM

THREE

Edited by

Kate Fleet, Gudrun Krämer, Denis Matringe,
John Nawas, and Everett Rowson

With

Roger ALLEN, Edith AMBROS, Thomas BAUER, Johann BÜSSOW,
Ruth DAVIS, Maribel FIERRO, Najam HAIDER, Konrad HIRSCHLER,
Nico KAPTEIN, Hani KHAFIPOUR, Alexander KNYSH, Corinne LEFÈVRE,
Scott LEVI, Roman LOIMEIER, Daniela MENEGHINI, M'hamed OUALDI,
D. Fairchild RUGGLES, Emilie SAVAGE-SMITH, Ayman SHIHADEH, and
Susan SPECTORSKY

BRILL

LEIDEN • BOSTON
2019

Library of Congress Cataloging-in-Publication Data

A C.I.P. record for this book is available from the Library of Congress.

EI3 is published under the patronage of the international union of academies.

ISSN: 1873-9830
ISBN: 978-90-04-38665-5

This book is printed on acid-free paper and produced in a sustainable manner.

LIST OF ABBREVIATIONS

A. PERIODICALS

AI = *Annales Islamologiques*
AIUON = *Annali dell' Istituto Universitario Orientale di Napoli*
AKM = *Abhandlungen für die Kunde des Morgenlandes*
AMEL = *Arabic and Middle Eastern Literatures*
AO = *Acta Orientalia*
AO Hung. = *Acta Orientalia (Academiae Scientiarum Hungaricae)*
ArO = *Archiv Orientální*
AS = *Asiatische Studien*
ASJ = *Arab Studies Journal*
ASP = *Arabic Sciences and Philosophy*
ASQ = *Arab Studies Quarterly*
BASOR = *Bulletin of the American Schools of Oriental Research*
BEA = *Bulletin des Études Arabes*
BEFEO = *Bulletin de l'Ecole Française d'Extrême-Orient*
BEO = *Bulletin d'Études Orientales de l'Institut Français de Damas*
BIE = *Bulletin de l'Institut d'Égypte*
BIFAO = *Bulletin de l'Institut Français d'Archéologie Orientale du Caire*
BKI = *Bijdragen tot de Taal-, Land- en Volkenkunde*
BMGS = *Byzantine and Modern Greek Studies*
BO = *Bibliotheca Orientalis*
BrisMES = *British Journal of Middle Eastern Studies*
BSOAS = *Bulletin of the School of Oriental and African Studies*
BZ = *Byzantinische Zeitschrift*
CAJ = *Central Asiatic Journal*
DOP = *Dumbarton Oaks Papers*
EW = *East and West*
IBLA = *Revue de l'Institut des Belles Lettres Arabes, Tunis*
IC = *Islamic Culture*
IHQ = *Indian Historical Quarterly*
IJAHS = *International Journal of African Historical Studies*
IJMES = *International Journal of Middle East Studies*

ILS = *Islamic Law and Society*
IOS = *Israel Oriental Studies*
IQ = *The Islamic Quarterly*
JA = *Journal Asiatique*
JAIS = *Journal of Arabic and Islamic Studies*
JAL = *Journal of Arabic Literature*
JAOS = *Journal of the American Oriental Society*
JARCE = *Journal of the American Research Center in Egypt*
JAS = *Journal of Asian Studies*
JESHO = *Journal of the Economic and Social History of the Orient*
JIS = *Journal of Islamic Studies*
JMBRAS = *Journal of the Malaysian Branch of the Royal Asiatic Society*
JNES = *Journal of Near Eastern Studies*
JOS = *Journal of Ottoman Studies*
JQR = *Jewish Quarterly Review*
JRAS = *Journal of the Royal Asiatic Society*
JSAI = *Jerusalem Studies in Arabic and Islam*
JSEAH = *Journal of Southeast Asian History*
JSS = *Journal of Semitic Studies*
MEA = *Middle Eastern Affairs*
MEJ = *Middle East Journal*
MEL = *Middle Eastern Literatures*
MES = *Middle East Studies*
MFOB = *Mélanges de la Faculté Orientale de l'Université St. Joseph de Beyrouth*
MIDEO = *Mélanges de l'Institut Dominicain d'Études Orientales du Caire*
MME = *Manuscripts of the Middle East*
MMIA = *Majallat al-Majmaʿ al-ʿIlmi al-ʿArabi, Damascus*
MO = *Le Monde Oriental*
MOG = *Mitteilungen zur Osmanischen Geschichte*
MSR = *Mamluk Studies Review*
MW = *The Muslim World*
OC = *Oriens Christianus*
OLZ = *Orientalistische Literaturzeitung*
OM = *Oriente Moderno*
QSA = *Quaderni di Studi Arabi*
REI = *Revue des Études Islamiques*
REJ = *Revue des Études Juives*
REMMM = *Revue des Mondes Musulmans et de la Méditerranée*
RHR = *Revue de l'Histoire des Religions*
RIMA = *Revue de l'Institut des Manuscrits Arabes*
RMM = *Revue du Monde Musulman*
RO = *Rocznik Orientalistyczny*
ROC = *Revue de l'Orient Chrétien*
RSO = *Rivista degli Studi Orientali*
SI = *Studia Islamica (France)*
SIk = *Studia Islamika (Indonesia)*
SIr = *Studia Iranica*

TBG = *Tijdschrift voor Indische Taal-, Land- en Volkenkunde* (of the Bataviaasch Genootschap van Kunsten en Wetenschappen)
VKI = *Verhandelingen van het Koninklijk Instituut voor Taal-, Land en Volkenkunde*
WI = *Die Welt des Islams*
WO = *Welt des Orients*
WZKM = *Wiener Zeitschrift für die Kunde des Morgenlandes*
ZAL = *Zeitschrift für Arabische Linguistik*
ZDMG = *Zeitschrift der Deutschen Morgenländischen Gesellschaft*
ZGAIW = *Zeitschrift für Geschichte der Arabisch-Islamischen Wissenschaften*
ZS = *Zeitschrift für Semitistik*

B. OTHER

ANRW = *Aufstieg und Niedergang der Römischen Welt*
BGA = *Bibliotheca Geographorum Arabicorum*
BNF = Bibliothèque nationale de France
CERMOC = Centre d'Études et de Recherches sur le Moyen-Orient Contemporain
CHAL = *Cambridge History of Arabic Literature*
CHE = *Cambridge History of Egypt*
CHIn = *Cambridge History of India*
CHIr = *Cambridge History of Iran*
Dozy = R. Dozy, *Supplément aux dictionnaires arabes*, Leiden 1881 (repr. Leiden and Paris 1927)
EAL = *Encyclopedia of Arabic Literature*
EI1 = *Encyclopaedia of Islam*, 1st ed., Leiden 1913–38
EI2 = *Encyclopaedia of Islam*, 2nd ed., Leiden 1954–2004
EI3 = *Encyclopaedia of Islam Three*, Leiden 2007–
EIr = *Encyclopaedia Iranica*
EJ1 = *Encyclopaedia Judaica*, 1st ed., Jerusalem [New York 1971–92]
EQ = *Encyclopaedia of the Qurʾān*
ERE = *Encyclopaedia of Religion and Ethics*
GAL = C. Brockelmann, *Geschichte der Arabischen Litteratur*, 2nd ed., Leiden 1943–49
GALS = C. Brockelmann, *Geschichte der Arabischen Litteratur, Supplementbände I–III*, Leiden 1937–42
GAP = *Grundriss der Arabischen Philologie*, Wiesbaden 1982–
GAS = F. Sezgin, *Geschichte des Arabischen Schrifttums*, Leiden 1967–
GMS = *Gibb Memorial Series*
GOW = F. Babinger, *Die Geschichtsschreiber der Osmanen und ihre Werke*, Leipzig 1927
HO = *Handbuch der Orientalistik*
IA = *İslâm Ansiklopedisi*
IFAO = Institut Français d'Archeologie Orientale
JE = *Jewish Encyclopaedia*
Lane = E. W. Lane, *Arabic-English Lexicon*
RCEA = *Répertoire Chronologique d'Épigraphie Arabe*
TAVO = *Tübinger Atlas des Vorderen Orients*
TDVIA = *Türkiye Diyanet Vakfi Islâm Ansiklopedisi*
UEAI = Union Européenne des Arabisants et Islamisants
van Ess, *TG* = J. van Ess, *Theologie und Gesellschaft*
WKAS = *Wörterbuch der Klassischen Arabischen Sprache*, Wiesbaden 1957–

A

ʿAbbāsid music

ʿAbbāsid music was that of the ʿAbbāsid dynastic period (132–656/750–1258). Little is known of ʿAbbāsid musical repertoire save for an *ʿūd* (lute) exercise by the philosopher al-Kindī (d. after 256/870), in which the notation is expressed in terms of fingers and frets, and transcriptions in the later ʿAbbāsid era by Ṣafī al-Dīn al-Urmawī (d. 693/1294) of songs and pieces in which durations and pitches are given [Illustration 1].

1. Notation

Musical notation in the early ʿAbbāsid era was apparently precise yet rarely used. We know of only two anecdotes touching the subject in the monumental *Kitāb al-aghānī* ("Book of songs") of al-Iṣfahānī (d. 360/971); Prince Ibrāhīm b. al-Mahdī (d. 224/839) asked Isḥāq al-Mawṣilī (d. 235/850) to send him the notation of a song the latter had recently composed; Isḥāq complied, and the notation apparently enabled Ibrāhīm to perform it as Isḥāq had composed it (10:105). We have sketchy details about the notation used, and was employed rarely, when the performer was far from the composer and thus unable to learn the song by ear. The notation included the rhythmic mode, the tonic, the course (melodic mode), melodic movement, and succession of notes, poetic feet, cadences and ends, durations and numbers of cycles. In addition to the type of notation mentioned above, al-Fārābī (d. 339/950) invented a precise syllabic notation for rhythm inspired by the fifth-century C.E. Byzantine treatise known now as the *Anonymous Bellermann* and complemented it with geometrical symbols [Illustration 2]. Three centuries later, Safī al-Dīn provided an easier and more precise rhythmic notation; essentially, he applied the prosodic circle notation to music, and interestingly, his circular system survived in Islamic music scholarship up to the early twentieth century [Illustration 3].

2. Sources

What ʿAbbāsid music lacked in notation, it more than made up for in extensive and reliable sources in music theory and literature. ʿAbbāsid music theory relied on the theories of practitioners, on models derived from Arabic and Persian letters

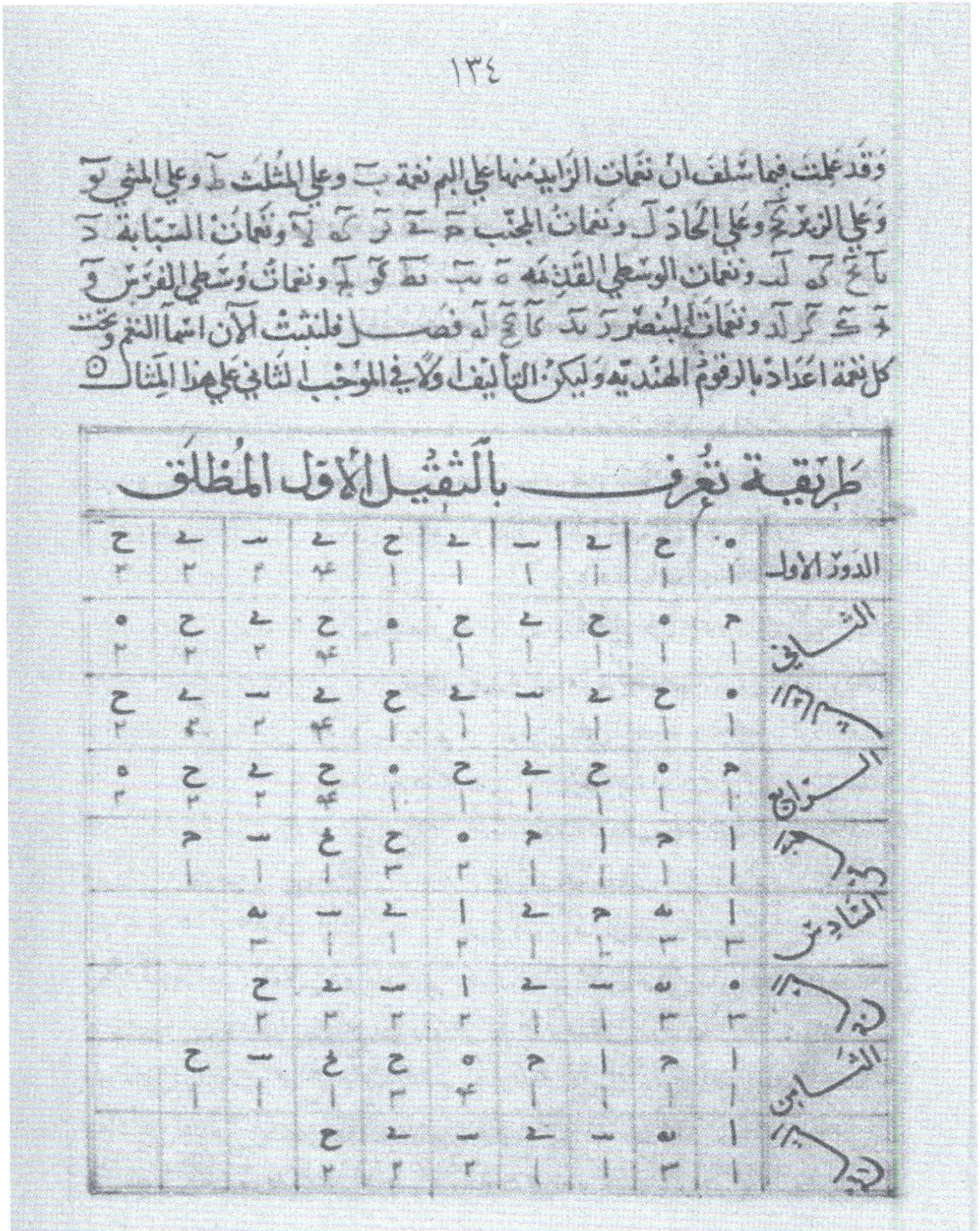
١٣٤

طريقة تعرف بالثقيل الأول المطلق

Illustration 1. A notation of a song from Ṣafī al-Dīn al-Urmawī, *al-Risāla al-Sharafiyya fī l-nisab al-taʾlīfiyya* ("Treatise dedicated to Sharaf al-Dīn on proportions in musical composition"). Istanbul, Topkapı Sarayı Müzesi, MS Ahmet III, 3460, fol. 67b.

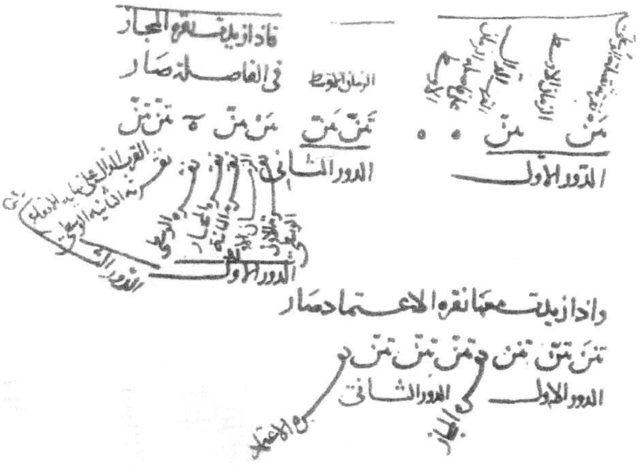

Illustration 2. Al-Fārābī's notation from *Kitāb Iḥṣāʾ al-īqāʿāt* ("Book on the basic comprehension of rhythms"). The notation exhibits syllabic and geometric symbols. Manisa Public Library, MS 1705, fol. 64a.

(grammar, phonology, prosody, poetics, rhetoric, and Qurʾānic sciences) and the methodology of Ancient Greek music theory, philosophy, and mathematics available in Arabic translations via Syriac. The first to fuse Greek and Arabic theory was al-Kindī; he was not a performing musician, so his work did not always reflect musical practice. Al-Fārābī, a performer as well as a logician, was more successful: his work dealt with intervals, consonance and dissonance, tetrachords, modes, melodic movement, composition, instruments, ornamentation, and performance practice. Other theorists include Ibn Sīnā (Avicenna, d. 428/1037), Ibn Zayla (d. 440/1048), al-Ḥasan b. Aḥmad ʿAlī al-Kātib (fl. fourth/tenth-eleventh century), Ibn al-Ṭaḥḥān (d. after 449/1057) and Ṣafī al-Dīn. Music literature, influenced by Persian and Arabic models, was included in many disciplines: *adab* (belles-lettres) and poetical literature; anthologies and anecdotal literature; *samāʿ* literature (concerning the lawfulness or unlawfulness of listening to music); bio-bibliographical literature; historical and geographical literature; dictionaries; and bureaucratic writing. The most important document in the music literature of the ʿAbbāsid, Umayyad, and early Islamic periods is the *Kitāb al-aghānī* of al-Iṣfahānī, compiled over a period of fifty years, with the support of an ʿAbbāsid patron, al-Muhallabī (d. 352/963), the *wazīr* of the *amīr* Muʿizz al-Dawla (r. in Iraq 334–56/945–67). The monumental collection, now in twenty-four volumes comprising ten thousand pages in the Cairo edition of 1927–74, treats in anecdotal form the activities of poets and musicians inside and outside the court from early Islam to the beginning of the fourth/tenth century. Al-Iṣfahānī's sources include oral and written history transmitted by poets and musicians and their descendants and friends. The anthology encompasses much material now lost and sheds light on anthropological aspects of musical practice, such as the socio-economic status of singers, uses and functions of songs, interaction of musicians and audience, criteria for evaluating

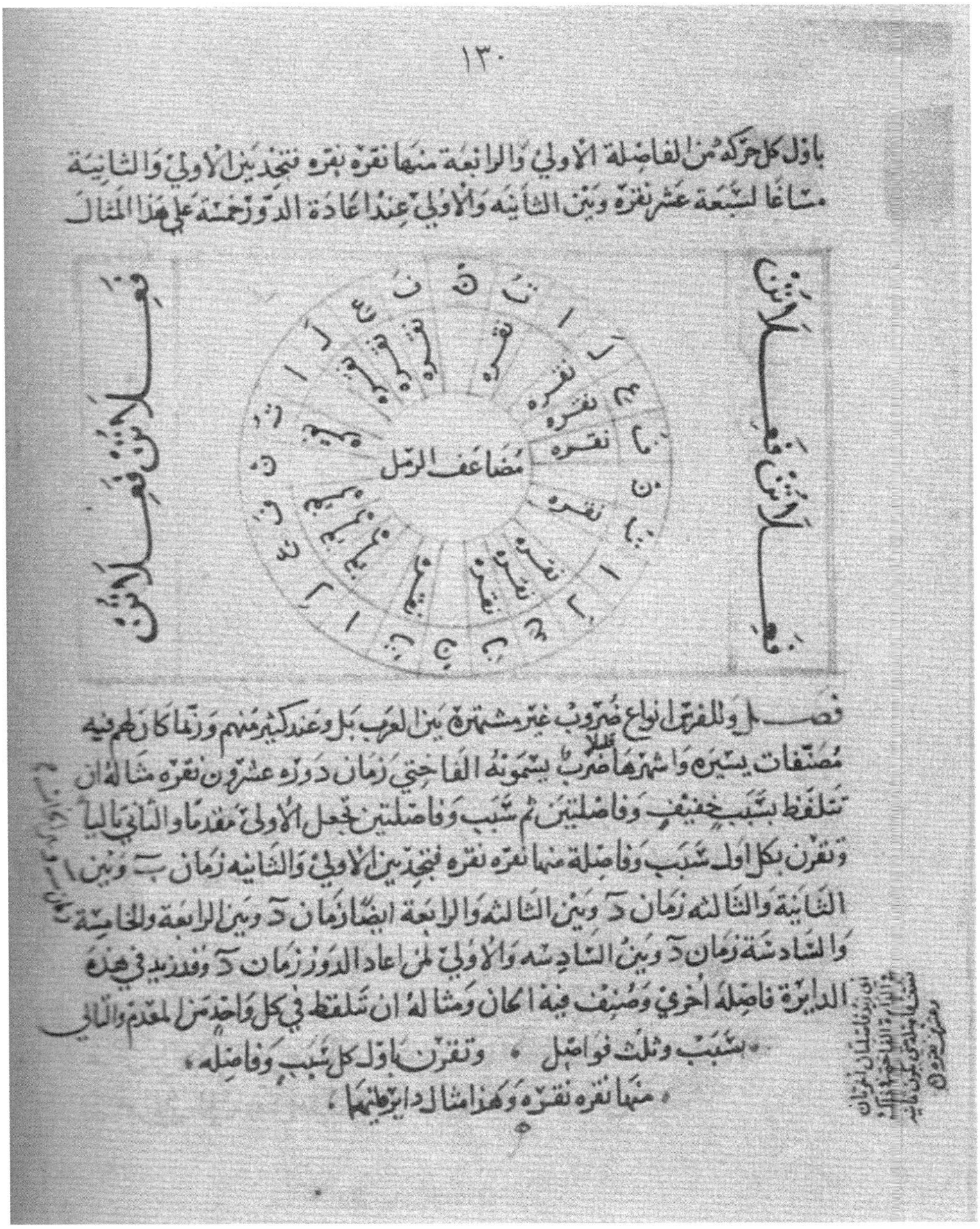

Illustration 3. A circular notation of rhythms from Ṣafī al-Dīn al-Urmawī, *al-Risāla al-Sharafiyya fī l-nisab al-taʾlīfiyya* ("Treatise dedicated to Sharaf al-Dīn on proportions in musical composition"). Istanbul, Topkapı Sarayı Müzesi, MS Ahmet III, 3460, fol. 65b.

musical excellence, processes of composition, improvisation, and ornamentation, and textual changes.

Since the period beginning with the second half of the fourth/tenth century, no collection as monumental as the *Kitāb al-aghānī* has survived. On a much smaller scale is the *Masālik al-abṣār* ("The roads to vision") of Ibn Faḍlallāh al-ʿUmarī (d. 749/1349), which includes biographies of musicians compiled from the *Kitāb al-aghānī* and, more importantly, from sources after the fourth/tenth century going beyond the era covered by it.

3. Cultural and social background

ʿAbbāsid music, like ʿAbbāsid culture more generally, was cosmopolitan and multicultural: music theorists and littérateurs came from a variety of ethnolinguistic backgrounds (speaking Aramaic, Arabic, Persian, and Turkish), skin colours (white, black, and mulatto), and creeds (Muslims, Christians, Jews, Sabians, and Zoroastrians). The music produced was a combination of musical styles (Near Eastern, Arabic, Persian, and Byzantine).

Male and female musicians came from a wide variety of social classes: slaves, freed slaves, freemen, princes and princesses. Several caliphs were distinguished composers, poets, and performers. A court musician was also a *nadīm* (boon companion), that is, a person well educated in literature, poetry, prosody, grammar, history, narration of anecdotes, the Qurʾān, *ḥadīth*, jurisprudence, astrology, medicine, cooking, the preparation of beverages, horse breeding, backgammon, and chess. Musicians also had to have the qualities of a *ẓarīf*, a gentleman of good behaviour and virtue and of elegance in conversation, clothing, and table manners. Such a background enabled them to befriend and educate the nobility and gain a permanent, well paid position at court. Some musicians became wealthy; this, along with their love songs and their drinking wine with the nobility, aroused the anger of some theologians who wrote treatises on the impermissibility of making or listening to music.

4. Performance context

Music making took place indoors, in palaces, the houses of poets and musicians, bathhouses, and taverns, and outdoors, in palace courtyards, parks, gardens, and the famous zoological gardens attached to the palace. The choice of songs was dictated by the makeup of the audience, the location, the scenery, and the context in which the songs were performed. Songs thus punctuated many aspects of social life, including birth, circumcision, wedding, love, farewell, greetings, and sickness; they described nature and wine; and they celebrated military victories and praised rulers on their accession to the caliphate and wazīrate. Improvisations were common and used sometimes to convey better the scenery and the mood of the audience. At court, the indoor *majlis* (social/musical gathering) took place in either of two ways, in the orderly *nawba* (turn to perform on a specific day of the week), in which a singer had a specific day of the week to perform, or haphazardly, in which singers were summoned to appear. In a *majlis* including many singers, they sang in turn and in cycles: each singer performed one song in a cycle or sang a series of songs in a single cycle; debates and fierce competitions took place, producing excellent performances and lively entertainment for the audience.

5. Modes

Songs were regulated metrically and tonally by eight rhythmic and eight melodic modes, which were classified and defined by the musician and theorist Isḥāq al-Mawṣilī. We know the nature of the eight rhythmic modes in the early ʿAbbāsid era thanks to al-Fārābī's precise definitions and notation [Illustration 2]: the *light hazaj* and *hazaj* were metres in 6/8, the *light hazaj* being the faster; the *ramal* and *light ramal* in 3/2 and 3/4, respectively; the *first heavy* and *first light heavy* in 4/2 and 4/4, respectively; and the *second heavy* and *second light heavy* in 5/2 and 5/4, respectively. These were rhythmic patterns of long and short durations tapped out by the composer to set his sung poem in a precise arrangement. The nature of the melodic modes is not well known; we can ascertain the first tetrachord of the modes but not the second (Sawa, *Music performance practice*, 76): F-G-A♭-B♭; F-G-A-B♭; G-A♭-B♭-C; G-A-B♭-C; A♭-B♭-C-D♭; A-B♭- C-D; B♭-C-D♭-E♭; B♭-C-D-E♭ (or, backwards, B♭-A♭-G-F; B♭-A-G-F). According to al-Fārābī, the A♭fret, known in the lute as the middle-finger fret, was 294 cents (a cent is one-hundredth of a semitone) from the open string (Sawa, *Music performance practice*, 79); it had, in practice, three more positions: two so-called Zalzal middle-finger frets, attributed to Manṣūr Zalzal (d. after 227/842), placed at 318 and 354 cents respectively from the open string (the latter is very close to the modern theoretical Arabic quarter tone), and the Persian middle-finger fret placed at 302 from the open string. These modes changed in the middle and late ʿAbbāsid eras.

6. Performance style

In a song, a singer either performed pre-composed ornaments or improvised them. Melodic ornaments consisted of replacing, adding, or removing notes. Rhythmic ornaments consisted of adding or removing notes, which occasionally altered the metre. Vocal timbral ornaments were named after human passions or after sensations corresponding to senses other than hearing or were named for the way air passes through the vocal tract. Vocal preludes consisted of textless singing, chanting, or interjection in a speech-like manner. A portion of the poem or interjection could be set to music syllabically and/or melismatically; it could be unrelated thematically to the song, and its rhythm contrasted with the song proper in tempo or by being set to a different rhythm.

The success of a performance depended on textual, musical, and extramusical factors. The latter consisted of a singer's combined qualities as *nadīm* and *ẓarīf*. Textual excellence depended on the skill of the singer in using a song in a proper situation, in catering to the audience's preference for poets and poetical styles, and on his ability to improvise poetry. Musical excellence comprised basic musicianship, a wide vocal range, a beautiful and powerful voice moving the audience to reach a state of *ṭarab* (acute joy or grief), the ability to accompany oneself on a stringed instrument, having a repertoire of at least five thousand songs, and being able to improvise and to alter the songs.

7. Instruments

The *ʿūd* (four- or five-stringed, short-necked Arab lute) was the most important instrument used to accompany a singer's performance. The singer often accompanied himself, and the *ʿūd* was important in helping the composer create his song; it was often said that it made him a better composer. The *ṭunbūr* (a two-stringed, long-necked lute) was also used for accompaniment. Open-stringed instruments were uncommon. The *ṣanj* (a harp) was rarely used. The *kankala* was a one-stringed, plucked instrument with a gourd-shaped box; of Indian origin it was introduced into the ʿAbbāsid court by ʿAbdallāh b. al-ʿAbbās b. al-Faḍl b. al-Rabīʿ (d. c.247/861). It occasionally replaced the *ʿūd* and the *ṣanj* and was used by the singer to accompany himself. The *miʿzafa* was a lyre, which the skilled singer Muḥammad b. al-Ḥārith b. Buskhunnar (d. after 232/847) used it to accompany his singing. Wind instruments included the *nāy* (a type of *mizmār*, or woodwind), a flute or a reed pipe that accompanied the singer. Percussion instruments included the *duff* (tambourine), the *ṣaffāqatān* (castanets), the *ṭabl* (hourglass-shaped, double-headed, laced drum) and the *qaḍīb*, which was a wand the singer used to tap the rhythm while singing or while composing, to ensure that the song fitted a rhythmic mode properly. Instruments used outside the court included the bowed *rabāb* (rebab), the *ṣanj* (cymbals or gong), *surnāy* (a high-pitched *mizmār)*, and the double *mizmār*. Ensemble music consisted of more than one *ʿūd* accompanying a singer or a combination of *nāy* and *ʿūd*. Vocal duets and responsorial singing were rare, while unaccompanied choruses and choruses accompanying themselves on *ʿūds* were common.

The Arabs' love of poetry made vocal music paramount. Al-Fārābī gave another reason: vocal music not only includes the melodic and rhythmic elements of instrumental music but also uses words that have meanings and therefore surpasses instruments in expressing emotions. The instruments thus played two subordinate roles to the voice—accompaniment to the vocal line, and preludes, interludes, and postludes to the songs. When accompanying the voice, the instrumentalist imitated the vocal line in octave or in unison, thereby supporting and guiding the singer's intonation and rhythm, and heterophonic textures resulted from the idiosyncratic melodic and rhythmic ornaments of the instrument. Preludes prepared the way for the singer's entry, and interludes gave the singer a rest; both were thematically related to the vocal part; postludes marked the end of a song. Pure instrumental music—that is, instrumental music not related to the voice—is, according to al-Fārābī, a type that the voice cannot sing. It falls short of perfection because it is wordless and consequently should be used in moderation. It consists of technical exercises, ear-training exercises, and preludes and interludes not related thematically to the vocal part.

Bibliography

Sources

Abū l-Faraj al-Iṣfahānī, *Kitāb al-aghānī*, 24 vols., Cairo 1927–74. For recordings of ʿAbbāsid music, see http://www.maisondesculturesdumonde.org/node/518

Studies

Henry George Farmer, *A history of Arabian music to the XIIIth century*, London 1929, repr. London 1973; Henry George Farmer, *The sources of Arabian music*, Leiden 1965; Henry George Farmer, *Studies in Oriental music*, ed. Eckhard Neubauer, Frankfurt am Main 1986 (a collection of most of Farmer's work); Hilary Kilpatrick, *Making the great Book of songs. Compilation and the author's craft in Abū l-Faraj al-Iṣbahānī's Kitāb al-aghānī*, London and New York 2003; Eckhard Neubauer, *Arabische Musiktheorie von den Anfängen bis zum 6./12. Jahrhundert. Studien, Übersetzungen und Texte in Faksimile*, Frankfurt am Main 1998; Eckhard Neubauer, Arabic writings on music. Eighth to nineteenth centuries, in *The Garland encyclopedia of world music*, vol. 6, *The Middle East* (New York 2002), 363–86; Eckhard Neubauer, *Musiker am Hof der frühen ʿAbbāsiden*,

Ph.D. diss., Goethe-Universität-Frankfurt 1965; George Dimitri Sawa, Classification of musical instruments in the medieval Middle East, in *The Garland encyclopedia of world music*, vol. 6, *The Middle East* (New York 2002), 395–99; George Dimitri Sawa, Fārābī, v. Music, *EIr;* George Dimitri Sawa, The *Kitāb al-aghānī*, in *The Garland encyclopedia of world music*, vol. 6, *The Middle East* (New York 2002), 351–6; George Dimitri Sawa, *Music performance practice in the early ʿAbbāsid era. 132–320 AH/750–932 AD*, Toronto 1989, Ottawa 2004²; George Dimitri Sawa, Musical humour in the *Kitāb al-aghānī*, in Roger M. Savory and Dionisius A. Agius (eds.), *Logos islamikos. Studia islamica in honorem Georgii Michaelis Wickens* (Toronto 1984), 35–50; George Dimitri Sawa, Paradigms in al-Fārābī's musical writings, in Nancy van Deusen and Alvin E. Ford (eds.), *Paradigms in medieval thought. Applications in medieval disciplines* (Lewiston NY 1990), 81–92; George Dimitri Sawa, The status and role of the secular musician in the *Kitāb al-aghānī*, *Asian Music* 17/1 (1985), 69–82; George Dimitri Sawa, Theories of rhythm and meter in the medieval Middle East, in *The Garland encyclopedia of world music*, vol. 6, *The Middle East* (New York 2002), 387–93; Amnon Shiloah, *Caractéristiques de l'art vocal arabe au moyen âge*, Tel Aviv 1963; Amnon Shiloah, *The theory of music in Arabic writings (c. 900–1900). Descriptive catalogue of manuscripts in libraries of Europe and the U.S.A.*, Munich 1979; Michael Stigelbauer, *Die Sängerinnen am Abbasidenhof um die Zeit des Kalifen al-Mutawakkil nach dem Kitāb al-aġānī des Abū-l-Farağ al-Iṣbahānī und anderen Quellen dargestellt*, Ph.D. diss., Universität Wien 1975; Suzanne Meyers-Sawa, Historical issues of gender and music, in *The Garland encyclopedia of world music*, vol. 6, *The Middle East* (New York 2002), 293–8; Suzanne Meyers-Sawa, The role of women in musical life, The medieval Arabo-Islamic courts, in *Canadian Woman Studies* 8/2 (1987), 93–5; Owen Wright, Ibn al-Munajjim and the early Arabian modes, *Galpin Society Journal* 19 (1966), 27–48; Owen Wright, *The modal system of Arab and Persian music. A.D. 1250–1300*, Oxford 1978.

George Dimitri Sawa

al-Aḥwal

Al-Aḥwal, Abū l-ʿAbbās Muḥammad b. al-Ḥasan b. Dīnār al-Hāshimī (d. 259/873?), was a lexicographer and an expert in poetry who spent most of his life in Baghdad. He was born in Baghdad shortly after 200/815. He transmitted poetry from Abū ʿUthmān Saʿdān b. al-Mubārak al-Ḍarīr (d. 220/835), Muḥammad b. Ziyād Ibn al-Aʿrābī (d. 231/846), and Abū l-Ḥasan al-Athram (d. 232/846), and became the teacher of prominent disciples, above all al-Yazīdī (d. 310/922), ʿAlī b. Sulaymān, known as al-Akhfash al-Aṣghar (d. 315/927), and Nifṭawayh (d. 323/935). He earned his living as a bookseller (*warrāq*) and copyist (*nāsikh*), copying, for example, the scientific books by Ḥunayn b. Isḥāq (d. 260/873). Al-Aḥwal was alive in 250/864, when al-Yazīdī studied the *dīwān* of ʿAmr b. al-Ahtam al-Minqarī (d. 57/676) under his guidance, and, since he was known to have been an older contemporary of al-Mubarrad (d. 285/898) and Thaʿlab (d. 291/904), he may have lived up to the beginning of the last quarter of the third/ninth century. According to al-Baghdādī, *Hadiyyat al-ʿārifīn*, 1:16, he died in 259/873, which sounds very plausible, but there is no proof that the date is correct because al-Baghdādī's source for this date is unknown.

According to the biographers al-Aḥwal wrote fewer than ten books, all of them apparently small lexicographical treatises, such as the *Kitāb al-dawāhī* (on synonyms of the word "misfortune"), which was incorporated by Ibn al-Qaṭṭāʿ (d. 515/1121) into the *dawāhī*-book of Abū ʿUbayda (d. c.210/825); see Weipert, 20–1; 55–64. Another example of his writings is the *Kitāb al-ābāʾ wa-l-ummahāt wa-l-abnāʾ wa-l-banāt*, a lexicon of phrases beginning with "Father, Mother, Son, or Daughter of" (*kunā*), which is partially extant via many quotations from the work in al-Suyūṭī (d. 911/1505), *al-Muzhir*, 1:506–16. The rest of his works, which include *Kitāb al-amthāl* (a collection of proverbs), *Kitāb mā ttafaqa lafẓuhu wa-khtalafa maʿnāhu* (on homonyms), and *Kitāb al-silāḥ* (on arms), have not come down to us.

His main activities, however, were devoted to studying poetry. It is said that al-Aḥwal collected the verses of 120 poets and edited them with a philological commentary in recensions of their *dīwāns*. Unfortunately only a handful of these are still available today. These are his recensions of the *dīwāns* of Dhū l-Rumma (*GAS* 2:395), the Banū Hudhayl (*GAS* 2:45) Kaʿb b. Zuhayr (*GAS* 2:230), al-Muthaqqib al-ʿAbdī (*GAS* 2:189), Salāma b. Jandal (*GAS* 2:193), and Suḥaym ʿAbd Banī l-Ḥasḥās (*GAS* 2:289). As W. Diem has shown in his study of the *Burda* poem of Kaʿb b. Zuhayr, al-Aḥwal's commentary on the *Dīwān Kaʿb b. Ẓuhayr* is very similar to the commentary of al-Sukkarī (d. 275/888). Since it is not clear whether it was al-Sukkarī who based his work on al-Aḥwal's or vice versa, or whether there was a mutual influence, an investigation into the relationship between the two commentaries remains highly desirable.

Bibliography

Sources

Ibn al-Nadīm, *al-Fihrist*, ed. Ayman Fuʾād Sayyid (London 1430/2009), 1/1:241; al-Zubaydī, *Ṭabaqāt al-naḥwiyyīn*, ed. Muḥammad Abū l-Faḍl Ibrāhīm (Cairo 1392/1973), 117, 208; al-Khaṭīb al-Baghdādī, *Taʾrīkh Baghdād*, ed. Bashshār ʿAwwād Maʿrūf (Beirut 1422/2001), 2:578–9; Ibn al-Anbārī, *Nuzhat al-alibbāʾ*, ed. Ibrāhīm al-Sāmarrāʾī (Baghdad 1970²), 119; Yāqūt, *Muʿjam al-udabāʾ*, ed. Iḥsān ʿAbbās (Beirut 1993), 3:1346, 6:2488–9; al-Qifṭī, *Inbāh al-ruwāt*, ed. Muḥammad Abū l-Faḍl Ibrāhīm (Cairo 1369–93/1950–73), 3:91–2; al-Yaghmūrī, *Nūr al-qabas*, ed. Rudolf Sellheim (Wiesbaden 1384/1964), 337; al-Yamānī, *Ishārat al-taʿyīn fī tarājim al-nuḥāt wa-l-lughawiyyīn*, ed. ʿAbd al-Majīd Diyāb (Riyadh 1406/1986), 306; al-Dhahabī, *Taʾrīkh al-Islām*, ed. ʿUmar ʿAbd al-Salām Tadmurī (Beirut 1411/1991), 21:256; al-Ṣafadī, *al-Wāfī bi-l-wafayāt*, ed. Sven Dedering (Wiesbaden 1394/1974), 2:344–5; al-Fīrūzābādī, *al-Bulgha fī tarājim aʾimmat al-naḥw wa-l-lugha*, ed. Muḥammad al-Miṣrī (Kuwait 1407/1987), 194; al-Suyūṭī, *Bughyat al-wuʿāt*, ed. Muḥammad Abū l-Faḍl Ibrāhīm (Cairo 1384/1964), 1:81–2; al-Baghdādī, *Hadiyyat al-ʿārifīn*, ed. Kilisli Rifat Bilge and Mahmud Kemal İnal (Istanbul 1951–5), 1:16; al-Suyūṭī, *al-Muzhir*, ed. Muḥammad Aḥmad Jād al-Mawlā et al. (Cairo n. d.), 1:506–16.

Studies

Werner Diem, *Studien zur Überlieferung und Intertextualität der altarabischen Dichtung. Das Mantelgedicht Kaʿb ibn Ẓuhayrs* (Wiesbaden 2010), index, s.v. al-Aḥwal; Charles Pellat, Muḥammad b. al-Ḥasan b. Dīnār, *EI2*; Reinhard Weipert, '*Ein Unglück kommt selten allein.' Vier arabische Synonymensammlungen zum Wortfeld* dāhiya, Munich 2004; *GAS* 8:138, 16:305–6.

Reinhard Weipert

ʿAllūya

ʿAlī b. ʿAbdallāh b. Sayf Abū l-Ḥasan (d. 236/850–1), known as **ʿAllūya** (ʿAllawayh), was a famous court singer of the early ʿAbbāsid era who performed for caliphs from al-Amīn (r. 193–8/809–13) to al-Mutawakkil (r. 232–47/847–61). He was a *mawlā* (client) of the ʿAbbāsids, whereas his grandfather, originally from Sughd (in present-day Tajikistan), was a freed slave of the Umayyads. He was a student of Ibrāhīm al-Mawṣilī (d. 188/804), whose son Isḥāq (d. 235/850) took his side against his rival Mukhāriq (d. 231/845 or

232/846). Isḥāq praised ʿAllūya as a good teacher and transmitter for his perfect, unadulterated renditions of songs but censured Mukhāriq's unreliability as a teacher for his constantly changing performances. The caliph al-Wāthiq (r. 227–32/842–7) considered ʿAllūya second best in three fields of musical performance—best composer, after Isḥāq al-Mawṣilī, best singer, after Mukhāriq, and best lutenist, after Thaqīf—thereby uniting several qualities found separately in other musicians. Al-Wāthiq compared the power and resonance of ʿAllūya's voice to that of a brass vessel reverberating in the ear for an hour after being struck. Despite having a repertoire of five thousand songs, a number required of most court singers, he was often at loss to find a proper song and sang instead inappropriate lyrics for which he was physically punished. Being left-handed, ʿAllūya strung his lute in the opposite direction from other musicians. His extra-musical qualities included being amiable, charming, pleasant at social gatherings, and jolly: on one occasion, being inebriated, he amused his audience by singing while dancing and clapping.

Bibliography

Source

Abū l-Faraj al-Iṣfahānī, *Kitāb al-aghānī* (Cairo 1927–74), 11:333–63.

Studies

Ignazio Guidi, *Tables alphabétiques du Kitâb al-aġânî* (Leiden 1900), 493; Eckhard Neubauer, *Musiker am Hof der frühen ʿAbbāsiden* (Ph.D. diss., Goethe-Universität-Frankfurt 1965), 168–9; George Dimitri Sawa, *Music performance practice in the early ʿAbbāsid era. 132–320 AH/750–932 AD* (Toronto 1989), index; Khayr al-Dīn al-Ziriklī, *al-Aʿlām* (Beirut 1979[4]), 4:303.

George Dimitri Sawa

Arzan

Arzan (Syriac: Arzōn; Armenian: Artsn, Arzn, Ałzn) was a town designated by the Arabs to be in the Arabian Peninsula, near the frontier with Anatolia. It was the seat of a Syriac bishopric between the first/seventh and fifth/eleventh centuries. Its location meant that it was often affected by the battles between the Byzantines and Persians in the centuries before Muslim domination. It was reportedly attacked by Lakhmid Arabs under al-Mundhir III around 520 C.E., and possibly again in 527 C.E. The town should not be confused with modern Erzurum (Arzan al-Rūm), which is sometimes referred to simply as Arzan in writings from the fifth/eleventh century onwards.

Arzan was of considerable age before its surrender in 20/640 to the Arab Muslims under the command of ʿIyāḍ b. Ghamn. Around 66/686 the town passed back to Byzantine rule as part of a treaty between the caliph ʿAbd al-Malik b. Marwān (d. 86/705) and the emperor Justinian II (d. 93/711). It later returned to the nominal control of the Arab Muslims, though it was directly ruled by Armenian notables closely allied to the Arabs. The town and its surrounding region produced the significant sum of 4.1 million *dirhams* in taxation from agriculture during the ʿAbbāsid period. Arzan was attacked and captured several times by the Byzantines in the mid-fourth/mid-tenth century.

Arzan grew in political importance during the fourth/tenth century as a result of its use as a base by the Ḥamdānid ruler Sayf al-Dawla (d. 356/967) for his attacks on Byzantine territory in Anatolia. At some point in the early 380s/990s—exactly when is unclear—the town passed back to the Byzantines, who, during their rearrangement of the defences of eastern Anatolia in the early fifth/eleventh century, had dismissed the Armenian Bagratid rulers. The town was sacked and permanently destroyed by the Seljūqs in 440–1/1049–50 (described in emotive and bloody detail by Matthew of Edessa) and the surviving population moved to nearby Erzurum. John George Taylor (fl. 1851–63) discovered the ruins of Arzan sometime in the period 1861–3.

Bibliography

Sources

Al-Balādhurī, *Kitāb futūḥ al-buldān*, ed. M. J. de Goeje (Leiden 1866), 176; Bar Hebraeus, *Chronography*, trans. E. A. Wallis Budge, London 1932; Ibn Khurradādhbih, *al-Masālik wa-l-mamālik*, ed. M. J. de Goeje (Leiden 1889), 245–6; Matthew of Edessa, *Armenia and the crusades. The chronicle of Matthew of Edessa*, trans. Ara E. Doustorian (Lanham MD 1993), 76–7; Yāqūt, *Muʿjam al-buldān*, ed. F. Wüstenfeld (Leipzig 1866–73), 1:205.

Studies

Marius Canard, *Sayf al Daula. Receuil de textes relatifs à l'émir Sayf al Daula le Hamdanide avec annotations* (Algiers 1934), 52, 57, 73, 79, 82, 96, 186, 213, 252; Marius Canard, *Histoire de la dynastie des Hamdanides* (Algiers 1951), 84, 240; Jean-Maurice Fiey, *Pour un oriens christianus novus. Répertoire des diocèses syriaques orientaux et occidentaux* (Beirut 1993), 170–1; R. N. Frye, Arzan, *EI2*; Joseph Marquart, *Die Enlstehung und Wiederherstellung der armenischen Nation* (Potsdam 1919), 33; Irfan Shahid, *Byzantium and the Arabs in the sixth century*, Washington DC 1995; J. G. Taylor, Travels in Kurdistan, with notices of the sources of the eastern and western Tigris, and ancient ruins in their neighbourhoods, *Journal of the Royal Geographical Society* 35 (1865), 21–58.

Alex Mallett

B

al-Bakrī, Abū l-Ḥasan

Abū l-Ḥasan Muḥammad b. Jalāl al-Dīn **al-Bakrī** al-Ṣiddīqī al-Shāfiʿī (898–952/1492–1545) was a leading religious scholar in tenth/sixteenth-century Cairo. He was the son of Jalāl al-Dīn al-Bakrī, a religious scholar who had a career in the administration of the Mamlūk state before turning to Ṣūfism under the influence of ʿAbd al-Qādir al-Dashṭūṭī (d. 924/1518), a holy fool who enjoyed the respect of the Mamlūk and Ottoman ruling elites. Jalāl al-Dīn administered the religious endowments established in al-Dashṭūṭī's name, including the White Mosque (Jāmiʿ al-Abyaḍ), which became the Bakrī family mosque. Al-Dashṭūṭī also encouraged Jalāl al-Dīn to place his son under the tutelage of Raḍī al-Dīn al-Ghazzī (d. 835/1529). The Ghazzīs, noted Shāfiʿī scholars and Ṣūfīs of the Qādirī order, played a role in Damascus similar to that played by the Bakrīs in Cairo.

Abū l-Ḥasan enjoyed a reputation as an outstanding jurist, Ṣūfī, and Qurʾān exegete. He associated himself with the Shādhilī order, and his descendants were usually considered a branch of that order (the Shādhiliyya, founded by the Moroccan Abū l-Ḥasan al-Shādhilī, d. 656/1258, is well established in North Africa and the central Middle East). ʿAbd al-Wahhāb al-Shaʿrānī (d. 973/1565), the Egyptian Ṣūfī, scholar, historian of Ṣūfism, and prolific writer on many religious subjects, portrays Abū l-Ḥasan as a legal expert unrestricted by school *(mujtahid muṭlaq)*, a view that appears also in a treatise on *ijtihād* (independent reasoning in Islamic law) by Abū l-Ḥasan's son Muḥammad (d. 994/1586). The idea that one could be an unrestricted legal expert while continuing to follow the Shāfiʿī school was adopted also by al-Shaʿrānī and the famous prolific scholar from Cairo Jalāl al-Dīn al-Ṣuyūṭī (d. 911/1505). Al-Shaʿrānī says that Abū l-Ḥasan was widely regarded as the axial saint (*quṭb*, lit., pole, axis) of his time.

In his poetry, Muḥammad al-Bakrī portrays his father Abū l-Ḥasan as the manifestation of the "reality" *(ḥaqīqa)* of Abū Bakr al-Ṣiddīq (d. 13/634), the senior Companion of the Prophet and his father-in-law and the first caliph. This idea, which draws on the concept of the Muḥammadan Reality *(al-ḥaqīqa al-Muḥammadiyya)* suggests that Abū l-Ḥasan was the first full manifestation of the metaphysical Abū Bakr since the latter's death. The lineage of the Cairene Bakrīs' descent from Abū Bakr can be found already in the Egyptian *ḥadīth* scholar and prosopographer al-Sakhāwī (d. 902/1497) (7:284), and Muḥammad al-Bakrī placed great emphasis on their maternal descent from al-Ḥasan b. ʿAlī b. Abī Ṭālib (d. 50/670) and, therefore, from the Prophet himself.

Abū l-Ḥasan wrote several works on Shāfiʿī law, several *ḥadīth* collections, and a popular work on *tafsīr* (Qurʾānic commentary) titled *Tashīl al-sabīl li-fahm maʿānī al-tanzīl* ("Easing the path to understanding the meaning of the revelation") or *Tafsīr al-Bakrī*. More than thirty manuscripts survive of this work, which was read throughout the Ottoman Empire. His *Ḥizb* was an influential prayer passed down by generations of Ṣūfīs until modern times. Abū l-Ḥasan was also an early advocate of the use of coffee by Ṣūfīs and wrote a treatise supporting it.

Shortly before his death, Abū l-Ḥasan named his son Muḥammad to succeed him in his teaching posts at the White Mosque and al-Azhar mosque (in Cairo). Their descendants, known as the Bakrī Lords (al-Sāda al-Bakriyya), were the most influential lineage of scholars in Ottoman Egypt.

Bibliography

Works of Abū l-Ḥasan al-Bakrī

Fatḥ al-mālik bi-sharḥ diyāʾ al-sālik, Riyadh, King Saud University, MS 345; *Hādī al-muḥtāj sharḥ al-Minhāj lil-Nawawī*, Riyadh, King Saud University, MS 7857; *Ḥizb*, Princeton University Library, MS Garrett 1254Y; *Iʿlām al-anām bi-faḍl al-ṣiyām*, Riyadh, King Saud University, MS 549; *Irshād al-zāʾirīn li-ḥabīb rabb al-ʿālamīn*, Princeton University Library, MS Garrett 1071H; *Iṣṭifāʾ al-ṣafwa li-taṣfiyyat al-qahwa*, University of Leiden Library, MS 1138; *Kashf al-labs fī munāṣaḥat al-nafs*, in Saʿīd ʿAbd al-Fattāḥ (ed.), *Rasāʾil fī l-nafs* (Cairo 1990), 149–205; Riyadh, King Saud University, MS 2186 (contains eleven *ḥadīth* anthologies); *al-Nafḥa al-daniyya ʿalā al-tuḥfa al-wardiyya*, Riyadh, King Saud University, MS 58; *Nubdha fī faḍl laylat al-niṣf min Shaʿbān*, Princeton University Library, MS Garrett 253Y, fols. 55a–60b; *Tafsīr al-Bakrī*, ed. Aḥmad Farīd al-Mazīdī Beirut 2010; *Risālat al-fāqa ilā al-fāqa*, MS Gotha A orient 1865, fols. 32b–70a; *Waṣīya*, Princeton University Library, MS Garrett 253Y, fols. 144a–145b.

Other sources

Aḥmad b. Zayn al-ʿĀbidīn al-Bakrī, *Qalāʾid al-minan wa-farāʾid al-zaman*, in Muṣṭafā Mughāzī and Ādam ʿAbd al-Ḥamīd Ṣabra (eds.), *Manāqib al-Sāda al-Bakriyya (Merits of the Bakrī Lords)* (Beirut 2015), 61–282; Ibn Abī l-Surūr al-Bakrī, *al-Kawkab al-durrī fī manāqib al-ustādh al-Bakrī*, in Muṣṭafā Mughāzī and Ādam ʿAbd al-Ḥamīd Ṣabra (eds.), *Manāqib al-Sāda al-Bakriyya (Merits of the Bakrī Lords)* (Beirut 2015), 7–60; ʿAbd al-Raʾūf al-Munāwī, *al-Kawākib al-durriyya fī tarājim al-Ṣūfiyya*, ed. ʿAbd al-Ḥamīd Ṣāliḥ Ḥamdān (Cairo 1994), 4:18–9; Najm al-Dīn al-Ghazzī, *al-Kawākib al-sāʾira bi-aʿyān al-miʾa al-ʿāshira*, ed. Khalīl Manṣūr (Beirut 1997), 2:192–6; ʿAbd al-Raḥmān al-Sakhāwī, *al-Ḍawʾ al-lāmiʿ*, Beirut 1966; Alī b. Yūsuf al-Ḥanafī al-Rūmī al-Shādhilī, *Kitāb nasamat al-nafaḥāt al-miskiyya fī dhikr al-baʿḍ min manāqib al-Sāda al-Bakriyya*, in Muṣṭafā Mughāzī and Ādam ʿAbd al-Ḥamīd Ṣabra (eds.), *Manāqib al-Sāda al-Bakriyya (Merits of the Bakrī Lords)* (Beirut 2015), 283–396; ʿAbd al-Wahhāb al-Shaʿrānī, *al-Ṭabaqāt al-ṣughrā*, ed. Saʿīd Hārūn ʿAbd al-Fattāḥ (Cairo 2003), 75–7.

Studies

Éric Geoffroy, Le diffusion du café au Proche-Orient arabe par l'intermédiaire des soufis. Mythe et réalité, in Michel Tuscherer (ed.), *Le commerce du café avant l'ère des plantations coloniales. Espaces, réseaux, sociétés (XVe–XIXe siècle)* (Cairo 2001), 7–15; Adam Sabra, Household Sufism in sixteenth-century Egypt. The rise of al-Sâda al-Bakrîya, in Rachida Chih and Catherine Mayeur-Jaouen (eds.), *Le soufisme à l'époque ottomane, XVIe–XVIIIe siècle* (Cairo 2010), 101–18.

Adam Sabra

al-Bakrī, Muḥammad b. Abī l-Ḥasan

Muḥammad b. Abī l-Ḥasan al-Bakrī al-Ṣiddīqī al-Shāfiʿī al-Ashʿarī Sibṭ Āl al-Ḥasan (b. 13 Dhū l-Ḥijja 930/12 October 1524, d. 14 Ṣafar 994/4 February 1586) was a leading religious scholar in Ottoman Cairo who was most famous for his mystical poetry. The son of the well-known Ṣūfī and jurist Abū l-Ḥasan al-Bakrī (d. 952/1545), he was a child prodigy who went on to have an even more illustrious career than his father. As his name indicates, his family traced its lineage back to Abū Bakr al-Ṣiddīq (d. 13/634) on the paternal side and the prophet Muḥammad through his grandson al-Ḥasan b. ʿAlī b. Abī Ṭālib (d. 50/670) through a maternal ancestor.

Muḥammad was celebrated by his contemporaries, such as ʿAbd al-Wahhāb al-Shaʿrānī (d. 973/1565), an Egyptian Ṣūfī, scholar, historian of Ṣūfism, and prolific writer on many religious subjects, who described him as "too famous to require identification." Al-Shaʿrānī even claimed to have had a dream validating his descent from Abū Bakr. Muḥammad taught at the family mosque (the White Mosque) as well as at al-Azhar mosque in Cairo. He made the pilgrimage to Mecca on numerous occasions and taught in the precincts of the Kaʿba and the Prophet's mosque in Medina. ʿAbd al-Qādir al-ʿAydarūs (d. 1038/1628), author of a biographical dictionary of scholars of the tenth/sixteenth century, describes Muḥammad al-Bakrī as teaching huge throngs of admirers. Ottoman soldiers accompanied him to protect him from the people who wanted to kiss his hand to receive *baraka* (beneficent force of divine origin). Al-ʿAydarūs claims that, although Muḥammad was designated by his father to succeed him, one of Muḥammad's leading students challenged his right to do so, because of his young age; he adds that Muḥammad prevailed in an examination by senior scholars.

Muḥammad al-Bakrī's *dīwān* of poetry, sometimes titled *Turjumān al-asrār* ("The interpreter of secrets") is devoted primarily to Ṣūfism. In some manuscripts, the *dīwān*'s introduction includes a paragraph distancing the author from the doctrine of the unity of being *(waḥdat al-wujūd)*, a theological position held by many interpreters of the works of Muḥyī l-Dīn Ibn al-ʿArabī (d. 638/1240), the major mystic of Andalusian origin; its adherents were sometimes accused of heresy. Nonetheless, it is clear that his poetry was influenced by the works of Ibn al-ʿArabī, Ibn al-Fāriḍ (d. 632/1235), the famous Ṣūfī Arab poet from Cairo, ʿAlī Wafā (d. 807/1405), the Ṣūfī *shaykh*, mystical poet, and head of a prominent family of Mamlūk Cairo, and possibly al-Būṣīrī (d. between 694–6/1294–7), the illustrious Egyptian poet of the Mamlūk period. Muḥammad celebrates his father Abū l-Ḥasan as the full manifestation of the "reality" *(ḥaqīqa)* of Abū Bakr, a concept derived from Ibn al-ʿArabī's use of the concept of the Muḥammadan Reality (the reality out of which the entire cosmos was created). Muḥammad al-Bakrī also uses his poetry to celebrate Ṣūfī saints such as Ibn al-Fāriḍ and the popular Egyptian saint Sayyid Aḥmad al-Badawī (d. 675/1276), to express his pride in his lineage and even to promote the use of coffee by Ṣūfīs in their rituals.

Muḥammad al-Bakrī's second major work is his collection of official correspondence *(inshāʾ)*. This is a large collection of official letters addressed to such officials as the Ottoman governors of Egypt, the Sharīfian rulers of the Ḥijāz, the Ottoman Shaykh al-Islām, the Ottoman grand vizier, and the Saʿdī rulers of Morocco. Some of these letters pertain to the Ottoman campaign (presumably of 977–8/1569–70) to conquer Yemen, while others appear to be letters of introduction written by Muḥammad al-Bakrī to recommend his disciples and clients to Ottoman officials in the hope of obtaining official positions or stipends for them. These letters show Muḥammad al-Bakrī to have been an influential political figure, as well as being, by reputation, a pious man and a mystical poet. Eleventh/seventeenth-century hagiographical sources also emphasise his role of an intercessor for *amīrs* with the Ottoman governor of Egypt.

The third body of work produced by Muḥammad al-Bakrī was a series of treatises dealing with various aspects of religious thought and practice. Most of these are devoted to Ṣūfism, but one deals with Abū l-Ḥasan al-Bakrī's claim to be a legal expert *(mujtahid)* unrestricted by legal school. Other topics include Ṣūfī audition *(samāʿ)*, spiritual guidance, the supreme divine name *(ism Allāh al-aʿẓam)*, the practices of the Saʿdī Ṣūfī network, and visiting the Prophet's tomb in Medina. Although many scholars claimed to have studied with him, his principle successors were his sons, especially Zayn al-ʿĀbidīn b. Muḥammad al-Bakrī (d. 1013/1604).

Bibliography

Works of Muḥammad al-Bakrī

Tanbīh al-awwāh li-faḍl lā ilāh illā Llāh, ed. Aḥmad Farīd al-Mazīdī, Cairo 2010; *al-Ijtihād al-muṭlaq*, ed. Salīm Fahd Shabʿāniyya, Damascus 1992; *Dīwān*, sometimes titled *Turjumān al-asrār* (principal MSS: Istanbul, Aya Sofya, MS 4164; Paris, BNF, MS arabe 3230; Erfurt, Gotha Library, MS O A 2326; Leipzig, Universitätsbibliothek, MS Vollers 0573; Berlin, Staatsbibliothek, MS we227); *Dustūr al-gharāʾib wa-maʿdan al-raghāʾib* (title varies between the principal MSS: Suhāj Library, MS Adab 227; Escorial Library, MS 532; Paris, BNF, MS arabe 4443); the Princeton University Library MS Garrett 253Y includes the following treatises: *Maʿāhid al-jamʿ fī mashāhid al-samʿ; al-Jawhara al-muḍīʾa fī tajwīz iḍāfat al-jāzim ʿalā al-mashīʾa*, dated 977 (1569–70) in Mecca; *Tarkīb al-ṣuwar wa-tartīb al-suwar; Akhbār al-akhyār*, dated 20–1 Dhū l-Qaʿda 959 (7–8 November 1552) in Mecca; *al-Jawāb al-ajall ʿan ḥikmat kurab al-Muṣṭafā ʿinda ḥulūl al-ajal; al-Fatḥ al-mubīn bi-jawāb baʿḍ al-sāʾilīn; ʿAqīlat al-ḥadhir wa-ʿaqīdat al-sirr; Hidāyat al-murīd lil-sabīl al-ḥamīd; al-Risāla al-murshida; al-Naṣīḥa; al-Naṣīḥa al-mawḍūʿa lil-shaykh Manṣūr; Nubdha fī l-kalām ʿalā āyat al-isrāʾ; Nubdha fī l-kalām ʿalā āyat al-Dukhān; Lawāmiʿ al-anwār wa-jawāmiʿ al-asrār fī l-kalām ʿalā al-duʿāʾ wa-faḍlihi wa-l-kalām ʿalā al-ism al-aʿẓam; Jawāb suʾāl fī maʿnā lafẓ "al-riḍā" fī qaṣīdat ʿAlī Ibn Abī l-Wafāʾ, Tanbīh al-awwāh li-faḍl lā ilāha illā Allāh; al-Iqtiṣād fī bayān marātib al-ijtihād*, dated end of Shawwāl 971 (c. 10 June 1564) in Mecca; *Jawāb ʿan suʾāl hal aṭlaʿa Allāh ḥabībahu Muḥammad ʿalā sāʾir maʿlūmātihi; Ṣādiḥat al-azal wa-nāṭiqat al-abad; Taʾbīd al-minna fī taʾyīd al-sunna*, dated 25 Muḥarram 959 (22 January 1552); *Jawāb suʾāl ʿan maʿnā qawlihi ṣallā Allāh ʿalayhi wa-sallam, innī aẓill ʿinda rabbi yuṭmiʿnī wa-yusqīnī; al-Risāla al-nāfiʿa; Aysar maṭlūb fī ziyārat akbar maḥbūb; al-Nuṣra al-ilāhīya lil-ṭāʾifa al-Saʿdiyya; Jawāb ʿan suʾāl hal aṭlaʿa Allāh ḥabībahu Muḥammad ʿalā sāʾir maʿlūmātihi; al-Sirr al-maktūm wa-l-durr al-manẓūm*, a poem not included in any of the manuscripts of the *dīwān; Ijāza lahu*, dated 7 Jumādā I 988 (20 June 1580); *Ṣīghat al-ṣalāh waradat ʿalā al-muṣṭafā; Tasbīḥāt wazzaʿa ʿalā ayyām al-usbūʿ; Tuḥfat al-sālik li-ashraf al-masālik*, dated 1 Dhū l-Qaʿda 951 (15 January 1545); *Nubdha fī aqsām al-bidaʿ wa-al-kalām ʿalayhā; Risāla murattaba fī bayān al-uslūb al-ḥakīm;* and *al-Mudhakkira*.

Other sources

ʿAbd al-Qādir b. Shaykh al-ʿAydarūs, *al-Nūr al-sāfir ʿan akhbār al-qarn al-ʿāshir*, ed. Aḥmad Ḥālū, Maḥmūd al-Arnāʾūṭ, and Akram al-Būshī, Beirut 2001; Aḥmad b. Zayn al-ʿĀbidīn al-Bakrī, *Qalāʾid al-minan wa-farāʾid al-zaman*, in Muṣṭafā Mughāzī and Ādam ʿAbd al-Ḥamīd Ṣabra (eds.), *Manāqib al-Sāda al-Bakriya (Merits of the Bakrī Lords)* (Beirut 2015), 61–282; Ibn Abī l-Surūr al-Bakrī, *Fayḍ al-mannān fī dawlat Āl ʿUthmān*, ed. ʿAbd al-Rāziq ʿAbd al-Rāziq ʿĪsā (Cairo 2011), 362–71; Ibn Abī l-Surūr al-Bakrī, *al-Kawkab al-durrī fī manāqib al-ustādh al-Bakrī*, in Muṣṭafā Mughāzī and Ādam ʿAbd al-Ḥamīd Ṣabra (eds.), *Manāqib al-Sāda al-Bakriyya (Merits of the Bakrī Lords)* (Beirut 2015), 7–60; Ibn Abī l-Surūr al-Bakrī, *al-Minaḥ al-raḥmāniyya fī l-dawla al-ʿUthmāniyya*, ed. Laylā al-Ṣabbāgh (Damascus 1995), 210–33; ʿAbd al-Raʾūf al-Munāwī, *al-Kawākib al-durriyya fī tarājim al-Ṣūfiyya*, ed. ʿAbd al-Ḥamīd Ṣāliḥ Ḥamdān (Cairo 1994), 4:125–6; Najm al-Dīn al-Ghazzī, *al-Kawākib al-sāʾira bi-aʿyān al-miʾa al-ʿāshira*, ed. Khalīl al-Manṣūr (Beirut 1997), 3:60–5; Alī b. Yūsuf al-Ḥanafī al-Rūmī al-Shādhilī, *Kitāb nasamat al-nafaḥāt al-miskiyya fī dhikr al-baʿḍ min Manāqib al-Sāda al-Bakriyya*, in Muṣṭafā Mughāzī and Ādam ʿAbd al-Ḥamīd Ṣabra (eds.), *Manāqib al-Sāda al-Bakriyya (Merits of the Bakrī Lords)* (Beirut 2015), 283–396; ʿAbd al-Wahhāb al-Shaʿrānī, *al-Ṭabaqāt al-ṣughrā*, ed. Saʿīd ʿAbd al-Fattāḥ (Cairo 2003), 119-20.; Studies; Khaled El-Rouayheb, *Islamic intellectual history in the seventeenth century. Scholarly currents in the Ottoman Empire and the Maghreb* (Cambridge 2015), 242–7; Muḥammad Sayyid Kīlānī, *al-Adab al-Miṣrī fī ẓill al-ḥukm al-ʿUthmānī, 922 H.-1220 H. (1517–1805 M.)* (Cairo 1965), 75–112; Adam Sabra, Household Sufism in sixteenth-century Egypt. The rise of al-Sâda al-Bakrîya, in Rachida Chih and Catherine Mayeur-Jaouen (eds.), *Le soufisme à l'époque ottomane, XVIe–XVIIIe siècle* (Cairo 2010), 101–18.

Adam Sabra

al-Ballanūbī

Abū l-Ḥasan ʿAlī b. ʿAbd al-Raḥmān b. Abī Bishr (al-Naḥwī) al-Anṣārī al-Kātibī **al-Ballanūbī** al-Ṣiqillī (d. c.470/1078), born in Sicily, made his name as a poet at the Fāṭimid court in Egypt. He apparently came from Ballanūba (Villanova), in Sicily. Yāqūt, in his geographic dictionary, in the entry on Ballanūba, mentions both al-Ballanūbī and his brother ʿAbd al-ʿAzīz, who originated from the same little Sicilian village, and includes one of the latter's poems (Yāqūt, 1:491). ʿAlī b. Abī Bishr left Sicily after the Norman conquest and went to Egypt, where he became a poet at the Fāṭimid court. Around 447/1055, he composed three laudatory poems on al-Nāṣir lil-Dīn Abū Muḥammad al-Ḥasan al-Yāzūrī, *wazīr* of the Fāṭimid caliph-*imām* al-Mustanṣir (r. 427–87/1036–94), which are preserved by the chancery clerk and anthologist Ibn al-Ṣayrafī (d. 542/1147).

Al-Ballanūbī was one of a group of Arab-Sicilian poets who were living in Sicily when the Normans conquered the island during the period 453–84/1061–91, a group that includes Ibn Ḥamdīs (d. 527/1133), who emigrated to Seville; and ʿAbd al-Raḥmān b. Abī l-ʿAbbās al-Atrābanishī (from Trapani), and al-Buthayrī (from Butera), both of whom remained in Sicily under the rule of the Norman king Roger II (r. 1130–54 C.E.).

The largest selection of al-Ballanūbī's poetry appears in the mediaeval anthology of Sicilian poets titled *al-Durra al-khaṭīra wa-l-mukhtār min shuʿarāʾ al-Jazīra* ("The precious pearl and the anthology of the poets of the Island"), collected by ʿAlī b. Jaʿfar b. ʿAlī al-Saʿdī al-Ṣiqillī, known as Ibn al-Qaṭṭāʿ (d. 515/1121). Another anthologist, ʿImād al-Dīn al-Iṣfahānī (d. 597/1201), secretary to the rulers Nūr al-Dīn (d. 569/1174) and Ṣalāḥ al-Dīn al-Ayyūbī (Saladin, r. 569–89/1174–93), included the works of some Sicilian-Arab poets of the fifth/eleventh and sixth/twelfth centuries in his anthology of the poetry of his age, the *Kharīdat al-qaṣr wa-jarīdat ahl al-ʿaṣr* ("The pearl of the palace and catalogue of the people of the epoch").

Most printed editions of *al-Durra*, especially the part concerning the poets of Sicily, begin with a large selection of al-Ballanūbī's poetry; he was apparently considered the most prominent Sicilian poet after Ibn Ḥamdīs, with many connections to the East as well as to Egypt and North Africa.

The first poem in ʿImād al-Dīn's selection of Sicilian verse is one composed in Egypt by the Andalusī poet Umayya b. al-Ṣalt (b. Denia 460/1068, d. Algeria 528/1134), in which Umayya expresses his admiration for al-Ballanūbī's eloquent style, citing his description of the Nile during the night of Mihrajān (24 June, celebrated by the Copts). He was inspired by some of al-Ballanūbī's lines of poetry that depict the sunlight reflected on the Nile at sunset as spear points on coats of mail (*Kharīda*, 6; ʿAbbās, *Muʿjam*, 111). Also a verse on this theme by the famous Andalusian poet Ibn Khafāja (d. 529/1134) is mentioned, with the gold of the sun reflecting on the silver of the water With this anecdote the section on al-Ballanūbī begins, with the selection of his poems that follows ordered alphabetically by rhyme letter. Another part of al-Ballanūbī's *Dīwān* was transmitted by Abū Muḥammad ʿAbdallāh b. Yaḥyā b. Ḥammūd al-Khuraymī (d. 514/1120), his pupil in Alexandria.

The biographical dictionary compiled by Iḥsān ʿAbbās, based on all the available sources on the Sicilian poets, is arranged alphabetically by poet. Al-Ballanūbī's poems appear at no. 91 (100–26), with perhaps the most notable being the poem that begins with the following lines: *wa-ghazālin mushannafin/ qad rathā lī baʿda buʿdī/ lammā raʾā mā laqītū* ("Many an ear-ringed gazelle/ had wept for me after my distance/ when he saw what grief I encountered") (ʿAbbās, *Muʿjam*, 102; ʿImād al-Dīn al-Iṣfahānī, 8–9). With the internal rhyme scheme abc/abc, etc., it contains five metres: *khafīf*, *majzūʾ al-khafīf*, *al-mujtathth*, *majzūʾ al-ramal*, and *manhūk al-ramal*, as explained by the editor of the *Kharīda* (8, note 2).

Other poems by al-Ballanūbī in the selections by Ibn Ḥammūd and Ibn al-Ṣayrafī contain laudatory poems on Egyptian dignitaries. One of his poems is an elegy on his mother, and other notable pieces are a poem on roses in a bowl (*ṭabaq*), one on a singer with a heavy voice (*thaqīl*), and others on female dancers, oranges, and other wine and love motifs.

Bibliography

Sources

al-Ballanūbī, *Dīwān* [MS Escorial 487], ed. Hilāl Nājī, Baghdad 1976; Iḥsān ʿAbbās, *Muʿjam al-ʿulamāʾ wa-l-shuʿarāʾ al-Ṣiqilliyyīn* (Beirut 1994), no. 91, 100–26; Ibn al-Qaṭṭāʿ, *al-Durra al-khaṭīra wa-l-mukhtār fī shuʿarāʾ al-Jazīra (jazīrat Ṣiqilliyya)*, ed. Bashīr al-Bakkūsh, Beirut 1995; Ibn al-Ṣayrafī, *Kitāb al-afḍaliyyāt*, ed. Walīd Qaṣṣāb and ʿAbd al-ʿAzīz b. Nāṣir al-Mānīʿ, Damascus 1982; ʿImād al-Dīn al-Iṣfahānī, *Kharīdat al-qaṣr wa-jarīdat al-ʿaṣr*, ed. Muḥammad al-Marzūqī, Muḥammad al-ʿArūsī al-Maṭwī, and Jīlānī b. al-Ḥājj Yaḥyā, *Qism shuʿarāʾ al-Maghrib* (Tunis 1966), vol. 1, part 2, section 4 (section on Sicily), 5–17; Abū ʿAbdallāh Muḥammad al-Nayfar, *ʿUnwān al-arīb* (Tunis 1352/1932), 1:126–38 (with Ibn al-Ṣayrafī's selection of Sicilian Arabic poetry); Yāqūt, *Muʿjam al-buldān* (Beirut 1374–6/1955–7), 1:491.

Studies

Iḥsān ʿAbbās, *al-ʿArab fī Ṣiqilliyya. Dirāsa fī l-taʾrīkh wa-l-adab*, Beirut 1975; Michele Amari, *Storia dei Musulmani di Sicilia*, 3 vols., ed. Giorgio Levi della Vida and Carlo Alfonso Nallino, Catania 1930–9; Francesca

Maria Corrao (ed. and trans.), *Poeti arabi di Sicilia*, Milan 1987; Antonino de Stefano, *La cultura in Sicilia nel periodo normanno*, Bologna 1954; Ignazio Di Matteo, *Antologia di poeti arabi siciliani* (Palermo 1935), 95–133; Jeremy Johns, Arabic sources for Sicily, in Mary Whitby (ed.), *Byzantines and Crusaders in non-Greek sources, 1025–1204* (London 2007), 341–60 (gives an up-to-date survey of the Arabic sources); Karla Mallette, Poetries of the Norman courts, in María Rosa Menocal, Raymond P. Scheindlin, and Michael Anthony Sells, *The literature of al-Andalus* (Cambridge 2000), 377–87; Karla Mallette, Arabic literature in Italy, in Christopher Kleinhenz (ed.), *Medieval Italy. An encyclopedia* (New York 2003), 45–6; Karla Mallette, *The Kingdom of Sicily, 1100–1250. A literary history*, Philadelphia 2005; Umberto Rizzitano, Un compendio dell'antologia di poeti arabo-siciliani, in *Atti dell'Academia Nazionale dei Lincei, Memorie*, series 8, vol. 8 (Rome 1958), 334–78; Arie Schippers, Liebesleid, Modelle und Kontakte. Arabische, hebräische und früh-romanische Dichter in Sizilien und die Minnesang, in Laura Auteri and Margherita Cottone (eds.), *Deutsche Kultur und Islam am Mittelmeer. Akten der Tagung Palermo 13.–15. November 2003* (Göppingen 2005), 61–75.

Arie Schippers

Barnāvī ʿAlāʾ al-Dīn Chishtī

Barnāvī ʿAlāʾ al-Dīn Muḥammad **Chishtī** (1007–88/1599–1677) wrote *Chishtiyya-yi bihishtiyya* ("The heavenly Chishtiyya," c. 1076/1665–6), a *tadhkira* (hagiographic compilation) of the lives of a subgroup of Chishtī Ṣūfīs who lived in Barnāvā and Raprī, towns near Shikohabad, in Uttar Pradesh. *Chishtiyya-yi bihishtiyya* was dedicated to Dārā Shikūh (d. 1069/1659), the eldest son of the Mughal emperor Shah Jahān (r. 1037–68/1628–57).

Little is known about the life of Shaykh ʿAlāʾ al-Dīn, but *Chishtiya-yi bihishtiya* is an important source on the Chishtīs of North India. It indicates the key role played by the Ṣūfīs, in particular Chishtīs such as the author's forefathers, in creating and sustaining Indo-Persian musical syncretism.

The teachings of the Chishtī order were brought to India by Shaykh Muʿīn al-Dīn Chishtī (d. 633/1236) who settled in Ajmer, in Rajasthan. The Chishtīs were known for their use of music in *samāʿ* (spiritual concert) to help them to enter ecstatic states. They associated with Hindus and welcomed them to their *khānqāh*s (Ṣūfī lodges). Ṣūfī gatherings became venues where the Turco-Persian music of the court fused with Hindu folk and devotional songs to create new genres of Indian vocal music.

Shaykh ʿAlāʾ al-Dīn's family, the Barnāvīs, originally migrated to India from Herat, in Afghanistan. An ancestor of Shaykh ʿAlāʾ al-Dīn, Shaykh Badr al-Dīn b. Sharaf al-Dīn Anṣārī (d. 788/1386), had been a pupil of the great Chishtī master Shaykh Nāṣir al-Dīn Maḥmūd, called Chirāgh-i Dihlī (lamp of Delhi, d. 757/1356). He was the first of the family to settle in Barnāvā, a village near Delhi. His successor, Shaykh Nāṣir al-Dīn (d. 856/1452) migrated to Raprī, east of Delhi, after Barnāvā was laid waste by Tīmūr's (r. 771–807/1370–1405) invasion in 800/1398. Pīr Buddhan (d. 903/1497–8), one of his sons, became the *pīr* (Pers., spiritual master (lit. 'old')) of Sulṭān Ḥusayn Sharqī of Jawnpur (r. 862–84/1458–79), a renowned musical connoisseur and composer. The family's involvement with music continued through successive generations, reaching its pinnacle with Shaykh Bahāʾ al-Dīn b. ʿAlāʾ al-Dīn (d. 1038/1628–9).

The collaboration between Ṣūfī and Hindu musicians is shown in *Chishtiyya-yi bihistiyya* through the life of Shaykh Bahāʾ

al-Dīn, a musical genius in the style of the great Indo-Persian Ṣūfī poet, scholar, and musician Amīr Khusraw (d. 725/1325), one of the earliest known composers of *khayāl*, a flexible form of Indian classical music providing great scope for improvisation. Amīr Khusraw, who was the pupil of the Chishtī *shaykh* Niẓām al-Dīn Awliyāʾ of Delhi (d. 725/1325), is considered the earliest and most celebrated Chishtī musician and poet to combine Arabic, Persian, Turkish, and Hindi to create new modes of artistic expression.

The Chokhs, a group of celebrated singers from the Deccan, were attached to the Barnāvī family from the time of Pīr Buddhan. The Chokhs and other musicians travelled with Shaykh Bahāʾ al-Dīn throughout Hindustan, as performers and as students of various forms of regional music. Shaykh Bahāʾ al-Dīn composed verses in Hindi, which were set to music and used by Hindus and Muslims alike to cure illnesses. The *shaykh* also composed tunes for the Vaishnavites (worshippers of Vishnu) and Bayrāgīs (Vaishnavite ascetics). Shaykh Bahāʾ al-Dīn had a close Bayrāgī friend, Dās Ghanun, who was the guru of Hindu notables.

The Barnāvīs served as a link between the classical and popular music and the poetry of India, allowing for new genres of musical and literary expression to develop from their original Indian, Persian, and Turkish roots.

Bibliography
Katherine Butler Brown, Evidence of Indo-Persian synthesis? The *tanbur* and *rudra vina* in seventeenth-century Indo-Persian treatises, *Journal of the Indian Musicological Society* 36–7 (2006), 89–103; Munis D. Faruqi, *The princes of the Mughal Empire 1504–1719*, Cambridge 2012; Nabi Hadi, *Dictionary of Indo-Persian literature*, New Delhi 1995; Nilay Kumar, Early Indo-Persian musical syncretism. The development of *khayal* (2014), http://docplayer.net/26867327-Early-indo-persian-musical-syncretism-the-development-of-khayal.html; Francesca Orsini, "Krishna is the truth of man." Mir Abdul Wahid Bilgrami's *Ḥaqāʾiq-i Hindī* (Indian truths) and the circulation of *dhrupad* and *bishnupad*, in Allison Busch and Thomas de Bruijin (eds.), *Culture and circulation. Literature in motion in early modern India* (Leiden 2014), 222–46; Saiyid Athar Abbas Rizvi, *A history of Sufism in India*, vol. 2, Delhi 1983; Hafiz Mahmud Sherani, Makhdum Shaikh Bahaʾud-Din Barnawi (in Urdu), *Oriental College Magazine* (1927), pt. 1, pp. 41–58, pt. 2, pp. 9–26.

Muneera Haeri

Beirut

The city of **Beirut**, Lebanon, despite modern invocations of its antiquity and its spectacular urban growth after independence, is a product of a convergence of political, economic, and cultural forces of the nineteenth century. "A beautiful ancient merchant city, it was one of the most important Syrian cities on the Roman coast. It rests on a nine-kilometrelong languet protruding into the Mediterranean Sea." This is how in 1875 Buṭrus al-Bustānī (1819–83), a leading figure in the nineteenth century *nahḍa*, the Arab Awakening, located his hometown on the global geo-historical grid in the entry "Bayrūt" for his Arabic encyclopaedia *Dāʾirat al-maʿārif*. Drawing on Latin sources and Arabic chronicles, al-Bustānī narrated the history of Beirut as a story of human resilience and urban triumph, culminating in his own modern Ottoman times. Subsequent historians of Beirut did not share al-Bustānī's cumulative view of history. Harvey Porter (d. 1923) at the Syrian Protestant College concluded in 1912 that by the mid-eighteenth century Beirut had "evidently declined." The Jesuit Orientalist Lūwis Shaykhū (Louis Cheikho, 1859–1927) lamented that the Ottomans had neglected Beirut's architectural heritage, and the *EI2* entry written by Nikita Elisséeff (1917–97) excised Ottoman history from Beirut's record altogether. Since then, scholarship has documented the city's transformation from a small port town of fewer than 8,000 inhabitants to a port-city vying with great Arab provincial and national capitals such as Aleppo and Damascus during the late-Ottoman and French Mandate periods. (See, for example, works by L. Fawaz, Davie, Eddé, Bodenstein, and Abou-Hodeib). Beirut's mid-twentieth century Lebanese internationalist architects dotted the city with concrete buildings that contrasted aesthetically with the lively downtown markets and the gardened-in, red-tiled, and triple-arched mansions above the old city (see, for example, Ruppert, Sarkis and Rowe, Arbid, Verdeil). By contrast, Beirut's Mamlūk and early-Ottoman histories remain less well documented and historians still rely to a large extent on the accounts of foreign travellers and Arabic chroniclers, such as al-Wāqidī (d. 207/822), Abū l-Fidā' (d. 732/1331), Ṣāliḥ b. Yaḥyā (d. 839/1436), Ḥamza b. Aḥmad Ibn Sibāṭ (d. 926/1520), Aḥmad al-Khālidī (1034/1625), and Isṭifān al-Duwayḥī (d. 1116/1704) (see, for example, Fuess).

Beirut's surface area expanded from 130 hectares in the 1840s to 350 hectares in the 1910s, while its population grew ten-fold over the course of the nineteenth century. From an estimated 10,000 inhabitants in the 1830s and 20,000 in the 1850s, the population jumped to 60,000 in the 1860s and peaked at 150,000 in 1914 (Fawaz, *Merchants*, 127–9; Davie, *Beyrouth et ses faubourgs*, 141). By World War I it had climbed to 220,000. Before 1860, Sunnīs constituted half the population. However, according to al-Bustānī in 1875, and Vital Cuinet in 1896, respectively, Beirut's demographic composition changed: more than two-thirds of the population was made up of Greek Orthodox (28/29%), Maronites (21/23%), Greek Catholics (8/7.5%), and Westerners (2.6/3.6%), as well as smaller contingents of Druze, Shīʿīs, Protestants and other Christians, and Jews. In the twentieth century, refugee streams added to Beirut's population mix. Thousands of Armenian, Assyrian, and Palestinian refugees settled in makeshift shelters and refugee camps on the outskirts of Beirut. At the outset of the twenty-first century, about one third of Lebanon's population of 4.5 million lived in Greater Beirut in an area of 7,600 hectares, but only around 400,000 in municipal Beirut (M. Fawaz).

Originally a Phoenician port, Beirut remained in the shadow of Byblos and Sidon. This changed when the Roman emperor Augustus (d. 14 C.E.) elevated Beirut to the status of a Roman colony in 14 B.C.E. and Augustus's powerful deputy Agrippa (d. 12 B.C.E.) built a large theatre, baths, and other urban amenities (Hall, 62–3). In 222 C.E., the Syrian-born emperor Alexander Severus (d. 235 C.E.) accredited Beirut's law school, which attracted jurists from across the empire and served as a repository of Roman jurisprudence for the next three centuries, culminating in the *Codex Justinianus*, completed in 534, which acknowledged Beirut as "the most beautiful city rightly considered the mother of laws" (*Codex Justinianus*, art. 7, in Jidejian, 1). The emperor Justinian (r. 527–65 C.E.) also Christianised Beirut, most notably by commemorating the martyrdom of Marthiana

(d. 303 C.E.), a "Beiruti martyr" who had struggled against the tyranny of Diocletian (al-Bustānī, 746).

A devastating earthquake and tsunami destroyed the region and ended Beirut's Roman prosperity in 551 (Darawcheh et al.). In 13/635 Yazīd b. Abī Sufyān (d. 18/639) conquered Beirut, along with Saida and Byblos/Jubayl (al-Wāqidī in Kassir, 71). The first prominent Muslim jurist to put Beirut on the cultural map of the expanding ʿAbbāsid empire was Abū ʿAmr al-Awzāʿī (d. 157/774), whose "living-tradition" approach to Islamic jurisprudence remained influential in Bilād al-Shām (Greater Syria) for two centuries (Judd, 26). During the reign of the ʿAbbāsid caliph Hārūn al-Rashīd (r. 170–93/786–809), the Banū Tanūkh—later known as Banū Buḥtur—took charge of Beirut and rebuilt its walls and citadel from the blocks of stone that were scattered all around, dating from Roman times (Nāṣir-i Khusraw, 9–11).

From 503/1110 to 690/1291, the Crusader conquests and Ayyūbid re-conquests again interrupted Beirut's prosperity. After a two-month long siege, King Baldwin of Jerusalem captured the city on 21 Shawwāl 503/13 May 1110 (William of Tyre, in Jidejian, 83). Salāḥ al-Dīn (Saladin, r. 564–89/1169–93) recaptured the city in 583/1187, but only ten years later it fell to the House of Ibelin (Ṣāliḥ b. Yaḥyā, 16–26).

Crusader kings ruled Beirut well into the Mamlūk era (r. 648–923/1250–1517), and the informal trade relations with the Buḥturids of the hinterland facilitated a measure of urban development. But in 690/1291, ʿAlam al-Dīn Sanqīr al-Shujāʿī conquered the city on behalf of the Mamlūk sultan in Egypt, killing many Crusaders, deporting the rest, and converting the recently built St. John's Church into a mosque. In contrast to the other coastal cities, which the Mamlūks either destroyed or demoted, Beirut became an administrative centre for the district of Baʿlabakk, in the province of Damascus, and maintained its status as a preeminent seaport for the region. The bubonic plague hit Beirut hard in 749/1348, and Genoese pirates marauded Beirut and its environs (Fuess, 160–71). The Mamlūks delegated the defence of Beirut to the Buḥturī *amīr*s of the southerly district of Gharb, in Damascus province, and to Turkmen troops, whom they settled in the northerly Kisrawān region of Tripoli province. Repairs to the two guard towers returned the city to its position as the main maritime trading outlet for the region (Ṣāliḥ b. Yaḥyā in Salibi, Buḥturids, 37).

After the Ottoman conquest of Bilād al-Shām in 922/1516, the Turkmen *amīr* Manṣūr al-ʿAssāf (r. 929–87/1523–79) and his troops brought Beirut under their control and built a government palace and a new mosque (Salibi, Northern Lebanon, 162). The Turkmens' southerly rival and successor, the *amīr* Fakhr al-Dīn Maʿn II (980–1045/1572–1635) made Beirut his winter residence and built Italianate gardens with water fountains as well as a control tower, Burj al-Kashshāf, on the southeastern side of the plain (al-Bustānī, 749). In the early twelfth/eighteenth century, governors from the Shihāb family, based in Mount Lebanon, built numerous intramural covered markets (sing. *qayṣariyya*) and *khān*s. However, political decisions were made at their court in Bayt al-Dīn and Bilād al-Shām's coastal capital Acre, where Ẓāhir al-ʿUmar (d. 1190/1775) and then Aḥmad Pasha al-Jazzār (d. 1219/1804) held the reins of regional power and a monopoly on Mediterranean trade (Abdel Nour, Philipp).

Acre's position was first challenged by a group of Beirut merchants who started to trade directly with European ships in 1808 (Philipp, 127–9; on eighteenth-century Beirut, see Qāʾidbay). Under Egyptian rule in the 1830s, a lazaretto—a facility where travellers could be quarantined upon arrival—was built on Beirut's harbour front (Boyer, 147–58). At the same time, steamships began to call, European consulates moved in, missionary schools cropped up on the outskirts of the old town, and a council of city notables was appointed to advise the Egyptian governor on urban affairs. The British and Austrians bombarded Beirut in 1840 to oust the Egyptians. This marked the beginning of the end of Beirut as a walled city. The first hotels opened on the seafront (Hanssen, 32, 120). In the 1850s, the Ottomans built the great *qishla* (military barracks) on the site of Burj Umm Dabbūs on Qanṭarī Hill overlooking the old town (Hanssen, 221, 241–5).

The civil war in Mount Lebanon and Damascus in the summer of 1860 brought thousands of Christian refugees as well as French soldiers and Western relief workers to the city. The Ottoman authorities reacted by building a military hospital alongside the *qishla* and by creating a local health council, which, in 1867, morphed into one of the empire's first municipal councils, whose twelve extramural electoral districts existed into the twentieth century. In 1864, Mount Lebanon became a *mutaṣarrifiyya*, an Ottoman province autonomous from both Beirut and Damascus, but under the joint supervision of the Ottoman Ministry of the Interior and a European council of diplomats. This arrangement endured until World War I (Akarlı). Meanwhile, Beirut's burgeoning intelligentsia reacted to the civil war by establishing a host of scientific associations and new schools, including al-Bustānī's own al-Madrasa al-Waṭaniyya in 1863 (Hanssen, 164–8). Soon the Syrian Protestant College (1866; the American University of Beirut since 1920) and the Jesuit Université de St. Joseph (1875) opened their gates to undergraduates. Financed by the booming silk trade in Mount Lebanon, well-to-do residents built triple-arched mansions on the hills above the old town (Bodenstein, 49–65), effectively staging Beirut's topography as an urban "amphitheatre" (Cuinet, 55).

Arabic newspapers started to proliferate, particularly during the governorship of Aḥmad Midḥat Pasha (1878–80) (Hanssen, 45). In 1884, the construction of the government palace on the former site of Fakhr al-Dīn's palace launched a revitalisation that turned the barren plain of Saḥlat al-Burj into the elegant Sāḥat al-Burj of fin de siècle postcards. Sūq Ṭawīla and Sūq Jamīl expanded the old city westward. Together, these activities fuelled an Ottoman civic spirit, which culminated in a campaign to make Beirut an Ottoman provincial capital (Hanssen, 35–52).

When Sulṭān Abdülhamid II (ʿAbd al-Ḥamīd II, r. 1876–1909) upgraded Beirut's status and attached the coastal regions of Tripoli and Latakia in the north and Acre, Haifa, and Nablus in the south to the new province of Beirut in 1888, the decision attracted local and international capital for major infrastructural development. Beirut's port enlargement, which cleared away the remnants of the Crusader castle and Mamlūk-era towers, was completed in 1893. Two years later the press hailed the new Beirut-Damascus railroad as a triumph of industry and a milestone in Beirut's regional ascendance. The Quarantine and slaughterhouses were moved out of the port area to make room for the first department store in Bilād al-Shām. International companies started to provide the city's main throughways with running water and with gas lighting in the 1890s. The Ottoman clocktower between the imperial barracks and the hospital, built by the local engineer Yūsuf Aftīmūs in 1899, signalled urban pride. In the 1900s, five tramway lines connected Nahr Bayrūt in the east to the new Lighthouse in Ra's Bayrūt in the west and the port and the old town to the Pine Forest and distant Furn al-Shubbāk in the south. These were the axes along which Beirut's urban expansion would take place during the twentieth century (Hanssen, 99–104).

During World War I, Ottoman governor general Cemal (Jamāl) Pasha had dozens of Arab intellectuals hanged on Sāḥat al-Burj for the crime of treason, amidst an Allied naval blockade and famine in Beirut and Mount Lebanon (Thompson, ch. 1; Fawaz, *Land*; Tanielian). Ottoman martial law enabled property expropriation and legalised boulevards cutting through Beirut's old urban tissue. When the League of Nations divided the Ottoman provinces of Bilād al-Shām into French and British Mandates of Lebanon, Syria, Transjordan and Palestine in 1922, France developed Beirut as its Levantine capital and perforated the old town by constructing Rues Foch, Weygand, and Allenby, invoking Ottoman wartime laws (Davie, *Beyrouth, 1825–1975*, 75–8). The Duraffourd Master Plan of 1926 razed much of Beirut's remaining eighteenth century urban fabric to build the Place de l'Étoile. Local architects were encouraged to experiment on public buildings. The engineer Yūsuf Aftīmūs built the iconic neo-Mamlūk Municipal building and the Grand Theatre across from it in the 1920s. In the 1930s, the architect Mardiros Altounian (1889–1958) designed the Parliament in neo-Mamlūk and the clocktower on Étoile Square in Art Deco style (Davie, *Beyrouth, 1825–1975*, 80–1). The National Museum of Beirut, which was designed by Antoine Nahas (1901–66) in neo-Pharaonic form, opened in 1942 (Tabet, 17; Kaufman, 122–5).

After Lebanese independence in 1943, Beirut acquired the sobriquets "Paris of the East" and "Merchant Republic" (Gates) as it came to function as a global hub in the circulation of petro-dollars and political intrigue. The international airport at Khalda opened in 1950, and the banking secrecy law of 1956 attracted Gulf capital and ushered in urban transformations that even the most visionary colonial master planner could not have foreseen. Automobile traffic increased as multi-lane highways cut through neighbourhoods, and the Haddad-Chehab Ring-Road encircled the downtown core. The Ḥamrā' District in Ra's Beirut became the local entertainment district and the regional centre for the Arabic and international press (Khalaf and Kongstad; Kassir, 453–71, 595–8). But neither the state nor the nation's capital was equipped to deal with the resultant massive immigration, as tens of thousands of Lebanese rural poor sought opportunities in the sprawling and precarious informal sectors of Beirut's economy. These migrant workers were Beirut's disenfranchised underclass in an electoral system that determined they vote in their village of origin and not in Beirut, their place of residence (Denoeux, 115–16; Johnson 2001, 156, 160). Beirut's financial bubble burst with the INTRA Bank crash of 1966 (Safieddine, ch. 5). The Israeli raid on the airport in 1968 and the Palestinian resistance's move from Jordan to Beirut in 1970 turned the city into an 'Arab Hanoi'. Leftist forces mobilised to overthrow the sectarian system of economic inequality. Instead, the ensuing Lebanese Civil War of 1975 to 1990 cost an estimated 150,000 Lebanese lives, bifurcated Beirut militarily, and reduced life to the protective confines of the neighbourhood (Mouzoune, 81–95, 139–57).

The postwar reconstruction efforts, led by billionaire Prime Minister Rafic Hariri (assassinated 2005), prioritised physical over social recovery. It was determined that the rebuilding of downtown Beirut would be the catalyst for economic revival (Khalaf and Khoury, 54). Under the motto of "Ancient City of the Future," SOLIDERE, the company Hariri formed to implement this vision through the reconstruction of downtown Beirut, evicted wartime squatters, expropriated property owners, commissioned the Spanish star architect Rafael Moneo with rebuilding the *sūq*s, and employed hundreds of Syrian limestone masons (Chalcraft). The choice for Mandate-era 'retro-chic' was a disavowal of both Beirut's Ottoman-era modernism and the international style of the 1950s (Sarkis and Rowe, 83–105). When late-Ottoman style did return to Sāḥat al-Burj between 2002 and 2008, it was with the disproportionately large Muḥammad al-Amīn Mosque, which projected the political claims of the slain former prime minister's Sunnī constituency to Beirut's future-past (Vloeberghs). Elsewhere, a few Ottoman buildings that survived the war- and postwar destruction in the pericentral districts were guarded as national treasures by heritage activists, while many others, like al-Bustānī's al-Madrasa al-Waṭaniyya in Zuqāq al-Blāṭ, crumbled into oblivion (Bodenstein et al.).

Bibliography

Toufoul Abu-Hobeib, *A taste for home. The modern middle class in Ottoman Beirut*, Stanford 2017; Antoine Abdel Nour, *Introduction à l'histoire urbaine de la Syrie ottomane (XVIe–XVIIIe siècles)*, Beirut 1982; Abū l-Fidāʾ, *al-Mukhtaṣar fī akhbār al-bashar*, 4 vols., Cairo 1998; Ḥāfiẓ Abū Muṣliḥ, *Tārīkh al-Durūz fī Bayrūt. 1017m–1975m*, Beirut 1998; Engin Deniz Akarlı, *The long peace. Ottoman Lebanon, 1960–1920*, London 1993; George Arbid, *Practicing modernism in Beirut: architecture in Lebanon, 1946–1970, PhD Thesis*, Cambridge, MA, 2002; Jean-Luc Arnaud (ed.), *Beyrouth, Grand Beyrouth*, Beirut 1997; Ralph Bodenstein et al., *History, space and social conflict in Beirut. The quarter of Zokak el-Blat*, Beirut 2005; Ralph Bodenstein, *Villen in Beirut. Wohnkultur und sozialer Wandel, 1860–1930*, Berlin 2012; Benoît Boyer, *Conditions hygiéniques actuelles de Beyrouth (Syrie) et de ses environs immédiats*, Lyon 1897; Buṭrus al-Bustānī, Bayrūt, in *Dāʾirat al-Maʿārif* (Beirut 1875), 5:744–53; John Chalcraft, *The invisible cage. Syrian migrant workers in Lebanon*, Stanford 2008; Saïd Chehabe ed-Dine, *Géographie humaine de Beyrouth, avec une étude sommaire sur les deux villes de Damas et Bagdad*, Beirut 1960; Dominique Chevallier, Signes de Beyrouth en 1834, in *Villes et travail en Syrie du XIX au XX siecle* (Beirut 1982), 9–28; Vital Cuinet, *La Turquie d'Asie*, vol. 2, *La Syrie, Liban et Palestine*, Paris 1896; Ryad Darawcheh, Mohamed Reda Sbeinati, Claudio Margottini, and Salvatore Paolini, The 9 July 551 AD Beirut earthquake, eastern Mediterranean region, *Journal of Earthquake Engineering* 4 (2000), 403–14; May Davie, *Beyrouth et ses faubourgs (1840–1940). Une intégration inachevée*, Beirut 1996; May Davie, *Beyrouth, 1825–1975. Un siècle et demi d'urbanisme*, Beirut 2001; Michael F. Davie, Maps and the historical topography of Beirut, *Berytus* 35 (1987), 141–63; Guilian Denoeux, *Urban unrest in the Middle East. A comparative study of informal networks in Egypt, Iran and Lebanon*, New York 1993; Isṭifān al-Duwayhī, *Taʾrīkh al-azmina*, ed. Buṭrus Fahd, Jūniyya 1976 [1699]; Carla Eddé, *Beyrouth. Naissance d'une capitale (1918–1924)*, Paris 2009; Nikita Elisséeff, Bayrūt, *EI2*; Leila Tarazi Fawaz, *Merchants and migrants in nineteenth-century Beirut*, Cambridge MA 1983; Leila Tarazi Fawaz, *A land of aching hearts. The Middle East in the Great War*, Cambridge MA 2016; Mona Fawaz, *Understanding slums. The case of Beirut, Lebanon*, https://www.ucl.

ac.uk/dpu-projects/Global_Report/pdfs/Beirut.pdf; Albrecht Fuess, *Verbranntes Ufer. Auswirkungen mamlukischer Seepolitik auf Beirut und die syro-palästinensische Küste (1250–1517)*, Leiden 2001; Toufic K. Gaspard, *A political economy of Lebanon, 1948–2002. The limits of laissez-faire*, Leiden 2004; Carolyn L. Gates, *The merchant republic of Lebanon. Rise of an open economy*, London 1998; Marlène Ghorayeb, *Beyrouth sous mandat français. Construction d'une ville moderne*, Paris 2014; Linda Jones Hall, *Roman Berytus. Beirut in late antiquity*, London 2004; Jens Hanssen, *Fin de siècle Beirut. The making of an Ottoman provincial capital*, Oxford 2005; Salīm Ḥasan Hashshī, *Durūz Bayrūt. Taʾrīkhuhum wa-maʾāsīhum*, Beirut 1985; Elizabeth Holt, *Fictitious capital. Silk, cotton, and the rise of the Arabic novel*, New York 2017; Ḥamza b. Aḥmad Ibn Sibāṭ, *Taʾrīkh al-Durūz fī ākhir ʿahd al-Mamālīk*, ed. Nāʾila Qāʾidbay, Beirut 1989; Nina Jidejian, *Beirut through the ages*, Beirut 1973; Michael Johnson, *Class & client in Beirut. The Sunni Muslim community and the Lebanese state, 1840–1985*, London 1986; Michael Johnson, *All honourable men; the social origins of war in Lebanon*, London 2001; Steven C. Judd, Competitive hagiography in biographies of al-Awzāʿī and Sufyān al-Thawrī, *JAOS* 122:1 (2002), 25–37; Ilyās J. Jurayj, *Wilāyat Bayrūt 1887–1914. Al-Tārīkh al-siyāsī wa-l-iqtiṣādī*, ʿAkkār 2004; Samir Kassir, *Histoire de Beyrouth*, Beirut 2003; Asher Kaufmann, *Reviving Phoenicia. The search for an identity in Lebanon*, London 2004; Samir Khalaf and Per Kongstad, *Hamra of Beirut. A case of rapid urbanization*, Leiden 1973; Samir Khalaf and Philip S. Khoury (eds.), *Recovering Beirut. Urban design and post-war reconstruction*, Leiden 1993; Aḥmad b. Muḥammad al-Khālidī [1625], *Lubnān fī ʿahd al-Amīr Fakhr al-Dīn al-Maʿnī al-Thānī*, ed. Asad Rustum and Fuʾād Afrām al-Bustānī, Beirut 1936; Nāṣir-i Khusraw, *Diary of a journey through Syria and Palestine*, trans. Guy Le Strange, London 1893; Muḥammad Mashnūq, *Ḥukūmat Bayrūt. Ishkāliyāt al-qiyāda al-ʿaṣriyya li-baladiyyat al-ʿāṣima*, Beirut 1995; Abdelkrim Mouzoune, *Les transformations du paysage spatio-communautaire de Beyrouth. 1975–1996*, Paris 1999; Thomas Philipp, *Acre. The rise and fall of a Palestinian city*, New York 2002; Harvey Porter, *The history of Beirut*, Beirut 1912; Nāʾila Qāʾidbay (ed.), *Mukhtaṣar taʾrīkh al-asāqifa alladhīna raqū martabat riʾāsat al-kahanūt al-jalīla fī madīnat Bayrūt*, Beirut 2002; Helmut Ruppert, *Beirut. Eine westlich geprägte Stadt des Orients*, Erlangen 1969; Hicham Safieddine, *Banking on the state. The financial foundations of Lebanon*, Stanford 2019; Robert Saliba, *Beirut 1920–1940. Domestic architecture between tradition and modernity*, Beirut 1998; Kamal S. Salibi, The Buḥturids of the Ġarb. Mediaeval lords of Beirut and of southern Lebanon, *Arabica* 8 (1961), 74–97; Kamal S. Salibi, Northern Lebanon under the dominance of Ġazīr (1517–1591), *Arabica* 14 (1967), 144–66; Kamal S. Salibi, The secret of the house of Maʿn, *IJMES* 4 (1973), 272–87; Hashim Sarkis and Peter Rowe (eds.), *Projecting Beirut. Episodes of the construction and reconstruction of a modern city*, Munich 1998; Lūwis Shaykhū, *Bayrūt. Taʾrīkhuhā wa-āthāruhā*, Beirut 1993; Jad Tabet (ed.), Portrait de ville. Beyrouth, *Archiscopie 17*, Paris 2001; Melanie Schulze Tanielian, Feeding the city. The Beirut municipality and the politics of food during World War I, *IJMES* 46 (2014), 737–58; Elizabeth Thompson, *Colonial citizens. Republican rights, paternal privilege, and gender in French Syria and Lebanon*, New York 2000; Éric Verdeil, *Beyrouth et ses urbanistes. Une ville en plans (1946–1975)*, Beirut 2009; Ward Vloeberghs, *Architecture, power and religion in Lebanon. Rafiq Hariri and the politics of sacred space in Beirut*, Leiden 2015; Muḥammad b. ʿUmar al-Wāqidī, *Futūḥ al-Shām*, Cairo 1955; Ṣāliḥ b. Yaḥyā, *Taʾrīkh Bayrūt. Récits des anciens de la famille de Buḥtur b. ʿAlī, emir du Gharb de Beyrouth*, ed. Kamal S. Salibi and Francis Hours, Beirut 1969.

Jens Hanssen

Boy Scout

The **Boy Scout** movement was founded in 1907–8 by General Sir Robert Baden-Powell as a means to strengthen character and physical fitness among British youths. In the years following its inception, the Scouting movement began to spread to Muslim countries, first through British colonial administrators and Protestant educational institutions. After World

War I, Scouts from other countries and communities, including French Catholics, equally became active among Muslims. Despite their insistence on being a peaceful organisation, the Boy Scout "troops" were structured along military lines, cultivating an ethos of loyalty and comradeship, together with religious virtues and a love of nature. In the Muslim world, Scouting was soon adopted by local modernising elites and regimes attempting to construct a nation-state, for example, in the Ottoman Empire after the 1908 revolution (later to be continued in republican Turkey), in Egypt and Iraq under their constitutional monarchies (1923–52 and 1921–58, respectively), and in Iran under the Pahlavi dynasty (1925–79). The term "Scouting" was translated into Turkish as *izcilik*, into Arabic as *kashshāfa*, and into Persian as *pīshahangī*. Originally devised in a Christian European (and not least, imperial) setting, the Scout rules were in part amended to suit the local context. Muslim Scouts commonly situate their founding principles in the Islamic faith and the practice of the prophet Muḥammad. Prophetic traditions (*aḥādīth*) mentioning the "strong believer" have sometimes been interpreted as referring also to physical strength, as acquired by Scouts. In an often-quoted *ḥadīth* transmitted by ʿAbdallāh b. ʿUmar b. al-Khaṭṭāb (d. 73/693), the Prophet admonishes believers to teach their children how to swim, ride a horse, and shoot arrows. Finally, explicitly Muslim Scouting associations translated the Boy Scout motto "Be prepared" by the Qurʾānic phrase "*wa-aʿiddū*," from Sūrat al-anfāl (Q 8:60).

Scouting helped to establish youth as a distinct social category and was linked to the emergence of an indigenous modern middle class in various parts of the Islamic world. Scouting activities were mostly centred on male youths, but not restricted to them. The presence of Girl Guides (the female equivalent of Boy Scouts) was of importance for modernisation and emancipation schemes, particularly among secular and leftist regimes, but also among Islamic reformers, such as the North African *iṣlāḥ* movements. In colonial settings, Scouting was part of the associational life of the new middle class, which was partly Westernised but, at the same time, professed an anti-colonial nationalism, exemplifying the specific ambiguity of the colonial situation.

In colonial settings from Mandate Syria and Palestine to French North and West Africa, the authorities deemed the Muslim Scouts potentially dangerous. In fact, the Algerian Scouting movement, which had originated in Islamic reformist circles during the 1930s, eventually became the backbone for the National Liberation Front (Jabhat al-Taḥrīr al-Waṭanī/Front de Libération Nationale, FLN) in its struggle for independence after 1954. In French West Africa, the Éclaireurs de France (the secular French Boy Scouts) were taken over, in time, by local nationalist elites.

While all French territories knew the split between secular and Catholic Boy Scouts (who all adhered to the international Baden-Powell organisation, though), countries with multiple ethnic and religious communities saw a further differentiation of organised Scouting. In Mandate Palestine, the Arab Scout associations, who sometimes, but not always brought together Muslims and Christians, competed with their British and Zionist counterparts, whereas in Syria and Lebanon the various Muslim and Christian communities each had their own organisations.

In the Lebanese confessional system this situation has endured to this day with religious-political movements, such as the Shīʿī Ḥizballāh, having their own Scouting organisations. In British India and the Netherlands East Indies (Indonesia), indigenous Scout movements, among them different Muslim organisations, developed from the 1920s onward—many of them not affiliated with the world movement founded by Baden-Powell, but tied to various local communities and political parties. Here, as elsewhere, the modernising post-colonial state tried to unify the Scout movement into a national organisation.

Today, there are more than nine million Muslim Scouts in the World Organization of the Scout Movement (WOSM). Among them are also a number of Muslim Scout troops in Western countries, such as Britain, France, Germany, and the United States.

Bibliography

Nicolas Bancel, Les Scouts de France et les Éclaireurs de France en AOF (1945–1960). Les conditions sociales et politiques du développement de deux mouvements de jeunesse en contacte colonial, in Évelyne Combeau-Mari (ed.), *Sport et loisirs dans les colonies, XIXe–XXe siècles. Asie, Pacifique, océan Indien, Afrique, Caraïbes* (Paris 2004), 219–38; Nicolas Bancel, Daniel Denis, and Youcef Fatès (eds.), *De l'Indochine à l'Algérie. La jeunesse en mouvements des deux côtés du miroir colonial, 1940–1960*, Paris 2003; Nelson R. Block and Tammy M. Proctor (eds.), *Scouting frontiers. Youth and the Scout movement's first century*, Newcastle 2009; Arnon Degani, They were prepared. The Palestinian Arab Scout movement 1920–1948, *BrisMES* 41/2 (2014), 200–18; Jennifer Dueck, A Muslim jamboree. Scouting and youth culture in Lebanon under the French Mandate, *French Historical Studies* 30/3 (2007), 485–516; Wilson Chacko Jacob, *Working out Egypt. Effendi masculinity and subject formation in colonial modernity, 1870–1940*, Durham NC and London 2011; Mikiya Koyagi, Moulding future soldiers and mothers of the Iranian nation. Gender and physical education under Reza Shah, 1921–41, *International Journal of the History of Sport* 26/11 (2009), 1668–96; Nazan Maksudyan, Agents or pawns? Nationalism and Ottoman children during the Great War, *Journal of the Ottoman and Turkish Studies Association* 3/1 (2016), 139–64; Pujo Semedi, Padvinders, Pandu, Pramuka. Youth and state in the 20th century Indonesia, *Africa Development* 36/3–4 (2011), 19–38; Sofia Maria Tagliabue, Inside Hezbollah. The al-Mahdi Scouts, education, and resistance, *Digest of Middle East Studies* 24/1 (2015), 74–95.

Jakob Krais

Bukhara, art and architecture

The **art and architecture** of **Bukhara** are marked by currents that were characteristic of Islamic art in general as well as regional and local elements, reflecting the city's role as a political and cultural centre in Islamic Central Asia. Ancient traditions of Central Asia were integrated with functional and formal developments from the capitals of the Arab caliphate. An intense exchange with Iran, and later with India, took place from the Sāmānid period (204–395/819–1005) and continued to the nineteenth century. With the Russian conquest of Central Asia, Bukhara remained a stronghold of tradition, where art was practised with few systemic changes until the Soviet conquest in 1920. Since then, modernism has held sway, with occasional references to regional traditions, while pre-modern arts and crafts practices continue as elements of folklore for tourists.

1. Architecture

With its great number of preserved monuments, the city of Bukhara (a

UNESCO World Heritage Site since 1993) can be seen as the major repertory of Islamic architecture in Central Asia, although much of its substance has been renewed or replaced in the twentieth and twenty-first centuries. These restorations have largely been ignored by architectural historians, so that monuments are frequently classified under a single period, although in many cases their features have been the product of multiple building phases. The citadel has archaeological traces from the city's pre-Islamic period, but for the most part the architecture of Bukhara before the Islamic conquest (from 91/710 onwards) and during the first centuries of Islamic rule can be reconstructed only from finds at neighbouring sites, such as Paykend and Varakhsha.

The city's Islamic architecture was apparently based on pre-Islamic regional traditions. In addition, building types and functions, particularly in the religious sphere, were adopted from the central Islamic lands. The connection with Iran was intimate and lasting, with builders and artists transferring innovations in techniques and motifs from one area to the other. The architecture of Bukhara, in turn, was crucial for and exerted influence over other locales in Central Asia. At the same time, it was also a source for Mughal architecture, a result of the migration of architects.

Construction was usually of brick and mud-brick or rammed earth, frequently on stone foundations. Wood was used for load-bearing and bracing elements, such as columns, lintels, ceilings, and frames within walls. Prior to the Mongol conquest in the seventh/thirteenth century, brick ornament was important for the design of surfaces, usually in conjunction with stucco and paint, but from the late eighth/fourteenth century onwards, glazed tiles became a dominating element of polychrome façade decoration. Sculptural ornament such as *muqarnas* was made of plaster or wood, and for interiors an intricate technique was developed of delicate stucco relief, with polychrome paint and gilding (nowadays termed *kundal*).

Little has been preserved of the city walls and the gates, which were protected by flanking half-round towers. The citadel (Pers. *arg*) [No. 1 in Illustration 1, Map of Bukhara], the fortified seat of the government over the centuries, certainly since the Hellenistic period, rises in the northwest of the old city. Its walls, currently consisting of battered curtain walls between strongly protruding round-front towers, have been rebuilt many times. The gateway on the west side gives access to the reception area, which contains a mosque and an audience courtyard. The east part of the citadel was completely destroyed in the 1920 Soviet siege of the city.

The Mausoleum of the Sāmānids [No.1.2 and Illustration 2], constructed in the first half of the fourth/tenth century, is of greatest importance for the history of Islamic funerary architecture. It was built in a cemetery that was originally outside the western city walls. The arrangement of the body of the building with a dome on a cubical base was a type of Islamic mausoleum that became widespread in different parts of the Islamic world. However, the slightly battered walls, the non-functional upper gallery, and the four small domes at the corners indicate an earlier, probably regional architectural source. The pointed-arch openings on all four sides have also been explained as derived from Sāsānian *chahār ṭāq* (the dome resting on four open arches, also used for Zoroastrian fire temples). The mausoleum is distinctive for its well-preserved decoration, with a combination of elaborate

Illustration 1. Map of Bukhara (after Parfenov-Fenin 1910), with monuments numbered. The enlargement of the city in the tenth/sixteenth century is shown in lighter shading.

1. Citadel
2. Mausoleum of the Sāmānids
3. Great Mosque (Masjid-i Kalān) with minaret
4. Mosque of Magok-i Attari
5. Namāzgāh
6. Mausoleum of Sayf al-Dīn Bākharzī
7. Mausoleum of Buyān Qulī Khān
8. Chashma Ayyūb
9. Madrasa of Ulugh Beg
10. Madrasa Mīr-i ʿArab, 933–43/1527–36
11. Tāq-i Ṣarrāfān, before 945/1539
12. Mosque of Vālida-i ʿAbd al-ʿAzīz Khān, c. 946–57/1540–50
13. Mausoleum of Ḥaḍrat-i Imām
14. Mausoleum of Turkī Jandī, probably first half of tenth/sixteenth century
15. Baland Mosque, probably first half of tenth/sixteenth century
16. Mosque and Khānqāh of Khvāja Zayn al-Dīn, probably before 957/1550
17. Madrasa Gāvkushān, 969–81/1562–73
18. Madrasa Mādar-i Khān, 974/1566–7
19. Madrasa Kūkaldāsh, 976/1568–9
20. Mosque of Gāvkushān, 986–92/1578–84
21. Madrasa Jūybārī Kalān, possibly 990/1582–3
22. Tāq-i Zargarān, 2nd half of tenth/sixteenth century
23. Tāq-i Tilpak Furūshān, 995/1587
24. Tīmche of ʿAbdallāh Khān, 1090s/1580s
25. Madrasa ʿAbdallāh Khān, 996–1000/1588–92
26. Khānqāh Faiḍābād, 1005–7/1597–9
27. Khānqāh Nādir Dīvān Begi, 1029/1619–20
28. Madrasa Nādir Dīvān Begi
29. Mosque of Magok-i Kurpa, 1047/1637
30. Madrasa of ʿAbd al-ʿAzīz Khān II, 1064/1654
31. Madrasa Sangīn Muḥammad Sharīf ("Ghāziyān"), 1142/1730
32. Madrasa of Chār Minār, 1222/1807
33. Mosque of Bālā Ḥauḍ, early twentieth century
34. Central Post Office, early twentieth century
35. Russian-Asian Bank, early twentieth century
36. School, early twentieth century
37. Ophthalmological clinic, early twentieth century
38. Shukhov Tower, after c. 1925

Illustration 2. Bukhara, Mausoleum of the Sāmānids. View from southwest, 2009. Photograph courtesy of G. Ruppert.

brick patterns for larger features, and terracotta and stucco for details (cf. Gabriele Stock, Das Samanidenmausoleum in Bukhara, *Archäologische Mitteilungen aus Iran* 22 [1989], 253–90; 23 [1990], 231–60; 24 [1991], 223–46).

The present location of the Great Mosque (Masjid-i Kalān) [No. 1.3] dates back to the Qarakhānid period (fifth-sixth/eleventh-twelfth century), as indicated by the minaret [Illustration 3]. The tower, nearly fifty metres high and with a diameter of nine metres at the base, was constructed by order of Arslān Khān, around 520/1127 (according to the fragmentary inscription). The combination of a voluminous, tapering shaft with a slightly splayed lantern gives the building its characteristic profile, which has become iconic for the silhouette of Bukhara and has served as a prototype for minarets in Central Asia. A sequence of patterned bands decorates the brick surface. The adjacent Great Mosque (126 × 81 metres) has a plan and some basic features that are generally assumed to go back to the Qarakhānid period, although the earliest parts of the existing structure can be

Illustration 3. Bukhara, Minaret of the Great Mosque (Kalān Minaret). View from Southwest. Photograph courtesy of Lorenz Korn.

dated only to the ninth/fifteenth century on the basis of their style. The portal with its large *ayvān* (Ar. *īwān*, hall open to the exterior or to a courtyard; here: monumental portal niche), half-octagonal in plan, was rebuilt under ʿUbaydallāh Sulṭān (Abūlkhayrid ruler of Bukhara, r. 918–46/1512–39) in 910/1514 (inscription). During the same period, part of the *qibla ayvān* was renewed and the *miḥrāb* (prayer niche indicating the direction of Mecca) decorated with faience mosaic, signed by the calligrapher Bāyezīd Pūrānī.

The Mosque of Magok-i Attari [No. 1.4] was built in the sixth/twelfth century and rebuilt in 953/1547 (according to the inscription, now mutilated). Speculation about the remnants of an ancient temple underlying the mosque has not been corroborated by excavations. The sixth/twelfth-century south portal is recessed in a deep niche, flanked with characteristic buttresses, and richly decorated with brick patterns and terracotta relief, with *muqarnas* filling the corners. Turquoise glaze highlights the inscription on the frontal arch; this is one of the earliest appearances of glazed ceramics in the architectural decoration of Central Asia. The existing prayer hall of three by four domed bays and the eastern entrance belong to the re-building under ʿAbd al-ʿAzīz Khān (r. 946–57/1540–50) (Tupev, II, 211–14). A similar scheme was realised in the eleventh/seventeenth century in the mosque of Magok-i Kurpa [No. 1.29].

The Namāzgāh [No. 1.5], located south of the old city, consists of a canopy of five vaulted bays arranged against the *qibla* wall, built in three distinct phases. While the core of the *qibla* wall has been dated to 513/1119–20 on the basis of a textual source, its surface was redecorated in the late eighth/fourteenth century. The pillars and vaults of the baldachin in their present shape belong to the tenth/sixteenth century.

In a former cemetery area east of the old city, the mausoleums of the Ṣūfī Sayf al-Dīn Bākharzī (586–659/1190–1261) and of the Chaghatayid ruler Buyān Qulī Khān (r. 749–60/1348–59) [Nos. 1.6–7] remain as two important monuments from the eighth/fourteenth century. They feature the typical Central Asian combination of a larger domed prayer hall with a smaller room containing the burial. With its glazed relief ceramics, the Buyān Qulī Khān Mausoleum is a key example of pre-Tīmūrid architectural decoration (Claus-Peter Haase, Buyan Quli Chan, Baudekor, *Damaszener Mitteilungen* 11 (1999 [2000]), 205–25).

The sanctuary of Chashma Ayyūb [No. 1.8], in the west of the city, was built in the Tīmūrid period (771–913/1370–1507), according to an inscription dated 785/1383–4. It was significantly expanded in the late tenth/sixteenth century, with vaults of variegated shapes. The only other Tīmūrid religious foundation was the Madrasa of Ulugh Beg (r. 850–3/1447–9) [No. 1.9], completed in 820/1417. A signature names the builder (*bannāʾ*) as having been Ismāʿīl b. Ṭāhir b. Maḥmūd al-Iṣfahānī. The two-*īwān* courtyard with cells arranged in two floors represents a reduced type, compared with its sister building in Samarkand. The decoration is characteristic of the Tīmūrid period.

During the tenth/sixteenth century, architecture in Bukhara flourished under the Abū l-Khayrid (Shaybānid, r. 906–1007/1500–99) dynasty. Patronage was shared among the ruler, the powerful men of the state (*amīrs*), and leaders of religious groups, most notably the *shaykhs* of

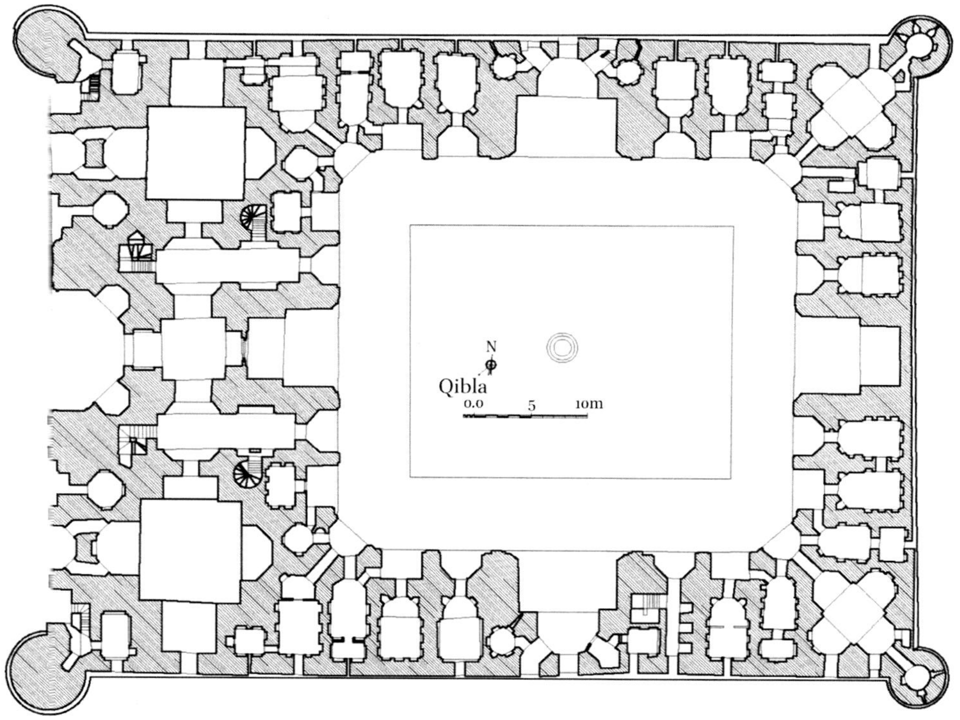

Illustration 4a. Bukhara, Madrasa Mīr-i ʿArab, ground plan (after Mustafa Tupev, Die Madrasa Mir-i Arab, *Bamberger Orientstudien* [Bamberg 2015], 533).

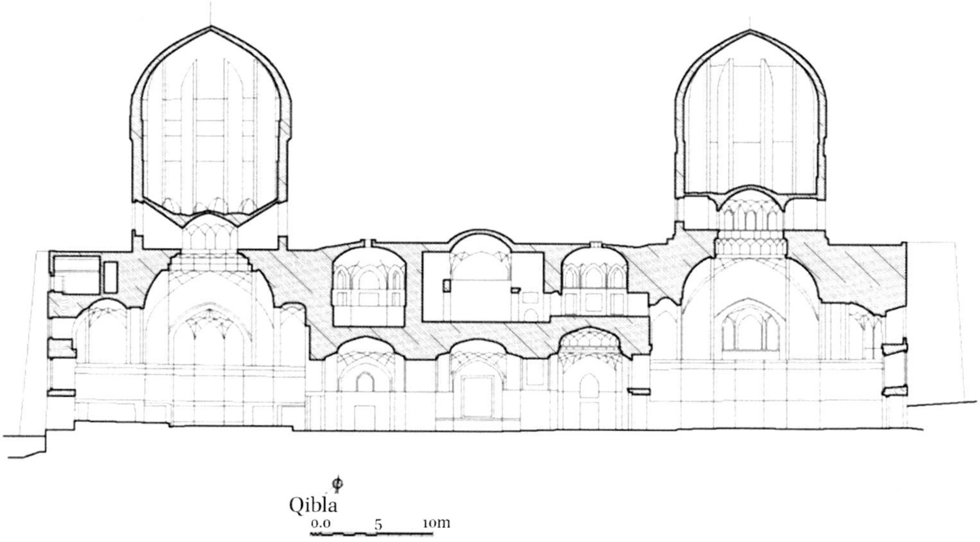

Illustration 4b. Bukhara, Madrasa Mīr-i ʿArab, section (after Mustafa Tupev, Die Madrasa Mir-i Arab, *Bamberger Orientstudien* [Bamberg 2015], 537).

the Naqshbandī and ʿIshqiyya Ṣūfī orders. The city was reshaped with architectural accents along its main roads and with clusters of monuments bordering public squares, sometimes with axial alignment of opposing façades. Apart from the Great Mosque, *madrasa*s and *khānqāh*s (Ṣūfī convents) were the most prestigious buildings. In the secular spaces of the bazaar and street, vaults and domed crossings (*ṭāq*) were built, an element of market infrastructure and urban beautification initiated by order of the rulers [Nos. 1.11; 1.22–24]. As another element of public infrastructure, the system of open water basins (sing. *ḥawḍ*) fed by channels was also extended.

*Madrasa*s followed the types established in the Tīmūrid period, with *ayvān*s and cells surrounding a rectangular courtyard, frequently with chamfered corners; new variations can be seen in the entrance blocks with U-shaped corridors and variegated shapes of vaulting covering the halls used for prayer, teaching, and burial. From its location, size, and architecture, the Madrasa of Mīr-i ʿArab [No. 1.10 and Illustrations 4a and 4b] can be attributed to ʿUbaydallāh Sulṭān (r. 918–46/1512–39) (Mustafa Tupev, Die Madrasa Mir-i Arab, *Bamberger Orientstudien* [Bamberg 2015], 517–74). Other large *madrasa*s are the Gāvkushān, built by the Jūybārīs, according to its inscription, in 978/1570–71 [No. 1.17]; the so-called Mādar-i Khān, probably donated by ʿAbdallāh Khān (r. 991–1006/1583–98) when he was crown prince, according to its chronogram of 974/1566–7 [No. 1.18]; the Madrasa of ʿAbdallāh's minister Qulbābā Kūkaldāsh, datable to 976/1568–9 [No. 1.19]; and the Madrasa Jūybārī Kalān (built probably by Khvāja Saʿd Jūybārī c. 990/1582–3) [No. 1.21]. At the end of the century, the full array of spatial arrangements was realised in the Madrasa of ʿAbdallāh Khān, c. 996–1000/1588–92 [No. 1.25].

An architectural form that was universally applied is the hall with a square plan and a dome construction over intersecting transversal arches, which can be seen in *madrasa* complexes, but also independently in *khānqāh*s [No. 1.5 and Illustration 5] and mausoleums, as, for example, the mausoleums of Ḥaẓrat-i Imām and of Turkī Jandī [Nos. 1.13–14]. A very similar kind of dome over intersecting arches (however, without the lantern) covers the *qibla ayvān* of the mosque of the mother of ʿAbd al-ʿAzīz Khān (r. 946–57/1540–50) [No. 1.12]. It was also used for the central bay of the Bukhara Namāzgāh, and even for commercial buildings, such as the Tāq-i Ṣarrāfān (inscription of 945/1539) [No. 1.11].

*Khānqāh*s of the tenth/sixteenth century show a variety of plans and elevations, partly a result of combinations with other functions, such as communal mosques. A monumental variation of the hall vaulted with intersecting arches was built by ʿAbd al-ʿAzīz Khān in 951/1544 at the tomb of Bahāʾ al-Dīn Naqshband (d. 791/1389) in a village east of the city. Around the turn of the eleventh/seventeenth century, the *khānqāh*s of the Ṣūfī *shaykh* Ḥākim Mullā Mīr (outside the city, in the village of Chilengu), and the one founded by a certain Dūst Dīvānbegī in 1007/1598–9 in the northeastern suburb of Faizabad (Fayḍābād) [No. 1.26] feature a large central domed hall flanked with small cells that open to the outside. This same scheme was taken up for the *khānqāh* of the minister Nādir Dīvān Begi in 1029/1619–20 [No. 1.27].

The city's residential quarters were equipped with small mosques, usually

Illustration 5. Complex of Chār Bakr, interior of *khānqāh* looking south, 2008. Photograph courtesy of Lorenz Korn.

consisting of an undivided prayer hall roofed either with a dome or with a flat roof on pillars, and with porticos on the outside (examples include the mosques of Āy Bināq and of Khvāja Tabband). However, the Baland Mosque (probably second quarter of tenth/sixteenth century, based on style) is considerably larger than the usual neighbourhood mosques and features elaborate decoration on the exterior and interior, with glazed tiles, stucco, painting, and a carved wooden ceiling [No. 1.15 and Illustration 6]. In the Mosque of Khvāja Zaynuddīn (probably 950s/1540s), the domed prayer hall is decorated with similar techniques; it is flanked by two large *muqarnas* niches on its east and west sides, while additional rooms indicate a combination of mosque and *khānqāh* [No. 1.16] (Jasmin Badr and Mustafa Tupev, The Khoja Zainuddin Mosque in Bukhara, *Muqarnas* 29 [2012], 213–43).

From the eleventh/seventeenth century onwards, monumental constructions became rarer. The Madrasa of ʿAbd al-ʿAzīz Khān II was built in 1064/1654 opposite the Madrasa of Ulugh Beg [No. 1.30]. Motifs on the polychrome tiles on the *pīshtāq* (large rectangular screen wall framing the portal) apparently reflect Iranian influence, matching the signature of a Qazvīnī artist in the wall paintings on the interior. One of the last monumental *madrasa* buildings is that of Sangīn Muḥammad Sharīf ("Ghāziyān") [No. 1.31], built in 1142/1730, with slight variation on traditional schemes. A different plan was followed by the Chār Minār Madrasa (1222/1807) in the east of the city, with its iconic four corner towers on the gatehouse. The Mosque

Illustration 6. Bukhara, Baland Mosque, wooden ceiling, 2009. Photograph courtesy of Lorenz Korn.

of Bālā Ḥawḍ, with its early twentieth-century pillared portico in front of a tenth/sixteenth-century domed mosque, appears entirely traditional.

Under Russian dominance, two suburban palaces were built for the *amīrs* of Bukhara. From 1895 to 1898, the palace near the Bukhara railway station at Kagan was constructed by the architect N. L. Benois (1813–98), with forms of Russian colonial architecture and additional elements of Moorish style. Between 1911 and 1914, the palace of Sitāra-i Māh-i Khāṣṣa [Illustration 7] was rebuilt by several architects in a hybrid mixture of styles. The combination of mirrors with stucco in the throne room, executed by stucco master Usto Shirin Murodov (1870–1957), was technically advanced. During the same period, some buildings *intra muros* display direct Russian influence in their architecture of baked brick with large windows, advertising their functions as bank, post office, school, and hospital [Nos. 1.34–37]. Some residential houses in newly built-up quarters were also constructed with gabled roofs, corner pilasters, and large exterior windows.

In a considerable number of the private houses in the inner city, old parts of the construction have been preserved: from the general layout, with the arrangement of rooms around one or more courtyards in a single storey, with some parts elevated above a cellar, to the construction using half-timber walls and wooden porticoes, and to the decoration with plastered wall niches, *muqarnas* cornices, and painted ornaments and inscriptions. Reception halls were obviously derived from palatial prototypes, transformed into a smaller scale.

During the Soviet period, modernism was slow to affect the old city of

Illustration 7. Bukhara, Sitāra-i Māh-i Khāṣṣa, courtyard to northwest, 2014. Photograph courtesy of Lorenz Korn.

Bukhara. The re-planning of the entire city, with apartment blocks and axes for motorised traffic, was only reluctantly implemented, limited by lack of resources. Some buildings were erected as landmarks on the margin of the old city, such as the hyperboloid steel grid tower with water container constructed by V. G. Shukhov (1853–1939) next to the citadel [No 1.38]. After World War II, administrative complexes, market halls, and the stadium were built south and east of the old city.

2. The art of the book

During the Tīmūrid period (ninth/fifteenth century), Transoxania received only weak impulses from the efflorescence of book painting that was taking place in the centres of Iran such as Herat and Shiraz very few works have been preserved. From the beginning of the tenth/sixteenth century onwards, the art of the book developed strongly in Bukhara. The evidence of preserved manuscripts and comments in written sources indicates that Shaybānī Khān (r. 907–16/1501–10) and ʿUbaydallāh Sulṭān (r. 918–46/1512–39) aspired to a patronage of fine arts in the Tīmūrid tradition, following the model of the Tīmūrid ruler of Herat, Ḥusayn Bāyqarā (842–911/1438–1506). However, the more important centre of manuscript production in the early tenth/sixteenth century seems to have been Shāhrukhiyya, c. 350 kilometres from Bukhara on the Syr Darya, at the court of the Abūlkhayrid prince Keldī Muḥammad (r. until 939/1532–3), where illustrated copies of Jāmī's *Haft Awrang*, the *Dīvān* of Navāʾī, and Kāshafī's *Anvār-i Suhaylī* were produced. The majority of illustrations represented a simplified variant of the Herat style, sometimes with a grand composition of a calm and harmonious atmosphere, but it remains an open question as to whether this indicated that artists from Herat were working in Bukhara. A work with some very original features that was perhaps produced in Bukhara is the *Fatḥnāma* of Mawlā Muḥammad Shādī, c. 907–13/1502–7 (Tashkent, Beruni Institute for Oriental Studies, MS 5369). Here, connections with the tradition of Shiraz appear stronger than with the Herat tradition. But this seems to have changed with ʿUbaydallāh's campaigns in Khurāsān, from where he brought artisans to Bukhara. The *Mihr va-Mushtarī* produced in 929/1522–3 (Washington DC, Freer Gallery, MS F1932.3–8) and Saʿdī's *Bustān*, illustrated circa 936/1530 (London, Royal Asiatic Society, MS M. 251), attest to this change. An undated *Manṭiq al-ṭayr* manuscript (London, British Library, MS Add. 7735) may well belong to the same group. The Herat style was probably further promoted when artisans from Shāhrukhiyya came to Bukhara after the death of Keldī Muḥammad in 939/1532–3.

With the reign of ʿAbd al-ʿAzīz (r. 946–57/1540–50), book production in Bukhara rose to an unprecedented level. Already during his time as governor, the prince had ordered a copy of Hātifī's *Haft Manzar*, dated 944/1538, in which illustrations were signed by Shaykhzāda, a student of the famed artist Bihzād (c. 854–942/1450–1535; Washington DC, Freer Gallery, MS F1956.14). The *Gulistān* of Saʿdī of 954/1547 (Fondation Bodmer, Geneva, MS 30) and other manuscripts display a creative use of the double page for paintings, in which a chronological sequence of events or a sequence of cause and effect were depicted. In general, book painting of the mid-tenth/sixteenth century was based on a rich array of design prototypes, successfully combining a great variety of elements in well-balanced compositions and displaying a high standard of craftsmanship, as in Navāʾī's *Lisān al-ṭayr* of 960/1552–3 (Paris, BNF, MS Suppl. turc 996) [Illustration 8] and in the *Gulistān* of Saʿdī of 974/1566–7 (Saint Petersburg, Saltykov-Shchedrin National Library, MS New Persian Series 110). The *Shāhnāma* of 964/1556–7, written for Ish-Muḥammad of Khiva, stands out, with its particularly inventive compositions and bold colours. In general, book production of the second half of the tenth/sixteenth century embraced illustrations as a desirable element in conjunction with calligraphy and illumination. In some cases, it seems that works of lower quality were produced on a large-scale for a broader market.

ʿAbdallāh Khān's conquests of Herat and Mashhad in 997/1588–9 facilitated new influences from Khurāsān during the late tenth/sixteenth century. On this basis the two artists Muḥammad Samarqandī and Muḥammad Sharīf revived the tradition attributed to Bihzād, with fresh attention to vivid facial expressions and gestures, as in the splendid manuscript of the *Majālis al-ʿUshshāq* dated 1015/1606 (Tashkent, Beruni Institute for Oriental Studies, MS IOS 3476). Some elements in Mughal style indicate that this manuscript was subject to alterations when it was taken to India. The reverse also seems to be true, in that Mughal book painting influenced the art of Bukhara, particularly during the eleventh/seventeenth century, perhaps as a result of the conquest of Bukhara by ʿAbd al-ʿAzīz II (r. 1055–91/1645–80) and his introduction of artists from his former residence in Balkh. While the *Shāhnāma* illustrated by Muḥammad Muqīm in 1075/1664

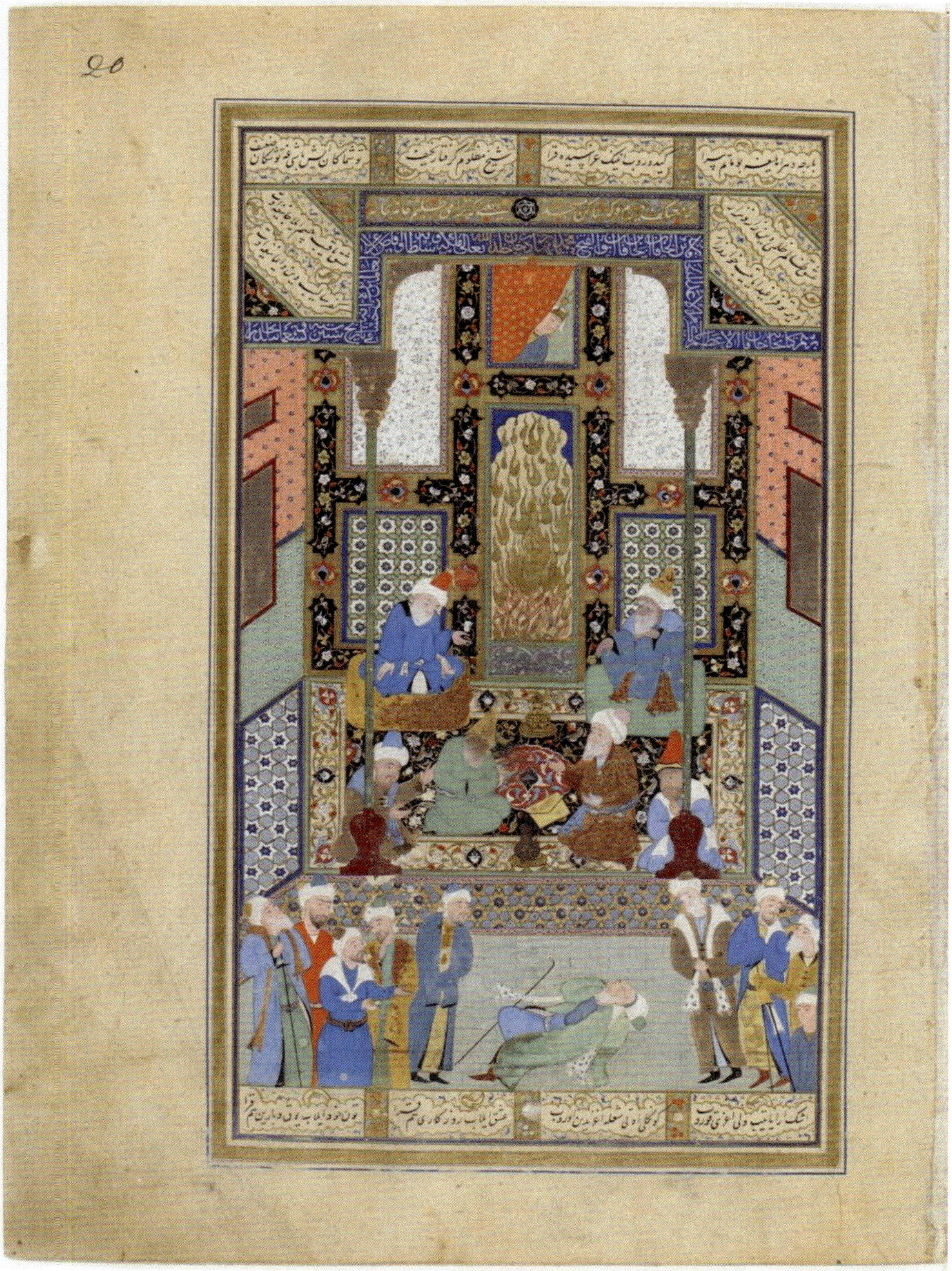

Illustration 8. Shaykh Ṣanʿān viewing the Christian girl. *Lisān al-ṭayr* of Navāʾī (Paris, BNF, MS Suppl. Turc 996, fol. 20a).

(Tashkent, Beruni Institute for Oriental Studies, MS IOS 3436) retains the Iranian-Transoxanian tradition, the *Khamsa* of Khvājū Kirmānī produced in 1078/1667–8 and attributed to a group of artists (Berlin, Museum of Islamic Art, MS I.1986.227) contains paintings that could well have been designed and executed in Mughal India, with respect to their figural style, architecture, details of draftsmanship, and colouring. In a different, more stylised manner, Indian prototypes can also be seen behind the *Khamsa* of Niẓāmī produced in 1058/1648 (Saint Petersburg, Saltykov-Shchedrin Library, MS New Persian Series 66), however interspersed with other paintings in purely Iranian-Transoxanian tradition. Even though the court workshop apparently ceased to exist soon after the death of ʿAbd al-ʿAzīz II in 1091/1580, figural book illustrations were still produced for a broader market. Calligraphy and illumination of Qurʾān manuscripts continued in a style characteristic of the Central Asian khānates until the early twentieth century.

3. Arts of the object

For the first centuries of Islam, metal objects from Bukhara can hardly be distinguished from Khurāsānian metalwork. Descriptions by geographers and travellers indicate that metalwork was traded in great quantities in the bazaar of Bukhara, but that not all of the metalwork was also produced there. Bronzes were cast with a very high level of technical skill, and the casting technique determined, to a large extent, the shapes of vessels and objects. Decorations were engraved or designed as openwork. A change can be seen in the sixth/twelfth century, when metal inlays became widespread as a technique of decoration. Simultaneously, sheet metal was used more frequently. This technical shift led to a change in the forms of vessels and objects, as well as to a change towards hammered decoration. Few metal objects can be attributed to Bukhara in the Īlkhānid and Tīmūrid periods. From the tenth/sixteenth century onwards, metalwork seems to have developed in close correspondence with Ṣafavid Iran. Metalwork from the nineteenth century has been preserved in greater quantities. Although the origin of the pieces that were acquired in Bukhara by travellers remains ultimately unclear, the extant material—for example, the Rickmers Collection in the Ethnologisches Museum in Berlin—gives a rather varied image of the rich culture of bronze objects that were used in Bukhara. Important groups comprise ewers and jugs for tea and water, ablution basins, hookahs, and other such items. The shapes of the ewers vary between extremely articulated models and more harmonious shapes in which body and neck merge into each other. Usually, the vessels are densely ornamented with a mesh of floral motifs, mostly organised in horizontal registers of vertical grooves (Sigrid Westphal-Hellbusch and Ilse Bruns, *Metallgefäße aus Buchara*, Berlin 1974).

Ceramic production of Bukhara was less important compared with other production centres, such as Afrasiyab (pre-Mongol Samarqand), a city from which glazed wares were imported. During the Tīmūrid period and later, blue-and-white ceramics were probably also produced in Bukhara, as in other places. During the twentieth century, ceramics from Ghijduvon (north of Bukhara) were very successful and replaced the production of Bukhara.

Like other Central Asian cities, Bukhara was a centre of textile production. Important examples of ikat (*abrbandi*) fabrics and embroidered cloths (*suzani*) from the nineteenth and twentieth centuries have been preserved (for the latter, cf. E. Tsareva, Suzanis of Central Asia, *Eothen* 2 [1994], 63–80). Carpets from the Bukhara region show geometrical motifs, frequently in brownish-red colours.

An outstanding example of carved woodwork has been preserved with the panels and doors from the tomb cover of Sayf al-Dīn Bākharzī (d. 659/1261), currently in the collection of the Bukhara Museum [Illustration 9]. Original parts dating from the eighth/fourteenth century have been supplemented with elements from later periods. The relief carving combines geometrical patterns in a polygon-star design, with vegetal ornament and inscriptions in various styles, typical of the eighth/fourteenth century.

Bibliography

(in addition to sources cited in the article)

General studies

E. Ernazarov, Akbar Khakimov, and Robert V. Almeev, *Buxoro Davlat badiiy-me'moriy muzey-qo'riqxona/The Bukhara State Architectural-Artistic Museum-Preserve*, Tashkent 2004; Johannes Kalter and Margareta Pavaloi (eds.), *Usbekistan. Erben der Seidenstraße*, Stuttgart 1995, English trans., *Uzbekistan. Heirs to the Silk Road*, London 1997; Liya Y. Man'kovskaia, *Bukhara*, Tashkent 1997.

Architecture and urbanism

Bakhtiyar Babadzhanov and Komildzhan Rakhimov (eds.), *O'zbekistan obidalarining epigrafik durdonalari/Masterpieces of architectural epigraphy of Uzbekistan*, 2 vols., Tashkent 201_; Anette Gangler, Heinz Gaube, and Attilio Petruccioli, *Bukhara, the eastern dome of Islam. Urban development, urban space, architecture and population*, Stuttgart and London 2004; Lisa Golombek and Donald N. Wilber, *The Timurid architecture of Iran and Turan*, 2 vols., Princeton 1988; Sergei G. Khmel'nitskii, *Mezhdu Arabami i Tyurkami. Ranneislamskaya arkhitektura Srednei Azii*, Berlin and Riga 1992; Sergei G. Khmel'nitskii, *Mezhdu Samanidami i Mongolami. Arkhitektura Srednei Azii XI-nachala XIII vv.*, 2 vols., Berlin and Riga 1996–7; Robert D. McChesney, Economic and social aspects of the public architecture of Bukhara in the 1560's and 1570's, *Islamic Art* 2 (1987), 217–42; Attilio Petruccioli (ed.), *Bukhara. The myth and the architecture*, Cambridge MA 1999; Galina A. Pugachenkova and Lazar' I. Rempel', *Istoriya iskusstv Uzbekistana*, Moscow 1965; Ol'ga A. Sukhareva, *K istorii gorodov Bukharskogo khanstva. Istoriko-etnograficheskie ocherki*, Tashkent 1958; Ol'ga A. Sukhareva, *Kvartal'naia obshchina pozdnefeodal'nogo goroda Bukhary*, Moscow 1976; Mustafa Tupev, *Kunsthistorische und historische Untersuchungen an Sakralbauten der Abulkhairiden (1494–1602)*, Ph.D. diss., University of Bamberg 2017; Valentina L. Voronina, *Architectural monuments of Middle Asia. Bukhara, Samarkand*, Leningrad 1969; Mavluda Yusupova, *Bukharskaya shkola zodchestva, XV–XVII veka*, Tashkent 2014; Mavluda Yusupova, L'évolution architecturale des couvents soufis à l'époque timouride et posttimouride, *Cahiers d'Asie Centrale* 3/4 (1997), 229–50; Boris N. Zasypkin, *Arkhitektura Srednei Azii*, Moscow 1948.

Book illustration

Oleg F. Akimushkin, Biblioteka Shibanidov v Bukhare XVI veka, in Ingeborg Baldauf and Michael Friederich (eds.), *Bamberger Zentralasienstudien* (Berlin 1994), 325–41; Mukaddema M. Ashrafi-Aini, *Bukharskaya shkola miniatyurnoy zhivopisi 40–70 gody XVI veka*, Dushanbe 1974; Mukaddema M. Ashrafi-Aini, The school of Bukhara to circa 1550, in Basil Gray (ed.), *The arts of the book in Central Asia* (Paris 1979), 249–72; Marie Efthymiou, *L'art du livre en Asie Centrale de la fin du XVIe siècle au début du XXe siècle. Étude des manuscrits coraniques de l'Institut d'Orientalisme Abū Rayḥān Bīrūnī*, Leiden 2014; Olympiada I. Galerkina, *Mawarannahr book painting*, Leningrad 1980; Muzaffar Khairullaev, *Oriental miniatures. The collection of the Beruni Institute of Oriental Studies of the Academy of Sciences of the Republic of Uzbekistan*, 3 vols., Tashkent 2001–4; Assadullah Souren Melikian-Chirvani, The anthology of a Sufi prince from Bokhara, in Robert Hillenbrand (ed.), *Persian painting. From the Mongols to the Qajars* (London and New York 2000), 151–69; Galina Pugachenkova and Olympiada I. Galerkina, *Miniatyury Srednei Azii*, Moscow 1979; Karin Rührdanz, Die Entwicklung der mittelasiatischen Buchmalerei vom 15. bis zum 17. Jahrhundert, *Eothen* 3 (1998), 109–22.

Lorenz Korn

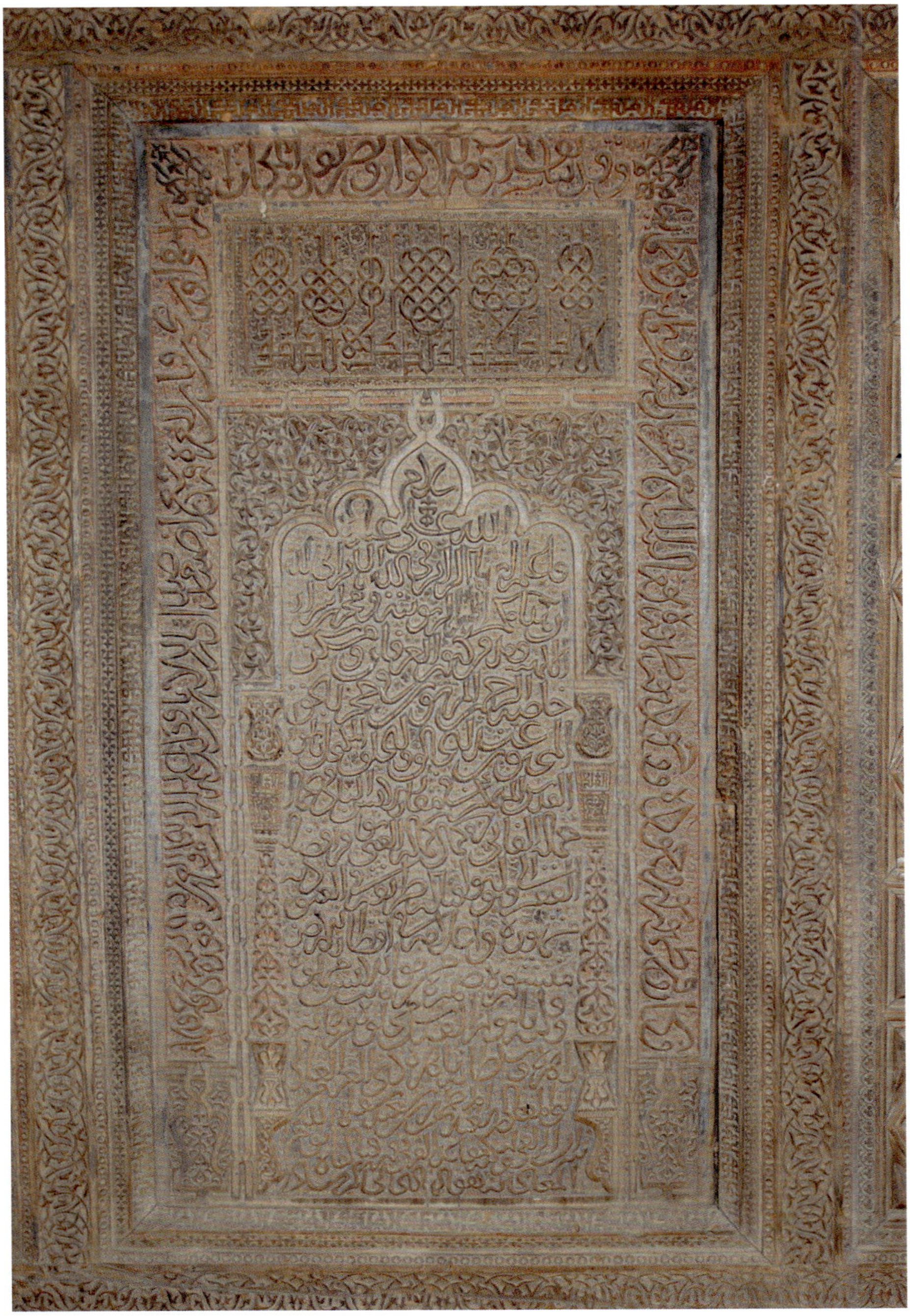

Illustration 9. Bukhara, central panel from the cenotaph of Sayf al-Dīn Bākharzī (Bukhara State Architectural-Artistic Museum-Preserve, with permission, 2008). Photograph courtesy of Lorenz Korn.

D

Daḥlān, Iḥsān Jampes

Iḥsān b. Muḥammad **Daḥlān** (1901–52), also known as Kyai Iḥsān **Jampes**, was a prominent Javanese Muslim scholar (*kyai*) and a prolific writer, recognised especially for his Arabic writings on Ṣūfism. He was born in Jampes, Kediri, East Java. His father was also a Muslim scholar and the founder of the Jampes *pesantren* (Islamic boarding school). Iḥsān Daḥlān grew up in the *pesantren* milieu and began his education under the tutelage of his father. He then went on to study with a number of prominent Muslim scholars in different *pesantrens* in Java, including his uncle, Kyai Khazin of Pesantren Bendo, Pare Kediri, East Java; Kyai Maksum of Pesantren Punduh, Magelang, Central Java; the celebrated Kyai Kholil of Bangkalan, Madura, East Java; and Kyai Daḥlān of Semarang. It is reported that unlike many other Muslim students (Javanese, *santri*) in his time, Iḥsān Daḥlān studied with these scholars only for a short period of time, just long enough to acquire the permission, or licence (*ijāza*), to transmit a particular subject of Islamic teaching. He died in 1952 in Jampes and was buried in the family graveyard close to his *pesantren* in Jampes.

In spite of the fact that unlike many other *ʿulamāʾ* from the Malay world, Kyai Iḥsān Daḥlān never lived in the Middle East and never studied with Middle Eastern *ʿulamāʾ* (he only made the pilgrimage to Mecca and Medina in 1926), he is one of the few Javanese Muslim scholars of his time who wrote most of his works in Arabic, producing at least twelve religious works in this language. His monumental *Sirāj al-ṭālibīn ʿalā Minhāj al-ʿābidīn ilā jannat Rabb al-ʿālamīn* is a commentary on the *Minhāj al-ābidīn* by al-Ghazālī (d. 505/1111), in which he like al-Ghazālī emphasised the reconciliation of Ṣūfism with *sharīʿa*. In his commentary, Iḥsān Daḥlān defines Ṣūfism as knowledge of the state of the soul (*nafs*) and its positive and negative attributes. According to him, the objective of Ṣūfism is for the heart to abandon remembrance of anything other than God and to attain the beautification of the heart by *mushāhada* (visions of God). He argues that the study of Ṣūfism is an individual obligation for every Muslim whose duty it is to fulfil the prescriptions of the *ʿulūm al-ẓawāhir* (sciences of the outward aspects of Islam), but also to study Islam's inner dimensions (*bāṭin*). The highest achievement for the *sālik* (mystic wayfarer) is to achieve *maʿrifa* (knowledge of God). In order to achieve *maʿrifa*, the *sālik* should be able not only to pass several stages but also to deal with temptations, one of which lies within the *sālik* himself or herself, which is usually called *nafs*. Iḥsān Daḥlān divides *nafs* into seven kinds, which he derives from relevant verses of the Qurʾān (Q 12:53; Q 75:2; Q 89:27–30; Q 91:7–8).

In 1930 Kyai Iḥsān Daḥlān published *Tasrīḥ al-ʿibārāt*, a commentary on *Natījat al-mīqāt* by Kyai Daḥlān of Semarang, a work that deals with astronomy. In response to the debate on smoking tobacco within his community, he wrote *Irshād al-ikhwān fī bayān aḥkām shurb al-qahwa wa-l-dukhān*, in which he discusses extensively the legal opinions of Muslim scholars on consuming tobacco and coffee. In 1944 he composed a book entitled *Manāhij al-imdād*, a commentary on the *Irshād al-ʿibād ilā sabīl al-rashād* by Zayn al-Dīn al-Malībārī (d. 982/1574). *Manāhij al-imdād* deals with the vast topic of *fiqh* (jurisprudence) and Islamic ethics including faith (*īmān*), prayer, almsgiving, fasting, pilgrimage, and repentance; the benefit of reciting and teaching the Qurʾān and of blessing the prophet Muḥammad; the condemnation of idolatry, divination, and fortune telling, adultery, false oaths, and false testimony, anger, envy, pride, lying, and usury; the prohibition of alcohol; the obligation of enjoining good and forbidding evil (*al-amr bi-l-maʿrūf wa-l-nahy ʿan al-munkar*); professional life, and marriage.

His *Sirāj al-ṭālibīn* made Iḥsān Daḥlān known as an expert in Ṣūfism, not only among Indonesian Muslim scholars but also abroad. It is reported that the *Sirāj al-ṭālibīn* was used as a reference work at al-Azhar in Cairo and that in 1934 King Fārūq of Egypt (r. 1936–52) invited him to teach at al-Azhar. He refused the king's offer, preferring to serve the community of his home country by teaching in the *pesantren*. In 1942, during the Japanese occupation of Indonesia, he established his own Islamic school and named it Madrasat Mafātīḥ al-Hudā, which attracted many students from different regions in Indonesia.

Through his extensive Arabic writings on various religious subjects, Iḥsān Daḥlān can lay claim to being one of twentieth-century Indonesia's Muslim scholars who contributed to maintaining the Islamic and *pesantren* tradition, particularly in Java and Madura. His books have been printed by publishing houses in Southeast Asia and the Middle East and for this reason have also become known outside the intellectual tradition of Indonesian *pesantrens*.

Bibliography

Ibnu Hazen (ed.), *100 ulama Dalam Lintas Sejarah Nusantara* (Jakarta 2015), 155–7; Ahmad Barizi, al-Ḥaraka al-fikriyya wa-l-turāth ʿinda l-Shaykh Ihsan Jampes Kediri. Mulāḥaẓa tamhīdiyya, *SIk* 11/3 (2004), 541–71; Jajat Burhanudin, Traditional Islam and modernity. Some notes on the changing role of the *ulama* in early twentieth century Indonesia, in Azyumardi Azra, Kees van Dijk, and Nico J. G. Kaptein (eds.), *Varieties of religious authority. Change and challenges in 20th century Indonesian Islam* (Singapore 2010), 66–8; Iḥsān Muḥammad Daḥlān, *Kitab kopi dan rokok. Untuk para pecandu rokok dan penikmat kopi berat*, Yogyakarta 2009.

Arif Zamhari

Darphane

The ***darphane*** (*ḍarbkhāne*, mint) was one of the longest established institutions in the Ottoman Empire, founded in the early days of the state. As the empire's boundaries expanded in Anatolia and Balkans, mints were opened in important administrative centres, near mines, in settlements on trade routes, and elsewhere. By the second half of the tenth/sixteenth century, Ottoman *darphane*s numbered more than fifty, and the most important was in Istanbul. During the financial crisis that began in the 990s/1580s under the effect of international monetary and metal movements and some domestic affairs, the *akçe (aqçe)*—the monetary unit of the Ottoman currency system—was debased and many mints closed, while those that survived became idle. Towards the end of the eleventh/seventeenth century, reform in the currency system by minting silver coins, such as large-sized European coins, and the use of mechanical methods in the *darphane* resolved the minting crisis, but most provincial *darphane*s were not reopened. Only the mints in Istanbul and Cairo, as well as a couple in North Africa, continued operating from the beginning of the twelfth/eighteenth century until the end of the empire.

Initially, mints were run either by *emanet* (*āmānet*, under the direction of a state-appointed official who received a salary) or as an *iltizam* (*ltizām*, tax farm). Occasionally, until the end of the eleventh/seventeenth century, a mixed method of administration that combined elements of both systems was also used. Over time, *iltizam* was discontinued and *emanet* became the sole method, and Muslim bureaucrats of the central administration began supervising the mint in Istanbul. After governmental ministries were created in the reign of Mahmud (Maḥmūd) II (r. 1223–55/1808–39), the Istanbul mint became a directorate within the ministry of finance.

Ottoman mints procured gold and silver from mines or the market. Mined metal cost less than gold and silver coins purchased from the market, but it was limited in quantity, and circulating coinage, though more expensive, provided a larger source of gold and silver. Since the Ottoman Empire was at an intersection of international trade routes, abundant foreign coins were available for sale to local mints.

The Ottomans used simple minting techniques until the introduction of modern technology at the end of the eleventh/seventeenth century. Through the efforts of Cerrah Mustafa (Muṣṭafā), a convert and *sahibiayar* (*ṣāḥib-i ʿayār*, assayer, here vice director of operations), imported European machinery that rapidly produced well-shaped coins with milled edges was set up at the Istanbul mint in 1099/1688, and this technology remained in use in Ottoman mints for about a century and a half. In the same period, largely stemming from a need to finance wars and reforms, especially during Mahmud II's reign, the *guruş* (*kuruş*, Ott. *ghuruş*)—which replaced the *akçe* as the monetary unit of the Ottoman currency system in the early twelfth/eighteenth century—was greatly debased. The consequent reform to resolve this problem was paralleled by the installation of steam-powered machinery at the Istanbul mint by experts from England. This technological renewal, finally completed in 1260/1844, raised the standards of the Istanbul mint up to the technical level of European mints.

Bibliography
Halil Sahillioğlu, *Kuruluştan XVII. asrın sonlarına kadar Osmanlı para tarihi üzerinde bir deneme*, Assoc. Prof. diss., Istanbul University 1958; Halil Sahillioğlu, *Studies on Ottoman economic and social history*, Istanbul 1999; Şevket Pamuk, *A monetary history of the Ottoman Empire*, Cambridge 2000; Garo Kürkman, *Sultan Abdülmecid dönemi Osmanlı darphane-i amire kuyumcu odası ve düzoğlu ailesi*, forthcoming; Ömerül Faruk Bölükbaşı, *XVIII. Yüzyılın ikinci yarısında darbhâne-i âmire*, Istanbul 2013; Ömerül Faruk Bölükbaşı, Osmanlı taşra darphaneleri (1697–1758), *Türk Kültürü İncelemeleri Dergisi 29* (2013), 27–76; Hüseyin Al and Şevket K. Akar, *Osmanlı finans sisteminde modernleşme. Osmanlı para reformu*, Istanbul 2014.

Ömerül Faruk Bölükbaşı

Dilāʾ

Dilāʾ is the name of an area on the western slopes of Morocco's Middle Atlas Mountains, located approximately 33 kilometres to the southwest of the city of Khenifra, which is best known as the site of the Dilāʾiyya Ṣūfī lodge (*zāwiya*). This *zāwiya* flourished as a scholarly, spiritual, and political centre during Morocco's so-called marabout crisis in the eleventh/seventeenth century. The word *dilāʾ* is the plural form of the Arabic word *dalw*, which means water pail; its use probably refers to this area's numerous freshwater springs. Despite its Arabic name, the Dilāʾ region is populated almost exclusively by Amāzīgh Berbers (Ḥajjī, al-Dilāʾ, 12:4066).

Around 974/1566, Abū Bakr b. Muḥammad b. Saʿīd al-Dilāʾī (d. 1021/1612) established a Ṣūfī lodge in Dilāʾ at the instruction of his teacher, Abū ʿUmar al-Qasṭalī l-Marrākushī (d. 974/1567), a disciple of the Jazūliyya Ṣūfī brotherhood (Ḥajjī, *al-Zāwiya*, 31–2). Under the leadership of Abū Bakr's son Muḥammad (d. 1046/1636), the Dilāʾiyya *zāwiya* rose to prominence as a refuge for Muslim religious scholars and intellectuals during the so-called marabout crisis, a decades-long civil war precipitated by the sudden death of the Saʿdid sultan Aḥmad al-Manṣūr in 1012/1603. As cultural life in Morocco's urban centres declined, rural Ṣūfī lodges, such as the Dilāʾiyya *zāwiya*, emerged as sanctuaries for religious and scholarly life in the country (Laroui, 260–1; El-Rouayheb). During this period, the Dilāʾiyya *zāwiya* hosted many of Morocco's leading Muslim scholarly figures such as the litterateur Aḥmad al-Maqarrī (d. 1041/1632) and the polymath and logician al-Ḥasan al-Yūsī (d. 1102/1691). As part of its charitable mission, the Dilāʾiyya *zāwiya* provided free room and board for scholars, students, and other travellers, in addition to supporting the livelihood of neighbouring communities (al-Nāṣirī, 6:97; Ḥajjī, *al-Zāwiya*, 48).

The Dilāʾiyya *zāwiya*'s fortunes began to change during the tenure of Muḥammad b. Abī Bakr's son and successor Muḥammad al-Ḥājj (d. 1082/1671). In 1046/1636, Muḥammad al-Ḥājj began a military campaign to establish political rule over Dilāʾ's surrounding region. By the 1050s/1640s, he had conquered the nearby cities of Meknès and Fez, the Atlantic port of Salé, Tétouan, along the Mediterranean Sea, as well as the fertile Tadlā plains along Morocco's Atlantic coast (al-Nāṣirī, 7:98). Dilāʾ grew as a political capital and commercial hub. An influx of residents led Muḥammad al-Ḥājj to establish a second Dilāʾī community at Aït Isḥāq, just to the north of the original *zāwiya* (Hajji, al-Dilāʾ, 12:4067). The Dilāʾī community flourished in this area until the first ʿAlawī sultan, Mawlay al-Rashīd

b. al-Sharīf al-ʿAlawī (r. 1076–82/1666–72), defeated Muḥammad al-Ḥājj's forces in 1078–9/1668. Consequently, Mawlay al-Rashīd exiled the Dilāʾī family to Tlemsan (Tilimsān), Algeria, and razed their *zāwiya* to the ground (al-Nāṣirī, 7:36–7).

The imprecise and contradictory nature of primary source accounts and the Dilāʾiyya *zāwiya*'s complete destruction by Mawlay al-Rashīd led modern historians to question the Dilāʾiyya *zāwiya*'s precise location (Henry). Based on fieldwork in the Middle Atlas, Moroccan historian Muḥammad Ḥajjī has concluded that ruins near present-day Aït Isḥāq correspond to the historical site of the Dilāʾiyya *zāwiya* (Ḥajjī, *al-Zāwiya*, 35–6). These are accessible by car via Morocco's National Route 8.

Bibliography

Sources

Aḥmad b. Khālid al-Nāṣirī, *Kitāb al-istiqṣā li-akhbār duwal al-Maghrib al-aqṣā*, ed. Jaʿfar al-Nāṣirī and Muḥammad al-Nāṣirī (Casablanca 1418/1997), 6:96–8.

Studies

Khaled El-Rouayheb, *Islamic intellectual history in the seventeenth century. Scholarly currents in the Ottoman Empire and the Maghreb* (Cambridge 2015), 147–53; Muḥammad Ḥajjī, al-Dilāʾ, in Muḥammad Ḥajjī et al. (eds.), *Maʿlamat al-Maghrib* (Salé, Morocco 1426/2005), 12:4066–7; Muḥammad Ḥajjī, *al-Zāwiya al-Dilāʾiyya*, Casablanca 1409/1988²; R. Henry, Où se trouvait la Zaouïa de Dilâ?, *Hespéris* 31 (1944): 49–54; Abdallah Laroui, *The history of the Maghrib. An interpretive essay*, trans. Ralph Manheim (Princeton 1977), 260–1.

Matthew Schumann

E

Elvan Çelebi

Elvan (Elvān) **Çelebi** (d. after 760/1358–9), an Ottoman poet, was the son of Âşık Ali (ʿĀşıq ʿAlī) Paşa (d. 13 Safer 733/3 November 1332), author of the *Garibname (Gharībnāme)*. His grandfather was Muhlis (Mukhliṣ) Paşa (d. 672/1273–4), and his great grandfather, Baba İlyas-i Horasani (Bābā İlyās-i Khurāsānī, d. 638/1240). Elvan Çelebi's exact date and place of birth are unknown, but he was probably born in Kırşehir, located in central Anatolia. Some sources identify him as "Ulvan" (ʿUlvān), but the Arabic epitaph on the tomb he had made for himself shows that his real name (also his pen-name) was Elvan.

After his father went to Egypt in 727/1326, Elvan Çelebi and his brother settled in the village known today as Elvançelebi, in the Mecitözü district of Çorum province. This village, mentioned in sources as Tananözü, Tanin, Tanık, Söğütlü, or Kavaklı, was also where Elvan died. *Keşf-el-zunun zeyli (Dhayl ʿalā Kashf al-zunūn)* and *Tuhfe-i Nâilî (Tuḥfe-i Nāʾilī)* record the year of his death as 770/1368, whereas Ahmet Yaşar Ocak indicates that he died a few years after 760/1358–9, but without giving a reason or source (Ocak, Elvan Çelebi, 63–4).

Elvan Çelebi's poems demonstrate that he was well educated. Besides three brothers, Selman (Salmān), Can, and Kızılca, he had a sister, Melek Hatun (Khātun). Neşet Köseoğlu recounts that he also had a son, Abdurrahman (ʿAbd al-Raḥmān) Çelebi; a grandson, Hayrüddin Halil (Khayr al-Dīn Khalīl) Bey; and two great grandsons, Abdülaziz (ʿAbd al-ʿAzīz) and Abdülmecid (ʿAbd al-Majīd) (Köseoğlu, 1439). His widespread fame in Çorum and Amasya lasted for centuries. Even today, his tomb is venerated by the inhabitants of Çorum and its surroundings, and receives many local visitors.

Works

Elvan Çelebi's only extant work is his *Menâkibu'l-kudsiyye fî menâsıbi'l-ünsiyye* (*Menāqıbu'l-qudsiyye fī menāṣibi'l-ünsiyye*, "Holy legends about esoteric ranks"), composed of 2,081 *beyt*s (couplets) in *mesnevi (methnevī)* rhyme, with *faʿilātun, mafāʿilun, faʿilun* metre. Written in 760/1358–9, this work is a vital source for eighth/fourteenth-century Anatolian Turkish history and the Babai (Bābāʾī) socio-religious movement of that period. Ümit Tokatlı prepared a doctoral dissertation about it in 1984. Ahmet Yaşar Ocak and İsmail E. Erünsal also published the work in the same year (1984), and Mertol Tulum published a revised version in 2000, to correct mistakes in the first publication.

Nine poems are attributed to Elvan Çelebi in anthologies (Ergun, 1230–1; Köksal). Some sources also mention a poem titled *Etvar-ı süluk (Eṭvār-ı sülūk)*, but M. Fuat Köprülü has affirmed that this work is Elvan-ı Şirazi's (Alvān-i Shīrāzī, d. after 829/1425–6) translation of *Gulshan-i rāz* (Köprülü, Âşık Paşa, 702). As for Mehmed Mecdi Efendi's statement in *Hadayık (Ḥadāʾiq)* that the poet "had a *divan*" (*dīvān*, collection of a poet's poems), Mecdi must have confused him with Elvan-ı Şirazi. Although Bursalı Mehmed Tahir and Mehmed Mecdi Efendi ascribed the work *Risāle fī l-iksīr* to Elvan Çelebi (Tahir, 110; Mecdi, 22), no copy has ever been found.

Elvan Çelebi wrote his *mesnevi* in a didactic, dry style, and his *gazels* are mystic in content. While the poet's didactic purpose is clearly perceptible in one part, he is completely amorous and sensual in another. Elvan Çelebi's father, Âşık Ali Paşa, and the Anatolian mystic and poet Yunus (Yūnus) Emre (fl. seventh/thirteenth and eighth/fourteenth centuries) clearly had a deep influence on him.

Bibliography

Şemseddīn Sāmī, *Qamūsü l-aʿlām*, (Istanbul 1311/1893–4), 4:3174; Mehmet Süreyya, *Sicil-i Osmani*, (Istanbul 1311/1893–4), 3:181; Bursalı Mehmed Tahir, *Osmanlı müellifleri* (Istanbul 1333/1914–5), 1:110; Sadettin Nüzhet Ergun, *Türk şairleri*, (Istanbul 1939), 3:1230–1; Neşet Köseoğlu, Elvan Çelebi III, *Çorumlu* 49 (1944), 1437–41; Mehmet Önder, Eine Neuen-deckte Quelle zur Geschichte der Seltschuken in Anatolien, *Wiener Zeitshrift für die Kunde Morgenlandes* 55 (1959), 84–8; Franz Taeschner, Das Heiligtum des Elvan Çelebi in Anatolien, *Wiener Zeitshrift für die Kunde Morgenlandes* 56 (1960), 227–31; Semavi Eyice, Çorum'un Mecidözü'nde Âşık Paşaoğlu Elvan Çelebi zaviyesi, *Türkiyat Mecmuası* 15 (1968), 211–46; Bağdatlı İsmail Paşa, *Keşf-el-zunun zeyli*, vol. 2, Istanbul 1972; Sadettin Buluç, Elvan Çelebi'nin Menakıb-namesi, *Türkiyat Mecmuası* 19 (1977–9), 1–6; Fuad Köprülü, *Türk edebiyatında ilk mutasavvıflar*, (Ankara 1981), 139; Elvan Çelebi, *Menâkıbu'l-kudsiyye fî menâsıbi'l-ünsiyye. Baba İlyas-ı Horasânî ve sül-Âlesinin menkabevî tarihi*, ed. İsmail E. Erünsal and Ahmet Yaşar Ocak (Istanbul 1984); Ümit Tokatlı, *Elvan Çelebi'nin Menakıbnamesi (metin-indeks-gramer)*, Ph.D. diss., Istanbul University, Institute of Social Sciences 1984; Ahmet Yaşar Ocak and İsmail E. Erünsal, Elvan Çelebi'nin Menâkıbnâme'si hakkında, *Türk Kültürü* 270 (1985), 374–81; Ahmet Yaşar Ocak and İsmail E. Erünsal, Elvan Çelebi'nin Menâkıbnâme'si hakkında, *Türk Kültürü* 270 (1985), 374–81; Ümit Tokatlı, Elvan Çelebi'nin eseri (El)-Menâkıbu'l-Kudsiyye fi' (il) Menâsıbi'l-Ünsiyye, *Erciyes Üniversitesi Sosyal Bilimler Enstitüsü Dergisi* 1 (1987), 165–71; Mehmed Mecdi Efendi, *Ḥadāʾiq al-shaqāʾiq*, ed. Abdülkadir Özcan, vol. 1 of *Şakaik-i nuʿmaniyye ve zeyilleri* (Istanbul 1989), 22; Mertol Tulum, *Tarihî metin çalışmalarında usul*, Menâkıbu'l- kudsiyye *üzerinde bir deneme*, Istanbul 2000; Mehmed Nail Tuman, *Tuhfe-i Nâilî. Dîvân şairlerinin muhtasar biyografileri*, facsimile ed. Cemâl Kurnaz and Mustafa Tatcı (Ankara 2001), 2:698; Ethem Erkoç, *Âşık Paşa ve oğlu Elvan Çelebi*, Çorum 2005; M. Fatih Köksal, *Klasik Türk şiiri araştırmaları* (Ankara 2005), 473–93; M. Fuat Köprülü, Âşık Paşa, *TDVİA* 1:701–6; Ahmet Yaşar Ocak, Elvan Çelebi, *TDVIA* 11:63–4.

M. Fatih Köksal

F

Fable, animal, in Muslim Southeast Asia

Many of the **animal fable**s in the two major literary traditions of **Muslim Southeast Asia** —Malay and Javanese— are translations and/or adaptations from foreign sources, primarily Arabic, Persian, and Indian, and, in the modern period, European. These works belong to the genre of edifying literature, designed to regulate the behaviour of Muslims (Braginsky, 340–1). They generally consist of collections of relatively short stories with animal characters endowed with human qualities, intended to teach moral lessons. Animal fables were also included to illustrate certain points in such didactic works as the *Bustān al-salāṭīn* by Nūr al-Dīn al-Rānīrī (d. 1069/1658–9), a Malay "mirror for princes" at the court of Aceh, in North Sumatra (Wormser). The *Hikayat bayan budiman* ("Tale of the wise parrot," 773/1371–2), attributed to a certain Kadi Hasan, is one of the oldest specimens in Malay literature and is based on a Persian version of the Sanskrit *Śukasaptati* ("Seventy tales of the parrot," Brandes; Winstedt). The Malay *Hikayat Kalilah dan Daminah* ("The tale of Kalila and Dimna" can be traced back, also through a Persian intermediary, to the Sanskrit *Pañcatantra*. In 1942, an Indonesian translation of the *Hikayat Kalilah dan Dimnah* was published by Ismail (Gelar Sutan Mangkuto) bin Jamil (d. 1948), based on the Arabic version of Ibn al-Muqaffaʿ (d. c.138/755–6).

There is, however, also a rich repertoire of indigenous, often orally transmitted, fables throughout insular Southeast Asia, which seem to belong to the oldest stratum of literary imagination (Brakel, 5–6). Christiaan Hooykaas (d. 1979) compiled a particularly rich collection of village stories and animal fables from Sasak literature (mainly from the island of Lombok) in the first half of the twentieth century (Marrison, 99–227). Most common are trickster stories in which a physically weak animal outwits its larger and more powerful adversaries. Although the tiger was called the king of the forest, the unassuming but clever mousedeer was his "real" master, ruling the animal kingdom (Drewes; Epskamp). As manuscripts with older Malay mousedeer stories show, such fables were not always just simple folk tales but could be much more sophisticated, even subversive and political (Proudfoot).

Since the late nineteenth century, the use of fables in schools has drastically altered their general perception, being relegated to the realm of children's tales without the satirical bite. For example, in the Javanese narrative poem *Babad kancil* ("History of the mousedeer," 1876), the wily mousedeer is a charming bookish creature, well read in school books on geography, mathematics, and Javanese grammar (Arps, 98–100). The Aesopic fables were adapted by Alang Ahmad bin Muhammad Yunus in his *Hikayat penerang hati* ("Story of the clear-sighted," 1896), to be used in the Malay schools as the basis for essay writing (Wahab Ali, 67). In the modern era, animal fables are routinely published as innocuous children's tales with cute illustrations. In recent years, Islamic publishers have brought out several full-colour illustrated children's books on wonder-exiting stories about animals in the Qur'ān, advertised as being full of inspirational examples and wisdom.

Traditional Malay literature boasts a special genre of narrative poem, in which animals (and flowers) talk and act like humans (Overbeck; Jusuf). Hans Overbeck (d. 1942) has suggested that these parodic animal romances perhaps allude to specific historical events, and this seems in some cases to be correct (Koster, 199–215). The *Syair raja tedung dengan raja katak* ("Poem of the cobra-king and the frog-king") may thus be interpreted as a political lampoon of historical events (Koster and Tol). At its simplest level, the poem teaches the importance of being able to distinguish friend from foe, but, read against eighteenth-century Malay history, the unflattering portrait of the foolish frog-king may be an allegory lampooning Sultan Sulaiman of Johor (r. 1134–74/1722–60). In the *Syair sang kupu-kupu dengan kembang dan balang* ("Poem of the butterfly with the flowers and the leaf insect"), written by Muhammad Bakir in Batavia at the end of the nineteenth century, the "marriage plot" of the anthropomorphic animals perhaps also refers to some historical situation (Overbeck, 145), but there is no non-textual support for that hypothesis. According to its author, the moral of the story was to teach readers and listeners about proper behaviour in the household (Wieringa).

In the post-colonial period, animal fables have only occasionally been intended for an adult readership in order to criticise political and social developments. The Javanese fable collection *Dongèng sato kéwan* ("Animal fables"), written by Prijana Winduwinata (d. 1969) in 1952 and translated into the national Indonesian language in 1954, is the most important literary work of satire in both Javanese and Indonesian (Anderson; Winduwinata). Its author, who served as Indonesia's minister of education and culture from 1957 to 1966, employed a characteristically Javanese kind of humour, with much wordplay, ridiculing the political rhetoric of the newly independent Indonesian state. In modern Indonesian literature the Islamic writer and academic Kuntowijoyo (d. 2005) published, in 1999, a collection of animal fables titled *Mengusir matahari. Fabel-fabel politik* ("Chasing away the sun. Political fables"), addressing the closing years of Suharto's authoritarian military regime (1968–98) and the beginning of the Reformasi (reform) era at the end of the 1990s.

Bibliography

A. Wahab Ali, *The emergence of the novel in modern Indonesian and Malaysian literature. A comparative study*, Kuala Lumpur 1991; M. M. M.

(Ben Anderson), Five animal tales by Pak Prijana Winduwinata, *Indonesia* 25 (1978), 81–114; Bernard Arps, Koning Salomo en het dwerghertje. Taalpolitiek, taalonderwijs en de eerste grammatica's in het Javaans, in Kees Groeneboer (ed.), *Koloniale taalpolitiek in Oost en West. Nederlands-Indië, Suriname, Nederlandse Antillen, Aruba* (Amsterdam 1997), 85–105; Vladimir Braginsky, *The heritage of traditional Malay literature. A historical survey of genres, writings and literary views*, Leiden 2004; L. F. Brakel, Die Volksliteraturen Indonesiens, in L. F. Brakel et al., *Handbuch der Orientalistik*, vol. 3, *Literaturen, Abschnitt 1* (Leiden and Cologne 1976), 1–40; J. Brandes, Lets over het papegaai-boek, zoals het bij de Maleiers voorkomt, *Tijdschrift voor Indische Taal-, Land- en Volkenkunde* 41 (1899), 431–97; G. W. J. Drewes, An Acehnese animal story, in Biancamaria Scarcia Amoretti and Lucia Rostagno (eds.), *Yād-nāma. In memoria di Alessandro Bausani* (Rome 1991), 2:355–62; Kees P. Epskamp, Ambiguous animals and their roguish tricks. Mouse deer stories in Indonesia, in R. de Ridder and J. A. J. Karremans (eds.), *The Leiden tradition in structural anthropology. Essays in honour of P. E. de Josselin de Jong* (Leiden 1987), 123–39; Jumsari Jusuf et al. (eds.), *Antologi syair simbolik dalam sastra Indonesia lama*, Jakarta 1978; G. L. Koster, *Roaming through seductive gardens. Readings in Malay narrative*, Leiden 1997; Gijs Koster and Roger Tol (eds.), *Syair raja tedung dengan raja katak. The poem of the cobra-king and the frog-king. A facsimile edition with transcription, translation and interpretation of manuscript KL. 161 in the library of the University of Leiden*, Leiden 2002; Geoffrey E. Marrison, *Catalogue of Javanese and Sasak texts (KITLV Or. 508)*, Leiden 1999; H. Overbeck, Malay animal and flower shaers, *Journal of the Malayan Branch of the Royal Asiatic Society* 12/2 (1934), 108–48; Ian Proudfoot, A "Chinese" mouse-deer goes to Paris, *Archipel* 61 (2001), 69–97; Edwin Wieringa, Der flatterhafte Schmetterling und die fröhlichen Früchte. Zwei malaiische Gedichte von Muhammad Bakir aus dem Batavia des ausgehenden 19. Jahrhunderts, in Susanne Schröter (ed.), *Körper und Identität. Ethnologische Ansätze zur Konstruktion von Geschlecht* (Hamburg 1998), 77–99; Pak Prijana Winduwinata, *Intrigues de jungle et lois de basse-cour au royaume des animaux de Java. Contes satiriques traduits de javanais par Marcel Bonneff*, Paris 2012; R. O. Winstedt, *Hikayat Bayan Budiman atau Cherita Khojah Maimun*, Singapore 1920; Paul Wormser, *Le Bustan-al-Salatin de Nuruddin ar-Raniri. Réflexions sur le rôle culturel d'un étranger dans le monde malaise au XVIIe siècle*, Paris 2012.

Edwin P. Wieringa

G

Grand vizier

The **grand vizier**, *vezir-i azam* (*vezīr-i āʿẓam*, "the greatest of the viziers"), or, from the mid-tenth/sixteenth century, *sadrazam* (*ṣadr āʿẓam*), was the second highest-ranking figure in the Ottoman state. Initially, grand viziers were selected from among the *ulema* (*ʿulamāʾ*), and they were given considerable authority during the reign of Orhan (Orkhān, r. c. 726–63/1326–62). Later, other dignitaries shared the rank of vizier, and although the grand vizier's entitlements were reduced, command of the military was added to his responsibilities. The *kanunname* (*qānūnnāme*) of Mehmed (Meḥmed) II (r. 848–50/1444–6 and 855–86/1451–81) raised the grand vizier to the status of the sultan's *vekil-i mutlak* (*vekīl-i muṭlaq*, plenipotentiary delegate), who held the sovereign's seal, dispensed justice in his name, presided over sessions of the *divan* (*dīvān*, council of state), and directed the higher echelons of the administration and army. The progressive expansion of the Ottoman administration, the establishment of the Sublime Porte in the second half of the eleventh/seventeenth century, the institution of ministries during the reign of Mahmud (Maḥmūd) II (r. 1223–55/1808–39), and the formation of a constitutional regime after 1326/1908 contributed to the evolution of the position of the grand vizier, who became a head of government, whose powers increased but were also limited by the very nature of his appointment. Under Mehmed II, the post was opened to the *kapı kulları* (*qapı qulları*, lit. "slaves of the Porte"), previously trained in the palace schools, and progressively closed to the Christian aristocrats of conquered lands, whose political integration was less crucial henceforth for control of the Balkans and Anatolia. In the eleventh/seventeenth century, the *devşirme* (*devşīrme*, the "collection" of boys from among Balkan and Anatolian Christian subjects) waned, while the number of dignitaries in imperial service from the Caucasus and from free families in Anatolia increased.

The role of the grand vizier was shaped by the development of the machinery of the state, which fostered the emergence of several dynasties, such as the Candarlı and the Köprülü; contributed to the procreation of civil elites, which intensified in the thirteenth/nineteenth century;

and benefited from the establishment of official bureaucratic regulations. Nevertheless, through the end of the Ottoman era, the grand vizier remained more the sultan's servant than his prime minister. Often, he was the ruler's closest associate, tied to him by special trust, friendship, or other bond (many grand viziers were also imperial sons-in-law). Conversely, the relationship could be distant; in the eleventh/seventeenth century, grand viziers sometimes suffered from having access to the sovereign only through written reports *(telhis/telkhīṣ)*. The grand vizier's authority hinged on the balance of power between the Sublime Porte and the palace, favourable at times (early twelfth/eighteenth century, during the Tanzimat/Tanẓīmāt), and unfavourable at others (early and late thirteenth/nineteenth century). It also depended on the individual personalities of the sultans, who were sometimes withdrawn from affairs (for example, in the era of the *valide sultan/vālide sulṭān*, mother of the reigning sultan), or, on the contrary, engaged in them—such as (Selim (Selīm) III (r. 1203–22/1789–1807), Mahmud II, or Abdülhamid (ʿAbd al-Ḥamīd) II (r. 1293–1327/1876–1909). If the sultan deemed that the grand vizier had exceeded his authority or privileges, or that the stability of the state required his removal, the ruler would not hesitate to confiscate his property and exile or execute him. (For instance, Süleyman (Süleymān) I (r. 926–74/1520–66) brutally did away with his old friend İbrahim (İbrāhīm) Paşa (d. 942/1536), whose hubris had offended him.) This explains the considerable number of executions up to the end of the twelfth/eighteenth century. There were periods of quick turnover in grand viziers (many years with several in the post) alternating with times of stability (with some viziers in the position for twelve to fifteen years), or a monopoly of the office (by a handful of ministers in the years 1255–65/1840–50). Despite the precariousness of the grand vizier's post, it was, nevertheless, a source of considerable profit. The grand vizier had substantial resources at his disposal, especially extensive *hass* (*khāṣṣ*, fiscal revenues), with which to build a fortune (similar to Rüstem Paşa or İbrahim Paşa), part of which he generally placed in a major *vakıf* (*waqf*, pious foundation).

Structured by career rules and steeped in *edep (adab)*, or the training and education of a competent dignitary, the grand vizier's role was defined by custom and practice, as confirmed by prosopographic analysis. Although several grand viziers were inexperienced when they assumed office (such as İbrahim, under Süleyman, and Mehmed Said (Meḥmed Saʿīd, d. 1332/1914), under Abdülhamid II), the majority were accomplished statesmen, generally former *beylerbeyi*s (*beğlerbeği*, governor) and viziers, or, in the thirteenth/nineteenth century, former ministers and governors-general, who were well seasoned in bureaucratic practice, if not in the profession of arms or diplomacy. They were able to build powerful estates reinforced by client relations and supported by the higher spheres of the state, especially prominent *ilmiye* (*ʿilmiyye*, the body of men learned in Islamic law). They did not ignore fraternal networks, the imperial family, or grand notables. Like the administration it headed, the grand vizierate was shaped by centuries of development in the machinery of the state, and its changing role was marked by an intensification and expansion of fiscal and administrative capacities; a lessening of religious and then military experience in favour of expertise acquired in the chancellery;

growing interest in the scientific disciplines and European techniques, languages, and diplomatic customs; and greater awareness of methods of inventorying resources and subjects.

Bibliography
Ali Akyıldız, *Tanzimat dönemi Osmanlı teşkilâtında reform*, Istanbul 1993; Sait Aşgın, *Osmanlı sadrazamları üzere bir inceleme*, master's thesis, Ankara University 1992; İsmail Hami Danişmend, *İzahlı Osmanlı tarihi kronolojisi*, 4 vols., Istanbul 1947–55; Carter V. Findley, *Bureaucratic reform in the Ottoman Empire. The Sublime Porte, 1789–1922*, Princeton 1980; Suraiya Faroqhi, Das Grosswesir-telhis. Eine aktenkundlliche Studie, *Der Islam* 45 (1969), 96–116; Pál Fodor, Sultan, imperial council, grand vizier. Changes in the Ottoman ruling elite and the formation of the grand vezieral *telhīṣ*, *Acta Orientalia Academiae Scientiarum Hungaricae* 47 (1994), 67–85; Pál Fodor, The grand vizieral *telhis*. A study in the Ottoman central administration 1566–1656, *Archivum Ottomanicum* 15 (1997), 137–88; İbnülemin Mahmud Kemal İnal, *Osmanlı devrinde son sadrazamlar*, 4 vols., Istanbul 1940–48; Mehmet İpşirli, Sadrazam, *TDVİA* 35:414–19; M. Kunt, Ṣadr-i Aʿẓam, *EI2*; Mouradgea d'Ohsson, *Tableau général de l'Empire ottoman* (Paris 1824, reprint Istanbul 2001), 7:221–36; Şefik Okday, *Büyükbabam son sadrazam. Ahmed Tevfik Paşa*, Istanbul 1986–7; Abdülkadir Özcan (ed.), *Kânûnnâme-i Âl-i Osman*, Istanbul 2003; Klaus Röhrborn, *Untersuchungen zir osmanischen Verwaltungsgeschichte*, Wiesbaden, Berlin, New York 1973; Aydın Taneri, *Osmanlı İmparatorluğu'nun kuruluş döneminde vezîr-i a'zamlık, 1299–1453*, Ankara 1974; Nazim Tektaş, *Osmanlı'da ikinci adam saltanâtı. sadrâzamlar*, Istanbul 2009; İsmail Hakki Uzunçarşılı, *Osmanlı devletinin merkez ve bahriye teşkilatı*, Istanbul 1948; İsmail Hakki Uzunçarşılı, *Çandarlı vezir ailesi*, Ankara 1974; Ahmet Emin Yaman, *Osmanlı İmparatorluğu'nda sadr-ı âzamlık (1876–1922)*, Ankara 1999.

Olivier Bouquet

Guruş

The **guruş** *(kuruş*; Ott. *ghuruş)* was an Ottoman silver coin that was minted from 1131/1719 to 1919 and served as the monetary unit of the Ottoman currency system until the end of the empire. Long before minting the *guruş*, the Ottomans used the term, which derives from *groschen* (Ger.)/*grosso* (It.), to name large European silver pieces that circulated in the empire, including *esedi* (*esedī*) *guruş* for the Dutch *leeuwendaalder* ("lion dollar") and *riyal* (*riyāl*) *guruş* for the Spanish *real de a ocho* ("Spanish dollar," or "piece of eight").

During the century-long crisis that began in the 990s/1580s, the *akçe (aqçe)*—the Ottoman monetary unit of that era—was debased, and foreign coins dominated the Ottoman market. At the end of the eleventh/seventeenth century, the Ottomans attempted to reform their currency system by introducing a new unit modelled on the large European silver pieces in circulation. The initiative started with the minting of the *zolota* (derived from the Polish *zloty*) in 1101/1690 and concluded with the introduction of the Ottoman *guruş* in 1131/1719.

*Zolota*s weighed 20.043 grams, contained sixty percent silver, and were valued at eighty *akçe*s. In the same period, a unit of account was created with a fixed value of one hundred and twenty *akçe*s. Called *esedi guruş*, it only appeared in accounting records and was not struck as a coin. This practise lasted for twenty-nine years, until the *ferman* (*fermān* [sultanic] order) of 6 Zilhicce (Dhū l-Ḥijja) 1131/20 October 1719, in the reign of Ahmed (Aḥmed) III (r. 1115–43/1703–30), when the *esedi guruş*, as a unit of account, was replaced by the *guruş*, a minted coin. The new silver piece (with a weight of 26.457

grams, sixty percent silver content, and value of one hundred and twenty *akçe*s) became the monetary unit, which marked the beginning of the *guruş* era in the Ottoman currency system. The value of the *zolota* was also raised from eighty to ninety *akçe*s under the same *ferman* (Istanbul, Başbakanlık Osmanlı Arşivi, *Darphane Defterleri*, no. 164).

The *guruş* was debased for the first time in 1150/1738, and further debasements occurred in the second half of the twelfth and early thirteenth centuries (second half of the eighteenth century), during political and financial turmoil prompted by military defeats. The situation reached a crisis point in the reign of Mahmud (Maḥmūd) II (r. 1223–55/1808–39), when the silver content of the *guruş*, which had been 15.874 grams in 1131/1719, was reduced to 0.54 grams. Currency reform resulted in the introduction of a bimetallic system in 1260/1844, when a new *guruş* (weighing 1,202 grams and containing about one gram of pure silver) was minted together with a gold *lira* (valued at one hundred *guruş*) that served as an upper monetary unit. The adjustment of the *guruş* was close to an improved standard introduced for the silver piece in 1249/1834, during Mahmud II's reign.

After the reform of 1844, debasement of the *guruş* ceased to be necessary since the Ottomans found different ways to finance their external debt and began printing banknotes. The coin preserved its value up to the late 1280s/early 1870s, when new silver deposits were discovered in North America and other states began adopting the gold standard. The increased supply of silver in world markets lessened the *gurus*'s value, which triggered chaos in the Ottoman monetary system. Minting of the *guruş* was discontinued in 1297/1880, but resumed three years later, and continued up to 1919. Traces of the Ottoman *guruş* (known as "piastre" in Western sources) remain evident today. For instance, the derived terms *kuruş* and *qirsh* are still used for coinage in Turkey and Egypt respectively.

Bibliography

Sources

Istanbul, Başbakanlık Osmanlı Arşivi, *Darphane Defterleri*, no. 164.

Studies

Halil Sahillioğlu, *Bir asırlık Osmanlı para tarihi, 1640–1740*, Ph.D. diss., Istanbul University 1965; Şevket Pamuk, *A monetary history of the Ottoman Empire*, Cambridge 2000; Edhem Eldem, Chaos and half measures. The Ottoman monetary "system" of the nineteenth century, in Edhem Eldem and Socrates Petmezas (eds.), *The economic development of south-eastern Europe in the 19th century* (Athens 2011), 251–305; Ömerül Faruk Bölükbaşı, *XVIII. yüzyılın ikinci yarısında darbhâne-i âmire*, Istanbul 2013; Hüseyin Al and Şevket Kamil Akar, *Osmanlı finans sisteminde modernleşme. Osmanlı para reformu*, 2 vols., Istanbul 2014.

Ömerül Faruk Bölükbaşı

H

Hagiography in South Asia

Tadhkira and *malfūẓāt* have been the major genres of **hagiography in South Asia**. *Tadhkira* describes the saintly lives of Ṣūfīs in the tradition of works written in the Middle East and Central Asia, whereas *malfūẓāt*, the recorded discourses of a Ṣūfī master, evolved in India.

The first Ṣūfī text written in South Asia, ʿAlī al-Hujwīrī's (d. 465–9/1073–7) *Kashf al-maḥjūb* ("The revelation of the veiled"), contained biographical sketches of pious Muslims and Ṣūfīs, yet none of them had lived in India. Local hagiographical tradition dates back to early eighth/fourteenth-century Delhi, where various genres of Ṣūfī literature began to flourish amongst the followers of the influential Chishtī *shaykh* Niẓām al-Dīn Awliyāʾ (d. 725/1325). The first full-fledged *tadhkira* was the Persian *Siyar al-awliyāʾ* ("Deeds of saints"), completed around 751/1350 by Amīr Khurd Kirmānī (d. 770/1368–9). The work, based largely on oral information transmitted by Niẓām al-Dīn's surviving disciples, documents extensively the life, teachings, and devotional regime of the master.

During the following centuries, the hagiographers' scope broadened from accounts of the lives of individual Ṣūfīs to hagiographical anthologies. Jamāl al-Dīn Kamboh Jamālī (d. 942/1535–6), the Suhrawardī Ṣūfī and poet laureate of Lodi sultans, recorded the biographies of thirteen Suhrawardī and Chishtī Ṣūfīs in *Siyar al-ʿārifīn* ("Deeds of the gnostics"), while *Akhbār al-akhyār* ("Reports of [the best] men") by the Mughal Ṣūfī scholar ʿAbd al-Ḥaqq Muḥaddith Dihlawī (d. 1052/1642) also included Qādirīs, Firdawsīs, Shaṭṭārīs, and Qalandarīs.

The hagiographic anthologies were also a means of promoting specific Ṣūfī lineages. ʿAbd al-Raḥmān Chishtī (d. 1094/1683) of Dhaniti, in North India, divided the Ṣūfīs into twenty-three generations *(ṭabaqāt)* in *Mirʾāt al-asrār* ("The mirror of secrets") completed in 1065/1655. By placing a Chishtī Ṣābirī master at the head of each generation, ʿAbd al-Raḥmān gave a literary expression to the sacred history of his Ṣūfī brotherhood that had been overshadowed by the Chishtī Niẓāmīs until the tenth/sixteenth century (Ernst and Lawrence, 58–64) (the Chishtiyya probably originated in Chisht, near Herat, towards the end of the sixth/twelfth century, and was introduced in India by Muʿīn al-Dīn Sijzī, d. 627/1230. From the ninth/fifteenth and twelfth/eighteenth centuries on, respectively, two main branches developed, the Ṣābiriyya, followers of ʿAlāʾ al-Dīn Ṣābir Kaliyarī, d. 690/1291, and the Niẓāmiyya, followers of Niẓām al-Dīn Awliyāʾ, d. 725/1325).

Documenting the lives of Ṣūfīs of a particular region became common during the twelfth/eighteenth century, and even *tadhkira*s with a universal scope acquired a local hue. *Mishkāt al-nubuwwat* ("The niche of prophethood") by Shāh Ghulām ʿAlī Qādirī (d. 1842–3) chronicles the lives of 660 saintly figures, beginning with the prophet Muḥammad himself. According to the author, the entire saintly tradition culminated in the Deccan, in the author's *shaykh*, Shāh Mūsā Qādirī (d. 1800–1).

Sometimes the regional *tadhkira*s blended hagiography with local history and urban geography by documenting also the architecture and festivities of the Ṣūfī shrines (e.g., Murād ʿAlī Ṭāliʿ, *Tadhkira-yi awliyāʾ-i Ḥaydarābād*, "Lives of the saints of Hyderabad," 1969–75). The influence of European literary genres inspired some nineteenth-century authors to write *tadhkira*s that resemble historical novels (e.g., Khᵛāja Ḥasan Niẓāmī, *Niẓāmī bāṇsurī*, "The bamboo flute of Niẓām al-Dīn," 1945).

The other major genre, *malfūẓāt*, also evolved amongst the followers of Niẓām al-Dīn Awliyāʾ. The first literary *malfūẓāt* collection was *Fawāʾid al-fuʾād* ("Benefits for the heart"), a Persian-language record of Niẓām al-Dīn's informal talks made by the poet laureate and Chishtī Ṣūfī Amīr Ḥasan Sijzī (d. 736/1335–6). The genre was a novel development in that it included only the discourses between the Ṣūfī master and his disciples, with no attempt to place them in the broader context of the former's life or teachings. The *malfūẓāt* do not attempt to reconcile the contradictory views presented by a Ṣūfī master at different times; at their best, they preserve the conversational spontaneity of actual teaching situations.

Fawāʾid al-fuʾād became instantly popular and was widely imitated. Soon, discourses of early Chishtī masters from Khᵛāja ʿUthmān Hārvanī (d. 617/1220) to Niẓām al-Dīn were available. Each of the *malfūẓāt* was allegedly recorded by the leading disciple of the master, although Niẓām al-Dīn had clearly stated that neither he himself nor any of his predecessors had written any books. Compared to the authentic *malfūẓāt*, the literary style of these texts is inferior, and they bear distinct signs of literary rather than oral transmission. Inauthentic *malfūẓāt* were probably written for readers who were not full-time Ṣūfīs. They contain valuable information about the popular aspects of Ṣūfism in eighth/fourteenth-century India (Lawrence, Afzal-ul-Fawa'id, 124–5). Today, these *malfūẓāt* are available in Urdu translation as a collection entitled *Hasht bihisht* ("Eight paradises").

Hagiographical texts are probably distributed and read in contemporary South Asia more widely than ever before. New *malfūẓāt* are produced, and even minor shrines publish *tadhkira*s of the Ṣūfīs buried in them. Some of these texts are only small booklets, but they have spread far and wide with pilgrims and through the Internet. Bookstalls around the shrines sell Urdu translations of Persian classics as well as the newly produced books, some of which are written in local vernaculars, such as Panjābī, Sindhi, Hindi, and Bengali.

The influence of the conventions of modern biographical literature on Ṣūfī hagiographies has remained marginal. With a few exceptions, the hagiographical texts have become increasingly formulaic. Instead of depicting Ṣūfīs as men or women who acquired their saintly qualities through their practice and training under their own masters, they portray them as born saints who manifest their inherent qualities through their actions and routinely perform miracles.

In addition to the Ṣūfī authors, royal chroniclers in South Asia have recorded the lives of Ṣūfīs in their works, seeking to emphasise the spiritual legitimation of the ruling dynasty. Most notably, Abū l-Faḍl-i ʿAllāmī (d. 1011/1602), adviser, biographer, and confidant of the Mughal emperor Akbar (r. 963–1014/1556–1605), describes in his *Āʾīn-i Akbarī* ("Rule of Akbar") various Ṣūfī orders and saints of the Mughal domain.

Bibliography

Sources

ʿAbd al-Ḥaqq Muḥaddith Dihlavī, *Akhbār al-akhyār fī asrār al-abrār*, Tehran 1383sh/2004–5; ʿAbd al-Raḥmān Chishtī, *Mirʾāt al-asrār* (Urdu), trans. Wahid Bakhsh Sial Rabbani, Lahore 1982; Abū l-Faḍl ʿAllāmī, *Āʾīn-i Akbarī*, ed. Syed Ahmad Khan, Delhi 1272/1855, repr. Aligarh 2005; *Hasht bihisht. Malfūẓāt-i khʷājagān-i chisht*, Delhi 2005; ʿAlī b. ʿUthmān al-Hujwīrī, *Kashf al-maḥjūb*, ed. Valentin Zhukovskiĭ, St Petersburg 1899; Amīr Khurd Kirmānī, *Siyar al-awliyāʾ*, Delhi 1302/1884–5; Khʷāja Ḥasan Niẓāmī, *Niẓāmī bānsurī*, Delhi 1945; Shāh Ghulām ʿAlī Qādirī, *Mishkāt al-nubuwwat* (Urdu), 8 vols., Hyderabad 1982–5; Amīr Ḥasan Sijzī, *Fawāʾid al-fuʾād*, ed. and trans. Khʷāja Ḥasan Ṣānī Niẓāmī, New Delhi 2007; Murād ʿAlī Ṭāliʿ, *Tadhkira-yi awliyāʾ-i Ḥaydarābād*, 4 vols., Hyderabad 1969–75.

Studies

Carl W. Ernst and Bruce B. Lawrence, *Sufi martyrs of love. The Chishti order in South Asia and beyond* (New York 2002), 47–63; Nile Green, *Indian Sufism since the seventeenth century. Saints, books and empires in the Muslim Deccan*, Abingdon and New York 2006; Nile Green, Making a "Muslim" saint. Writing customary religion in an Indian princely state, *Comparative Studies of South Asia, Africa and the Middle East* 25/3 (2005), 617–33; Bruce B. Lawrence, Afzal-ul-Favaʾid. A reassessment, in Zoe Ansari (ed.), *Life, times and works of Amīr Khusrau Dehlavi. Seventh centenary* (New Delhi 1975), 119–31; Bruce B. Lawrence, *Notes from a distant flute. Sufi literature in pre-Mughal India*, Tehran 1978; Amina Steinfels, His master's voice. The genre of *malfūẓāt* in South Asian Sufism, *History of Religions* 44/1 (2004), 56–69; Mikko Viitamäki, Retelling medieval history for twentieth-century readers. Encounter of a Hindu prince and a Sufi master in Khwaja Hasan Nizami's *Nizami bansuri*, in Raziuddin Aquil and David L. Curley (eds.), *Literary and religious practices in medieval and early modern India* (New Delhi 2016), 191–212.

Mikko Viitamäki

Ḥātim al-Aṣamm

Abū ʿAbd al-Raḥmān **Ḥātim** b. ʿUnwān (or Ḥātim b. Yūsuf or Ḥātim b. ʿUrwān b. Yūsuf) **al-Aṣamm** (the deaf; d. 237/851–2) was a native of Balkh, where he spent most of his life. A disciple of Shaqīq al-Balkhī (d. 194/809–10), he is considered one of the earliest spiritual masters of Khurāsān.

Abū Saʿd al-Samʿānī (d. 562/1166), the important Arab biographer from Merv, mentions in his *Kitāb al-ansāb* ("The book of origins") other relevant men who bear the same sobriquet (al-Samʿānī, *Ansāb*, 1:294–8). Ḥātim, however, seems to be the only one known metaphorically as "deaf" and not because of any physical defect. Ḥātim pretended not to hear in order to protect the honour of an old lady who accidentally farted in his presence (al-Qushayrī, 1:63; Gramlich, *Sendschreiben*, §1.13). This episode might be considered proof of Ḥātim's adherence to the ethical values of the *fityān* (Ar. plur. of *fatā*, lit., boy, manservant, slave; the *futuwwa* was a social and spiritual movement to which his spiritual master, Shaqīq al-Balkhī, probably also belonged) (al-Qushayrī, 1:56; Gramlich, *Sendschreiben*, §1.9). Shaqīq played a decisive role in Ḥātim's spiritual and religious education. The disciple spent considerable time with his master—thirty years, according to Ibn al-Jawzī (4:135)—and accompanied him in war against pagan Turks. His training as a fighter is often cited by hagiographical sources as a distinctive feature (al-Qushayrī, 1:57, 1:62; Gramlich, *Sendschreiben*, §1.9, §1.13). Ḥātim eventually died in a *ribāṭ* (a small fort, of the sort often used as Ṣūfī monasteries) called Ra's Sarwand, near the city of Wāshajird (al-Sulamī, *Ṭabaqāt*, 80). The experience of *jihād* helped him to define his spiritual doctrine of life and death. War is an experience that can guide a man to absolute confidence in God *(tawakkul)*. One of the the most important legacies of his teacher, Shaqīq, this concept was refined and disseminated by Ḥātim al-Aṣamm in his teachings (Radtke, 542; Gramlich, *Alte Vorbilder*, pt. 2, 68, Knysh, *Islamic mysticism*, 33). This radical attitude towards life and death is also visible in other aspects of his life. He had a large family—four wives and nine children—and an anecdote shows that concern for their support did not lessen his trust in God (Abū Nuʿaym, 8:79). Ḥātim was known also for his travels, as attested in an encounter with a Christian monk (Gramlich, *Alte Vorbilder*, pt. 2, 81, from al-Shaʿranī, *al-Ṭabaqāt al-kubrā*).

Despite his distrust of men and his fame as an ascetic *(zāhid)*, he was active as a preacher and, according to some hagiographical sources, was a popular spiritual adviser (Wāʿiẓ-i Balkhī, 1:176; Gramlich, *Alte Vorbilder*, pt. 2, 76). His teachings often derive from his own exegesis of Qurʾānic passages concerning readiness to die and absolute sincerity towards God (ʿAṭṭār, *Tadhkira*, 1:246, Gramlich, *Alte Vorbilder*, pt. 2, 79). Al-Sulamī (d. 412/1021), the important Ṣūfī hagiographer and Qurʾān commentator, quotes him twice in his collection of mystical exegesis titled *Ḥaqāʾiq al-tafsīr* ("True realities of Qurʾānic exegesis") in reference to Q 3:188 and Q 57:14. Ḥātim was aware of the role and influence of the religious establishment, and he acknowledged the evil that corrupt religious authorities could generate. He did not hesitate to admonish powerful men publicly (Gramlich, *Alte Vorbilder*, pt. 2, 87ff.), as in his criticism of the rulers and religious scholars of Medina (Abū Nuʿaym, 8:82–3). At the same time, he held in high esteem Aḥmad Ibn Ḥanbal (d. 241/855), the celebrated theologian, jurist, traditionist, and founder of one of the four major Sunnī schools, whom he visited in Baghdad (Abū Nuʿaym, 8:82; Khaṭīb al-Baghdādī, 8:242). Besides his oral teachings, he appears to have also composed some treatises that are no longer extant (al-Hujwirī, trans. Nicholson, 115).

Ḥātim is a pivotal figure in the history of Islamic spirituality. Later sources recognised a line of spiritual transmission originating with his companionship with Shaqīq. Ḥātim's own disciples, including Aḥmad b. Khiḍruyya (d. 240/854–5) and Abū Turāb al-Nakhshabī (d. 245/859), were part of the same chain of authority (cf. Gril, 40). In his *logia*, one sees also the emergence of codified practices that would later become signs of a Ṣūfī adept, such as the investiture with the patched cloak *(muraqqaʿa)*, called the "green death" (al-Qushayrī, 1:64; Gramlich, *Sendschreiben*, §1.13), or with the woollen mantel *(ʿabāʾ)* (al-Sulamī, *Ṭabaqāt*, 85). He was bilingual in Arabic and Persian. Because he was not fluent in classical Arabic (Abū Nuʿaym, 8:82), his teachings were probably all systematised in Arabic after his death (Gramlich, *Alte Vorbilder*, pt. 2, 63). Later local historiography, such as Ṣafī al-Dīn Wāʿiẓ-i Balkhī's *Faḍāʾil-i Balkh* ("The merits of Balkh"), testifies to the veneration of Ḥātim after his death. Ṣafī al-Dīn Wāʿiẓ-i Balkhī narrates some of Hātim's miraculous qualities attested to by local people; he also visited Ḥātim's hermitage (Gramlich, *Alte Vorbilder*, pt. 2, 66, 92–3).

Bibliography

Sources

Abū Nuʿaym al-Iṣbahānī, *Ḥilyat al-awliyāʾ wa-ṭabaqāt al-aṣfiyāʾ* (Cairo 1932–8), 8:73–83; ʿAbdallāh b. ʿUmar al-Wāʿiẓ-i Balkhī, *Faḍāʾil-i Balkh*, ed. ʿAbd al-Ḥayy-i Ḥabībī, Tehran 1350sh/1971; Farīd al-Dīn Muhammad ʿAṭṭār, *Tadhkirat al-awliyāʾ*, ed. Reynold Nicholson, 2 vols., Leiden 1905–7; al-Hujwirī, *Kashf al-maḥjūb*, ed. Mahmūd ʿĀbidī, Tehran 1383sh/2004–5; al-Khaṭīb al-Baghdādī, *Taʾrīkh Baghdād*, 14 vols., Cairo 1349/1931; al-Qushayrī, *Risāla al-qushayriyya*, ed. ʿAbd al-Ḥālīm Maḥmūd and Maḥmūd Ibn al-Sharīf, 2 vols., Cairo 1966, repr. 1990–4, trans. Richard Gramlich, *Das Sendschreiben al-Qušayrīs über das Sufitum*, Stuttgart 1989; al-Samʿānī, *al-Ansāb*, ed. ʿAbd al-Raḥmān b. Yaḥyā al-Muʿallimī, 12 vols., repr. Cairo 1980–4; al-Sulamī, *Ṭabaqāt al-ṣūfiyya*, ed. Johannes Pedersen, Leiden 1960; al-Sulamī, *Tafsīr al-Sulamī* (= *Ḥaqāʾiq al-tafsīr*), ed. Sayyid ʿImrān, 2 vols., Beirut 2001.

Studies

Richard Gramlich, *Alte Vorbilder des Sufitums*, pt. 1, *Scheiche des Westens*, Wiesbaden 1995; Richard Gramlich, *Alte Vorbilder des Sufitums*, pt. 2, *Scheiche des Ostens*, Harrassowitz, Wiesbaden 1996; Denis Gril, Compagnons ou disciples? La *ṣuḥba* et ses exigences. L'exemple d'Ibrāhīm b. Adham d'après la *Ḥilyat al-awliyāʾ*, in Geneviève Gobillot and Jean-Jacques Thibon (eds.), *Les maîtres soufis et leurs disciples, IIIe–Ve siècles de l'hégire (IXe–XIe s.). Enseignement, formation et transmission* (Damascus 2013), 35–53; Alexander D. Knysh, *Islamic mysticism. A short history*, Leiden 2000; Alexander D. Knysh, *Al-Qushayri's epistle on Sufism*, Reading 2007; Louise Marlow, A translation from the *Ḥilyat al-awliyāʾ wa-tabaqāt al-aṣfiyāʾ* by Abū Nuʿaym al-Iṣfahānī. The life of Ḥātim al-Aṣamm, *al-ʿArabiyya* 19 (1986), 29–46; Reynold A. Nicholson, *Kashf al-maḥjúb of Hujwírí. The oldest Persian treatise on Súfism*, Leiden 1911, London 1976; Bernd Radtke, Theologen und Mystiker in Ḫurāsān und Transoxanien, *ZDMG* 136 (1986), 536–69; Aluma Solnik-Dankowitz, On the life and teachings of the mystic Ḥātim al-Aṣamm. An example of Sufi anecdotes in Jewish sources (in Hebrew), in *Sefunot. Studies and Sources on the History of the Jewish Communities in the East* n.s. 23 (2003), 75–97; Georges Vajda, Une réplique rarement attestée de Ḥātim al-Aṣamm, *Arabica* 23 (1976), 88–90.

Francesco Chiabotti

Ḥusayn, Muḥammad Kāmil

Muḥammad Kāmil Ḥusayn (1901–77) was an Egyptian surgeon, novelist, and writer. He was born in Subk al-Daḥḥāk, a village in the Delta governorate of al-Munūfiyya, to a learned family with peasant roots. After the death of his father—a teacher of Arabic language and friend of the prominent reformer Muḥammad ʿAbduh (d. 1905)—Ḥusayn's elder brother took care of him and provided him with a secular education in Cairo. He graduated from medical school in 1923, then went on a government sponsored study mission to London in 1925. While there, he sent back articles to the weekly *al-Siyāsa* under the penname "Ibn Sīnā," a reference to the famed physician and philosopher known in the West as Avicenna (d. 428/1037). Ḥusayn returned to Egypt in 1931, with a membership in the Royal College of Surgeons and a master's degree in orthopaedic surgery, a discipline that he helped establish in Egypt. A brilliant surgeon, he was known for his interest in clinical issues and his close relationship with his patients. "To him, medicine [was] a complete culture" (Expert-Bezancon, 27).

In addition to his busy schedule as doctor, professor of orthopaedic surgery, and rector of ʿAyn Shams University (from 1951 to 1954), Ḥusayn was also an active writer. He published more than thirty books and articles on medicine, philosophy, literature, and Arabic language and grammar. He is the author of an edition of al-Rāzī's (Rhazes, d. 313/925 or 323/935) major medical treatise, *Kitāb al-ḥāwī* ("The comprehensive book"); in this famed Persian physician and philosopher he saw a free-thinker and forefather of modern clinical theory, whose vision of medicine resonated with his own. He counted among his friends the well-known Egyptian liberal intellectuals Aḥmad Luṭfī l-Sayyid (1872–1963) and Ṭāhā Ḥusayn (1889–1973).

In his writing he presented a critical approach to religious texts and the classical Arabic heritage, systematically questioning statements by "traditional Qurʾānic commentators." In *al-Wādī l-muqaddas* ("The hallowed valley," 1968), he displayed "an intriguing ambivalence about traditional Islamic understanding of revelation, prophethood, worship, prayer and liturgy" (Cragg, 7). His reading of Arabic classical poetry insisted on its universal and human aspects, privileging *shiʿr al-ṭabʿ* (poetry of nature) over *shiʿr al-iḥtirāf* (poetry of craft). He also showed a particular interest in the work and complex personality of the renowned poet al-Mutanabbī (d. 354/965). As a member of the Majmaʿ al-Lugha al-ʿArabiyya (Academy of the Arabic Language), he suggested many detailed reforms to Arabic grammar that aimed to simplify its rules.

Ḥusayn published one novel, for which he was awarded the Egyptian State Prize in Literature in 1957. (He was later awarded the State Prize in Science, in 1966). *Qarya ẓālima* (published in 1954 and later translated into English as *City of wrong. A Friday in Jerusalem*), whose title refers to Qurʾānic verse 4:75, is a philosophical narrative recounting Jesus's last day, discussing the dynamics that led to the crucifixion. *Qarya ẓālima* offers a deeply philosophical meditation on the responsibility of every individual whose deeds eventually led to Christ's murder, thus avoiding theological debates between Muslims and Christians about the actual crucifixion. The reception of this novel contributed to establishing the reputation of a discreet intellectual, someone who devoted his life, first and foremost, to his patients. He remained unmarried until his death, in March 1977.

Bibliography

Works by Muḥammad Kāmil Ḥusayn

al-Taḥlīl al-biyūlūjī lil-taʾrīkh, Cairo 1950; *Mutanawwiʿāt*, Cairo 1951, 1960²; *Qarya ẓālima*, Cairo 1954, English trans., *City of wrong. A Friday in Jerusalem*, trans. Kenneth Cragg, New York 1966, French trans. *La cité inique. Récit philosophique*, trans. Roger Arnaldez and Jean Grosjean, Paris 1973; *Waḥdat al-maʿrifa*, Cairo 1958; *al-Wādī l-muqaddas*, Cairo 1968, English trans., *The hallowed valley. A Muslim philosophy of religion*, trans.

Kenneth Cragg, Cairo 1977; *al-Shiʿr al-ʿArabī wa-l-dhawq al-muʿāṣir*, Cairo 1970; *al-Lugha al-ʿArabiyya al-muʿāṣira*, Cairo 1977; with the Arab League Educational, Cultural, and Scientific Organisation, Idārat al-thaqāfa, *al-Mūjaz fī taʾrīkh al-ṭibb wa-l-ṣaydala ʿind al-ʿArab*, Cairo n.d.; with Muḥammad ʿAbd al-Ḥalīm ʿUqbī, *Ṭibb al-Rāzī. Dirāsa wa-taḥlīl li-Kitāb al-ḥāwī*, Beirut and Cairo 1977.

Studies

Marc Chartier, La pensée religieuse de Kâmil Husayn, *IBLA 133* (1974), 1–44; Hélène Expert-Bezancon, Notes biographiques sur le docteur Kâmil Husayn, *IBLA 155* (1985), 19–43; Kenneth Cragg, Translator's introduction, in Muḥammad Kāmil Ḥusayn, *The hallowed valley. A Muslim philosophy of religion*, Cairo 1977; Muḥammad Muḥammad al-Jawādī, *al-Duktūr Muḥammad Kāmil Ḥusayn. ʿĀliman wa-mufakkiran wa-adīban*, Cairo 1979; Oddbjørn Leirvik, *Human conscience and Muslim-Christian relations. Modern Egyptian thinkers on al-ḍamīr*, London and New York 2006; Oddbjørn Leirvik, *Images of Jesus Christ in Islam*, London and New York 2010.

Dina Heshmat

I

Ibn ʿAṭāʾallāh al-Iskandarī

Tāj al-Dīn Abū l-Faḍl (also Abū l-ʿAbbās; Ibn Farḥūn, *Dībāj*, 1:242) Aḥmad b. Muḥammad b. ʿAbd al-Karīm **Ibn ʿAṭāʾallāh al-Iskandarī** (b. before 657/1259, d. 709/1309) was an Egyptian Ṣūfī and scholar of the Ayyūbid-Mamlūk period, author of the *al-Ḥikam* ("The aphorisms"), and successor of al-Mursī (d. 686/1287) and al-Shādhilī (d. 656/1258) as head of the Shādhilī order.

1. Life

Primary sources for his life consist of autobiographical information scattered through the author's *Laṭāʾif al-minan* ("Subtle blessings") and of the brief entries in various biographical dictionaries, such as those by Tāj al-Dīn al-Subkī (d. 771/1370), the leading scholar from Cairo, who lived mostly in Damascus (9:23–4), Ibn Farḥūn (1:242) (d. 799/1397), an influential Mālikī jurist, al-ʿAsqalānī (d. 852/1449), the Egyptian *ḥadīth* scholar, judge, and historian (1:273–5), and al-Suyūṭī (d. 911/1505), a prolific teacher of *ḥadith*, jurist, philologist, historian, and Ṣūfī from Cairo (1:524). Al-Shaʿrānī (d. 973/1565), a major representative and author on Ṣūfism in early Ottoman Egypt (2:18–9), mentions him only briefly, probably because of his fame. Al-Kūhin (b. 1915) summarises various sources (94–6). A longer notice is found in al-Shāriʿī's (d. 615/1218) guide for visiting saints' graves in the Qarāfa cemetery of Cairo (*Murshid*, 2:12; Massignon, 67).

For secondary literature on his life, see, in Arabic, Abū l-Wafā al-Taftazānī, in English, Victor Danner and especially Mary Ann K. Danner, and in French, Paul Nwyia and Samia Touati.

Little is known about Ibn ʿAṭāʾallāh's early life. He was born in Alexandria, probably before 657/1259 (Touati, 38–40) into the Banū Ibn ʿAṭāʾallāh, a distinguished family of religious jurists (*fuqahāʾ*) mentioned by Ibn Khaldūn (d. 784/1382), the famous historian and philosopher of Arabo-Andalusian origin, as one of the three most important scholarly dynasties of Alexandria (*Taʾrīkh*, 4:813). The family originally moved to Alexandria during the early Muslim conquests and is of Arab descent, as indicated by the *nisba* al-Iskandarī of the Arab tribe al-Judhāmī. Ibn Khaldūn (4:813) stresses the significance of Alexandria for the Mālikī tradition of Egypt, and Ibn ʿAṭāʾallāh's family played an important role in this respect. His grandfather, ʿAbd al-Karīm Ibn ʿAṭāʾallāh (d. 612/1215), a renowned scholar of his time and the author of works on linguistics and jurisprudence, was hostile to Ṣūfism (Ibn Farḥūn, 1:167; al-Suyūṭī, 1:456; al-Taftazānī, 14–6; Danner, *Ṣūfī aphorisms*, 2). On the other hand, the father of Ibn ʿAṭāʾallāh, Muḥammad Ibn ʿAṭāʾallāh (date of death unknown), was a disciple of Abū l-Ḥasan al-Shādhilī.

Besides the instruction within his family, Ibn ʿAṭāʾallāh received an intense and excellent education in the Islamic sciences from the most distinguished scholars of Alexandria (Danner, *Ṣūfī aphorisms*, 3), such as Muḥyī l-Dīn al-Mārūnī (d. 693/1294) for Arabic grammar, Sharaf al-Dīn al-Dimyāṭī (d. 705/1306) for *ḥadīth*, Makīn al-Dīn al-Asmar (d. 692/1293) for Qurʾān recitation, and Shams al-Dīn al-Iṣfahānī (d. 688/1290) for Ashʿarī *kalām* (speculative theology) and *uṣūl al-fiqh* (principles of jurisprudence). In *fiqh* (jurisprudence), he received training from both Mālikī and Shāfiʿī scholars. Except for al-Subkī (9:23), however, who vacillates between the two schools, all the sources consider him a Mālikī scholar.

Ibn ʿAṭāʾallāh himself eventually became a distinguished specialist in Mālikī jurisprudence, Qurʾānic exegesis, theology, and Prophetic tradition (al-Suyūṭī, 1:524). Some of his teachers, such as al-Asmar, had Ṣūfī connections or even direct contact with Abū l-Ḥasan al-Shādhilī (from Morocco, d. c.656/1258), the founder of the Shādhilī order. According to Ibn ʿAṭāʾallāh's own testimony (*Laṭāʾif*, 102), however, he received his religious and scholarly education in a milieu mistrustful of Ṣūfism (Nwyia, 20; Geoffroy, *Hagiographie*, 11). He recounts (*Laṭāʾif*, 105) that he was initially critical of Ṣūfism; his association with Ṣūfism and the Shādhilī order in particular was, in fact, the result of his encounter at the age of seventeen with Abū l-ʿAbbās al-Mursī (d. 686/1288), the successor of the founder of the Shadhilī order. This first encounter was triggered by a dispute with one of al-Mursī's disciples. Being much impressed by the teaching of al-Mursī, Ibn ʿAṭāʾallāh decided to visit him regularly and finally became his disciple in 674/1276. An anecdote recounts how he found himself facing the dilemma of having to choose between his scholarly pursuits and the company of his *shaykh*, al-Mursī. It shows al-Mursī advising him against abandoning his studies and telling him to "persevere, by God, for you will be surely a master in both disciplines" (*la-takūnanna muftiyan fī l-madhhabayn; Laṭāʾif*, 106), that is, in the religious sciences and Ṣūfism. The anecdote captures the novelty and the peculiarity of the Shādhiliyya approach in a context of tension between the Ṣūfī orders and the scholars (Mary Ann K. Danner, 5–6; Gril, 104; Geoffroy, *Ésotérisme*, 118). Ibn ʿAṭāʾallāh, the most scholarly of the earlier authorities of the Shādhiliyya, appears as a personification of this Shādhilī emphasis on harmonising the requirements of scholarly knowledge with those of spiritual practice.

Having spent twelve years in the company of al-Mursī, Ibn ʿAṭāʾallāh succeeded him upon his death, in 696/1287, as head of the Shādhiliyya in Cairo (for the circumstances and problems associated with this succession, see Hofer, 117) where he was already active as a foremost religious authority of his day. As a scholar, he taught at the Manṣuriyya *madrasa* and gave public sermons at the Azhar mosque. Although it is known that he also instructed his disciples in smaller private groups, there is no *zāwiya* (Ṣūfī lodge) associated with his name (Mary Ann K. Danner, 8). Ibn ʿAṭāʾallāh's *Tāj al-ʿarūs* ("The bridegroom's crown") and the notes of one of his disciples, Rāfiʿ b. al-Shāfiʿ (death date unknown), offer direct testimony of his oral and public teaching (Gril; Shoshan, 12–6). They show him to have been both a spiritual master and a preacher who integrated Ṣūfī doctrines—such as perpetual repentance *(tawba)*, the abandonment of self-management *(isqāṭ al-tadbīr)*, and the reality of sainthood—into a hortatory discourse addressed to a popular audience. According to Gril (103–4), testimonies of famous scholars such as the historian and *ḥadīth* scholar from Damascus al-Dhahabī (d. 749/1348) portray Ibn ʿAṭāʾallāh as a much appreciated preacher who had a profound effect on his listeners (see also al-ʿAsqalānī, 1:274). His popularity was not, however, limited to scholars or to the common people amongst whom he seems to have had many followers (al-ʿAsqalānī, 1:274). His advice was sought by all classes of Egyptian society, and, from his own testimony (*Laṭāʾif*, 175), we know that he counselled the Mamlūk sultan ʿAbd al-Mālik al-Manṣūr (r. 696–8/1296–8).

His influence and his role as a widely recognised authority in both religious sciences and Ṣūfism are evident from an incident with the Ḥanbalī theologian, jurisconsult, and reformer Ibn Taymiyya (d. 728/1328) (Shoshan, 16, 92 n. 102; Johansen, 103–14; Hofer, 167–73) in 707/1307, when he joined the master of the Saʿīd al-Suʿadāʾ Ṣūfī lodge and other Ṣūfīs along with more than five hundred people in a march to the citadel in order to complain to the authorities about Ibn Taymiyya's public attacks against Ṣūfism. During the council that took place as a result of the march, Ibn ʿAṭāʾallāh played a decisive role in the condemnation of Ibn Taymiyya and his expulsion from Cairo (al-ʿAsqalānī, 1:73; Ibn Kathīr, 14:45). In this incident Ibn ʿAṭāʾallāh positions himself as a defender of Ibn ʿArabī's doctrines and of Ṣūfism in general. The anecdote must be situated in the wider context of the various scholarly disputes in Mamlūk Egypt over the doctrines of the famous Ṣūfī of Andalusian origin Muḥyī l-Dīn Ibn ʿArabī (d. 637/1240) and indicates the controversies between Ṣūfīs and their critics more generally. It illustrates Ibn ʿAṭāʾallāh's role as a mediator between Ṣūfīs and exoteric *ʿulamāʾ*, a role that made him, in al-ʿAsqalānī's words, a recognised spokesman of Ṣūfism in his days (*al-mutakallim ʿalā lisān al-ṣūfiyya fī zamānih; Durar*, 1:273). As such, he serves as a paradigm for later generations and for other Shādhilī scholars, such as Ibn ʿAbbād al-Rundī (d. 793/13901), Zarrūq (d. 899/1494), and Aḥmad Ibn ʿAjība (d. 1809), all of whom wrote commentaries on his *al-Ḥikam*. The influence and success of Ibn ʿAṭāʾallāh were sustained by a political context favourable to Ṣūfism in the early Mamlūk era and by the cultural influence that Cairo exerted as far as the Maghrib and the Middle East after the destruction of Baghdad by the Mongols (656/1258).

Ibn ʿAṭāʾallāh died at around sixty years of age, in Jumāda II 709/November 1309, in the Manṣūriyya *madrasa* in Cairo. His funeral was a major public event in Cairo, and his tomb in the Qarāfa cemetery in Cairo became a place of pilgrimage, as it remains today (al-Shāriʿī, 2:12).

2. Significance

Considered during his lifetime as "the wonder of his time in expressing the teachings of Ṣūfism" (Ibn Farḥūn, 70), Ibn ʿAṭāʾallāh was one of the most influential advocates of Islamic spirituality and, because of his crucial importance for the constitution and the spread of the Shādhilī order (Nwyia; Hofer), a major figure in the consolidation and formalisation of Ṣūfism. According to Hofer (112–3), Ibn ʿAṭāʾallāh played a decisive role in the emergence of "the institutionalised identity" of Shādhilī Ṣūfism, thereby contributing substantially to the establishment and articulation of an authoritative Shādhilī tradition: "While both al-Shādhilī and al-Mursī did much to publicise their message and bring it to the people, it was surely al-Iskandarī who mass-produced that message and thereby precipitated the institutionalisation of the Shādhilī *ṭarīqa*" (Hofer, 165).

Several eminent disciples of Ibn ʿAṭāʾallāh are known (Danner, *Ṣūfī aphorisms*, 11–2), including al-Subkī's father, Taqī al-Dīn Abū l-Ḥasan ʿAlī (d. 756/1355) (al-Subkī, 5:176; al-Suyūṭī, 1:524; Taftazānī, 26), the aforementioned Rāfiʿ b. al-Shāfiʿ, and the *ḥadīth* transmitter Shihāb al-Dīn Ibn Maylaq (d. 750/1349). The Mālikī scholar Dāwūd al-Bākhilī (d. 732/1332) is mentioned in the usual Shādhilī chain of transmission as the successor of Ibn ʿAṭāʾallāh.

Ibn ʿAṭāʾallāh figures in the most widely disseminated *silsila* (chain of transmission) of the Shādhiliyya order. From this filiation emerged the major Shādhilī ramifications, such as the Zarrūqiyya, the Mīlyāniyya, the Fāsiyya, the Nāṣiriyya, the Darqāwiyya, and the ʿAlāwiyya. He is known also as a transmitter of *aḥzāb* (litanies; al-Shawkānī, 3:1447–8).

3. Works

The main characteristics, and probably the reasons for the success of his writings, are their concision and force of expression, the accessibility of his style, the combination of the doctrinal and the practical dimensions of Ṣūfī teaching, and the remarkable clarity with which he articulated complex Ṣūfī ideas in a language acceptable to the exoteric scholarly tradition and intelligible to common people. The writings (for an overview, see Danner, *Ṣūfī aphorisms*, 12–4), all of which have been translated into European languages, deal with the rules of the spiritual path, the practice of *dhikr* (remembrance of God), and the doctrine of sainthood.

While the oral teachings of al-Shādhilī and al-Mursī constitute the primary source of Ibn ʿAṭāʾallāh's thought, the influence of major Ṣūfī authors is evident. Besides *Iḥyāʾ al-ʿulūm al-dīn* ("The revivification of religious sciences") by the famous Ṣūfī and theologian al-Ghazālī, d. 505/1111), *Qūt al-qulūb* ("The sustenance of hearts") by al-Makkī (d. 386/996), a Ṣūfī and traditionist who frequented the Ṣūfīs of Mecca, Basra, and Baghdad, as well as the works of the traditionist and exponent of the Ṣūfī doctrine of sainthood from Central Asia al-Ḥakīm al-Tirmidhī (d. c.285/898) and those of Ibn ʿArabī seem to have had a lasting impact on him, especially in his conceptions of prophetology, sainthood, and the unity of being (Gobillot; Geoffroy, *Influence*; Geoffroy, *Hagiographie*, 60–6). Ibn ʿAṭāʾallāh's achievement lies in the fact that he expressed these and other complex doctrines in an accessible way and in a way that puts at the forefront the implications of these doctrines for spiritual practice. He embedded the Shādhilī conception of Ṣūfism and sainthood into the idea of a spiritual Muḥammadan heritage (*al-warātha al-nabawiyya*, Geoffroy, *Hagiographie*, 51–7) which he expounds at the beginning of his *Laṭāʾif al-minan* (21–2). Ibn ʿAṭāʾallāh thus highlights the Prophetic source and identity of the Shādhiliyya as its peculiar characteristics. In Ibn ʿAṭāʾallāh's thought, this explicitly Muḥammadan orientation implies the search for harmony between the esoteric and exoteric dimensions of Islamic practice, which is characteristic of Shādhilī Ṣūfism. In addition to this doctrinal orientation, according to Hofer (130), "Ibn ʿAṭāʾallāh's entire corpus reflects a larger project to shape, disseminate and popularise the Shādhilī *ṭarīqa* (lit., way, hence Ṣūfī order) in Egypt." In fact, he seems to have considered it his mission to formalise and fix in writing the central teachings of the Shādhiliyya in a manner that would be acceptable to the scholarly tradition and would establish the pattern for the future generations of the order. There are indications that the writings of Ibn ʿAṭāʾallāh exerted some influence even outside the milieu of Sunnī scholarship and Ṣūfism. While the Spanish scholar Miguel Asín Palacios suggested that Saint John of the Cross (d. 1591 C.E.) may have been influenced by the writings of Ibn ʿAṭāʾallāh, William Chittick has discovered in Shīʿī literature passages adopted from his writings.

Al-ḥikam ("The aphorisms") is an anthology of 264 aphorisms about spiritual practice and doctrine. It is Ibn ʿAṭāʾallāh's most widely known work and a landmark of Arabic Ṣūfī literature (Nwyia, 35–49). The critical edition was prepared by Nwyia in 1972 and has been translated into the several European languages (into French by Nwyia, English by Danner, and German by Schimmel). The oft repeated saying that, if it were possible to recite in the canonical prayer any other text than the Qurʾān, it would be the *Ḥikam* (Nwyia, 3), illustrates the inspirational quality attributed to the work. From a literary point of view, the *Ḥikam* was perhaps inspired by the aphorisms of Abū Madyan (d. 594/1198), a famous Ṣūfī of Andalusian origin (Nwyia, 51–2), while synthetising the common doctrinal heritage of formative Ṣūfism with the teachings of the early Shādhiliyya. Al-Mursī is reported to have said to Ibn ʿAṭāʾallāh that the *Ḥikam* contains the core teachings *(maqāṣid)* of al-Ghazālī's famous *Iḥyāʾ al-ʿulūm al-Dīn* "and beyond" (Nwyia, 3), while the commentator Ibn ʿAbbād al-Rundī (d. 793/1391) affirms that "it absolves one of referring to many other books about Sufism" (Nwyia, 4). The anthology obviously intends to offer precepts for the introspection and the interior education of the disciple, but it concerns also common topics such as ritual prayer, repentance, virtues and vices, and supplication, as well as more sophisticated elaborations on metaphysical contemplation and mystical insight. The success of the *Ḥikam* is due to the concision, intelligence, and richness of its language, as well as to the unique psychological perspicacity and spiritual depth of its teaching. While it reflects the characteristic suspicion of the Shādhiliyya towards external piety, scholastic erudition, and asceticism, the *Ḥikam* condenses the principal teachings of conventional Ṣūfism and stays in line with the teachings of al-Makkī and al-Ghazālī. In most editions, the aphorisms themselves are followed by "letters to certain disciples" and finally the *Munājāt* ("Intimate conversations [with God]"), a series of thirty-five (Nwyia, 208–28) supplications summarising the main ideas of the *Ḥikam*. The remarkable popularity of the *Ḥikam*, even amongst non-Ṣūfī scholars, is documented by the many commentaries prepared up to the contemporary period, constituting a veritable tradition in Ṣūfī literature that is yet to be studied. The most influential commentaries are those of Ibn ʿAbbād al-Rundī, Aḥmad Zarrūq (d. 899/1493), and particularly the *Īqāẓ al-himam* ("The wakening of aspiration") by the Moroccan Ṣūfī Aḥmad Ibn ʿAjība (d. 1809). Even contemporary non-Ṣūfī scholars such as Ramaḍān al-Būṭī (d. 2013) from Syria wrote a popular commentary that has been translated into French (De Vos et al.).

Laṭāʾif al-minan fī manāqib al-shaykh Abī al-ʿAbbās al-Mursī wa-shakykhihi al-Shādhilī Abī al-Ḥasan ("The subtle blessings in the saintly lives of Abū l-ʿAbbās al-Mursī and his master Abū l-Ḥasan al-Shādhilī"). This "foundational text of the *ṭarīqa* Shādhiliyya" was written after 698/1298 and, Ibn ʿAṭāʾallāh's last work, may be considered his "spiritual testament" (Geoffroy, *Hagiologie*, 51, 66). After the *Ḥikam*, the *Laṭāʾif al-minan* is his most widely acclaimed writing. Like all of his works, the *Laṭāʾif al-minan* exists in multiple editions, the most notable being that by the former chief *muftī* of al-Azhar ʿAbd al-Ḥalīm Maḥmūd. There is a French translation by Geoffroy *(Sagesse)*, an English translation by Roberts, and a Spanish translation by Tabuyo and López. Intended as a "defence and illustration of sainthood in Islam, by showing that the Muslim saint does nothing else than to conform himself in a profound way to the prophetic model" (Geoffroy, *Hagiographie*, 50), the work expounds a doctrine of sainthood that shows more visibly than in any other of Ibn ʿAṭāʾallāh's writings the influence of al-Tirmīdhī and Ibn ʿArabī (Geoffroy, *Hagiographie*, 65). It thus combines hagiographical narratives with hagiological expositions in order to elucidate in accessible language the reality of sainthood through the example of his master, al-Mursī, and the latter's master, al-Shādhilī. In addition to this general intent, the work aimed at "providing his readers with a narrative model for their devotions and doctrines" and thus "formulated the contours of what it meant to follow al-Shādhilī and be a Shādhilī Sufi" (Hofer, 113). The particularity of this hagiographic work lies also in the fact that it bases the authority of al-Shādhilī and al-Mursī less on spiritual filiation through a *silsila* than on their sainthood and their initiatic function as spiritual poles *(quṭb)* of their times (*Laṭāʾif*, 90). It thereby highlights the outstanding status of the new *ṭarīqa* established by al-Shādhilī and al-Mursī. At the same time, the work constitutes a legitimation of Ibn ʿAṭāʾallāh's own succession to al-Mursī (Hofer, 116–8). This is particularly obvious in the conclusion, in which he affirms that "it is from him (al-Mursī) that we derive our spiritual lights and it is him whose traces we follow; it is he who has rapidly disclosed to us our own secret *(sirr)* and who has loosened our tongue" (204).

Al-tanwīr fī isqāṭ al-tadbīr ("The illumination through the abandonment of self-management") is a treatise on the Ṣūfī virtue of trust in God and satisfaction with divine decrees. It elucidates for a larger audience (Jean-Jacques Thibon, introd. to French trans., ed. Penot, 32–3) one of the most distinctive core teachings of the Shādhiliyya, thus reflecting the interiorisation of Ṣūfī practice promulgated by al-Shādhilī. The text argues that the spiritual virtues exemplified by former Ṣūfī manuals aim, in fact, at the realisation of existential servitude *(al-ʿubūdiyya)* towards God, the essence of which consists in the attitude of *isqāṭ al-tadbīr* (abandonment of self-management; *Isqāṭ*, 52–5). The text attempts to show that the *isqāṭ al-tadbīr* represents no more than the practical consequence of the spiritual realisation of *tawḥīd* (divine unity). It asserts that seeking a livelihood does not conflict with the virtue of total trust in God and that, when practised with *isqāṭ al-tadbīr*, is even to be considered a form of spiritual exercise that deepens the disciple's consciousness of his ontological dependence on God (*Isqāṭ*, 120–8). Ibn ʿAṭāʾallāh thereby puts at the very centre of Ṣūfī education the attitude of leaving to God the direction of one's affairs while being engaged in ordinary social activities and thus proposes a specifically Shādhilī reorientation of classical Ṣūfī teaching. The text continued to be quoted by later authors of the Shādhiliyya, such as Ibn ʿAjība and Ibn ʿAbbād; the latter writes that "it contains the quintessence of everything that has been written about mystical life" (Nwyia, 4). The *Tanwīr* has been translated into French (Penot) and English (Kugle).

Tāj al-ʿarūs al-ḥāwī li-tahdhīb al-nufūs ("The bridegroom's crown, containing instructions on refining the self"), called also *Tāj al-ʿarūs wa-qamʿ al-nufūs* ("The bridegroom's crown and the restraint of the self"), is an anthology of oral discourses, perhaps recorded by a disciple, which might originally have been public sermons delivered at the Azhar mosque in Cairo (Shoshan, 12–6; Hofer, 166) or teaching sessions reserved to the disciples of the author (Cecere, 105). In his translation, Jackson (9–12) argues that the teaching recorded in this work was intended for a non-Ṣūfī audience. The text follows no apparent thematic order and exposes numerous elements of spiritual education, such as repentance, the imitation of the Prophet's example, trust in God's decrees, detachment from worldly matters, and the purification of the heart, developing thereby a teaching about the realisation of uncompromising sincerity towards God.

ʿUnwān al-tawfīq fī ādāb al-ṭarīq ("The sign of success concerning the etiquettes of the way") is a commentary on a poem about the etiquette of Ṣūfism attributed to Abū Madyan. The *ʿUnwān* appears as a an actualisation of a teaching that was both preparative and constitutive for the emergence of the Shādhilī tradition. In the context of the institutionalisation of Ṣūfism in the Mamlūk period, this "Shādhilisation of Abū Madyan's teachings" represents an attempt to "co-opt the legacy of Abū Madyan in Egypt" (Hofer, 116–7). Above all, however, the *ʿUnwān* seeks to furnish the adepts of the Shādhiliyya order with a referential text about the essential attitudes and forms of behaviour towards one's spiritual master and fellow disciples.

Miftāḥ al-falāḥ wa-miṣbāḥ al-arwāḥ ("The key of salvation and the lamp of souls") and *al-Qaṣd al-mujarrad fī maʿrifat al-ism al-mufrad* ("The exclusive purpose concerning the knowledge of the unique name") are treatises about the Ṣūfī practice of *dhikr* or invocation of God (on the authenticity of their attribution to Ibn ʿAṭāʾallāh, see Hofer, 130). The *Miftāḥ* is general and practical, while the *Qaṣd* deals specifically with the invocation of the divine name "Allāh," a practice in which the advanced Shādhilī disciple is initiated by his master and which is considered in the Shādhilī tradition to constitute the highest form of *dhikr*. In addition to asserting the orthodoxy of the Ṣūfī practice of *dhikr*, the two treatises both explain and establish the doctrinal foundation for the distinctive *dhikr* practice of the Shādhiliyya, on the basis of which it claims its superiority to other orders.

Other texts are mentioned in *GALS* (2:147) and individual Arabic sources (ʿAlī

Zahrī, 7–12), but these are presumably falsely attributed to Ibn ʿAṭāʾallāh. These include the *Tartīb al-sulūk* (ed. ʿAlī Zahrī, Beirut 2004), whose attribution to the Ṣūfī and scholar from Nīshāpūr al-Qushayrī (d. 465/1072) is discussed by Fritz Meier (1963), and *al-Tanbīh fī ṭarīq al-qawm* ("The admonition concerning the way of the people, i.e., the Ṣūfīs") and *al-Ṭarīqa al-jāda fī nayl al-saʿāda* ("The paved way concerning the acquisition of happiness," MS 12902 Rabat).

Bibliography

Works by Ibn ʿAṭāʾallāh al-Iskandarī

Laṭāʾif al-minan, ed. ʿAbd al-Ḥalīm Maḥmūd, Cairo 1974, repr. 1992; *al-Qaṣd al-mujarrad fī maʿrifat al-ism al-mufrad*, ed. Khālid Muḥammad Khamīs, Cairo 2008; *Tāj al-ʿarūs al-ḥāwī li-tahdhīb al-nufūs*, Cairo 2005; *al-Tanwīr fī isqāṭ al-tadbīr*, ed. Muḥammad Amīn ʿAbd al-Hādī, Damascus 2002[2]; *al-Tanwīr fī isqāṭ al-tadbīr*, ed. Muḥammad ʿAbd al-Raḥmān Shāghūl, Cairo 2007; *Tartīb al-sulūk*, ed. ʿAlī Zahrī, Beirut 2004; *ʿUnwān al-tawfīq fī ādāb al-ṭarīq*, ed. Khālid Zahrī, Beirut 2004.

Translations of works by Ibn ʿAṭāʾallāh al-Iskandarī

Mohammed Saïd Ramadân al-Bouti, *Paroles sublimes, exégèse des sagesses d'Ibn ʿAtâʾ Allâh as-Sakandarî*, trans. Idrîs de Vos, ʿAbd Allâh Penot, and Samia Touati, 3 vols., Paris 2011; Abd-ar-Rahmâne Buret, *Hikam. Paroles de sagesse, suives d'un choix d'Épîtres et des Entretiens confidentiels*, Milan 1999; Victor Danner, *Sūfī aphorisms. Kitāb al-Ḥikam*, Leiden 1973; Victor Danner and Wheeler M. Thackston, *The book of wisdom*, New York 1978; Éric Geoffroy, *La sagesse des maîtres soufis (= Latâʾif al-minan fī manâqib al-shaykh Abî l'Abbâs al-Mursî wa shaykhi-hi al-Shâdhilî Abî l-Hasan)*, Paris 1998; Maurice Gloton, *Traité sur le nom Allāh*, Paris 1981, repr. 1989; Juan José González, *Sobre el abandono de sí mismo (= Kitāb at-tanwir fī isqaṭ at-tadbir. Tratado de sufismo sàdilī)*, Madrid 2006; Ibrahim Hakim, *Illuminating guidance on the dropping of self-direction*, Charlottesville 2007; Sherman Jackson, *Sufism for non-Sufis? Ibn ʿAṭāʾ Allāh al-Sakandarī's Tāj al-ʿarūs*, Oxford 2012; Mary Ann Koury Danner, *The key to salvation & the lamp of souls (= Miftāḥ al-falāḥ wa-miṣbāḥ al-arwāḥ)*, Cambridge 1996; Scott Kugle, *The book of illumination (= Kitāb al-tanwīr fī isqāṭ al-tadbīr)*, Louisville 2005; Agustín López and María Tabuyo, *La enseñanza de los maestros sufíes*, Madrid 2008; Riordan Macnamara, *La clef de la réalisation spirituelle et l'illumination des âmes (= Miftāḥ al-falāḥ wa-miṣbāḥ al-arwāḥ)*, Beirut 2002; Paul Nwyia, *Ibn ʿAṭāʾ Allāh (m. 709/1309) et la naissance de la confrérie šādilite*, Beirut 1972; ʿAbd Allâh Penot, *De l'abandon de la volonté propre*, introd. Jean-Jacques Thibon, Lyon 1997; Nancy Roberts, *The subtle blessings in the saintly lives of Abū al-ʿAbbās al-Mursī and his master Abū al-Ḥasan al-Shādhilī (= Laṭāʾif al-minan)*, Louisville 2005; Annemarie Schimmel, *Bedrängnisse sind Teppiche voller Gnaden (= Ḥikam)*, Freiburg 1987; Caterina Valdré, *Sentenze e colloquio mistico*, Milan 1993; Abū l-Wafā al-Taftazānī, *Ibn ʿAṭāʾallāh al-Sakandarī wa-taṣawwufuhu*, Cairo 1958.

Other sources

Ibrāhīm Ibn Farḥūn, al-*Dībāj al-mudahhab li-maʿrifat aʿyān ʿulamāʾ al-madhhab*, ed. Muḥammad al-Aḥmadī, 2 vols., Cairo 1975; Ibn Ḥajar al-ʿAsqalānī, *al-Durar al-kāmina fī aʿyān al-miʾat al-thāmina*, ed. Muḥammad ʿAbd al-Muʿīd Ḍān, 5 vols., Beirut 1997; Ibn Kathīr, *al-Bidāya wa-l-nihāya*, ed. ʿAlī Shīrī, 14 vols., Beirut 1988; Ibn Khaldūn, *Taʾrīkh al-ʿallāmat Ibn Khaldūn*, ed. Yūsuf Asʿad Dāghir, 6 vols., Beirut 1956–61; Muwaffaq al-Dīn al-Shāfiʿī al-Shāriʿī, *Murshid al-zuwwār ilā qubūr al-abrār*, Cairo 1994; al-Shaʿrānī, *al-Ṭabaqāt al-kubrā*, ed. Aḥmad ʿAbd al-Raḥīm al-Sāyiḥ, 2 vols., Cairo 2005; al-Shawkānī, *al-Fatḥ al-rabbānī min fatāwā al-Imām al-Shawkānī*, ed. Muḥammad Ṣubḥī Ḥasan Ḥallāq, 12 vols., Ṣanʿāʾ 2002; Tāj al-Dīn al-Subkī, *Ṭabaqāt al-Shāfiʿiyya al-kubrā*, ed. Maḥmūd Muḥammad al-Ṭanāḥī and ʿAbd al-Fattāḥ Muḥammad al-Ḥilw, 10 vols., Cairo 1992; al-Suyūṭī, *Ḥusn al-muḥāḍara fī akhbār* (or *taʾrīkh) Miṣr wa-l-Qāhira*, ed. Muḥammad Abū l-Faḍl Ibrāhīm, 2 vols., Cairo 1967.

Studies

Ernst Bannerth, *Dhikr* and *khalwa* d'après Ibn ʿAtâ Allâh, *MIDEO* 12 (1974), 65–90; Guiseppe Cecere, Le charme discret de la Shādhiliyya ou l'insertion sociale d'Ibn ʿAtāʾ

Allāh al-Iskandarī, in Giuseppe Cecere, Mireille Loubet, and Samuela Pagani (eds.), *Les mystiques juives, chrétiennes et musulmanes dans l'Egypte médiévale (*VIIe–XVIe *siècles)* (Cairo 2013), 63–93; Guiseppe Cecere, Santé et sainteté. Dimensions physiologiques de la vie morale et spirituelle chez Ibn ʿAṭāʾ Allāh al-Iskandarī (m. 709/1309), in Pauline Koetschet and Abbès Zouache (eds.), *Le corps dans l'espace islamique médiéval*, *AI* 48 (2014), 206–36; Guiseppe Cecere, Se faire nourrir par les mécréants? Soufisme et contact inter-religieux dans les *Laṭāʾif al-minan* d'Ibn ʿAṭāʾ Allāh al-Iskandarī, in Giuseppe Cecere, Mireille Loubet, and Samuela Pagani (eds.), *Les mystiques juives, chrétiennes et musulmanes dans l'Egypte médiévale (*VIIe–XVIe *siècles)* (Cairo 2013), 189–207; Guiseppe Cecere, *Il Tâj al-ʿarûs. Discorsi persuiasivi del "Maestro" Ibn ʿAtâ Allâh al-Iskandarî*, Ph.D. diss., Università degli Studi di Florence 2007; William C. Chittick, A Shadhili presence in Shiʿite Islam, *Sophia Perennis/Jāvīdān Khirad* 1/1 (1975), 97–100; Benjamin G. Cook, *Understanding Sufism. Contextualising the content*, Ph.D. diss., University of Tasmania 2014; Victor Danner, *Ibn ʿAtâʾ Allâh. A Sufi of Mamluk Egypt*, Ph.D. diss., Harvard University 1970; Victor Danner, Ibn ʿAṭāʾ Allāh, in Mircea Eliade (ed.), *The encyclopedia of religion* (New York 1987), 557–8; Éric Geoffroy, De l'influence d'Ibn ʿArabī sur l'école shādhilie (époque mamelouk), *Horizons Maghrébins* 41(2000), 83–90; Éric Geoffroy, Entre hagiographie et hagiologie. Les *Laṭāʾif al-minan* d'Ibn ʿAṭāʾ Allāh, *Annales d'Islamologie* 32 (1998), 49–66; Éric Geoffroy, Entre ésotérisme et exotérisme. Les Shâdhilis, passeurs de sens (Égypte XIIIe–XVe siècles), in Éric Geoffroy (ed.), *Une voie soufie dans le monde. La Shâdhiliyya* (Paris 2005), 117–29; Geneviève Gobillot, Présence d'al-Hakîm al-Tirmidhî dans le pensée shâdhilî, in Éric Geoffroy (ed.), *Une voie soufie dans le monde. La Shâdhiliyya* (Paris 2005), 31–52; Denis Gril, L'enseignement d'Ibn ʿAtâʾ Allâh al-Iskandarî, d'après le témoignage de son disciple Râfiʿ Ibn Shâfiʿ, in Éric Geoffroy (ed.), *Une voie soufie dans le monde. La Shâdhiliyya* (Paris 2005), 93–106; Nathan Hofer, *The popularisation of Sufism in Ayyubid and Mamluk Egypt, 1173–1325*, Edinburgh 2015; Julian Johansen, *Sufism and Islamic reform in Egypt. The battle for Islamic tradition*, Oxford 1996; al-Ḥasan al-Kūhin, *Ṭabaqāt al-Shādhiliyya al-kubrā*, Cairo 1347/1928; Louis Massignon, La Cité des Morts au Caire, *BIFAO* 57 (1958), 25–79; Fritz Meier, Qushayrī's *Tartīb al-sulūk*, in *Essays on Islamic piety and mysticism*, trans. John O'Kane (Leiden 1999), 93–133; Julie Scott Meisami, Ibn ʿAṭāʾ Allāh (d. 709/1309), in Julie Scott Meisami and Paul Starkey (eds.), *Encyclopedia of Arabic literature* (London 1998), 313–4; Miguel Asín Palacios, *Un precursor Hispanomusulman de San Juan de La Cruz*, Madrid 1933; Yunus Wesley Schwein, *Illuminated arrival in the Hikam al-ʿaṭāʾiyyah and three major commentaries*, master's thesis, University of Georgia 2007; Boaz Shoshan, *Popular culture in medieval Cairo*, Cambridge 1993; Samia Touati, *Le péché et son rôle salvateur chez le maître soufi égyptien Ibn ʿAtâʾ Allâh al-Iskandarî (m. 709/1309)*, Ph.D. diss., University of Strasbourg 2014; *GALS*.

Ruggero Vimercati Sanseverino

Ibn Bāna, ʿAmr

ʿAmr Ibn Muḥammad b. Sulaymān b. Rāshid (d. 278/891) was a *mawlā* of the Thaqīf tribe and **Bāna** was his mother's name. His father was in charge of an administrative governmental office and a prominent ʿAbbāsid secretary. ʿAmr lived in Baghdad and died in Sāmarrāʾ. He was a good poet as well as a good singer endowed with a beautiful and heart-rending singing style. He followed the singing style of Ibrāhīm b. al-Mahdī (d. 224/839), that is, taking liberty to change the older repertoire to suit his taste and abilities. His compositional output was small and of medium quality. He failed to reach the level of the top composers because he did not play an instrument, nor accompanied himself on a melody instrument while singing. He did not claim to be a professional musician and it is reported that he said to Isḥāq al-Mawṣilī (d. d. 235/850): "I cannot be compared to you because you learned singing to earn a living, whereas I learned it for the love of the emotions *(taṭarrub)* it has. I used to be beaten so as not to learn it, and you used to be beaten until you learned it!" (al-Iṣfahānī, 15:270). His storytelling was much admired; his teachings skills were outstanding, and the few who were able to study with him became excellent singers. He dedicated one of his untitled book of songs to the caliph al-Wāthiq, but he did not include the melodic or rhythmic modes of the songs. His other book of songs, titled *Kitāb fī l-aghānī* ("A book about songs"), in which he mentions the rhythmic and melodic modes, was one of the foundations on which other books were written. There were two systems, one by Ibrāhim b. al-Mahdī and one by Isḥāq al-Mawṣilī; their main differences pertain to the first and second heavy rhythms and their respective lights: the first heavy is in 4/2 and the second heavy is in 5/2. Ibrahim mixed them up and mixed up their respective lights. In this work he followed the modal theory of Ibrāhim b. al-Mahdī and not Isḥāq al-Mawṣilī's, even though, it was the latter with which he studied. ʿAmr revised the modal theory and followed the system of Isḥāq. Al-Iṣfahānī called this revised book *Nuskhat ʿAmr Ibn Bāna al-thāniya* ("The second copy of ʿAmr Ibn Bāna"). ʿAmr was among the few notable boon-companions of the caliphs of his day. It was also said that he was haughty, vain, and conceited.

Bibliography

Henry George Farmer, *A history of Arabian music to the XIIIth century*. London 1929 (reprinted 1973); Ignazio Guidi, *Tables alphabétiques du Kitâb al-aġânî*, Leiden 1900; Abū Aḥmad Yaḥyā b. ʿAlī Ibn al-Munajjim, *Risāla fī l-mūsīqā*, ed. Zakariyya Yūsuf, Cairo 1964; Abū l-Faraj al-Iṣfahānī, *Kitāb al-aghānī*, Cairo 1927–74; ʿUmar Riḍā Kaḥḥāla, *Muʿjam al-muʾallifīn. Tarājim muṣannifī al-Kutub al-ʿArabiyya*, 15 vols., Damascus 1957–61; Hilary Kilpatrick, *Making the great "Book of songs." Compilation and the author's craft in Abū l-Faraj al-Iṣbahānī's "Kitāb al-aghānī,"* London and New York 2003; Eckhard Neubauer, *Musiker am Hof der frühen ʿAbbāsiden*, Ph.D. diss., Goethe-Universität Frankfurt am Main 1965; George Dimitri Sawa, *An Arabic musical and socio-cultural glossary of "Kitāb al-aghānī,"* Leiden 2015; George Dimitri Sawa, *Music performance practice in the early ʿAbbāsid era. 132–320 AH / 750–932 AD*, Toronto 1989 (reprinted Ottawa 2004); Khayr al-Dīn al-Ziriklī, *al-Aʿlām. Qāmūs tārājim li-ashhar al-rijāl wa-l-nisāʾ min al-ʿArab wa-l-mustaʿribīn wa-l-mustashriqīn*, 8 vols., Beirut 1979[4].

George Dimitri Sawa

Ibn Ḥamdīn

Ibn Ḥamdīn was the name given in the biographical dictionaries and histories for the two most notable of the three members of the Banū Ḥamdīn who served as *qāḍīs* (judges) in the Andalusī city of Córdoba (Qurṭuba) during the Almoravid dynasty (r. in al-Andalus during the late fifth/eleventh century and first half of the sixth/twelfth).

The first to serve as *qāḍī* of Córdoba was Abū ʿAbdallāh Muḥammad b. ʿAlī Ibn Ḥamdīn (d. 508/1114–5). He is known mainly for leading opposition to *Iḥyāʾ ʿulūm al-dīn* ("The revival of the religious sciences") by the scholar, theorist, mystical and pastoral theologian, and author Abū Ḥāmid al-Ghazālī (d. 505/1111) during a controversy over this work in al-Andalus. Biographies written by contemporaries who had met Muḥammad Ibn Ḥamdīn, such as Ibn ʿAṭiyya (d. 541/1147) and al-Qāḍī ʿIyāḍ (d. 544/1149), mention his several refutations of al-Ghazālī, of which one fragment survives in *Siyar aʿlām al-nubalāʾ* ("The lives of noble figures"), the major encyclopaedia of biographical history by al-Dhahabī (d. 748/1348), the Shāfiʿī *ḥadīth* scholar from Damascus. It alternates between a critique of the *Iḥyāʾ* itself and of an unnamed jurist who, inspired and guided by the *Iḥyāʾ*, took up Ṣūfī practice and became the leader of a group of Ṣūfīs referred to as al-Ghazāliyya. The fragment displays Ibn Ḥamdīn's knowledge of several sections of the *Iḥyāʾ*.

Sources from the subsequent Almohad dynasty describe a public burning of the *Revival*, and some charge Muḥammad Ibn Ḥamdīn with orchestrating it. The pro-Almohad *Naẓm al-jumān li-tartīb mā salafa min akhbār al-zamān* ("The stringing of pearls in the arrangement of the accounts of times bygone") by the Moroccan scholar Ibn al-Qaṭṭān (d. 650/1252) claims that Ibn Ḥamdīn presided over the burning of the *Iḥyāʾ* in early 503/1109, at the western gate of the Umayyad mosque in Córdoba. But Ibn al-Qaṭṭān presents his account for the purpose of introducing the myth that Ibn Tūmart (d. 524/1130), the founder of the Almohad regime, was present with al-Ghazālī when the latter learned of the burning of his book by the Almoravids and tasked Ibn Tūmart with taking revenge on their regime. This is one of several fantastic tales regarding al-Ghazālī in al-Andalus and the Maghrib and the burning of the *Iḥyāʾ*. The lateness and tendentiousness of these later sources and the absence of any mention of Ibn Ḥamdīn's role in a burning in the earlier ones has led some scholars to doubt that it ever occurred.

Muḥammad had two sons who served as *qāḍī* after him, Abū l-Qāsim Aḥmad b. Muḥammad b. ʿAlī Ibn Ḥamdīn (d. 521/1127), and Abū Jaʿfar Ḥamdīn b. Muḥammad b. ʿAlī Ibn Ḥamdīn (d. 547/1152). Ḥamdīn Ibn Ḥamdīn served two, non-consecutive, appointments as *qāḍī*, between 521/1127 and 532/1137–8. Popular riots in 535/1140 led the *qāḍī* of the city to flee. A year later, when the Almoravid sultan ʿAlī b. Yūsuf b. Tashufīn (r. 500–537/1107–42) allowed the people of Córdoba to choose their own judge, they chose Ḥamdīn Ibn Ḥamdīn. In 539/1144, the Córdobans rose against the crumbling Almoravid regime and appointed Ḥamdīn Ibn Ḥamdīn as their ruler. In Ramaḍān 539/February 1145, the elite and commoners of the city gathered in the mosque and swore an oath of allegiance to him, not only as *qāḍī* but as *raʾīs* (head of the city). He adopted the regnal titles Amīr al-Muslimīn (commander of the Muslims) and Nāṣir al-Dīn (defender of the religion) and took up residence in the Umayyad caliphal palace, although he did pledge allegiance to the ʿAbbāsid caliph. Coins were minted and Friday prayers said in his name in other cities of al-Andalus as well. His rule lasted only eleven months. Expelled by the Almoravids, Ḥamdīn sought the help of Alfonso VII of Castile (r. 1126–57) to restore him to power. Alfonso's troops took the city in Dhū l-Ḥijja 540/May 1146, but, when he heard that the Almohads had crossed the Straits of Gibraltar, he returned the city to Almoravid rule. Ḥamdīn took refuge with a former ally in Málaga, where he died a natural death in 546/1161. When the Almohads conquered al-Andalus, they exhumed and crucified his body.

Bibliography

al-Dhahabī, *Siyar aʿlām al-nubalāʾ*, ed. Shuʿayb al-Arnāʾūt and Ḥusayn al-Asad, 25 vols., Beirut 1982–93; Maribel Fierro, The Qāḍī as ruler, in *Saber religioso y poder politico en el Islam* (Madrid 1994), 71–116; Saʿd Ghrāb, Ḥawla iḥrāq al-murābiṭīn li-*Iḥyāʾ* al-Ghazālī, in *Actas del IV Coloquio Hispanico-Tunecino* (Madrid 1983), 133–63; Delfina

Serrano-Ruano, Why did the scholars of al-Andalus distrust al-Ghazālī? Ibn Rushd al-Jadd's *fatwā* on *Awliyā' Allāh*, *Der Islam* 83 (2006), 137–56.

Kenneth Garden

Ibn Ḥamdīs

Abū Muḥammad ʿAbd al-Jabbār b. Abī Bakr b. Muḥammad b. Ḥamdīs al-Azdī al-Ṣiqillī (b. c.447/1055, d. c.527/1133), known as **Ibn Ḥamdīs**, was an Arab-Sicilian poet renowned for his rootlessness and his life-long sentiment, expressed in his poetry, of longing for home (*ghurba*).

Ibn Ḥamdīs contextualised most of his poems in personal and historic terms (Ibn Ẓāfir, 71), providing in his *dīwān* (collected poetry) a primary source on his life. He was born in Noto, near Syracuse, Sicily, to a wealthy family that traced its lineage to the Banū Azd of Yemen. Following a privileged upbringing, during which he already showed poetic inclinations, he left for al-Andalus some years in advance of the Norman occupation of Syracuse (479/1086–7). At that time, the court of al-Muʿtamid Ibn ʿAbbād (r. 461–84/1069–91) in the *ṭāʾifa* kingdom of Seville was a place that held great attraction for poets. After some difficulties, Ibn Ḥamdīs settled in Seville around 472/1079, where he distinguished himself in the circle of protégés for his talent in improvisation and his refinement. He left al-Andalus for the Maghrib when the Almoravids took the city in 484/1091 and deported the king to Aghmāt, where the poet went to visit him just before al-Muʿtamid's death in 488/1095 (*Dīwān*, no. 153). He spent the second half of his life, almost another forty years, at various locations in northern Africa, offering panegyrics at the courts in the region, always turning his back on the Almoravids. The city of Béjaïa (Bijāya) appears to have been the final refuge of the by-then blind octogenarian poet (*Dīwān* no. 300, 301), and his demise can be dated to approximately 527/1133, as maintained by Ibn Khallikān (3:215).

The poems of Ibn Ḥamdīs range across all genres except satire (*hijāʾ*), which he expressly rejected (*Dīwān* no. 60, 328). His verses provide a great fresco of the western Mediterranean culture of his time, thanks to his masterful descriptions (*waṣf*) of foods, objects, animals, events, customs, and diseases. His euphuistic lexicon nevertheless engages in everyday language; his phrasing is elegant and eloquent, and the ingenuity of his figures of speech gave new life to the classic *topoi*. In al-Andalus, under the patronage of al-Muʿtamid, he developed his bacchic (*khamriyya*), amorous (*ghazal*), and panegyric (*madīḥ*) poetry, the latter particularly fine in terms of composition and rhetoric but with a rather neoclassical coldness. However, Ibn Ḥamdīs achieved his finest work in the verses dealing with the *ghurba*, or rootlessness, that pervaded his life, far from his home in Sicily and, later, far from al-Andalus. Sicily inspired his poems on *fakhr*, pride for his homeland, coupled with a fury against the Norman occupiers, and al-Andalus is the setting for his *qaṣīda*s on bygone carefree times. Subsequently, he composed tender elegies (*rithāʾ*) on the deaths of many of his relatives, and in his old age he cultivated the ascetic poem (*zuhd*).

The poetry of Ibn Ḥamdīs was appreciated and recited by his contemporaries, as chronicled by Ibn Bassām (d. 542/1147–8) and Ibn Ẓāfir (d. 613/1216), although his contemporary, the Andalusian polygraph Ibn Abī Ṣalt (d. 529/1134), described him as a plagiarist (ʿImād al-Dīn al-Iṣfahānī, 2:196). He likewise received acclaim later, both in the Arab world and in the West, for the way in which he personalised his poetry, which seems strikingly modern.

Two manuscripts from his *dīwān* are preserved: one in the Vatican, in Maghribī script, containing 5,292 verses, and the other in St. Petersburg, recorded in Damascus in 1006/1598, containing 2,165 verses. These manuscripts share only 1,510 verses. The manuscript preserved in the Vatican, however, spans Ibn Ḥamdīs's entire lifetime. Celestino Schiaparelli undertook to publish the complete collection from these two texts and some poems from other sources (*Il canzoniere di ʿAbd Al Ǵabbār Ibn Abī Bakr Ibn Muḥammad Ibn Ḥamdīs poeta arabo di Siracusa (1056–1133)*, Rome 1897), which was revised and completed by Iḥsān ʿAbbās (*Dīwān Ibn Ḥamdīs*, Beirut 1960).

Bibliography

Sources

Ibn Ḥamdīs, *Diwan di Abu Muhammad ʿAbdalgabbar (b. Abu Bakr) [sic] Ibn Hamdis as-Siqilli*, Rome, Vatican Library, MS Ar. 447; Ibn Ḥamdīs, *Dīwān Ibn Ḥamdīs*, St. Petersburg, Institute of Oriental Manuscripts, MS C-30; Ibn Ḥamdīs, *Il Canzoniere*, trans. Celestino Schiaparelli, ed. Stefania Elena Carnemolla, Palermo 1998; Ibn Bassām al-Shantarīnī, *al-Dhakhīra fī maḥāsin ahl al-Jazīra*, ed. Iḥsān ʿAbbās (Beirut 1978–9), 4:320–42; Ibn Khallikān, *Wafayāt al-aʿyān*, ed. Iḥsān ʿAbbās (Beirut 1968), 3:212–5 = no. 396; Ibn Ẓāfir al-Azdī, *Badāʾiʿ al-badāʾih*, ed. Muḥammad Abū l-Faḍl Ibrāhīm, Cairo 1970; ʿImād al-Dīn al-Iṣfahānī, *Kharīdat al-qaṣr wa-jarīdat al-ʿaṣr. Qism shuʿarāʾ al-Maghrib wa-l-Andalus*, ed. Ādhartāsh Ādhurnūsh, Muḥammad al-Marzūqī, Muḥammad al-ʿArūsī al-Maṭwī, and al-Jilānī b. al-Ḥājj Yaḥyā (Tunis 1986²), 2:194–207 = no. 52.

Studies

Michele Amari, *Biblioteca arabo-sicula*, Frankfurt am Main 1994; Francesco Gabrieli, *Dal mondo dell'Islam. Nuovi saggi di storia e civiltà musulmana*, Milan and Naples 1954; Luz Gómez García, Ibn Hamdis, in Jorge Lirola Delgado and José Miguel Puerta Vilchez (eds.), *Biblioteca de al-Andalus* (Almería 2004), 3:268–72; William Granara, Ibn Ḥamdīs and the poetry of nostalgia, in María Rosa Menocal, Raymond P. Scheindlin, and Michael Sells (eds.), *The literature of al-Andalus* (Cambridge 2000), 388–403; Umberto Rizzitano, Ibn Ḥamdīs, *EI2*; Saʿd Shalabī, *Ibn Ḥamdīs al-Ṣiqillī. Ḥayātuh min shiʿrih*, Cairo n.d.; Zayn al-ʿĀbidīn al-Sanūsī, *ʿAbd al-Jabbār Ibn Ḥamdīs*, Tunis 1983.

Luz Gómez García

Ibn Isḥāq

Abū ʿAbdallāh or Abū Bakr Muḥammad **Ibn Isḥāq** (d. c.151/768) *ṣāḥib al-sīra/ṣāḥib al-maghāzī* (the compiler of the monograph on the Prophet's biography/battles) compiled the most widespread mediaeval biography of the prophet Muḥammad, known to us mainly through an abridged and censored version produced by Ibn Hishām (d. 218/833 or 213/828).

Ibn Isḥāq was a *mawlā*, that is, a descendant of a manumitted slave. His grandfather Yasār was among a group of Jewish boys taken captive in the village of Nuqayra, near ʿAyn al-Tamr (modern Shithātha, some 50 kilometres west of Karbalāʾ), during the caliphate of Abū Bakr (r. 11–3/632–4). Ibn Isḥāq's paternal uncles Mūsā and ʿAbd al-Raḥmān, and his brothers Abū Bakr and ʿUmar (d. 154/771) transmitted *ḥadīth*. His father-cum-teacher, Isḥāq, provided him with written materials *(kutub)* concerning the *maghāzī* (the Prophet's battles) and other topics, which Ibn Isḥāq transmitted on his father's authority (*kutub Ibn Isḥāq ʿan abīhi fī l-maghāzī wa-ghayrihā*; al-Dhahabī, 7:39). Ibn Isḥāq followed his father in taking a lax attitude toward mentioning his immediate informants—this was common practice in his father's generation and remained common practice in certain types of Islamic literature, including historiography. Instead of the informant's name we find "men from Banū so-and-so," sometimes followed by the name of a specific earlier informant, for example: *qāla/ʿan Ibn Isḥāq/Muḥammad b. Isḥāq: wa-ḥaddathanī abī/wālidī Isḥāq ibn Yasār ʿan rijāl min banī Māzin ibn al-Najjār/ʿan baʿḍ banī Māzin, ʿan Abī Dāwud al-Māzinī* (Ibn Isḥāq: my father, Isḥāq b. Yasār, told me, quoting people from the Banū Māzin b. al-Najjār/quoting one of the Banū Māzin, from Abū Dāwūd al-Māzinī); Ibn Hishām, 2:286; Qiwām al-Sunna al-Iṣfahānī, 228). In other cases there is no mention of an earlier informant, as in this passage, quoted in al-Bayhaqī: *wa-ʿan Ibn Isḥāq qāla ḥaddathanī wālidī Isḥāq b. Yasār ʿan rijāl min banī Salima* (Ibn Isḥāq: my father, Isḥāq b. Yasār, told me, quoting people from Banū Salima) (al-Bayhaqī, 3:291); and in this, quoted in Ibn al-Athīr: *ʿan Ibn Isḥāq ʿan abīhi Isḥāq b. Yasār ʿan rijāl min banī Saʿd b. Bakr* (Ibn Isḥāq: quoting his father, Isḥāq b. Yasār, quoting people from Banū Saʿd b. Bakr); (Ibn al-Athīr, 1:622). Another important teacher of Ibn Isḥāq, ʿAbdallāh b. Abī Bakr (d. 130/748 or 135/753), quotes an unspecified informant, who in turn names his informant: *qāla Ibn Isḥāq: wa-ḥaddathanī ʿAbdullāh b. Abī Bakr ʿan baʿḍ banī Sāʿida ʿan Abī Usayd Mālik b. Rabīʿa*... (Ibn Isḥāq: ʿAbdallāh b. Abī Bakr told me, quoting a member of Banū Sāʿida, from Abū Usayd Mālik b. Rabīʿa...) (Ibn Hishām, 2:286).

In addition to his father, two of Ibn Isḥāq's many teachers and informants merit special mention for their role in the history of Islamic literature, namely Abān b. ʿUthmān b. ʿAffān (d. between 101/720 and 105/724; he was the son of the third caliph, ʿUthmān) and Ibn Shihāb al-Zuhrī (d. 124/742). The *Muwaffaqiyyāt* by al-Zubayr b. Bakkār (d. 256/870) has a fictitious anecdote from an Anṣārī source censuring the Umayyad caliph ʿAbd al-Malik b. Marwān (r. 65–86/685–705) for his alleged disregard of Muḥammad's biography, motivated by narrow political concerns. The other protagonist of the anecdote, which is placed in 82/701, is the twenty-eight-year-old heir apparent, Sulaymān b. ʿAbd al-Malik. Sulaymān asked Abān to write down for him the *siyar* and *maghāzī* of the prophet Muḥammad, only to find out—so the anecdote goes—that Abān had a collated copy of a *siyar* and *maghāzī* book, which he had received from a trustworthy source (*hiya ʿindī qad akhadhtuhā muṣaḥḥaḥa mimman athiqu bihi*. I have it. I received it, after it had been collated, from someone I trust); al-Zubayr b. Bakkār, 275). That the book existed seems credible: it provides the backdrop for the fictitious anecdote, and it is there to lend it credibility. Abān's book, regardless of its content, form, and readership, must have had an impact on his pupil's work.

Ibn Shihāb al-Zuhrī and Ibn Isḥāq had mutual respect for one another, despite the age difference and the huge gap in social status between the famous and powerful member of Quraysh on the one hand and the *mawlā* on the other. Yet another fictitious anecdote has it that al-Zuhrī complained to Ibn Isḥāq about the latter's tardiness (*fa-ʾstabṭaʾahu*). Ibn Isḥāq replied: "Can anyone reach you with that doorkeeper of yours?" Zuhrī instructed the doorkeeper to let the young man in without delay (al-Dhahabī, 7:36). The existence of the doorkeeper as a character in this anecdote is a plausible detail. Al-Zuhrī's literary contribution to the field of *maghāzī* is of special interest to us here. According to al-Darāwardī (d. 187/803), who both taught Ibn Isḥāq and learned from him, al-Zuhrī's *sīra* was the first to be compiled in Islam (*wa-dhakara l-Zuhrī fī siyarihi wa-hiya awwal sīra ullifat fī l-Islām* (al-Zuhrī mentioned in his *Siyar*, which was the first *sīra* compiled in Islam); al-Suhaylī, 2:239–40). The quotation from al-Zuhrī's *siyar*/*sīra* mentioned in al-Suhaylī concerns Muḥammad's marriage to Khadīja. Several sources quote from, or refer to, *Kitāb al-Zuhrī*. There is, of course, more than one way to interpret this phrase from al-Suhaylī, but when the quotations and references are linked to Muḥammad and his time, they may well relate to al-Zuhrī's *siyar* quoted in al-Suhaylī. There are several attestations of it in the literature. For example, Abū l-Qāsim al-Baghawī (d. 317/929), a scholar who compiled a dictionary dedicated to Muḥammad's Companions, rejects the alleged participation of a certain slave in the battle of Badr, citing *Kitāb al-Zuhrī* and *Kitāb Ibn Isḥāq*, both of which do not include that particular slave in the list of Badrīs (*wa-laysa lahu dhikr fī-man shahida Badr*[an] *fī kitāb al-Zuhrī wa-lā fī kitāb Ibn Isḥāq*; Ibn Kathīr, 5:339). Abū Nuʿaym al-Iṣfahānī (d. 430/1039), another compiler of a Companion dictionary, rejects the claim that a certain Anṣārī participated in the ʿAqaba meeting and in the battle of Badr, on the grounds that he is not listed among the ʿAqabīs and Badrīs in *Kitāb al-Zuhrī* and in Ibn Isḥāq's book (*wa-lam ara lahu dhikr*[an] *fī kitāb al-Zuhrī wa-lā Ibn Isḥāq fī l-ʿAqaba wa-Badr*; Abū Nuʿaym, 2:409). These quotations indicate that Zuhrī's book included lists of ʿAqabīs and Badrīs. Such lists were among the most sensitive social and political topics in Muḥammad's biography—the people mentioned in them had a secure place in history. *Kitāb al-Zuhrī* also included an account of the beginning of revelation: (*wa-fī kitāb al-Zuhrī anna rasūl Allāh lammā atāhu l-waḥy*... (in Zuhrī's book it is said that the Messenger of God, when the Qurʾān was revealed to him...); al-Maqdisī, 5:34), and it probably did not end with the Prophet's death but continued into the *ridda* wars, which took place after the death of the Prophet (*wa-fī kitāb al-Zuhrī: thumma laḥiqū aṣḥāb Ṭulayḥa* (in Zuhrī's book it is said: then they chased after Ṭulayḥa's followers); al-Diyārbakrī, 2:207, line 26). Whatever its content, form, and readership, al-Zuhrī's book must have had an impact on Ibn Isḥāq's work.

Ibn Isḥāq travelled to Alexandria in 115/733, where he taught and studied for several years. He returned to Medina, and sometime after the ʿAbbāsid revolution, which brought about the end of the Umayyad dynasty and the establishment of the ʿAbbāsid in 132/750, he joined the caliph al-Manṣūr in Hāshimiyya (also called Hāshimiyyat al-Kūfa), between Kufa and Ḥīra, where Manṣūr's citadel (*madīna*, including *qaṣr al-imāra*) was located. This took place after Manṣūr's accession in 136/754 as the second ʿAbbāsid caliph. Sometime later, but not before 142/759, Ibn Isḥāq was sent to ʿAbbās b. Muḥammad, Manṣūr's brother, who was his governor in the Jazīra and the *thughūr* (the Byzantine frontier province) between 142–55/759–72. One assumes that the intellectual who was by now in his late fifties or sixties was not sent there as a warrior; in the conflict zone of *al-thughūr* he could best contribute to the war effort as a "morale officer," and his *maghāzī* could be a source of inspiration for both commanders and troops. Subsequently Ibn Isḥāq became the tutor to the heir apparent, al-Mahdī (r. 158–69/775–85), in Rayy. He spent his last years in Baghdad.

In an account which is panegyric rather than history, al-Masʿūdī (d. 345/956) implies—in somewhat vague terms—that the caliph Manṣūr (r. 136–58/754–75) was somehow associated with the creation of Ibn Isḥāq's biography of Muḥammad: "In his time Muḥammad b. Isḥāq composed *(waḍaʿa) Kitāb al-maghāzī wa-l-siyar wa-akhbār al-mubtadaʾ*; before that the stories of Muḥammad's life had not been collected, known, or arranged systematically (*wa-lam takun qabla dhālika majmūʿa wa-lā maʿrūfa wa-lā muṣannafa*; al-Masʿūdī, 5:211, no. 3446). It is not clear what the caliph's book included. However, Ibn Isḥāq's *maghāzī* had existed in book form well before his departure from his hometown Medina. This fact is at the background of a boastful statement made by his disciple Ibrāhīm b. Saʿd (d. 184/800), whose recension of Ibn Isḥāq's book came into being in Medina: "Muḥammad b. Isḥāq 'undid' the *maghāzī* three times, and I observed and witnessed all of this" (*naqaḍa Muḥammad ibn Isḥāq l-maghāziya thalāth marrāt kullu dhālika ashhaduhu wa-aḥḍuruhu*; Lecker, When did Ibn Isḥāq compose his *maghāzī*?). Ibrāhīm was actually claiming that his recension was most accurate, since he had had several opportunities to correct it, weed out its errors, and bring it as close as possible to Ibn Isḥāq's original.

Bibliography

Sources
Abū Nuʿaym, *Maʿrifat al-ṣaḥāba*, ed. Muḥammad Ḥasan Ismāʿīl and Masʿad ʿAbd al-Ḥamīd al-Saʿdanī, Beirut 1422/2002; al-Bayhaqī, *Dalāʾil al-nubuwwa*, ed. ʿAbd al-Muʿṭī Amīn Qalʿajī, Beirut 1405/1985; al-Diyārbakrī, *Taʾrīkh al-khamīs*, Cairo 1283/1866; al-Dhahabī, *Siyar aʿlām al-nubalāʾ*, ed. Shuʿayb al-Arnāʾūṭ et al., Beirut 1401–9/1981–8; Ibn al-Athīr, *Usd al-ghāba fī maʿrifat al-Ṣaḥāba*, ed. ʿAlī Muḥammad Muʿawwaḍ and ʿĀdil Aḥmad ʿAbd al-Mawjūd, Beirut 1415/1994; Ibn Hishām, *al-Sīra al-nabawiyya*, ed. Muṣṭafā al-Saqqā, Ibrāhīm al-Ibyārī, and ʿAbd al-Ḥāfiẓ Shalabī, Cairo 1355/1936; Ibn Kathīr, *al-Bidāya wa-l-nihāya*, Beirut 1412–3/1992–3; al-Maqdisī, *al-Badʾ wa-l-taʾrīkh*, ed. Clément Huart, Paris 1899–1919; al-Masʿūdī, *Murūj al-dhahab*, ed. Charles Pellat, Beirut 1966–79; Qiwām al-Sunna al-Iṣfahānī, *Dalāʾil al-nubuwwa*, ed. Muḥammad b. Muḥammad al-Ḥaddād, Riyadh 1409/1988; al-Suhaylī, *al-Rawḍ al-unuf*, ed. ʿAbd al-Raḥmān al-Wakīl, Cairo 1387–90/1967–70; al-Zubayr b. Bakkār, *al-Akhbār al-muwaffaqiyyāt*, ed. Sāmī Makkī al-ʿĀnī, Beirut 1416/1996.

Studies
Josef Horovitz, *The earliest biographies of the Prophet and their authors*, ed. Lawrence I. Conrad, Princeton 2002; J. M. B. Jones, Ibn Isḥāḳ, *EI2*; Michael Lecker, Muḥammad ibn Isḥāq *ṣāḥib al-maghāzī*. Was his grandfather Jewish?, in Andrew Rippin and Roberto Tottoli (eds.), *Books and written culture of the Islamic world. Studies presented to Claude Gilliot on the occasion of his 75th birthday* (Leiden 2015), 26–38; Michael Lecker, When did Ibn Isḥāq compose his *maghāzī*? forthcoming; Wim Raven, Biography of the Prophet, *EI3*; Gregor Schoeler, *The biography of Muḥammad. Nature and authenticity*, New York and London 2011; Rudolf Sellheim, Prophet, Chalif und Geschichte. Die Muhammed-Biographie des Ibn Isḥāq, *Oriens* 18/19 (1965/1966), 33–91.

Michael Lecker

Ibn Jāmiʿ

Ismāʿīl **Ibn Jāmiʿ** (fl. late second/eighth century), born in Mecca, came from a noble family related to the Quraysh tribe. He was pious and knew the Qurʾān by heart. His mother married Siyāṭ (d. c.169/785), the singer and composer from whom Ibn Jāmiʿ learned his craft. He also learned from Yaḥyā l-Makkī (d. c.218/833).

Ibn Jāmiʿ was poor and he left Mecca for Medina in search of a better life. From Medina Ibn Jāmiʿ later moved to Baghdad where he was strongly reprimanded by the caliph al-Mahdī (r. 158–69/775–85) for singing, together with Ibrāhīm al-Mawṣilī (d. 188/804), for his son Mūsā l-Hādī (r. 169–70/785–86). The caliph had Ibrāhīm beaten but spared Ibn Jāmiʿ owing to Ibn Jāmiʿ's Qurayshī lineage. Nevertheless, Ibn Jāmiʿ was scalded by the caliph: "May God disgrace you! You sing even though you are a Qurayshī!" (al-Iṣfahānī, 4:303). After al-Mahdī's death, Ibn Jāmiʿ was welcomed by al-Hādī and Hārūn al-Rashīd (r. 170–193/786–809). In his first performance for Hārūn, Ibn Jāmiʿ impressed him by capably embellishing a well-known song. He further impressed Hārūn by singing difficult songs known to test the skills of slave girls before purchase.

A strong rivalry occurred between Ibn Jāmiʿ and Ibrāhīm al-Mawṣilī. Annoyed at the success of Ibrāhīm in a *majlis*, Ibn Jāmiʿ followed him by singing without the help of instrumental accompaniment, and excelled. He was protective of his songs and would change his performance to prevent Ibrāhim from learning them. Ibrāhīm resorted to a ruse in order to learn and steal Ibn Jāmiʿ's songs, hiring Muḥammad al-Zaff (d. c.193/809) who was endowed with amazing learning speed. Muḥammad learned the songs of Ibn Jāmiʿ and then taught them to Ibrāhim.

Ibn Jāmiʿ was renowned for a strong and loud voice, his singing had a powerful effect on people, apparently causing them to hit their heads on walls and columns! He is also said to have had an amazing sense of rhythm. Barṣawmā (d. after 188/804) the wind player said about Ibn Jāmiʿ's voice and composition that they were akin to a receptacle full of honey: whether you open its mouth or tear its side you will only get honey (al-Iṣfahānī, 4:297)!

Bibliography

Henry George Farmer, *A history of Arabian music to the XIIIth century*. London 1929 (reprinted 1973); Ignazio Guidi, *Tables alphabétiques du Kitâb al-aġânî*, Leiden 1900; Abū l-Faraj al-Iṣfahānī, *Kitāb al-aghānī*, Cairo 1927–74; Hilary Kilpatrick, *Making the great "Book of songs." Compilation and the author's craft in Abū l-Faraj al-Iṣbahānī's "Kitāb al-aghānī,"* London and New York 2003; Eckhard Neubauer, *Musiker am Hof der frühen ʿAbbāsiden*, Ph.D. diss., Goethe-Universität Frankfurt am Main 1965; George Dimitri Sawa, *An Arabic musical and socio-cultural glossary of "Kitāb al-aghānī,"* Leiden 2015; George Dimitri Sawa, *Music performance practice in the early ʿAbbāsid era. 132–320 AH / 750–932 AD*, Toronto 1989 (reprinted Ottawa 2004); Khayr al-Dīn al-Ziriklī, *al-Aʿlām. Qāmūs tarājim li-ashhar al-rijāl wa-l-nisāʾ min al-ʿArab wal-mustaʿribīn wa-l-mustashriqīn*, 8 vols., Beirut 1979⁴.

George Dimitri Sawa

Ibn al-Māshiṭa

Abū l-Ḥasan ʿAlī b. al-Ḥasan **Ibn al-Māshiṭa** (d. after 311/923) was an ʿAbbāsid bureaucrat and author. Nothing is known of his origins other than his nickname ("son of the hairdresser") which, however, seems to have been an insult rather than a reference to his family (Ibn al-Nadīm). He had a long career as an accountant in charge of wages (this seems the most probable meaning of al-Tanūkhī's *kāna yataqalladu... al-ʿamālāt*, although the reference does not seem to be a separate sub-bureau in the administrative manuals). Already at an advanced age, he was appointed head of the state treasury *(dīwān bayt al-māl)* during the wazīrate of Ḥāmid b. al-ʿAbbās (in office 306–11/918–23, d. 311/923). It is unclear whether he served in this capacity until Ḥāmid's fall from grace in 311/923, but he seems to have been imprisoned after being removed from his post (al-Marzubānī). None of the extant chronicles cites his name in the list of appointments by a new *wazīr*, nor do they relate accounts of his doings in office. His precise date of death is unknown: al-Marzubānī mentions meeting him as an old man after 311/923, and he apparently lived to be a hundred (al-Tanūkhī). Al-Masʿūdī says that his history of *wazīrs* reached the end of the caliphate of al-Rāḍī (r. 322–9/934–40). This would suggest a date of death after 329/940, which is confirmed by Ibn al-Nadīm, who, writing in 377/987–8, says that Ibn al-Māshiṭa lived in recent times.

Ibn al-Nadīm lists three works by him on administrative practices: *Kitāb jawāb al-muʿnit*, a short *Kitāb al-kharāj*, and a *Kitāb taʿlīm naqd al-muʾāmarāt* that Ibn al-Nadīm claims to have seen. Al-Masʿūdī is the only source to mention Ibn al-Māshiṭa—alongside Ibn al-Jarrāḥ (d. 296/908–9), al-Ṣūlī (d. 335/947), and al-Jahshiyārī (d. 331/942–3)—as the author of *Akhbār al-wuzarāʾ*, a history of *wazīrs*. None of his works is known to be extant, although Ibn al-Ṣayrafī (d. 542/1147) quotes a story from *Kitāb jawāb al-muʿnit*, a book about chancery practices, on the honesty of an archivist *(khāzin)* in refusing a bribe and reporting it to the *wazīr* ʿAlī b. ʿĪsā (d. 334/946). Al-Tanūkhī cites Ibn al-Māshiṭa as a source, and al-Marzubānī ascribes three short pieces of poetry to him.

Bibliography

Ibn al-Nadīm, *Kitāb al-fihrist*, ed. Aymān Fuʾād Sayyid (London 2009), 1:2 420–1; Ibn al-Ṣayrafī, *Qānūn dīwān al-rasāʾil*, ed. ʿAlī Bahjat (Cairo 1905), 36–7, trans. Henri Massé, Code de la Chancellerie d'État (période fâtimide), *BIFAO* 11 (1911), 65–120, here 110–1; al-Marzubānī, *Muʿjam al-shuʿarāʾ*, ed. ʿAbd al-Sattār Aḥmad Farrāj (Cairo 1960), 155; al-Masʿūdī, *Kitāb al-tanbīh wa-l-ishrāf*, ed. ʿAbdallāh Ismāʿīl al-Ṣāwī (Cairo 1938), 298, 305; al-Masʿūdī, *Murūj al-dhahab*, trans. Barbier de Meynard, Pavet de Courteille, and Charles Pellat (Beirut 1965–79), 1:15 (§12); al-Tanūkhī, *Nishwār al-muḥāḍara*, ed. ʿAbbūd al-Shālijī (Beirut 1971–3), 4:54, 8:17, trans. D. S. Margoliouth, The table-talk of a Mesopotamian judge, *IC* 3 (1929), 487–522, here 494; Yāqūt, *Muʿjam al-udabāʾ*, ed. Iḥsān ʿAbbās (Beirut 1993), 4:1674–5.

Letizia Osti

Īlkhānids

The **Īlkhānids** were a Mongol dynasty that ruled much of the Middle East from the mid-seventh/thirteenth to the mid-eighth/fourteenth century. Nomads had been active in the politics of the eastern Islamic lands since the arrival of the Saljūq Turks in the early fifth/eleventh century, but the elimination of the ʿAbbāsid caliphate (656/1258) at the hands of the first Īlkhān, Hülegü (r. 654–63/1256–65), was a watershed in the political and social history of the Middle East. The Īlkhāns were the first Islamic dynasty compelled to legitimise their worldly power in the absence of a caliphate. This effort, facilitated by new channels of artistic and commercial exchange opened by the Mongol conquest, made the Īlkhānate and its aftermath a period of remarkable artistic, intellectual, and political innovation.

The title 'īlkhān' is generally understood to mean 'subordinate khan,' referring to Hülegü's original status relative to his brother, the Mongol Great Khān Qubilay (also transliterated Qubilai, r. 658–93/1260–94). Īlkhāns continued to recognise Qubilay's suzerainty until the latter's death in 693/1294. However, the name Īlkhān appears inconsistently in contemporary textual and numismatic sources, tending to disappear as the dynasty realised political independence from its sibling dynasty in China.

This article is organised according to major topics of interest to the historian of the Īlkhānate: conquest, administration and finance, religious conversion and scholarship, and art and architectural patronage. While all these topics pertain to the entire period, they are here treated in the order in which they are most historically pertinent. The sections therefore offer a roughly chronological overview of dynastic history; further detail may be found in separate articles on individuals mentioned here.

1. Conquest

The irruption of the Mongols into the Islamic lands was the most consequential of a series of Turko-Mongol incursions from the steppes of Inner Asia between the early fifth/eleventh century and the beginning of the eleventh/seventeenth century. Turks led by the descendants of Saljūq b. Duqāq (d. c.399/1009) had previously established a military dynastic state that formally depended on the sanction of ʿAbbāsid caliphs. The military power of the both the Turks and the Mongols lay in their mastery of horsemanship, particularly horse archery, with which the Saljūq Turks provided needed military support to the ailing caliphate.

The habit among nomadic dynasties to treat the state as joint property of the ruling family caused a rapid fragmentation of Saljūq sovereignty. By the beginning of the seventh/thirteenth century, Saljūq rule had dissolved everywhere except Anatolia. Meanwhile, the ʿAbbāsid caliph al-Nāṣir (r. 575–622/1180–1225) struggled to reassert his office's authority against Khwārazmshāh Muḥammad (r. 596–617/1200–20). In 616/1219, after Inalchik (d. 617/1220), Muhammad's governor in Utrār (Otrar, in present-day southern Kazakhstan) executed a trade embassy from Chinggis Khān (Genghis Khan, r. 602–26/1206–29), the latter launched a retributive raid against the Khwārazmshāh. Having overrun the cities of Central Asia, a Mongol army pursued Muḥammad across the southern littoral of the Caspian Sea. A separate force led by Chinggis Khān and his son Toluy (Tolui, d. 629/1232) chased the Khwārazmshāh's son Jalāl al-Dīn (d. 628/1231) through Khurāsān and Afghanistan as he fled to India. Contemporary Arabic and Persian accounts relate in apocalyptic terms the sudden and destructive nature of this first invasion. While the casualties reported for the cities of Khurāsān are surely exaggerated, Chinggis Khān's nomadic army severely disrupted the fragile agricultural infrastructure on which these cities depended. Writing more than a century later, Ḥamdallāh Mustawfī (d. c.744/1343) asserted that even a millennium of peace would not allow the land to recover.

Chinggis Khān's son and successor Ögedey (Ögedei or Ögödey, r. 626–39/1229–41) dispatched a second army under the general Chormaghun (d. c. 639/1241) to deal with the same Khwārazmī Jalāl al-Dīn, now resurgent. Chormaghun again overran the eastern and northern provinces of Iran and then established a military headquarters on the Mughan plain, in Azerbaijan. Like Mongol armies across Eurasia, Chormaghun's force included units from the patrimony of each branch of Chinggis Khān's family. This system invested the entire ruling clan in the ongoing expansion of the empire. From his headquarters and winter camp in Azerbaijan, Chormaghun campaigned into Georgia and Armenia between 632/1235 and 637/1240. At the same time, Batu (r. 624–53/1227–55), grandson of Chinggis Khān through his oldest son, Jochi (d. 624/1227), led an army against the cities of Russia and eastern Europe to establish his own patrimonial state, known as the Ulus of Jochi, or Golden Horde. Batu may have considered his campaign and that of Chormaghun as two parts of a united effort, as he and his descendants repeatedly claimed Chormaghun's conquests for themselves.

Chormaghun also campaigned against the remaining Saljūq sultanate of Rūm, which became a client state to the Mongols after 641/1243. While the Mongol army increasingly dominated the Middle East, the region became fiscally important to the central court on the Mongolian steppe. When certain elements of Middle Eastern society, in particular the network of Nizārī Ismāʿīlī strongholds in the regions of Alamut and Quhistān, resisted Mongol taxation efforts, the new Great Khān, Möngke b. Toluy (r. 649–57/1251–59) appointed his youngest brother Hülegü to lead a third Mongol expedition to the region.

Hülegü sent his deputy Ket Buqa (Kitbuqa, d. 658/1260) ahead to lay siege to the Ismāʿīlī fortresses, entering the region himself only in 654/1256. At that time, the scholar Naṣīr al-Dīn Ṭūsī (d. 672/1273) joined Hülegü's service and negotiated the surrender of his former patron, the Ismāʿīlī Imām Rukn al-Dīn Khurshāh (d. 655/1257). After securing the surrender of other Ismāʿīlī strongholds, Hülegü moved against Baghdad, justifying his action by the fact that the caliph al-Mustaʿṣim (r. 640–56/1242–58) had failed to provide assistance against the Ismāʿīlīs. In Muḥarram-Ṣafar 656/January-February 1258, Baghdad was seized and al-Mustaʿṣim executed. Arabic and Persian sources lament the fall of Baghdad and speak of a thorough sacking of the city by Mongol troops. Unlike the cities of Khurāsān, however, Baghdad remained vibrant, quickly resuming its role as a major economic and cultural centre. The contrast between the effect of Hülegü's campaign and that of his grandfather demonstrate how much Mongol attitudes towards the Middle East changed as the Mongols came to appreciate its potential as a source of tax revenues.

The presence of Nestorian Christians amongst the wives of the ruling Mongols raised the hopes of crusading Latin Christians for an alliance against the Mamlūks. Both Pope Innocent IV (r. 1243–54) and King Louis IX (r. 1226–70) of France dispatched ambassadors to the central Mongol court and to its generals stationed in the Middle East in an attempt to secure such an alliance. After the Mongol conquest of Baghdad, Hülegü pressed his advance into northern Syria with the support of King Het'um I (r. 1226–70) of Cilician Armenia and the Norman crusader Prince Bohemond VI (r. 1251–75) of Antioch. During the second half of the seventh/thirteenth century, members of the Armenian clergy and ruling family played an especially significant role in trying to broker further alliances between the Mongols and the

Latin West. In so doing, they produced a significant body of sources recording various accounts of Mongol origins, political and social organisation, and even language.

The Mongol campaign was halted in Galilee by the forces of the Mamlūk sultanate at the battle of ʿAyn Jālūt on 25 Ramaḍān 658/3 September 1260. Hülegü had withdrawn eastward in order to intervene if necessary in the selection of a new Great Khān after Möngke's death, leaving Ket Buqa and a much reduced army to maintain the expanding frontier. Unlike the armies of the Khwārazmshāh or the local levies of Iran and Iraq, the Mamlūk army consisted mostly of enslaved Turkic nomads from the Pontic steppe, and thus matched the Mongols in its training, tactics, and professionalism. The defeat at ʿAyn Jālūt initiated recurring conflicts between the Mamlūks and the Īlkhāns that lasted more than sixty years.

In 660/1261–62, a second military front opened between Hülegü and Batu's brother Berke (r. 655–65/1257–67) over their competing claims to grazing rights in Azerbaijan. Hülegü's assumption of sole authority over the formerly joint Mongol military operation in the Middle East and his execution of al-Mustaʿṣim had alienated him from Berke, who had converted to Islam before taking the Jochid throne. The course of these wars and the diplomatic correspondences and alliances that they inspired are treated by Reuven Amitai (Abāqā, *EI3*).

2. Administration

Hülegü established his capital at Marāgha, in Azerbaijan. The later Īlkhans moved the capital to Tabriz and then to Sulṭāniyya, but it stayed within the high pastures of northern Iran, which had played such an important role in supporting the Mongols' nomadic lifestyle as they conquered and ruled the Middle East. In the long scope of Iranian history, this marks a significant shift of political activity from established centres in the south and east—Mesopotamia, Fārs, and Khurāsān—to the northwest. Here a comparison can be drawn to Qubilay, whose own new capitals in China ultimately drew the political centre of that state northwards.

The new political centre in northern Iran facilitated access for Italian merchants, operating through the Black Sea port of Trebizond, to trading networks in Inner Asia. As a result, Tabriz became, during the Īlkhānid period, a major trading centre and an entrepot of Asian luxury goods into European markets. After the decline of the Īlkhānate in 736/1335, the descendants of Chūbān Suldūz (see below) proved less amenable to trade. This change in political climate and the increasing importance of grain from the Volga basin for the survival of the Italian cities led Italian merchants to favour northern Black Sea trade routes, severely restricting Iranian contact with emerging mercantile systems in the West.

To manage his state, Hülegü appointed the same Naṣīr al-Dīn Ṭūsī as vizier, part of a larger pattern in which Mongols across Eurasia employed local administrative specialists to manage affairs of state. During the period of Chormaghun's military governorship, Chin Tīmūr (d. 633/1235–6), of the Khitan (Qidan, Liao dynasty of northern China), had built the first civil administration for the Mongol Middle East, just as his compatriot Yeh-lü Ch'u-ts'ai (Yelü Chucai, d. 1244) was doing the same for the central regions of the empire. Chin Tīmūr had appointed

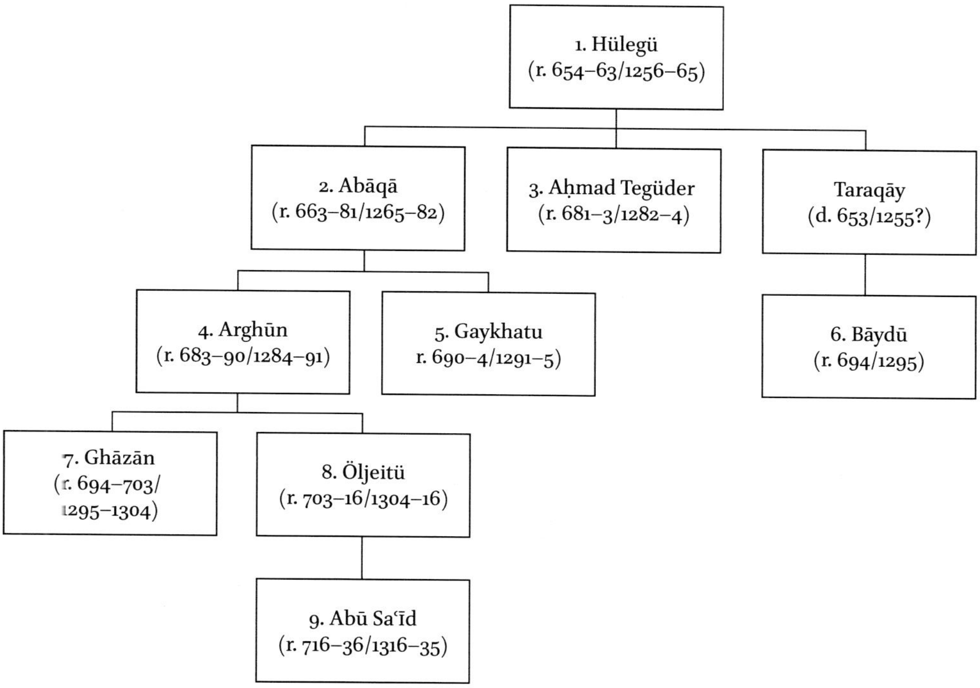

Illustration 1. Genealogical tree of the Īlkānid dynasty.

as his *ṣāḥib-dīwān* Bahāʾ al-Dīn Juvaynī (d. 651/1253), whose family had served the Khwārazmī state. Juvaynī became the trusted deputy of the last non-royal governor of the Middle East, the Oyirat Mongol Arghūn (d. 673/1275), and assumed executive authority when the latter travelled to the central court in Mongolia. When Hülegü came to the Middle East, Arghūn entrusted three members of his own entourage, including Bahāʾ al-Dīn's son, ʿAlāʾ al-Dīn Juvaynī (d. 681/1283), with assisting the prince.

In 657/1259, Hülegü assigned ʿAlāʾ al-Dīn Juvaynī to govern Baghdad. Three years later, he appointed a younger son of Bahāʾ al-Dīn, Shams al-Dīn Juvaynī (d. 683/1284), as *ṣāḥib-dīwān*. Between 658/1260 and 683/1284, the two Juvaynī brothers developed an administrative corps for the Īlkhānate. Their efforts to manage the state were hampered by the long-term effect of the Mongol conquest. On top of the destruction of the first invasion under Chinggis Khān, the early Īlkhāns imposed new and often arbitrary tax burdens on their subjects. Much of these funds were needed to pay for military operations, against the Mamlūks and Jochids and against a series of local revolts in Khurāsān and invasions by the Chaghatayid Mongols of Central Asia.

During the period of the Juvaynīs' administration, and in parallel with similar practices in China, Islamic bureaucrats were frequently paired in office with Mongol overseers, so that the management of the Īlkhānid state was marked by a blend of nomadic and bureaucratic practices and by political factions that cut across ethnic and social lines. This factionalism, combined with the unsustainable fiscal situation of the state, destabilised the politics and administration of the Īlkhānate during the period following Abāqā's death in 681/1282. Between then and 694/1295, there were five changes in ruler, each accompanied by revolt, princely opposition, and/or fiscal disaster. One of these, in 683/1284, was accompanied by the deaths of both Juvaynī brothers and the gradual dismantling of the administrative apparatus they had developed (for details of this complicated but formative period, see Aubin, 29–51).

3. Religious conversion and scholarship

The years following Abāqā's death also saw a gradual realignment in Īlkhānid religious identity, culminating in the conversion to Islam of Ghāzān Khān (r. 694–703/1295–1304) in Shaʿbān 694/June 1295. Hülegü was a devout Buddhist, and his descendants were raised in that religion, although some of them also embraced Christianity for at least part of their lives, under the influence of their Nestorian mothers. Contemporary chronicles connect the period's political instability with changes in the Īlkhāns' religious preferences, regularly attributing the success or failure of the reigns of individual rulers to their associations with figures from one or another faith community. These narratives, chiefly those of Rashīd al-Dīn Ṭabīb (d. 718/1318) and the fiscal administrator and court panegyrist of Fārs, Shihāb al-Dīn Waṣṣāf (fl. 702–27/1302–27), were, however, written under the patronage of Ghāzān, and they reflect an Islamising ideology, by which animism and Buddhism, and, to a lesser degree, Judaism and even some forms of Islamic practice are denigrated in order to celebrate Ghāzān's position as the converter king.

Ghāzān was not the first Muslim Īlkhān. Arghūn's brother Tegüder (Takūdār, r. 681–3/1282–4) had converted in his youth, taking the Arabic name Aḥmad. His choice of faith does not seem to have been an obstacle to his accession, indicating that conversion was at least acceptable to the Mongol elite. In his short reign Aḥmad Tegüder attempted to end the ongoing conflict with the Mamlūks. He dispatched two embassies to Cairo, although nothing came of them before his reign ended with the revolt of his Buddhist nephew Arghūn b. Abaqa (r. 683–90/1284–91).

Aḥmad Tegüder cultivated relationships with Ṣūfīs, and during his reign Ṣūfī institutions and practices presented a new political context in which the Mongol dynasty could be integrated into Islamic society. The religious experience of the Īlkhāns was not a one-way process of conversion but a bilateral acculturation between the indigenous society and its new political and military elite. In Rashīd al-Dīn's portrayal of Tegüder, however, Ṣūfīs play a sinister role. The Īlkhān neglects affairs of state in order to sit in audience with a dervish, Īshān Ḥasan Menglī (d. 690/1291). This depiction serves, in part, to justify Arghūn's rebellion against Aḥmad Tegüder, during which Hasan Menglī was boiled alive.

The Buddhist Arghūn had long opposed the Juvaynīs and their Persianate administrative system, and both brothers were dead within a year of his accession. Arghūn initially appointed in their place two Mongol brothers, Buqa and Aruq of the Jalayir clan. They were soon replaced and ultimately purged in early 688/1289 after Buqa led a rebellion against Arghun in the name of Arghun's cousin Jushkeb. With Islamic and Mongol administrations recently discredited, Arghūn appointed as vizier the Jew Saʿd al-Dawla Abharī (d. 690/1291), who repopulated the administration with members of his own family and faith. His extreme concentration of authority, however, alienated both Mongol elites and Islamic scholar-bureaucrats. Saʿd al-Dawla was executed as Arghūn lay dying. The resentment felt against him was turned against other Jews, sparking the first systematic religious persecutions of the young state.

The reign of Gaykhatu (Geikhatu, r. 690–4/1291–5) saw a return to the basic pattern that prevailed under the first two Īlkhāns, with a Buddhist ruler assisted by Persian Muslim administrators. Gaykhatu's vizier, Ṣadr al-Dīn Zanjānī (d. 697/1298), worked to stabilise the state apparatus, appointing judicial and financial agents and attempting to increase tax revenues and rein in his patron's exorbitant spending. His efforts could not compensate for systemic problems, and, in late 693/1294, he took the desperate step of introducing a paper currency modelled on the Chinese *chao*. Despite decrees requiring its implementation, the *chao* was widely opposed and soon abandoned. Gaykhatu was deposed and executed by a rebellion that put his cousin Bāydū b. Taraqāy (Bāidū, d. 1295) on the throne for about seven months in 694/1295. Bāydū was, in turn, overthrown by his nephew, Ghāzān b. Arghūn (r. 694–703/1295–1304). Since the beginning of Arghūn's reign, Ghāzān had served as governor of the eastern provinces of Khurāsān and Māzandarān and had faced raids by the rebel *amīr* Nawrūz (d. 696/1297), who was an ardent Muslim. After his surrender to Ghāzān in the winter of 694/1294–5, Nawrūz became part of Ghāzān's inner circle and convinced the prince to adopt Islam as part of his rebellion against Bāydū.

Mediaeval and modern historians single out Ghāzān's conversion as the great watershed of Īlkhānid history, and it formed a central plank of his ideological platform. Other of Ghāzān's measures helped stabilise the finances and administration of the state. He had already publically rejected the *chao* while governing the eastern provinces, claiming that the humidity of Māzandarān made paper currency unfeasible. As Īlkhān, Ghāzān implemented a series of administrative and financial reforms, reported in differing ways by Waṣṣāf, Ḥamdallāh Mustawfī, and Rashīd al-Dīn. The latter's account of these reforms is the fullest, containing the text of numerous decrees, although it is unclear to what degree these measures were implemented.

The first years of Ghāzān's reign saw religious persecutions more systematic than those that had accompanied the fall of Saʿd al-Dawla. Between 694/1295 and 696/1297, Christian, Jewish, and Buddhist places of worship were targeted. These persecutions were probably pursued under the influence of Nawrūz, and they ended around the time of his fall from grace and execution, in 696/1297. From the accession of Ghāzān, the Īlkhānate became a Sunnī Muslim state, although Ghāzān exhibited particular interest in the special status of the family of the prophet Muḥammad. His brother and successor, Öljeitü (Ūljāytū, r. 703–16/1304–16) adopted Twelver Shīʿism for at least part of his reign, largely under the influence of al-ʿAllāma al-Ḥillī (d. 726/1325), one of the most productive and influential exponents of Shīʿī doctrine of all time. Al-Ḥillī was a member of a mobile college of Islamic scholars that Öljeitü maintained to debate questions of faith, following a tradition of Mongol patronage of court religious debate documented from the early empire until the time of the Mughal emperor Akbar (r. 963–1014/1556–1605).

Beyond Öljeitü's mobile college, theoretical sciences developed rapidly during the Īlkhānid period, as the collapse of the caliphate created an opportunity for Shīʿī scholars, amongst others, to re-examine the relationship between Islam and worldly power. Emblematic of this new wave of theology, philosophy, and theosophy is Quṭb al-Dīn Shīrāzī (d. 710/1311), the first to align the peripatetic philosophy of Ibn Sīnā (Avicenna, d. 428/1037) with the Illuminationism of Abū Najīb ʿAbd al-Qādir Suhrawardī al-Maqtūl (d. 563/1168).

4. Art and architectural patronage

Both Qutb al-Dīn Shīrāzī and al-ʿAllāma al-Ḥillī had entered Īlkhānid patronage early in the dynasty's history. Hülegü had instructed his vizier Ṭūsī to build an astrological observatory at Marāgha in order to determine auspicious horoscopes for court events. The community of scholars that Ṭūsī attracted developed the science of planetary theory beyond their official mandate, most notably in Shīrāzī's commentaries on Tūsī's earlier work, where he proposed a new solution for modeling the movement of Mercury.

Marāgha was just the first in a series of urbanisation projects that established the Īlkhānid footprint in Azerbaijan. This simultaneously signalled Īlkhānid rule of the region to their Jochid rivals and invested the new, nomadic elite in the built environment of their subject people. During Abāqā's reign, a palace was built over the ruins of the Zoroastrian fire temple of Azerbaijan, at a site that had come to be known as the Takht-i Sulaymān (throne of Solomon) [Illustration 2]. While the ruins of this palace are striking, its significance as a witness to historical events is best demonstrated by the glazed tiles now distributed amongst various public and private collections. Many of these tiles refer to the *Shāh-nāma* (completed c. 400/1009–10) of Abū l-Qāsim Firdawsī (d. 409/1019 or 416/1025), through both textual citation and visual reference, suggesting that the ideological programme of the early Īlkhānid court included an association with the heroes of Iranian tradition.

Arghūn is probably responsible for an unfinished rock-cut precinct at Viar, near the pastures of Qonqur Öleng northeast of Takht-i Sulaymān, that reflects Islamic architectural styles but carries Buddhist decorative motifs [Illustration 3]. He also monumentalised two urban sites: a neighbourhood in Tabriz and a new city at Qonqur Öleng. These were completed by Arghūn's sons Ghāzān and Öljeitü. Ghāzān continued developing the district in Tabriz into the shrine-city of Shanb, containing his own tomb, a new astronomical observatory, and numerous charitable foundations. Öljeitü turned his father's foundation at Qonqur Öleng into his new capital of Sulṭāniyya. There he built his own mausoleum, which was the largest domed space in its time and remains the most remarkable testament to the architectural achievements of the Īlkhānate [Illustration 4]. Several smaller shrines and mosques in cities across Iran have preserved Īlkhānid decorative programmes more fully than the royal establishments in the capitals. Sites at Ardabil,

Illustration 2. The ruins of the palace of Takht-i Sulaymān (throne of Solomon). Photograph courtesy of Dan Waugh.

Natanz [Illustration 5], and Yazd demonstrate significant advances in the use of glazed tile, including the development of *lajvardina*, a type of lustreware in which gold and coloured enamels were painted over lapis glaze.

The royal shrine-cities of Shanb and Sulṭāniyya find parallels in the building projects of non-royal persons, particularly the viziers who managed the state finances and benefited from direct royal patronage. Most famous in this regard is the Rabʿ-i Rashīdī built by Rashīd al-Dīn on the outskirts of Tabriz. The surviving original *waqf* (charitable endowment) document leaves detailed instructions for the maintenance of a mosque, *madrasa*, scriptorium, and hospital, as well as Rashīd al-Dīn's tomb and other scholarly and charitable institutions. After Rashīd al-Dīn was executed in 718/1318, on charges of having poisoned Öljeitü, the Rabʿ-i Rashīdī was ransacked; it was partially restored during the vizierate of his son Ghiyāth al-Dīn Muḥammad (served 727–36/1327–36). Rashīd al-Dīn's co-vizier during his later life was Tāj al-Dīn ʿAlī Shāh (served 711–24/1312–24), who also commissioned major building projects as a way to secure his position in government. One wall of ʿAlī Shāh's massive congregational mosque still stands in Tabriz [Illustration 6].

Other hallmarks of Īlkhānid art include richly decorated metalwork and a new style of manuscript painting and illumination drawing on influences as diverse as the Mongol empire. The most famous examples of these were produced in Tabriz, at the scriptorium in the Rabʿ-i Rashīdī. Surviving copies of the *Jāmiʿ al-tawārīkh* (discussed below) and of Rashīd al-Dīn's contributions to the theological debates of Öljeitü's court show that large teams of artists at his scriptorium produced books on an unprecedented scale and at unprecedented expense. The combination of large urban endowments with scriptoria for the production of deluxe manuscripts became a central component for later Tīmūrid, Ṣafavid, and Ottoman displays of sovereign power.

5. Literary legacy

The *Jāmiʿ al-tawārīkh* is the most famous entry in a prodigious catalogue of historical writing produced during the Īlkhānate. Rashīd al-Dīn presented the completed *Jāmiʿ* to Öljeitü in 706/1307. The first volume of the work was a dynastic history of the Mongols prepared originally for Ghāzān, after whom it was titled *Taʾrīkh-i mubārāk-i Ghāzānī*. The second volume, the *Taʾrīkh-i ʿĀlam*, contains a history of the Perso-Islamic world up to the Mongol conquest, supplemented by

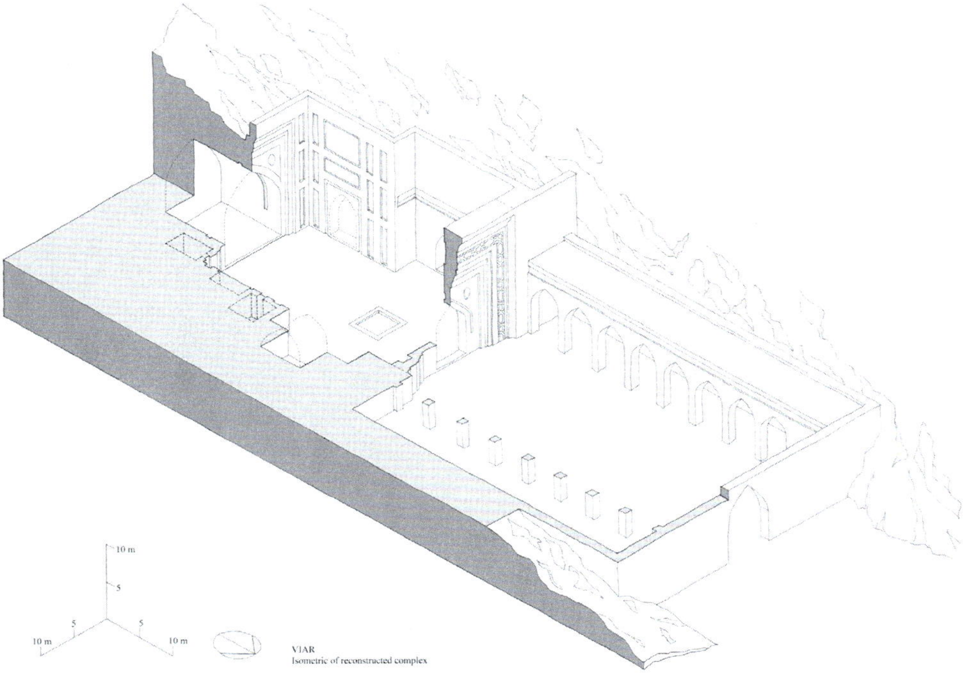

Illustration 3. Isometric reconstruction of unfinished rock-cut precinct at Viar. Image by Nicholas Warner, provided courtesy of Sheila Blair.

Illustration 4. The mausoleum of Öljeitü at Sulṭāniyya. Photograph courtesy of Dan Waugh.

Illustration 5. The Īlkhānid shrine complex at Natanz. Composite photograph courtesy of Dan Waugh.

Illustration 6. The wall of ʿAlī Shāh's congregational mosque in Tabriz. Photograph courtesy of Dan Waugh.

a series of short histories of the Oghuz Turks, Chinese, Jews, Franks, and Indians. In his general introduction to the *Jāmiʿ al-tawārīkh*, Rashīd al-Dīn also describes a third volume consisting of a gazetteer of all the lands treated in the first two volumes, but no copies of this have survived.

The *Jāmiʿ al-tawārīkh* bears Rashīd al-Dīn's name, but, as the surviving works of Abū l-Qāsim Qāshānī become available, they tend to validate Qāshānī's accusations that Rashīd al-Dīn stole his work. Qāshānī makes these claims in his *Taʾrīkh-i Ūljāytū*, an important work as the only contemporary narrative of Öljeitü's reign and for the light it sheds on court historiography under the Īlkhāns. It was evidently compiled from administrative journals recording the daily activities at court. No such journals survive, but they were probably also the sources for much of the *Taʾrīkh-i mubārāk-i Ghāzānī*.

In addition to his commissions of Rashīd al-Dīn and Qāshānī, Ghāzān took Shihāb al-Dīn Waṣṣāf under his patronage. Waṣṣāf had begun his *Tajziyat al-amṣār wa-tazjiyat al-aʿṣār* independently, as a continuation of ʿAlāʾ al-Dīn Juvaynī's *Tārīkh-i jahāngushā*, which recounts the rise of the Mongols and the fall of the Khwārazmian dynasty. Like Waṣṣāf, Juvaynī wrote his history without a royal patron in mind. These and other Persian-language histories of the early Mongol period were the products of local scholar-bureaucrats trained in the institutional culture of previous dynasties but indebted to the Mongols for employment and patronage. Such histories written by, and largely for, administrators, include the *Niẓām al-tawārīkh* of

Qāḍī al-Bayḍāwī (d. 719/1319), the anonymous *Akhbār-i Mughūlān*, and the *Awāmir al-ʿalāʾiyya fī l-umūr al-ʿalāʾiyya* commissioned by ʿAlāʾ al-Dīn Juvaynī from Ibn Bībī (d. after 684/1285), an administrator for the Saljūqs of Rūm. Such works are important as witnesses to Mongol history and the history of the late Saljūq world but also for beginning to integrate the Mongols into Islamic traditions of historical writing.

The last years of the Īlkhānate saw a shift in historical writing and artistic patronage, with renewed interest in Firdawsī's *Shāh-nāma*, both in its own right and as a model for new historical works. One of Rashīd al-Dīn's administrative appointees, Ḥamdallāh Mustawfī, produced two new universal histories, the prose *Tarīkh-i guzīda* and the *Ẓafar-nāma*. The latter was written as a continuation of the *Shāh-nāma*, using Firdawsī's epic metre and style. Other individuals produced verse histories in the same vein, culminating in Niẓām al-Dīn Shāmī's (d. before 812/1409) own *Ẓafar-nāma* versification of Tīmūr's life. The earliest illustrated copies of the *Shāh-nāma* also date to the late Īlkhānate, particularly to the 730s/1330s, as the dynasty died out. During this time, the so-called Great Mongol *Shāh-nāma*, one of the most spectacular examples of early Persian book painting, was produced in Tabriz, and the Injūid court of Shiraz (discussed below) became one of the first to imitate Īlkhānid patterns of patronage by producing deluxe *Shāh-nāma* manuscripts as part of an effort to express political independence from the moribund Mongol dynasty [Illustration 7].

6. Regions and aftermath

The last Īlkhān to hold effective rule was Abū Saʿīd Bahādur Khān (r. 716–36/1316–35), son of Öljeitü. His reign was the longest and most stable of any of the Īlkhāns and is remembered fondly by writers who outlived it. While the long-running war with the Mamlūks ended with a treaty in 722/1322, the state was troubled by periodic incursions by the Ulus of Jochi and the Chaghatayids of Central Asia, as well as by internal rebellions amongst Mongol *amīrs*. These revolts signal the beginning of a transition in authority from royal Īlkhānid sovereignty to various non-Chinggisid families. The most immediate of these successor dynasties were the descendants of *amīr* Chūbān of the Suldūz tribe (d. 728/1327). Chūbān had been Abū Saʿīd's leading general. He married two of the sultan's sisters and gained near total command of Abū Saʿīd's military and administrative apparatus as long as the sultan remained too young to oppose him. Abū Saʿīd eventually turned against the general and his family, executing Chūbān and several of his sons. The political and military prominence of the family, however, allowed his descendants to seize control of Azerbaijan, the capital region, after Abū Saʿīd died without an heir.

Throughout the Īlkhānate, dynastic power had been concentrated in Azerbaijan. In peripheral regions of the state, dynamics of Mongol aristocratic culture combined with pre-existing local structures of authority to create the circumstances for diverse successor states. Anatolia, troubled by local rebellion and by Mamlūk interference, had been a theatre of Mongol military activity since Chormaghun's arrival. From here, Mongol *amīrs* of the Jalayirid and Suldūz tribes had played prominent roles in the Īlkhānid military and civil administration since the final decades of the seventh/thirteenth century.

Illustration 7. Bahrām Gūr fights the Horned Wolf, illustrated folio from the Great Īlkhānid *Shāh-nāma* ("Book of Kings"), c. 730–40/1330–40, an example of early Persian book painting. Harvard Art Museums/Arthur M. Sackler Museum, Bequest of Abby Aldrich Rockefeller, 1960.19[illegible]. Photograph courtesy of Imaging Department, © President and Fellows of Harvard College.

After Abū Saʿīd's death, their descendants attempted to perpetuate the Mongol state, first by supporting members of the Mongol royal family and then by seizing independent sovereignty for themselves. While the Chūbānids held Azerbaijan, the Jalayirids, based in Baghdad, oversaw the longest-lasting and most significant continuation of Mongol political culture, falling to the Turkmen confederacy of the Qarā Qoyūnlū in 835/1432.

In southern Iran, non-Mongol houses took a different approach to establishing independent rule in the wake of the Īlkhānate. In both Shiraz and Yazd, local dynasties of atabegs (*atābaks*) appointed by Saljūq sultans had recognised Mongol suzerainty on Hülegü's arrival. The Salghurids of Fārs were patrons to numerous poets and scholars, including Quṭb al-Dīn Shīrāzī, al-Bayḍāwī, and Waṣṣāf, all of whom later found work under Īlkhānid patronage. After a movement for local independence was put down in 683/1284, the Mongol court took direct control of the region. At the beginning of Öljeitü's reign, the administration of Fārs was again delegated, this time to Sharaf al-Dīn Maḥmud Shāh (r. c.725–36/c.1325–36), whose family became known as the Injūids in reference to the *injü* (royal estate) that they managed on behalf of their Mongol patrons.

In Yazd, a dynasty of atabegs appointed by the Saljūqs was overthrown in 719/1319 by Mubāriz al-Dīn (d. 765/1363), the son of Sharaf al-Dīn Muẓaffar (d. 713/1314). Abū Saʿīd confirmed Mubāriz al-Dīn in his position, and the latter aggressively pursued expansion, particularly after Abū Saʿīd's death, capturing Shiraz from the Injūids in 754/1353. While the Muẓaffarid dynasty itself did not survive the arrival of Tīmūr (d. 807/1405) in the region in 795/1393, they pursued a programme of patronage, particularly of illuminated books, which had begun under the Injūids and which helped make Shiraz one of the great centres of early book art and a main influence on Tīmūrid efforts in that area.

The Īlkhāns, like previous Middle Eastern dynastic states, found it difficult to maintain control of the provinces of Khurāsān and Māzandarān. As had been the practice under the Achaemenids and Sāsānids, members of the royal family were regularly delegated as viceroys of the East. In addition to this royal presence, the Kart dynasty (r. 643–791/1245–1389) of Herat maintained some independence right through the Īlkhānate, a result of their prompt submission to Mongol suzerainty. The Kart *maliks* proved their loyalty to the Īlkhānid dynasty on several occasions: both Nawrūz (in 696/1297) and Chūbān (in 727/1327) fled to Herat after falling out of favour at court, and both were executed rather than protected. In Sabzavār, various groups banded together in the wake of the Īlkhānate to form a government led by local Shīʿī *shaykhs* known as the Sarbadārs. This name has been alternately interpreted as "(one with his) head in the gallows," "reckless ones," and "refactory," all with the sense of rebelliousness. (Considering the decentralized nature of this confederacy, perhaps "headless" approaches the sense of the name.) From the decline of the Īlkhānate to the rise of Tīmūr, other areas of Khurāsān continued to host a Mongol military elite largely unchanged from that which had entered the region over a century earlier.

Despite this political fragmentation after 736/1335, all these successor states looked, in one way or another, to the Īlkhānid legacy to justify their own claims to authority. Furthermore, the geographic reach of Īlkhānid rule had a lasting impact on subsequent dynastic states. Chronicles written during the Īlkhānate revived the use of the term "Iran" as a geo-political designation of the state. This looked back to late antique Sāsānid precedent and forward to the Ṣafavid state, making the Īlkhānate an important moment for maintaining the idea of Iranian cultural and political continuity.

Bibliography

Sources

Abū l-Fidāʾ, *al-Mukhtaṣar fī akhbār al-bashar*, 4 vols. in 2, Istanbul 1286/1869–70, repr., 4 vols. in 1, Cairo 1907–8; Anon., *Akhbār-i Mughūlān (650–683) dar anbāna-yi Mullā Quṭb. Az majmūʿa-yi khaṭṭī muvarrikh-i 685, Kitābkhāna-i Āyatallāh al-ʿUẓmā Marʿashī Najafī (Qum)*, ed. Īraj Afshār, Qum 2010; Karīm al-Dīn Āqsarāyī, *Musāmarat al-akhbār wa-musāyarat al-akhyār*, ed. Ömer Turan, Ankara 1944; Nūr al-Dīn b. Muḥammad Nūrī Azhdarī, *Ghāzān-nāma-yi manẓūm*, ed. Maḥmūd Mudabbirī, Tehran 1381/sh2002; Fakhr al-Dīn Abū Sulaymān Dāvūd Banākatī, *Tārīkh-i Banākatī. Rawḍat ūlī al-albāb fī maʿrifat al-tavārīkh al-akābir wa-l-ansāb*, ed. Jaʿfar Shiʿār, Tehran 1348sh/1969; Bar Hebraeus, *The chronography of Gregory Abû'l Faraj*, trans. Ernest A. Wallis Budge, 2 vols., London 1932; Robert P. Blake and Richard N. Frye (Armenian text ed. and trans.), History of the nation of archers (the Mongols) by Grigor of Akanc, *Harvard Journal of Asiatic Studies* 12/3–4 (1949), 269–399; Ibn al-Fuwaṭī, *Majmaʿ al-ādāb fī muʿjam al-alqāb*, ed. Muḥammad al-Kāẓim, 6 vols., Tehran 1416sh/1995–6; Kirakos Gandzakets'i, *Kirakos Gandzakets'i's history of the Armenians*, trans. Robert Bedrosian, New York 1986; Ḥāfiẓ Abrū, *Dhayl-i jāmiʿ al-tavārīkh*, ed. Khānbābā Bayānī, 2 vols., Tehran 1317sh/1938; Ibn Bībī, *Avāmir al-ʿalāʾiyya fī l-umūr al-ʿalāʾiyya*, ed. Adnan S. Ezri, *el-Evāmirü'l-ʿalāʾiyye fī'l-umūri'l-ʿalāʾiyye*, Ankara 1956; ʿAlāʾ al-Dīn ʿAṭā Malik Juvaynī, *Tārīkh-i jahāngushā*, ed. Muḥammad b. ʿAbd al-Wahhāb Qazvīnī, 3 vols., Leiden 1912–37, trans. John Andrew Boyle, *The history of the world conqueror*, Manchester UK and Cambridge MA 1958; Abū l-Qāsim ʿAbdallāh b. Muḥammad Qāshānī, *Tārīkh-i Uljāytū*, ed. Mahīn Hambalī, Tehran 1348sh/1969; Ḥamdallāh Mustawfī Qazvīnī, *Tārīkh-i guzīda*, ed. ʿAbd al-Ḥusayn Navāʾī, Tehran 1983; Ḥamdallāh Mustawfī Qazvīnī, *Ẓafar-nāma*, ed. Naṣrallāh Pūrjavādī and Nuṣratallāh Rastagār, 2 vols., Vienna 1999; Ḥamdallāh Mustawfī Qazvīnī, *Dhayl-i Ẓafar-nāma*, ed. V. Z. Piriiev, Baku 1978; Ḥamdallāh Mustawfī Qazvīnī, *Nuzhat al-qulūb*, ed. and trans. Guy Le Strange, *The geographical part of the Nuzhat-al-qulūb*, Leiden and London 1915; Rabban Sauma, *The history of Yaballaha III, Nestorian patriarch, and of his vicar, Bar Sauma, Mongol ambassador to the Frankish courts at the end of the thirteenth century*, trans. from the Syriac by James A. Montgomery, New York 1927; Igor de Rachewiltz (trans.), *The secret history of the Mongols. A Mongolian epic chronicle of the thirteenth century*, 3 vols., Leiden 2004–13; Rashīd al-Dīn Faḍlallāh Ṭabīb, *Jāmiʿ al-tawārīkh*, ed. Muḥammad Rawshan and Muṣṭafā Musavī, Tehran 1373sh/1994; Rashīd al-Dīn Faḍlallāh Ṭabīb, *Jāmiʿ al-tawārīkh*, trans. Wheeler Thackston, *Compendium of chronicles*, Cambridge MA 1998; Rashīd al-Dīn Faḍlallāh Ṭabīb, *Vaqf-nāma-yi Rabʿ-i Rashīdī*, ed. Īraj Afshār and Mujtabā Minuvī, Tehran 1350sh/1971 (facs.), 2536/1977 (edited text); A. A. Seyed-Gohrab and S. McGlinn, *The treasury of Tabriz. The great Il-khanid compendium*, Amsterdam 2007; Muḥammad b. ʿAlī b. Muḥammad Shabānkāraʾi, *Majmaʿ al-ansāb*, ed. Mīr Hāshim Muḥaddith, Tehran 1363sh/1984–5; Ibn Faḍlallāh al-ʿUmarī, *Masālik al-abṣār fī mamālik al-amṣar*, ed. Fuat Sezgin et al., 30 vols., Frankfurt 1408/1988; ʿAbdallāh b. Faḍlallāh Waṣṣāf, *Tajziyat al-amṣār wa-tazjiyat al-aʿṣār*, Qazvīn 1835.

Studies

Denise Aigle, *L'Iran face à la domination mongole*, Tehran 1997; Denise Aigle, *The Mongol empire between myth and reality. Studies in anthropological history*, Leiden 2014; Thomas T. Allsen, *Mongol imperialism. The policies of the Grand Qan Möngke in China, Russia, and the Islamic lands, 1251–1259*, Berkeley 1987; Thomas T. Allsen, *Culture and conquest in Mongol Eurasia*, Cambridge 2001; Reuven Amitai, Il-Khanids I. Dynastic history, *EIr*; Reuven Amitai, *The Mongols in the Islamic lands. Studies in the history of the Ilkhanate*, Aldershot UK and Burlington VT 2007; Reuven Amitai, *Mongols and Mamluks. The Mamluk-Īlkhānid war, 1260–1281*, Cambridge 1995; Reuven Amitai-Preis and David O. Morgan, *The Mongol empire and its legacy*, Leiden 1999; Jean Aubin, *Emirs, mongols et vizirs persans dans les remous de l'acculturation*, Paris 1995; Michal Biran, *Qaidu and the rise of the independent Mongol state in Central Asia*, Surrey 1997; Sheila S. Blair, Il-Khanids II. Architecture, *EIr*; Sheila Blair, *A compendium of chronicles. Rashid al-Din's illustrated history of the world*, London 1995; J. A. Boyle, *The Cambridge history of Iran*, vol. 5, *The Saljuq and Mongol periods*, Cambridge 1968; Stefano Carboni, Il-Khanids III. Book illustration, *EIr*; Bayarsaikhan Dashdondog, *The Mongols and the Armenians (1220–1335)*, Leiden 2011; Joseph Hammer-Purgstall, *Geschichte der Ilchane*, 2 vols., Darmstadt 1842–3; Hans Henning von der Osten and Rudolph Naumann, *Takht-i-Suleiman. Vorläufiger Bericht über die Ausgrabungen 1959*, Berlin 1961; Birgitt Hoffmann, *Waqf im mongolischen Iran. Rašīduddīns Sorge um Nachruhm und Seelenheil*, Stuttgart 2000; Peter Jackson, *The Mongols and the Islamic world. From conquest to conversion*, New Haven 2017; Peter Jackson, *The Mongols and the West, 1221–1410*, Harlow 2005; Hani Khafipour, A hospital in Ilkhanid Iran. Toward a socio-economic reconstruction of the Rabʿ-i Rashidi, *Journal of the International Society for Iranian Studies* 45/1 (January 2012), 97–117; Judith G. Kolbas, *The Mongols in Iran. Chingiz Khan to Uljaytu, 1220–1309*, London 2006; Linda Komaroff, *Beyond the legacy of Genghis Khan*, Leiden 2006; Linda Komaroff and Stefano Carboni, *The legacy of Genghis Khan. Courtly art and culture in western Asia, 1256–1353*, New York 2002; Dorothea Krawulsky, *Īrān, das Reich der Īlḫāne. Eine topographisch-historische Studie*, Weisbaden 1978; C. P. Melville, *The fall of Amir Chupan and the decline of the Ilkhanate, 1327–1337. A decade of discord in Mongol Iran*, Bloomington 1999; David Morgan, *The Mongols*, Oxford 1986, Malden MA and Oxford and Cambridge MA 2007[2]; Peter Morgan, Il-Khanids IV. Ceramics, *EIr*; Constantin d'Ohsson, *Histoire des Mongols, depuis Tchinguiz-Khan jusqu'a Timour Bey, ou Tamerlan*, 4 vols., The Hague 1834–5; Judith Pfeiffer, *Politics, patronage, and the transmission of knowledge in 13th-15th century Tabriz*, Leiden 2014; H.R. Roemer, The Jalayirids, Muzaffarids and Sarbadārs, in Peter Jackson (ed.) *The Cambridge history of Iran*, vol. 6, *The Timurid and Safavid periods*, Cambridge 1986, 1–40. J. J. Saunders, *The history of the Mongol conquests*, New York and London 1971, Philadelphia 2001; J. Masson Smith, Jr., *The history of the Sarbadār dynasty 1336–1381 A.D. and its sources*, The Hague 1970; Bertold Spuler, Īlkhāns, *EI2*; Bertold Spuler, *Die Mongolen in Iran. Politik, Verwaltung und Kultur der Ilchanzeit, 1220–1350*, Berlin 1939, 1955[2], 1968[3], Leiden 1985[4]; Patrick Wing, *The Jalayirids. Dynastic state formation in the Mongol Middle East*, Edinburgh 2016.

STEFAN KAMOLA

Indonesia: Java from the coming of Islam to 1942

Evidence of Islamisation in **Java** first appears in the fourteenth century. By the late eighteenth century, Islam was the majority faith of Javanese.

1. The early stages of Islamisation in Java

The earliest surviving evidence of Islam amongst the Javanese is in the form of gravestones at Trawulan and Tralaya, in East Java, near the site of the Hindu-Javanese court of Majapahit (late thirteenth-early sixteenth centuries). They are Muslim gravestones, since Hindus were cremated. The stones have quotations from the Qurʾān and pious formulae, yet they bear dates in the Indian Śaka calendar rather than the Muslim *hijrī* and use Old Javanese rather than Arabic numerals. The earliest is dated Ś 1290 (1368–9 C.E.). They also have decorations associated with the Majapahit dynasty. This evidence persuaded Damais (Études javanaises I) that these were probably the graves not of Muslim immigrants or foreigners but of distinguished Javanese, perhaps even members of the royal family.

This is all the more remarkable because this period was the apogee of Majapahit's glory and power, celebrated in the famous Old Javanese work by the Buddhist author Prapañca titled *Deśawarṇana* (formerly called *Nāgarakṛtāgama*), written in Ś 1287 (1365 C.E.); this work makes no reference to a Muslim presence, suggesting that Islam was not welcomed in all court circles.

Our knowledge of the history of Majapahit's later years and of Islam amongst the Javanese during that time is limited. Majapahit apparently endured a civil war (unconnected with Islam) in 1405–6, a disputed succession in the 1450s, and a princely rebellion in 1468. The Majapahit royal line, or a branch of it, seems to have survived these events. According to Javanese historical traditions, Islam was spread during this period by holy men known as the nine saints *(wali sanga)*, whose graves remain major pilgrimage sites but whose identities and histories are enveloped in myths.

The Chinese Muslim traveller Ma Huan visited the north coast of Java in 816–8/1413–5 and recorded the presence of Muslims from western Asia, China, some of whom were Muslims like himself, and Java, whom he described as heathens. This suggests that Islam had begun its spread amongst the Javanese elite of East Java but was not yet a significant presence amongst the Javanese of the coast. The Portuguese apothecary Tomé Pires (d. first half of sixteenth century) visited the coast a century later and observed a cultural transition. The Javanese-speaking heartland of Central and East Java was still ruled, in principle, by a Hindu-Buddhist king, then resident at Daha (Kediri) in East Java. On the north coast, however, there were twin cultural changes under way: Javanese were converting to Islam, and foreign Muslims were adopting Javanese cultural styles (and no doubt spouses) and were, in effect, becoming Javanese. Thus were laid the foundations of a hybrid culture in Java, making Islam there different in style from what was found in much of the rest of the Indonesian archipelago and the Malay Peninsula.

The Portuguese were the first Europeans to reach Java, in the early sixteenth century, but their impact was insignificant there and, except for Pires, their sources tell us little. In 1596, the first Dutch voyage reached Java's coast. Over the succeeding years, the increasing Dutch involvement in Java makes the documents of the Dutch East India Company (Vereenigde Oost-Indische Compagnie, VOC, est 1602, bankrupt 1799) more valuable for historians, especially after the foundation of the VOC headquarters at Batavia (present-day Jakarta) in 1619 and particularly after the first major VOC military intervention in the interior of Java, in the 1670s. During the eighteenth century, Javanese-language sources also become more voluminous, informative, and reliable.

2. The period of Islamised states

Several Muslim-ruled states emerged on the north coast in the sixteenth century. According to semi-historical Javanese legends, the most important of these was Demak. In about 1527, Demak conquered the remnants of Majapahit. Demak seems to have imposed some degree of hegemony over the remaining Central and East Javanese principalities around 1529–46, campaigns that ended when Demak's "sultan" Trenggana was apparently murdered in 1546.

In the 1520s, Demak supported the growth of both Cirebon and Banten as significant Muslim states in West Java.

The semi-legendary figure of Sunan Gunungjati (one of the nine saints) reputedly played the major role in these events. In about 1579, Pajajaran, the last Hindu-Buddhist state of West Java, fell to forces from Banten.

In the second half of the sixteenth century, two Islamised powers emerged in the interior of Central Java: Pajang and Mataram. The history of Pajang (in the area of present-day Surakarta) is almost entirely unknown, there being no surviving contemporary evidence. The state of Mataram (near present-day Yogyakarta) appears to have been founded in the 1570s, and it was there that the dynasty was established that survives today in the persons of the sultan of Yogyakarta, the Susuhunan of Surakarta, and the subsidiary Mangkunagara and Pakualam princes. The foundations of Mataram's hegemony over Central and East Java were evidently laid by a semi-legendary figure known as Panembahan Senapati Ingalaga (r. c.1584–1601). Chronicles describe a sequence of military successes and supernatural events that linked him to autochthonous forces: a falling star that descended above his head as he slept, and the three days he spent in liaison with the Goddess of the Southern Ocean (Ratu Kidul). There were also Islamic aspects to his legend, for one of Senapati's principal advisers was said to be Sunan Kalijaga, one of the nine *walis*. Senapati was succeeded by his son Seda ing Krapyak (r. c.1601–13), about whom somewhat more is known, primarily through VOC reports.

The first Mataram ruler concerning whom we have significant reliable information was Sultan Agung (lit., great sultan, r. 1613–46). He was indeed the greatest of the early Mataram monarchs and a major figure in the reconciliation of Islamic and indigenous traditions. He confirmed Mataram's hegemony by finally conquering Surabaya, Mataram's greatest competitor, in 1625. Other recalcitrant lords were also brought to heel by military action, but his two attempts in 1628–9 to expel the VOC from its new headquarters at Batavia failed. This failure destroyed the myth of his invincibility and sparked indigenous rebellions against him from 1630 to 1636, all of which he crushed.

The most significant rebellion against Sultan Agung occurred in 1630. It was evidently led by religious teachers based at Tembayat, the location of the grave of Sunan Bayat, the *wali* of south-central Java. Agung crushed the rebellion but thereafter took actions that were apparently intended to position the supernatural power of Islam as a pillar of the Mataram dynasty rather than as a threat to it. He made a pilgrimage to Tembayat in 1633, where he erected an inscribed ceremonial gateway. He also changed the calendar at this time, abandoning the Hindu Śaka era, which the court was still using, for an Islamic lunar calendar but continuing the previous counting of the year sequence, thus producing the hybrid Javanese calendar (AJ, anno Javanico). Legends say that Agung received instruction in mystical knowledge from the spirit of Sunan Bayat. He ordered the production of the literary works *Serat Yusup* (based on the Qurʾānic story of Joseph in Egypt), *Carita Sultan Iskandar* (an elaborated version of the Qurʾānic tale of Dhū l-Qarnayn), and *Kitab Usulbiyah* (a more locally idiosyncratic version of Islamic hagiography). He also evidently wrote *Suluk Garwa Kancana* ("Song of the house of gold"), known only in a copy from the 1730s, which seems to represent Agung's own political philosophy from the 1630s. This reconciled Javanese concepts of the warrior king with Ṣūfī ideas of *al-jihād al-akbar*, the "greater holy war" against one's own carnal appetites. Sultan Agung thus played a signal role in the reconciliation of indigenous Javanese and Islamic traditions.

The most serious remaining threat resting on a religious basis was the holy site of Giri (near Surabaya), where the *wali* Sunan Giri is buried. Agung destroyed resistance there in 1636 and then took his final symbolic step, sending an ambassador in 1639 to Mecca, who returned in 1641 with authority—from whom is not clear—for him to adopt the title of "sultan." By the end of his days, Agung had acquired a reputation as a holy man. Nevertheless, legends continued to associate him with his supernatural wife, the Goddess of the Southern Ocean.

After Agung, however, there followed a period in which the Mataram dynasty faced Islamically inspired resistance and rebellion. Agung's son and successor Amangkurat I (r. 1646–77) sought to consolidate the Mataram empire, crushing all countervailing sources of authority. To this end, he invited the kingdom's Islamic leaders with their families to his court and there, according to the contemporary Dutch visitor to the court, Rijklof van Goens, five thousand to six thousand of them were slaughtered. He chose not to call himself "sultan" but used instead the Javanese title Susunan Ratu.

Amangkurat I's tyranny was murderous. In 1675 this precipitated a rebellion led by the Madurese prince Trunajaya and supported by Raden Kajoran, a spiritual leader in Central Java reputed to have supernatural powers. The rebellion failed, partly because of the military intervention of the VOC, which would soon have cause to regret its entanglement in Javanese affairs. The next five decades were marked by internal dynastic conflict (notably the first and second Javanese wars of succession, 1704–8 and 1719–23), and Islamically inflected resistance to a dynasty that appeared to be so lacking in legitimacy that it had to rely on non-Muslim military support.

A second attempt to reconcile the Mataram dynasty with Islamic sensibilities occurred during the reign of Pakubuwana II (1726–49). The major figure in this was not the new and ineffectual sixteen-year-old monarch but his grandmother, Ratu Pakubuwana (d. 1732). She was a pious Ṣūfī, a master of the occult life of the court who was reputed to possess supernatural protection and to be grandmother to almost all the younger generation who dominated court life. This second reconciliation of indigenous and Islamic traditions involved notably the production of new versions of the works of Sultan Agung's time—*Serat Yusup*, *Carita Sultan Iskandar*, and *Kitab Usulbiyah*—which were credited with supernatural powers to make the reign of Pakubuwana II perfect. A new version of *Suluk Garwa Kancana* was produced at the same time.

Pakubuwana II was shaped into the ideal Ṣūfī monarch of holy war when he joined the anti-VOC side in the so-called Chinese War (1740–3). In 1741 he attacked the VOC garrison at the court of Kartasura, killing some thirty-five Europeans, including the commandant, and forcing the VOC survivors to convert to Islam. But this apparent triumph was brief, as the tide of war turned in the Company's favour. Pakubuwana II then sought reconciliation with the VOC, which, understandably, had little trust in him. The rebel forces then turned against the inconstant monarch, and Kartasura fell twice in 1742: first in June, when the rebels conquered it and put Pakubuwana II to flight, and then in November, when Madurese forces allied to the Company took it from the rebels. On both occasions it was sacked, leading to the loss of many cultural treasures.

Kartasura was replaced by the court of Surakarta in 1746, but the chaos continued. That year marked the beginning of the Third Javanese War of Succession (1746–57), followed by further bloody, bitter, and devastating civil war. The main combatants were the VOC and, on the rebel side, the princes Mangkunagara (who became Prince Mangkunagara I of Surakarta, r. 1757–95) and Mangkubumi (r. 1749–92; in 1755 he became Sultan Hamengkubuwana I of Yogyakarta). The Surakarta sovereigns Pakubuwana II and Pakubuwana III (r. 1749–88) played insignificant roles in this conflict, until Mangkubumi was placated by being awarded half of the realm in 1755, whereupon he established his new court at Yogyakarta. Courtiers then began to return to the court of Surakarta, which reemerged as a significant participant in the politics of Central Java.

From 1755 to 1757, Mangkunagara I was pursued by the combined forces of Surakarta, Yogyakarta, and the VOC. He was on the defensive and had no prospect of defeating all these enemies, but they, too, found it exhausting trying to capture and kill him. In 1757, Pakubuwana III, feeling at a disadvantage in facing his more battle-hardened uncle Hamengkubuwana I, came to an agreement with his older and equally battle-hardened cousin Mangkunagara I for the latter to settle in Surakarta as a senior and semi-independent prince, whose experience and maturity would, the king hoped, strengthen the Surakarta side in standing up to Yogyakarta. The VOC gratefully withdrew from its military commitments in the countryside but retained fortified posts at Surakarta and Yogyakarta. The Company hoped to concentrate on its commercial concerns although it was now, in fact, tumbling towards bankruptcy at the end of the eighteenth century.

From 1757 to 1825, Java enjoyed the longest period of peace since at least the early sixteenth century. During this time we see the dominance of a style of Islam that may be called the mystic synthesis. Within the capacious boundaries of Ṣūfism, this rested on three pillars: 1) A strong sense of Muslim identity: to be Javanese was to be Muslim (even though there were still some small pre-Islamic communities in Java). 2) Observance of the five pillars of Islamic orthopraxy (the confession of faith, the fivefold daily prayer, the giving of alms, fasting in Ramaḍān, and the pilgrimage to Mecca for those able to undertake it). 3) Despite the above, acceptance of the reality of local spiritual forces, from major figures such as the Goddess of the Southern Ocean (Ratu Kidul) and the spirit of Mount Lawu (Sunan Lawu), to the spectral denizens of caves and forests, were-tigers and evil spirits who stole children in the night.

While our evidence concerns mainly the aristocratic class, there is some concerning ordinary folk, and it appears that this mystic synthesis (not to be confused with the *abangan* version of Islam described below) was the dominant form of Islamic belief across all levels of Javanese society.

A major crisis erupted in 1788–90, associated with Pakubuwana IV's ascension to the throne of Surakarta (r.1788–1820). He gathered about him a group of divines about whom we have only imperfect knowledge, as all the surviving evidence derives from their enemies. They evidently claimed to have supernatural powers that could be deployed to make Surakarta the senior court in Java, reducing Yogyakarta to a secondary position. The king elevated them to senior positions, replacing members of the court elite. These so-called *santris* (students of religion) may even have had plans to slaughter all Europeans in Java, although that seems unlikely and may have been a rumour concocted by their enemies. Where they stood within the spectrum of Islamic faith and practice is not clear, but at least one source charges that they were a deviant section of the Shattariyah (Ar., Shaṭṭāriyya) Ṣūfī order. The crisis came to a head in late 1790, when armed forces of Yogyakarta, Prince Mangkunagara I, and the VOC surrounded and prepared to attack the Surakarta court. Pakubuwana IV relented, thus narrowly escaping deposition, and his new advisers were soon on their way into exile. The established elite of the kingdom was restored to authority.

Pakubuwana IV again dallied with religious idiosyncrasy during the British interregnum (during the Napoleonic Wars) in Java (1811–6). He plotted with disaffected Indian Hindu Sepoys in British service to destroy both the European government in Java and Yogyakarta, on the basis of supposedly shared religious heritages. The plot was discovered, the Sepoys were court-martialled—seventeen were shot, the rest sent back to India in irons—and Pakubuwana IV once again narrowly escaped deposition.

3. The colonial period c. 1830–1942

From 1800, in the wake of the VOC's bankruptcy, its positions in the Indonesian archipelago were taken over by the Netherlands government. This made little difference at first. With the arrival in Batavia (now Jakarta) of the Napoleonic Marshal H. W. Daendels as governor-general (1808–11), however, power relations between the Europeans and the Javanese began to tilt towards something more recognisably colonial in nature. Daendel's bluster was backed by more powerful armed forces than the VOC had been able to mobilise for many decades, and Javanese potentates found themselves suddenly treated not as allies but as subjects. This trend continued and strengthened under the British interregnum of 1811–6 led by Lieutenant-Governor Thomas Stamford Raffles (d. 1826) (there was no position of governor-general in Java under the British). This change in circumstances culminated in the British sack of the court of Yogyakarta in 1812, the only time in Javanese history when a court was attacked and conquered by a European power. This humiliation of Yogyakarta signalled clearly the beginning of a new colonial era.

Resistance to the new regime culminated in the rebellion of Prince Dipanagara of Yogyakarta (d. 1855) in 1825, another prominent figure who embodied the mystic-synthesis style of Javanese Ṣūfism. He was a devout Muslim who clearly felt himself part of the global Muslim *umma* (community). He moved in the circles of religious schools (*pesantren*, lit., place of the *santri*, the Javanese term for students of religion), studied Islamic religious texts, and was steeped in Javanese literature and traditions. But he also wrote in his autobiography of his encounter with the Goddess of the Southern Ocean. Dipanagara was alienated from the intrigue, immorality, decadence, and corrupting European influence that he perceived at the court of Yogyakarta. The Java War (1825–30) that followed the launch of his rebellion marked the decisive watershed from precolonial to colonial eras in Java. Dutch power in Java was seriously threatened during this rebellion, but the colonial side finally prevailed, at a heavy cost to itself and to Javanese society. The colonial side lost eight thousand European and seven thousand Indonesian soldiers. At least 200,000 Javanese died. When Dipanagara agreed to negotiate with the Dutch in 1830 he was instead arrested and spent his remaining years a prisoner in exile in Indonesia's eastern islands.

After Dipanagara's defeat, the Dutch introduced a new system to exploit Java's natural resources and, it was hoped, finally to make a profit. This was known as the *cultuurstelsel* (cultivation system, sometimes called the culture system). This was hardly a system at all, with wide local variations, unclear and changing principles, and much corruption. It did, however, make an immense amount of money for the Dutch and may be one of the most successful exploitative systems in the history of European colonialism, resting, as it did, on the compulsory labour of Indonesian—especially Javanese and Sundanese—peasants. This was accompanied by significant population growth. There is no certainty about the total indigenous population (the majority being Javanese) on the island of Java circa 1800, but it was probably somewhere between three and five million. By 1850 it had reached 9.5 million, by 1870 it was 16.2 million, and by 1890 it had reached 23.5 million. In the census of 1930, the heartland of the Javanese—Central and East Java—had an indigenous population of 30.4 million.

The *cultuurstelsel* relied on the conservative Javanese social elite for its enforcement and on compulsory labour from peasants for its profits. It monopolised the main areas of economic activity but also facilitated significant social change. There were pockets of opportunity where local entrepreneurs played significant roles, as in such enterprises as pottery and gunnysack-making, textile production, bricklaying, entertainment, smithing, agricultural processing, land transport, and shipbuilding. Local markets flourished from the 1850s. After 1870, a shift in colonial policy encouraged more paid (as opposed to compulsory) labour. In 1900, sixteen percent of working adult males were engaged exclusively—and another fifteen percent partially—in non-agricultural work. These figures did not include women, who had long dominated market trading. Thus emerged a nascent proletariat and middle class amongst the Javanese, who played a significant role in religious change.

The first signs of Islamic reform movements to emerge in the Indonesian archipelago were in Sumatra, where the so-called Padri movement appeared in the 1780s. Similar evidence did not appear in Java until about the 1850s. The emerging Javanese commercial middle class, based largely in the urban centres of the north coast, often had connections with Arab traders, amongst whom were supporters of Islamic reform movements. The increasing wealth of this nascent Javanese bourgeoisie meant that more of them could undertake the *ḥajj*. The advent of steam shipping and the opening of the Suez Canal in 1869 also facilitated links with the Middle East. Dutch colonial statistics are not entirely reliable but do chart a dramatic growth in the numbers of those undertaking the pilgrimage. In 1850, fewer than fifty pilgrims were recorded as leaving Javanese-speaking areas for Mecca. By 1858 that number had grown to 2200, in 1898 to more than 5300, in 1911 to more than 7600, and in 1914 to more than ten thousand.

Not all of these Javanese came back as committed reformers. Not a few prospered as landowners and usurers, but some were reformers, and they, along with other religious leaders, contributed to an explosion in the numbers of *pesantrens*. In 1862, colonial records noted the existence of nearly 94,000 Javanese *pesantren* students. A decade later the figure was put at over 162,000. In 1893 there were reckoned to be nearly eleven thousand *pesantrens* in Javanese-speaking areas, with more than 272,000 students. Today, such *pesantrens* are a ubiquitous feature of the Javanese-speaking towns and countryside. More orthodox Ṣūfī movements also spread, as the Naqshbandiyya and the hybrid Qādiriyya wa-Naqshbandiyya competed with and tended to replace the previously dominant Shaṭṭāriyya.

Not all Javanese responded favourably to pressures for greater Islamic orthodoxy and orthopraxy. There emerged—again, beginning in the 1850s—a group in Javanese society, particularly amongst the rural majority, who began to reduce their commitment to Islam. These were castigated by the pious (who called themselves, amongst other things, the *putihan*, lit., the white ones) as *abangan* (lit., the brown or red ones). Why this term was chosen is unclear: it may refer to peasants' colourful clothing or even the red-stained teeth of betel-chewers. The term was soon adopted proudly by the *abangan* themselves who, by the end of the nineteenth century, constituted the majority of Javanese. They tended to see themselves as more authentically Javanese than the pious *putihan* Muslims, with their more Arab-influenced dress and Arabic terminology. The previously dominant mystic synthesis thus came under pressure and even attack from various Javanese Muslim communities. There were even some Javanese who came to regard Islamisation itself as a civilisational mistake; beginning in the 1860s and 1870s anti-Islamic books appeared that depicted modern European learning as a means to restore a more authentically Javanese pre-Islamic culture.

Javanese society was growing more polarised at the beginning of the twentieth century. For the first time, some Javanese even embraced Christianity. By 1900 there were probably about twenty thousand indigenous Christians in Central and East Java, only 0.1 percent of all Javanese. Social-religious polarisation was increased by the appearance in Java of modernist Islam beginning in the first decade of the twentieth century, with its commitment to return to the Qurʾān and *ḥadīth* as the authentic means of understanding the Islamic revelation and its willingness to embrace modern, European-style education and schools to achieve this. The Arab community of Batavia founded the Benevolent Society (Jamiat Kheir, Ar. Jamʿiyyat Khayr) in 1901, which opened a modern-style school with instruction in Malay. Indigenous reformers followed cautiously.

The most significant modernist movement was the Muhammadiyah (Ar., Muḥammadiyya) founded in Yogyakarta in 1912 by Kyai Haji Ahmad Dahlan (1868–1923). Returning from Mecca in 1890, he was determined to reform Islam as he saw it in Java. The Muhammadiyah founded schools and welfare organisations and launched a missionary programme to counter the efforts of Christian missions and to end the dominance of local superstitions amongst the Javanese. In 1917, Dahlan established a women's section called Aisyiyah, after the prophet Muḥammad's wife ʿĀʾisha. The Muhammadiyah met much opposition from old-fashioned religious teachers, government-recognised religious hierarchies, and pious Muslims who rejected modernist ideas. By 1925, it had only four thousand members, fifty-five schools with four thousand students, two clinics, one poorhouse, and one orphanage. Its leadership then fell to dynamic Minangkabau (Sumatran) leaders who oversaw a dramatic expansion. In 1938 it claimed 250,000 members throughout the archipelago, had 834 mosques and prayer houses, thirty-one public libraries, and 1774 schools. It deployed 5516 male and 2114 female proselytisers *(muballigh)*.

The first decades of the twentieth century were a time also of rapid political polarisation, as various anti-colonial parties contended. They generally reflected the socio-religious polarisation described above. Thus, Sarekat Islam (est. 1912) was led by modernist intellectuals, many with roots in the Muhammadiyah. The Indonesian Communist Party (est. 1920) was led by more secular intellectuals with an *abangan* popular base. In 1926, Muslim leaders who rejected both modernism and communism formed their own organisation, the Nahdlatul Ulama.

The colonial government felt increasingly threatened by the social and political turmoil that it faced, not only in Java but also elsewhere in the archipelago. When the Communist Party—by then thoroughly penetrated by police informers and with most of its leadership in exile or police hands—launched a Quixotic rebellion in 1925–6, the government cracked down forcefully on all political movements. Thereafter, all popular organisations and movements were closely monitored, and significant action was restricted until the Japanese invasion of 1942.

Bibliography

General references

M. C. Ricklefs, *A history of modern Indonesia since c. 1200*, Basingstoke 2008[4]; M. C. Ricklefs, *Islamisation and its opponents in Java. A political, social, cultural and religious history, c. 1930 to the present*, Singapore 2012; M. C. Ricklefs, *Mystic synthesis in Java. A history of Islamisation from the fourteenth to the early nineteenth centuries*, Norwalk CT and White Plains NY 2006; M. C. Ricklefs, *Polarising Javanese society. Islamic and other visions c. 1830–1930*, Singapore 2007.

Early Islamisation in Java, from the fourteenth century

Muḥammad b. Faḍlallāh Burhānpūrī, *The gift addressed to the spirit of the Prophet*, ed. and trans. A. H. Johns, Canberra 1965; Armando Cortesão (ed. and trans.), *The Suma Oriental of Tomé Pires ... and the book of Francisco Rodrigues*, 2 vols., London 1944; Louis-Charles Damais, L'épigraphie musulmane dans le sud-est asiatique, *BEFEO* 54 (1968), 567–604; Louis-Charles Damais, Études javanaises I. Les tombes musulmanes datées de Trålålåja, *BEFEO* 48/2 (1957), 353–415; G. W. J. Drewes (ed. and trans.), *The admonitions of Seh Bari*, The Hague 1969; G. W. J. Drewes (ed. and trans.), *An early Javanese code of Muslim ethics*, The Hague 1978; G. W. J. Drewes (ed. and trans.), *Een Javaanse primbon uit de zestiende eeuw*, Leiden 1954; A. H. Johns, Sufism as a category in Indonesian literature and history, *JSEAH* 2/2 (1961), 10–23; Ma Huan, *Ying-yai sheng-lan. "The overall survey of the ocean's shores (1433),"* ed. and trans. J. V. G. Mills, Cambridge 1970; Prapañca, *Deśawarṇana (Nāgarakṛtāgama)*, trans. Stuart Robson, Leiden 1995.

The period of Islamised states

Azyumardi Azra, *The origins of Islamic reformism in Southeast Asia. Networks of Malay-Indonesian and Middle Eastern 'ulamā' in the seventeenth and eighteenth centuries*, Crows Nest, New South Wales 2004; Martin van Bruinessen, *Tarekat Naqsyabandiyah di Indonesia. Survei historis, geografis dan sosiologis*, Bandung 1992; P. B. R. Carey, *The power of prophecy. Prince Dipanagara and the end of an old order in Java, 1785–1855*, Leiden 2007; P. B. R. Carey, The sepoy conspiracy of 1815 in Java, *BKI* 133/2–3 (1977), 294–322; H. J. de Graaf, *De regering van Panembahan Sénapati Ingalaga*, The Hague 1954; H. J. de Graaf, *De regering van Sultan Agung, vorst van Mataram 1613–1645* [sic] *en die van zijn voorganger Panembahan Séda-ing-Krapjak, 1601–1613*, The Hague 1958; H. J. de Graaf, *De regering van Sunan Mangku-Rat I Tegal-Wangi, vorst van Mataram, 1646–1677*, 2 vols., The Hague 1961–2; H. J. de Graaf (ed.), *De vijf gezantschapreizen van Rijklof van Goens naar het hof van Mataram, 1648–1654*, The Hague 1956; H. J. de Graaf and Th. G. Th. Pigeaud, *De eerste Moslimse vorstendommen op Java. Studiën over de staatkundige geschiedenis van de 15de en 16de eeuw*, The Hague 1974; A. D. Cornets de Groot, Bijdragen tot de kennis van de zeden en gewoonten der Javanen, *Tijdschrift van Nederlandsch Indië* 14/2 (1852), 257–80, 346–67, 393–422; J. Noorduyn, Majapahit in the fifteenth century, *BKI* 134/2–3 (1978), 207–74; Th. G. Th. Pigeaud and H. J. de Graaf, *Islamic states in Java, 1500–1700. Eight Dutch books and articles by H. J. de Graaf, as summarised by Theodore G. Th. Pigeaud, with a comprehensive list of sources and a general index of names composed by H. J. de Graaf*, The Hague 1976; M. C. Ricklefs, Dipanagara's early inspirational experience, *BKI* 130/2–3 (1974), 227–58; M. C. Ricklefs, *Jogjakarta under Sultan Mangkubumi, 1749–1792. A history of the division of Java*, London 1974; M. C. Ricklefs, *The seen and unseen worlds in Java, 1726–1749. History, literature and Islam in the court of Pakubuwana II*, St Leonards, New South Wales 1998; M. C. Ricklefs, *War, culture and economy in Java 1677–1726. Asian and European imperialism in the early Kartasura period*, Sydney 1993; P. J. Zoetmulder, *Pantheism and monism in Javanese suluk-literature. Islamic and Indian mysticism in an Indonesian setting*, ed. and trans. M. C. Ricklefs, Leiden 1995.

The colonial period circa 1830–1942

G. W. J. Drewes, *Drie Javaansche goeroe's. Hun leven, onderricht en messiasprediking*, Leiden 1925; G. W. J. Drewes, The struggle between Javanism and Islam as illustrated by the Sěrat Děrmagandul, *BKI* 122/3 (1966), 309–65; R. E. Elson, *Village Java under the cultivation system 1830–1870*, Sydney 1994; C. Fasseur, *The politics of colonial exploitation. Java, the Dutch and the cultivation system*, trans. R. E. Elson and Ary Kraal, Ithaca NY 1992; Nancy K. Florida, Reading the unread in traditional Javanese literature, *Indonesia* 44 (1987), 1–15; C. Guillot, *L'affaire Sadrach. Un essai de christianisation à Java au XIXe siècle*, Paris 1981; Muhamad Hisyam, *Caught between three fires. The Javanese pangulu under the Dutch colonial administration, 1882–1942*, Jakarta 2001; V. J. H. Houben, *Kraton and Kumpeni. Surakarta and Yogyakarta, 1830–1870*, Leiden 1994; Sartono Kartodirdjo, *The peasants' revolt of Banten in 1888. Its conditions, courses and sequel. A case study of social movements in Indonesia*, The Hague 1966; Sartono Kartodirdjo, *Protest movements in rural Java. A study of agrarian unrest in the nineteenth and twentieth centuries*, Singapore 1973; A. P. E. Korver, *Sarekat Islam 1912–1916. Opkomst, bloei en structuur van Indonesië's eerste massabeweging*, Amsterdam 1982; George D. Larson, *Prelude to revolution. Palaces and politics in Surakarta, 1912–1942*, Dordrecht and Providence 1987; Ruth T. McVey, *The rise of Indonesian communism*, Ithaca NY 1965; Ruth T. McVey, Taman Siswa and the Indonesian national awakening, *Indonesia* 4 (1967), 128–49; Akira Nagazumi, *The dawn of Indonesian nationalism. The early years of the Budi Utomo, 1908–1918*, Tokyo 1972; Deliar Noer, *The modernist Muslim movement in Indonesia, 1900–1942*, Singapore 1973; C. Poensen, *Brieven over den Islām uit de binnenlanden van Java*, Leiden 1886; Takashi Shiraishi, *An age in motion. Popular radicalism in Java, 1912–1926*, Ithaca NY 1990; Robert Van Niel, *The emergence of the modern Indonesian elite*, The Hague and Bandung 1960; Robert Van Niel, *Java's northeast coast 1740–1840. A study in colonial encroachment and dominance*, Leiden 2005; Michael C. Williams, *Communism, religion and revolt in Banten*, Athens OH 1990.

M. C. Ricklefs

Indonesia: Islam and politics since 1942

The relationship between **Islam and politics in Indonesia since 1942** has often been reshaped, alternating between government co-optation and repression, expansion and contraction. During the Japanese occupation of 1942–5, Muslims in general were sought as a source for support, but in the first phase of Indonesia's independence, President Sukarno (in office 1945–67) strove to keep Islam out of politics. Following the regime change that brought General Suharto to power (in office 1967–98), Muslim activists were first used to counter communism and then violently repressed. Religious piety was encouraged, while the public sphere was kept secular. In the post-Suharto era, Islam has been increasingly present in politics, society, and popular culture, as both a conservative and a progressive force.

1. The Japanese occupation (1942–5)

The Japanese landed on Java and Sumatra in 1942, and the Dutch surrendered quickly to the occupier. As short-lived as it was, the Japanese occupation was formative for the East Indies' political leadership. The Japanese reorganised the territory's local and national bureaucratic apparatus and transformed existing political parties—mostly by rallying members around local, ethnic identities—into broader mass organisations coordinated at the national level. This led to the politicisation of the rural population and the formation of an Indonesian national identity that went beyond regional and ideological lines.

Japan openly attempted to confirm a partnership with Java's Muslim population. Japanese officers trained traditionalist rural Muslim leaders (*kyais*) in their vision of an East Asia Co-Prosperity Sphere and pan-Asian ideology while calling more broadly upon the Indonesian people to fulfil "their duty to defend themselves as an Asiatic race, to defend the religion, the sovereignty, and justice as Muslems [sic], and to support the realisation of *hakko itjoe* [Japanese *hakkō ichiu*, figuratively, the world as one house] as ordained by Allah" (Muhammad Zain Djambek, quoted in M. Slamet, *The holy war "made in Japan,"* Batavia 1946, 12–3).

All Islamic parties dating from the Dutch era were abolished. The Muslim religious leadership was initially merged into a subdivision of the secular mass organisation Gerakan Tiga A (Triple A Movement) called Persiapan Persatoean Oemmat Islam (Preparation of the Unification of the Islamic Community). Beginning in January 1943, this organisation was restructured to form the Majelis Islam A'la Indonesia (MIAI, Islamic Superior Council of Indonesia). Fearing that the MIAI was garnering too much power, the Japanese disbanded it in November of the same year and established in its place the Majelis Syuro Muslimin Indonesia (Masyumi, Consultative Council of Indonesian Muslims).

The new Islamic organisations effected important changes in the religious-political leadership of the country, as the factionalism of colonial-era parties was forcibly eliminated and career politicians were sidelined by religious scholars, whose main interests were in societal issues. With the transition from MIAI to Masyumi, Japan reduced the influence and power of political Islam. Masyumi's leadership was entrusted to members of the country's two civil-society organisations, the modernist Muhammadiyah and the traditionalist Nahdlatul Ulama (NU, lit., Revival of the Ulama), which had emerged in Java in 1912 and 1926, respectively. The Japanese saw them as less politicised than the parties from the colonial era. This shift in approach, granting importance and power to the *kyai*s and *ulama*, has been deemed "the most important aspect of Japanese Islamic politics in 1943" (Benda, 135).

In late December 1944, Japan made a last attempt to embrace Islam. As its defeat drew closer, its propaganda office framed the defence of the occupation regime as a holy war, and Masyumi was eventually allowed its own armed wing, Barisan Hizbullah (lit., Army of God's Party). At this point, Muslim activists were ready to lead the defence of Java against Dutch attempts to reconquer the colony and to shape the politics of an independent Indonesia.

2. Sukarno's leadership: Marginalising Islam (1945–67)

Japan had entrusted Sukarno with the task of leading the nationalist project. In mid-1945, the Panitia Persiapan Kemerdekaan Indonesia (Preparatory Committee for the Independence of Indonesia) was set up, with Japanese consent, as a platform for discussing the foundations of the Indonesian state-to-be. Its religious wing—represented by Sarekat Islam (Islamic Union), Masyumi, and other groups—advocated the formal recognition of Islam's importance in the country's identity and the inclusion in the constitution of a requirement for all Muslims to follow *sharīʿa* law. This demand, which came to be known as the Jakarta Charter, was opposed by the secular nationalists in the Komite Nasional Indonesia Pusat (Central Indonesian Committee), which had supplanted the earlier Preparatory Committee on 29 August 1945. Eventually, the Central Indonesian Committee succeeded in substituting for the Jakarta Charter a broad statement on freedom of religion and Sukarno's non-confessional state philosophy called Pancasila (Five Principles). During a speech delivered on 1 June 1945, Sukarno described Pancasila as the call for a nation based on nationalism *(kebangsaan)*, humanitarianism *(perkemanusiaan)*, deliberation amongst representatives *(permusyawaratan-perwakilan)* social welfare *(kesejahteraan)*, and belief in the one and only God *(ketuhanan yang maha Esa)*. Sukarno saw this as the only suitable strategy for keeping Indonesia united from Aceh to Timor. As the Islamist movement continued to oppose this solution, belief in the one and only God became the first principle.

To appease further those who called for a stronger presence of Islam in the new state's structure, Sukarno declared that the 1945 text was to be considered a "temporary" constitution (Endang Saifuddin Anshari, *Piagam Jakarta 22 Juni 1945. Sebuah konsensus nasional tentang dasar negara Republik Indonesia 1945–1959*, Jakarta 1997[2], 48), suggesting that the Indonesian people could later elect members of parliament committed to the institutionalisation of Islam through legal and constitutional reform. This promise resonated also with other political constituencies. Expecting a first round of elections in the near future, the Islamic parties advanced an aggressive propaganda in favour of an Islamic state. Muslim religious scholars, politicians, and intellectuals became involved in a debate on the relationship between Pancasila and Islam. Many books and pamphlets were published, either affirming the compatibility of these two frameworks and reassuring pious Muslims that a Pancasila state would allow them to freely pursue devout lives, or arguing that, in order to fulfil their religious duties, they had to establish an Islamic state. Efforts in the latter direction went beyond parliamentary politics, as the 1940s and 1950s witnessed an archipelago-wide Islamist movement referred to as Darul Islam that fought for the creation of an Islamic state of Indonesia (Negara Islam Indonesia).

Japan's defeat in the Second World War and its sudden withdrawal from the archipelago presented the Dutch with an opportunity to attempt to regain control of their former colony. However, the Dutch invasion of Java and Sumatra in July 1947 and Sukarno's agreement to interact with them through diplomatic channels ignited grassroots protest. Youth and leftist groups as well as Islamist activists took militant action against the Dutch and advanced their respective political agendas: members of the Communist Party proclaimed a communist republic in Madiun, East Java, in 1948, and Darul Islam proclaimed an Islamic republic in West Java in 1949. The decade following Sukarno's proclamation of independence was thus characterised by militancy across the archipelago, with part of the population fighting to make Indonesia an Islamic state. The Madiun movement was crushed immediately, but Darul Islam remained active in Java, Sumatra, and Kalimantan until 1965.

Although political parties had been formed as early as October 1945, elections for parliament and the constitutional assembly were not held until 1955, against the background of the non-aligned movement's Asia-Africa conference in Bandung. The four major parties included Masyumi, which retained its mixture of traditionalist and modernist Muslims; the Partai Sosialis (Socialist Party); the Partai Komunis Indonesia (PKI, Indonesian Communist Party); and the Partai Nasional Indonesia (PNI, Indonesian Nationalist Party), from which Sukarno hailed. By 1955, Nahdlatul Ulama (NU) had split from Masyumi. The former acted as a Java-based organisation representing mostly rural Muslims, while the latter represented modernist urban Muslims across the nation. This split was reflected in the elections: Masyumi dominated election results outside of Java and came in second at the national level, Nahdlatul Ulama came in third, while two other largely Java-based parties, the Indonesian Nationalist Party and the Communist Party, came in first and fourth (in Java, the PKI was the second-largest party).

The results of the parliamentary elections of 1955 and regional elections of 1957–8 gave the impression that communism was poised to achieve power at the national level, further fuelling social tensions. Regional rebellions in Sumatra, Java, and Kalimantan continued to challenge the central authority of the Jakarta government. In 1957 Sukarno declared martial law and soon thereafter disbanded the cabinet to form an emergency government that excluded both the Communist Party and Masyumi (which would eventually be dissolved in 1960, largely because of its involvement in the regional rebellions). At about the same time, Sukarno had begun to elaborate a new political philosophy, known as Guided Democracy. Sukarno's commitment to this new ideology, the deterioration in his health, and conflict with Malaysia seemed to leave Nahdlatul Ulama as the last bastion against a communist takeover. Violent clashes between NU affiliates and Communist Party members had begun in Java as early as 1963–4, preparing the ground for the involvement of rural Muslims in the anti-communist violence of 1965. Sukarno's rule faded gradually, as the army launched an anti-communist campaign and took political control under the leadership of General Suharto. Sukarno had marginalised Islam in the 1950s and early 1960s, but the emerging new regime was able to co-opt disaffected Muslims, although the alliance would be short-lived.

3. Suharto's New Order: Co-opting Islam (1967–98)

Suharto came to power in the aftermath of the alleged communist coup of 30 September 1965. The formal transfer of power from Sukarno to Suharto was only completed in 1967, but Suharto undertook efforts to eradicate communism immediately after the alleged coup. There are unconfirmed estimates that between 500,000 and two million people (actual and suspected members of the PKI and their families and many ethnic Chinese) were killed in the following twelve months; many more were tortured, assaulted, or raped. As several army battalions in Java were thought to be infiltrated by the Communist Party, much of the violence was committed by ordinary citizens mobilised by various actors, including members of Muhammadiyah, the Nahdlatul Ulama's youth wing (NU Ansor), rural *kyai*s, and former Darul Islam activists. Communists were labelled *kuffar* (unbelievers), and killing them was equated with participating in holy war.

The political instrumentalisation of Islam continued throughout the 1970s and 1980s. Beginning in 1966, the government deliberated over the obligation for all Indonesians to declare affiliation with one of five officially recognised religions (Islam, Catholicism, Protestantism, Hinduism, and Buddhism), and, in its five-year development plan, it dedicated funds to the building of mosques throughout the country, village by village. At the same time, the regime encouraged individual piety as a marker of anti-communism. In 1975 Suharto supported the establishment of the Majelis Ulama Indonesia (MUI, Indonesian Ulama Council) which was to serve as a government-sponsored body in charge of legitimising Suharto's policies in Islamic terms. These policies went in parallel to the religious revival that was taking shape across the Muslim world following the resurgence of Egypt's Muslim Brotherhood under the presidency of Anwar al-Sādāt (1970–81), the Wahhābī emergence on the global scene, Zia-ul-Haq's Islamisation drive in Pakistan, the Iranian Revolution, and the Soviet invasion of Afghanistan. As Muslim groups adopted an increasingly activist stand, the distinction between piety and politics became increasingly difficult to maintain. One early move of the regime was to stop sending Indonesians to study in the Middle East (Cairo, Mecca, and Medina had been favourite destinations) and to privilege graduate programmes in the United States, Canada, Europe, and Australia in order to create a new elite of religious intellectuals committed to a "modern" approach to Islam and to the separation between religion and politics.

To counter Suharto's policies, former Masyumi leader Mohammad Natsir (d. 1993) founded in 1967 the Dewan Dakwah Islamiyah Indonesia (Indonesian Islamic Mission Council) as an Islamising force "from below," although its ultimate goal remained to create a stronger link between Islam and the state. The broadening of its activities from the 1970s onwards was made possible primarily through Saudi Arabian support which followed the increase in petroleum prices and the distribution of petrodollars across the global *umma*. A different strategy was embraced by other former Masyumi members who had joined Parmusi (Partai Muslimin Indonesia, Indonesian Muslims' Party): under the impression that the regime had chosen Islam as its political ally, they requested, unsuccessfully, in 1968 the reintegration of the Jakarta Charter into the constitution.

To ensure full control of the political sphere and to keep political Islam from gaining ground, the Suharto New Order regime counterbalanced co-optation with repression. Suharto distanced himself from Islamic piety, and the government increased the number of Christians in the military and the administration and created an environment that privileged Christianity (rather than Islam) amongst Communist Party sympathisers. Nahdlatul Ulama had enjoyed the regime's favour under Sukarno and initially Suharto, too, but it was marginalised after coming out of the 1971 national elections as the second-strongest party, losing control of the Ministry of Religion (which it had held since 1953) and suffering funding cuts to its religious-education programmes. In 1973–4 the government proposed a new marriage bill that replaced the various religious laws by a unified national law, causing much discontent and unrest among Muslims, especially Muslim students. In 1973, Islamic parties formed the new Partai Persatuan Pembangunan (PPP, United Development Party).

In anticipation of the 1977 elections, the regime further restricted the impact of Islam as a social and political force in the country. The army crushed the militant underground group Komando Jihad, which had, in the mid-1970s, challenged government control; in response to the marriage bill protests, the government issued the Normalisation of Campus Life ordinance, which centralised all campus associations and deprived them of both autonomy of action and choice of leadership. After a few years of "Pancasila indoctrination" courses for the general population, the government announced in 1983 the policy of *asas tunggal* (lit., the one and only principle), which required all organisations to declare Pancasila their sole foundational principle.

The strategy of de-politicisation of religion was quite successful. The prominent Muslim intellectual Nurcholish Madjid (d. 2005), who had graduated with a Ph.D. degree from the University of Chicago, sanctioned this approach in 1970, with the slogan "Islam yes, Islamic party no!" By 1984 Nahdlatul Ulama left politics, withdrew from the Partai Persatuan Pembangunan, and returned to a purely socio-religious agenda. The effects were visible in the PPP's electoral results: the Islamic party won just under thirty percent of the vote in 1977, less than twenty-eight percent in 1982, and only sixteen percent in 1987. Yet at the same time the repression of university activism pushed student discontent underground and into mosques, fuelling the emerging Tarbiyah (lit., education) movement. Organising young Muslims in study groups, the Tarbiyah movement would become the basis for the later emergence of Islamist groups, such as the Partai Keadilan Sejahtera (PKS, Justice and Prosperity Party) and Hizb ut Tahrir Indonesia (HTI, Liberation Party–Indonesia branch).

Beginning in the late 1970s and continuing through the 1980s and 1990s, students in high schools and universities became active in Islamist groups, which were largely inspired by Egypt's Muslim Brotherhood. In addition to the works of Ḥasan al-Bannā (d. 1949), they also read and discussed Abū l-Aʿlā Mawdūdī (d. 1979) and the Iranian intellectual ʿAlī Sharīʿatī (d. 1977), the Iranian Revolution having provided additional inspiration to Sunnī activists. Some of the groups aspired to create an Islamic state of Indonesia, often forging connections to the older Darul Islam movement, but many of them were concerned solely with spiritual renewal and *dakwah* (Ar., *daʿwa*, appeal for adherence and support, missionary work). By 1990, Sunnī orthodoxy had become prevalent at the expense of both "Javanism" and other alternative, local, expressions of piety.

After twenty-five years of marginalisation of Islam in the public sphere, Suharto changed his approach in order to capitalise on the electoral potential of Muslim voters. Since the 1977 elections, the pro-Suharto Partai Golongan Karya (Party of the Functional Groups, Golkar) had brought in many Islamic teachers and leaders, using them to counter the Partai Persatuan Pembangunan's argument that Muslims must always choose an Islamic party (R. William Liddle, Indonesia 1977. The New Order's second parliamentary election, *Asian Survey* 18, 1978, 181). From the late 1980s onwards, however, Suharto's New Order regime began to openly support grassroots Islamisation and to re-enlist the help of Islam in countering "latent" communism. In 1989 the government reinforced religious education in public schools, and in 1991 it lifted the ban on headscarves in government schools and offices. Throughout the 1990s Islamic courts were given powers equal to those of civil and military courts, and Christian military officers were replaced with "green generals" (high-ranking officers known to be sympathetic towards Islam). The presidential family undertook the *ḥajj* to Mecca, and Suharto discontinued the national sports lottery, supported the opening of the first Islamic bank, and endorsed the creation of the Ikatan Cendekiawan Muslim se-Indonesia (ICMI, All-Indonesia Union of Muslim Intellectuals), under the leadership of B. J. Habibie (b. 1936). The government also recognised the Palestinian Authority as a state.

This strategy allowed the regime to enlist the support of both moderate and extremist Muslim groups during the political campaign of 1996–7. Anti-regime intellectuals, students, NGO workers, and "ordinary citizens" had organised themselves in small political groups, but, with the elections approaching, they coalesced around the Partai Demokrasi Indonesia (PDI, Indonesian Democracy Party) and Megawati Sukarnoputri (b. 1947), Sukarno's daughter and a pro-democracy politician in her own right.

Suharto's co-optation strategy was largely successful. His opposition to Megawati's movement relied heavily on the military and on Muslim organisations, including the Majelis Ulama Indonesia, the ICMI, the Dewan Dakwah Islamiyah Indonesia, and numerous leaders from the Nahdlatul Ulama and the Muhammadiyah. Following the riots that destroyed the Partai Demokrasi Indonesia headquarters in Jakarta, Amien Rais (b. 1944), then chairman of Muhammadiyah and head of ICMI's council of experts, stated that "people power was unacceptable to Indonesia's cultural traditions and … Muhammadiyah's masses could be brought in to counteract the anti-regime forces" (Porter, 175). The head of NU Ansor Youth declared that its members were "ready to help [the military] to eliminate the new communist movement" (Porter, 176). Abdurrahman Wahid (d. 2009), long-time chairman of Nahdlatul Ulama and later to become president, declared his support for Golkar, because it protected the unity of the Muslim vote. In reality, the Muslim vote was split: the Partai Persatuan Pembangunan took a mildly anti-regime stand and absorbed part of the PDI's Muslim electorate, and Golkar won the elections.

4. Reformasi: Reforming Islam (1998–2017)

The 1997 financial crisis that had begun with the fall of the Thai *baht* currency eventually reached Indonesia, further fuelling domestic discontent. Students continued to demonstrate, demanding Suharto's resignation. When Suharto eventually stepped down on 21 May 1998 and Vice-President B. J. Habibie took over, the protests did not stop. At the same time, the nomination of Habibie, the former minister of research and technology and head of ICMI, appeared to appease those among the newly emergent pious middle class critical of the Suharto regime and seeking change.

The Habibie presidency lasted only seventeen months (1998–9) but oversaw the country's first free and fair elections since 1955. Of the forty-eight parties that participated in the 1999 elections, at least fifteen had an explicitly Islamic profile, but only three made it into parliament, together gaining thirty-two percent of the vote. The Islamic party that would become most influential in Indonesian politics in the following decades, the Partai Keadilan Sejahtera (PKS, formerly the Patai Keadilan, PK, Justice Party), did not initially garner enough votes to enter parliament. The party received less than two percent of the vote in 1999, but, by 2004, the PKS was the seventh largest party, with 7.3 percent, and in 2009 the fourth largest, with 7.9 percent. Following several scandals, however, the PKS won only 6.8 percent of the elections of 2014, whereas the Islamic vote had generally increased compared to previous elections, returning to the thirty-two percent of 1999. Despite a general Islamisation of society and politics, Islamic parties had been unable, by the late 2010s, to establish themselves as a stable presence in parliament. This was a result partly of the large number of parties and their inability to overcome their differences and partly of the fact that by the early 2000s religious training had become so prevalent across all parties that many Muslims did not feel the need to vote for an explicitly Islamic party.

The PKS had its roots in the Tarbiyah movement of the 1980s and was caught between the necessity to commit to the democratic process it participated in and its advocacy for a stronger presence of Islam in the political and legal fields, or even an Islamic state. This dilemma led the party to engage in a variety of activities, ranging from secular-nationalist to openly Islamist, and occasionally even violent. Thus the PKS joined events organised by radical groups, such as the Majelis Mujahidin Indonesia (MMI, Indonesian Mujahidin Council), the Front Pembela Islam (FPI, Islamic Defenders' Front), and Hizb ut Tahrir Indonesia (see more on this below).

The resurgence of Islam notwithstanding, the first post-Suharto elections saw the victory of secular parties, as Megawati's Partai Demokrasi Indonesia Perjuangan (PDI-P, Indonesian Democracy Party of Struggle) and a "new" Golkar obtained most of the votes. Parliament nominated as president the chairman of Nahdlatul Ulama, Abdurrahman Wahid (in office 1999–2001). An advocate of religious tolerance, Wahid promoted the formation of the first Shīʿī civil-society organisation, the Ikatan Jama'ah Ahlul Bait Indonesia (All-Indonesian Assembly of *ahl al-bayt* Associations) and the inclusion of Confucianism as a sixth official religion and, more generally, appointed "liberal" Muslims, secularists, and Christians to important cabinet positions. After just twenty-one months, however, he was impeached, and Megawati, Wahid's vice-president, was nominated president (in office 2001–4). As in much of the post-Suharto era, Megawati forged an alliance with the religious constituency by nominating as vice-president Hamzah Haz (b. 1940), the chairman of the Partai Persatuan Pembangunan. It was under her presidency that parliament debated, although eventually rejected, the proposal to insert the Jakarta Charter into the constitution, which would have required Muslims to follow Islamic law.

Susilo Bambang Yudhoyono (b. 1949) was the first president to be directly elected, and he held office for two consecutive terms (2004–14). Under his presidency, with the Islamist Partai Keadilan Sejahtera joining his coalition, Islamism gained increasing sway over Indonesian society, mostly at the expense of liberally minded Muslims and religious minorities. His successor Joko "Jokowi" Widodo (b. 1961) adopted a different approach. Unlike Yudhoyono, Jokowi avoided close association with any Islamic group and forged alliances with non-Muslims. More generally, he curbed the activities of Islamist groups and encouraged Nahdlatul Ulama's campaign to promote a localised approach to Islam as a tolerant counter-discourse to rising extremism. Still, for the presidential elections of 2019 he chose as his running mate Ma'ruf Amin (b. 1943), head of Nahdlatul Ulama's *syuriah* council and chairman of Majelis Ulama Indonesia.

5. Current issues in Islam in Indonesia

The years following the fall of Suharto witnessed an advance in democratic practices, especially in formal politics, but also a further rise of Islamism and various reactions to it.

The immediate post-Suharto years were marked by several violent confrontations between Muslims and non-Muslims, usually referred to as "communal," "sectarian," or "ethno-religious" and later framed as either *jihād* or terrorism. These clashes, which took place most notably in Java, Kalimantan, and the Moluccas, witnessed the instrumentalisation of religion, both Islam and Christianity, as a force to mobilise masses along communal lines. Research has shown that the tensions arose from resource-driven land-ownership competition, shifts in patron-client relations, and village-level disagreements.

Under the Wahid and Megawati presidencies, a law was passed allowing greater regional autonomy, paving the way for the gradual spread of religiously inspired local regulations. In the early 2000s, municipalities across the archipelago passed laws determining, amongst other things, female dress-codes and night-time freedom of movement and requiring that public servants be proficient in Qurʾān recitation. This law also facilitated the resolution of the decades-long conflict between the national government in Jakarta and the westernmost province of Aceh; the brokered peace agreement following the 2004 Indian Ocean tsunami granted regional autonomy to Aceh, enabling the implementation of Islamic law.

At the same time, an Islamic popular culture emerged. In late 2013, the chairman of Partai Kebangkitan Bangsa (National Awakening Party) chose Rhoma Irama (b. 1946) as their presidential candidate for the 2014 elections. Dubbed "the king of *dangdut*," Rhoma Irama had popularised this musical art form as a tool of *daʿwah* in the 1970s and 1980s, finding its roots in a combination of Arab-inspired Malay orchestral performance and Islamic content. His religious commitment and political involvement—he had campaigned for the Partai Persatuan Pembangunan in the late 1970s—earned Irama the opposition of the Suharto regime. Since the fall of Suharto, *dangdut* was one of many avenues that made Islam accessible to broad audiences; the loosening on censorship facilitated the spread of religious literature (in fiction, newspapers, and Islamist magazines), while a view of spiritual piety as "urban" and "modern" encouraged a return to Ṣūfism.

Islamic extremism thrived in the twenty years after Suharto's fall. In the early 2000s several terrorist attacks across the archipelago targeted churches, hotels, and other civilian locations. Amongst the many incidents, the Bali bombing of 12 October 2002 caused the greatest numbers of victims and had the largest impact on the media. Because of its timing and other evidence, it is believed that the perpetrators were members of Jemaah Islamiyah (see below) and had connections with al-Qāʿida. There were also groups such as the Front Pembela Islam (FPI), formed in August 1998, which enjoyed the support of the army and police, who deployed members of the group in the attacks on pro-democracy activists. FPI's stated aim was to fulfil the Qurʾānic mandate of *al-amr bi-l-maʿrūf wa-l-nahy ʿan al-munkar* (enjoining good and preventing evil), and its members regularly raided Jakarta's night clubs and bars, revealing their roots in urban thuggery *(premanisme)*.

The Majelis Mujahidin Indonesia (MMI) had stronger Islamist ties. It was established in August 2000, when about two thousand people gathered to discuss the necessity of implementing Islamic law and establishing an Islamic state in Indonesia. The leading figure at the congress was Abu Bakar Ba'asyir (b. 1938), an Indonesian of Ḥaḍramī descent who had been involved in organising radical Muslims since the 1970s, mostly through the operation of the conservative Islamic boarding school Pesantren Mukmin in Solo (Surakarta, in central Java), which he ran with Abdullah Sungkar, another Ḥaḍramī. Both had been arrested in 1978 for their involvement with the Islamist *jihādī* group Jemaah Islamiyah but had, after a self-imposed exile in Malaysia, returned to Indonesia. Because of the connection between Majelis Mujahidin Indonesia and Jemaah Islamiyah and MMI's own links to al-Qāʿida affiliates, MMI was classified as a terrorist organisation by the United States Department of State in June 2017.

Another important Islamist organisation was the Indonesian branch of Hizb ut Tahrir (Ar., Ḥizb al-Taḥrīr), founded by the Jordanian Islamist Taqī al-Dīn al-Nabhānī (d. 1977) in 1953, in Jerusalem. Present in the archipelago since the 1980s as part of the underground Tarbiyah movement, Hizb ut Tahrir Indonesia (HTI) came into the open in the post-Suharto era. In 2007, Jakarta hosted the first international Caliphate Conference, including about 100,000 Indonesians. In the following decade the group expanded considerably throughout society, regularly calling for the implementation of *sharīʿa* law and the establishment of a caliphate. Hizb ut Tahrir Indonesia was eventually banned in July 2017 (see below).

Islamist groups became increasingly vocal during the Yudhoyono presidency of 2004–14. One of the reasons lies in the growing influence of Majelis Ulama Indonesia (MUI), which was encouraged by Yudhoyono himself. After Reformasi, MUI had come to be seen as a quasi-legislative body charged with ensuring Indonesian Muslims' conformity to a "correct" version of Islam and with providing guidance to various government offices. MUI came to play a central role in matters concerning Islam (Yudhoyono, in Ricklefs, 285). Perhaps its most impactful *fatwā* so far (issued 2005) has been the one condemning pluralism, liberalism, and secularism as Western and un-Islamic. Exacerbating religious and social intolerance, it also gave rise to a country-wide wave of violence against Aḥmadīs and Shīʿīs that lasted for more than a decade. Supported by another *fatwā* (also issued 2005), which specifically condemned the Aḥmadīs as heretics, local governments went further, limiting their freedom and forbidding them from teaching their creed and worship; the minister of religious affairs even suggested that all Shīʿīs should be forcibly "converted" to Sunnī Islam.

Mounting extremism also gave rise to growing opposition, which manifested itself in many ways, mostly amongst youth belonging to the traditionalist organisation Nahdlatul Ulama. Youth groups promoting progressive and "liberal" Islamic agendas had emerged from the Nahdlatul Ulama throughout the 1980s and 1990s, but it was only in the post-Suharto era that they found it possible to be more assertive. Building on previous experiments, the Jaringan Islam Liberal (Liberal Islamic Network) formed in 2001 and openly challenged views held by Indonesian Muslims in order to promote Qurʾānic interpretations that took into consideration social context and circumstance (Luthfi Assyaukanie, in Ricklefs, 357). Similar progressive groups were formed by young leaders of the reformist Muhammadiyah, although the Jaringan Intelektual Muda Muhammadiyah (Muhammadiyah Young Intellectuals' Network) remained less influential.

Another counter-discourse appeared under the label "Islam Nusantara" (lit., Islam of the archipelago), a scholarly approach to Islam in Indonesia. It was made popular by Nahdlatul Ulama's 2015 congress and received considerable attention internationally, largely because Indonesians appeared to have been less involved with the Islamic State/Daesh (Dāʿish) than did Muslims in other countries. Islam Nusantara rested on the historical narrative that Islam gained a foothold in Southeast Asia gradually, blending with existing cultural and devotional expressions and allowing the emergence of an Islam that was inherently "more tolerant" than Islam in the Middle East (in this context largely equated with Saudi Wahhābism) and an antidote to radical, *jihādī* groups. Although it emerged from the scholarly tradition of Nahdlatul Ulama, Islam Nusantara was embraced by government anti-terror agencies in their anti-radicalisation programmes; by the Ministry of Religion, to teach Islam as a peaceful, moderate, and compassionate force; and by President Jokowi and Vice-President Jusuf Kalla (b. 1942), who advocated its exportation to the Middle East. Critique of this approach was also widespread, especially amongst Muslims who felt that localised Islam was a deviation from Islamic orthodoxy originating in the Arabian Peninsula.

Bibliography
Harry Jindrich Benda, *The crescent and the rising sun. Indonesian Islam under the Japanese occupation, 1942–1945*, The Hague 1958; Julia Day Howell, Modernity and Islamic spirituality in Indonesia's new Sufi orders, in Martin van Bruinessen and Julia Day Howell (eds.), *Sufism and the "modern" in Islam*, London 2007; Christopher R. Duncan, *Violence and vengeance. Religious conflict and its aftermath in eastern Indonesia*, Ithaca 2013; Greg Fealy and Sally White (eds.), *Expressing Islam. Religious life and politics in Indonesia* (Singapore 2008), 174–91; R. Michael Feener, *Muslim legal thought in modern Indonesia*, Cambridge 2007; Chiara Formichi, *Islam and the making of the nation*, Leiden 2012; David D. Harnish and Anne K. Rasmussen, *Divine inspirations. Music and Islam in Indonesia*, New York 2011; James B. Hoesterey, ACI Indonesia—Rebranding Islam. Public diplomacy, soft power, and the making of "moderate Islam," 20 April 2016 (https://sites.nd.edu/contendingmodernities/2016/04/20/aci-indonesia-rebranding-islam-public-diplomacy-soft-power-and-the-making-of-moderate-islam/); Carool Kersten, *Cosmopolitans and heretics. New Muslim intellectuals and the study of Islam*, London and New York 2011; Donald J. Porter, *Managing politics and Islam in Indonesia*, London and New York 2002; Merle C. Ricklefs, *Islamisation and its opponents in Java. A political, social, cultural and religious history, c. 1930 to the present*, Honolulu 2012.

Chiara Formichi

Iram

Iram is an ancient Arabian name most commonly associated in modern writing with a lost city in southeastern Arabia, the capital of the pre-Islamic people of ʿĀd, whom God destroyed for their disbelief (Cobb, 2:559; Clapp). The meaning of "Iram" has, however, undergone a complex evolution of varied and debated interpretations in both Muslim and European narratives.

Pre-Islamic Nabatean epigraphy uses *ʾrm* as a toponym in northwestern Arabia (Savignac, 591; Macdonald, 3:76, n. 171; Hoyland, 39–40), near the modern border between Jordan and Saudi Arabia. The inscriptions support Sprenger (144), who postulated that Iram was in the Ḥismā region, based on its identification as an Arabised form of the "Aramaya" listed in Ptolemy's geography (vi, 7, 27). The historian-geographer al-Hamdānī (d. c.333/945) notes a well, Biʾr Iram, in the Ḥismā (*Ṣifat*, 243), also suggestive that Iram was a pre-Islamic northern Arabian locale.

1. Iram in the Qurʾān

The name "Iram" also appears in Q 89:6–8, where it is mentioned with a pre-Islamic people, the ʿĀd, as an example of God's power to smite tyrants. Whether the Qurʾānic "Iram" was intended to refer to the pre-Islamic northern Arabian toponym is unclear: the precise meaning of the verses hinges on deciphering their ambiguous vocabulary and case vocalisations, and early Muslim Qurʾān readers adopted several possibilities (al-Khaṭīb, 10:418–20, has a list of attested vocalisations). One tradition reads the phrase in verses 89:6–7 as ʿĀd^{in} Iram^{a}, implying that the Iram were a people related to the ʿĀd. An alternative reading has the verses ʿĀd^{i} Iram^{a}, a possessive construction that could make "Iram" the name of the ʿĀd's city. The description in Q 89:7 of Iram as *dhāt al-ʿimād* also gave rise to disagreement. Some exegetes interpreted it as meaning that the Iram were giants, whereas others interpreted the words to mean either "of columns" (suggesting that Iram was a substantial city) or "of tent poles" (suggesting that the Iram were a nomadic people). Each interpretation is grammatically permissible, and most pre-modern exegetes remained undecided as to whether Iram denoted a city or a tribe (Muqātil, 5:687–8; al-Akhfash, 2:578; al-Ṭabarī, *Jāmiʿ*, 30:218–20; al-Qurṭubī, 20:30–2).

The context of the verses in Q 89 supports an interpretation of Iram as a location inhabited by the ʿĀd, and al-Biqāʿī (d. 885/1480), one of the few pre-modern exegetes to adopt an expressly narrative (not syntactic) interpretation of the Qurʾān, asserts that Iram was the ʿĀd's city, not a tribe (8:416). Conversely, "Iram" appears frequently in pre-Islamic poetry as a reference to a bygone people and never as a reference to a city. Pre-Islamic poets cite Iram, often with ʿĀd and occasionally with names of other ancient peoples, to express the idea that all things, even powerful peoples, inevitably pass away (Imruʾ al-Qays, 208; ʿAmr b. Qamīʾa, in al-Buḥturī, *al-Ḥamāsa*, 1:327; Jandal b. Ashmaṭ al-ʿAnazī, in Abū Tammām, 162; Labīd, 34, 108, 209, 378). The Iram also feature metaphorically in violent threats, in which a poet boasts he will dispatch his enemies to perdition, whence they will join the dead Iram (Rashīd b. Rumayḍ al-ʿAnazī, in al-Baṣrī 1:320; see also the early Muslim-era ʿAmr b. Maʿdī Karib, 184). Al-Ḥārith b. Ḥilizza (fl. 550–60 C.E.) uses the adjective *iramī* to connote age, physical strength, or noble equanimity (Ibn al-Anbārī, 492; al-Tabrīzī, 472). Al-Aghlab al-ʿIjlī (d. c.20/641), a pre-Islamic poet whose long career extended into the early Islamic era, compares a leader to the Iram, also possibly as a metaphor of nobility (Ibn al-Anbārī, 493). The coupling of Iram with ʿĀd in Q 89:6–7 may thus be drawing from the familiar poetic lexicon for bygone peoples, converting names synonymous in poetry with ancient might into warnings of God's power to annihilate unbelievers.

Umayyad and early ʿAbbāsid-era poets also cite Iram as a bygone people, with the same formulae as pre-Islamic poets and with additional allusions to the Qurʾān (al-Qaṭāmī, 100, 103; al-Ḥuṭayʾa, 262; al-Aḥwaṣ al-Anṣārī, in al-Buḥturī *al-Ḥamāsa*, 1:298). Likewise, early genealogists (Ibn Qutayba, 28; al-Ṭabarī, *Taʾrīkh*, 1:204, 207, 216) and lexicographers (al-Khalīl, 8:296; Ibn Durayd, 2:1068) endorsed the definition of the Iram as a people related to the ʿĀd. Al-Khalīl's (d. 175/791) *al-ʿAyn* additionally defines *iram* as a way-marker and/or grave cairn of the ʿĀd, but these definitions are not cited in glosses on Q 89:6–8, and extant texts suggest that most early Muslims probably interpreted the Qurʾān's "Iram" as a powerful nomadic tribe from the ancient Arabian past.

2. Iram becomes a city

The process by which writers reinterpreted Qurʾānic "Iram" as a city had a complex evolution. The toponymic association may have originated to justify the alternative vocalisation, ʿĀd[i] Iram[a], of Q 89:6–7. Al-Azharī's (d. 370/980) *Tahdhīb al-lugha*, the first dictionary to state that "Iram" might refer to the city of the ʿĀd (11:254), cites the Qurʾān scholar al-Farrāʾ (d. 207/822–3) as the source of this interpretation. Al-Farrāʾ's *Maʿānī al-Qurʾān* does argue for the possibility of interpreting "Iram" as a city to explain why Qurʾān readers vocalised Q 89:6–7 as a possessive (3:268), but neither al-Farrāʾ nor al-Azharī is dogmatic, and they accept that "Iram" could also mean a nomadic people related to the ʿĀd.

The impetus for an exclusive interpretation of Iram as a substantial city perhaps derives from factional competition in early Islam. During the Umayyad and early ʿAbbāsid caliphates, an elite faction identified as the Yamāniyya (Southerner Arabs) articulated a boastful communal history in which they portrayed their pre-Islamic forebears as proto-Muslim urban empire-builders, in contrast to their rivals, the Northerner Arabs (known as Maʿadd, Nizār or, later ʿAdnān), whose ancestors they denigrated as primitive nomads (Webb). The Yamāniyya counted the ʿĀd amongst their ancestors, and they interpreted the Qurʾānic Iram as a splendid, many-columned imperial city constructed by the ancient ʿĀd's putative king Shaddād b. ʿĀd, where he lived for the latter part of what was reckoned a reign of five hundred years (Wahb b. Munabbih, 74; Ibn Sharya, 338; al-Hamdānī, *Iklīl*, 8:183; al-Masʿūdī, §827). The location of this Iram was variable: because the Yamāniyya accorded Shaddād a world empire, some placed Iram in Yemen (near Abyan, outside of Aden, or in the Ḥaḍramawt, near modern Oman), while others identified it as the original settlement of Alexandria or Damascus, interpreting those cities' ruined Hellenistic pillars as the remains of Shaddād's "Iram" (al-Masʿūdī, §926, §1143; al-Bakrī, 1:140; al-Andalusī, 1:45–6, 104). Such narratives are ascribed to the first/seventh-century Yamānī scholars Wahb b. Munabbih and ʿUbayd b. Sharya, but the texts probably coalesced in the early third/ninth century, and it was in that century that "Iram" appears in Arabic poetry as a city rather than a tribe (al-Buḥturī, *Dīwān*, 817; al-Hamdānī, *Iklīl*, 8:38; al-Buḥturī elsewhere, *Dīwān*, 1759, follows the older tradition of citing Iram as a tribe).

3. Iram in South Arabia

Whilst third-fourth/ninth-tenth century Iraqi writers remained tentative in identifying Iram variously as a tribe (al-Ṭabarī, *Taʾrīkh*, 1:204, 207; al-Jawharī, 2:1068) or with Damascus, Alexandria, or Yemen (Ibn Khurdādhbih, 76; al-Masʿūdī, §1414; al-Ṭabarī, *Jāmiʿ*, 30:222–3 prefers Yemen), Yemeni writers promoted the interpretation of Iram as a fabulous South Arabian city. The lexicographer Nashwān al-Ḥimyarī (d. 573/1178) rejected the Damascus/Alexandria options in favour of either Aden or Ḥaḍramawt (1:230). The historian-geographer al-Hamdānī (d. c.333/945) was expressly critical of Iraqi historical narratives and placed Iram near Aden (*al-Iklīl*, 8:33, 183). Al-Hamdānī's text is also the earliest extant attestation of wondrous associations with Iram. He noted that storytellers in Ṣanʿāʾ told of Iram's treasures and added a tale that Iram disappeared into the sands, reappearing only once, with its bejewelled splendour intact, to a Bedouin during Muʿāwiya's caliphate (41–60/661–80) (al-Hamdānī, *al-Iklīl*, 8:33, 119, 183; al-Masʿūdī, §1414).

The mystique of Iram as a specifically South Arabian "lost city" gained increasing currency after the story's fourth/tenth-century emergence and appeared in elaborate forms in Iraqi, Syrian, and Egyptian writing (al-Zamakhsharī, 4:735–6; Yāqūt, 1:155–7; al-Ibshīhī, 2:232–3). And the story changed: the initial Yamānī boast of Shaddād as a proto-Muslim subsided, and he was recharacterised into a tyrant who ordered Iram's construction to rival Paradise, only to be smote by God on the eve of the city's completion. The tale borrows motifs from the *Thousand and one nights*, and scholars were roundly critical of its embellishment, rejecting its historicity (al-Masʿūdī, §§1415–6; Yāqūt 1:157; Ibn Khaldūn 1:20–2; Ibn Ḥajar 11:82). Most exegetes contemporary with the growth of Iram's legend in the mediaeval period also criticised the tales and maintained equivocal interpretations of Iram as either a city or a nomadic people (al-Qurṭubī, 20:30–1; Ibn Kathīr, 4:478; al-Bayḍāwī, 2:594).

4. Iram in the Western imagination

The latest chapter of Iram's memorialisation, which decidedly promoted the impression of Iram as a lost South Arabian city, occurred in modern Western literature. Whilst Sprenger echoed the mediaeval Muslim scholarly circumspection when he chided the legendary Yemeni Iram narratives as "nonsense" (199), Washington Irving embraced the marvellous facets of the Arabic tales, and included "Irem" as a fabulous story in his 1832 *The Alhambra* (115–6). The British explorer Charles Doughty travelled through Ḥismā in 1876 and noted Sprenger's placement of Iram in that region, but Doughty added some of Irving's mythopoeic flair, coining a new interpretation of Iram as "the city of columns, the terrestrial paradise" (1:93–4). Doughty influenced twentieth-century British travellers to Arabia, and the orientalist mystique he invoked of romantic adventure about a lost city in inhospitable sands inspired exploration. The efforts of Philby and Thomas to locate the site added a novel conflation of Iram with a second lost-city tradition, that of Ubār/Wabār (Philby 575–6; Thomas 260–5). Mediaeval Arabic literature narrated wondrous tales about Wabār in Arabia's Empty Quarter but did not equate it with the name in Q 89:6–8 (Ibn Qutayba, 27–8; al-Ṭabarī, *Taʾrīkh*, 1:203–4; Yāqūt, 5:356–9). The stories' similar themes, however, merged in English writings, which located Iram-Ubār ("Atlantis of the Sands") in southeastern Arabia. Expeditions uncovered the ruins of a late-mediaeval trading centre in southern Oman, which, despite its late date, became associated in the popular imagination with the pre-Islamic "Qurʾānic Iram" (Fiennes; Clapp). Twentieth-century Muslim Qurʾānic exegesis eschewed such romance: Sayyid Quṭb (d. 1966), like earlier exegetes interprets Iram as an ancient nomadic people (8:156), but Arabic literary figures embrace the wondrous, invoking Iram in mystical narratives as an enigmatic lost city (Jubrān; Ṣaḥrāwī). Archaeologists have sought to reinterpret Q 89:6–8 via excavations in Jordan and have proposed that the Qurʾān's *Iram dhāt al-ʿimād* means a temple of "Iram on a high mount," which they place at a site in the Wādī Rum (Wādī Iram) (Zayadine and Farès-Drappeau, 256), adducing yet another possible interpretation of the Iram puzzle.

Bibliography

Sources

Abū Tammām, *Dīwān al-Waḥshiyyāt*, ed. ʿAbd al-ʿAzīz al-Maymanī, Cairo 1989; al-Akhfash, *Maʿānī al-Qurʾān*, ed. Hudā Maḥmūd Qarrāʿa, 2 vols., Cairo 1990, repr. 2010; ʿAmr b. Maʿdī Karib, *Dīwān*, ed. Muṭāʿ al-Ṭarābīshī, Damascus 1985; Ibn Saʿīd al-Andalusī, *Nashwat al-ṭarab*, ed. Naṣrat ʿAbd al-Raḥmān, 2 vols., Amman 1982; al-Azharī, *Tahdhīb al-lugha*, ed. Muḥammad ʿAbd al-Raḥmān Mukhaymir, 12 vols., Beirut 2004; al-Bakrī, *Muʿjam mā istaʿjam*, ed. Muṣṭafā al-Saqqā, 4 vols., Cairo 1947; Ṣadr al-Dīn al-Baṣrī, *al-Ḥamāsa al-baṣriyya*, ed. ʿĀdil Sulaymān Jamāl, 4 vols., Cairo 1999; al-Bayḍāwī, *Anwār al-tanzīl wa-asrār al-taʾwīl*, 2 vols., Beirut 1999; Burhān al-Dīn al-Biqāʿī, *Naẓm al-durar*, ed. ʿAbd al-Razzāq Ghālib al-Mahdī, 8 vols., Beirut 1995; al-Buḥturī,

Dīwān, ed. Ḥasan Kāmil al-Sayrafī, 5 vols., Cairo 1965–78; al-Buḥturī, *Dīwān al-Ḥamāsa*, ed. Muḥammad Nabīl Ṭarīfī, 2 vols., Beirut 2009; al-Farrāʾ, *Maʿānī al-Qurʾān*, ed. Aḥmad Yūsuf Najātī and Muḥammad ʿAlī al-Najjār, 3 vols., Cairo 1955–71; al-Hamdānī, *al-Iklīl*, vol. 8, ed. Nabīh Amīn Fāris, Princeton 1940; *Ṣifat Jazīrat al-ʿArab*, ed. Muḥammad b. ʿAlī al-Akwaʿ, Ṣanʿāʾ 1990; al-Ḥuṭayʾa, *Dīwān*, ed. Nuʿmān Amīn Ṭāhā, Cairo 1987; Ibn al-Anbārī, *Sharḥ al-qaṣāʾid al-sabʿ al-ṭiwāl al-jāhiliyyāt*, ed. Muḥammad ʿAbd al-Salām Hārūn, Cairo 1963, repr. 2005; Ibn Durayd, *Jamharat al-lugha*, ed. Ramzī Munīr Baʿalbakī, 3 vols., Beirut 1987–8; Ibn Ḥajar al-ʿAsqalānī, *Fatḥ al-bārī*, ed. Naẓar Muḥammad al-Faryābī, 17 vols., Riyadh 2011; Ibn Kathīr, *Tafsīr*, 4 vols., Beirut 1994; Ibn Khaldūn, *al-ʿIbar*, 7 vols., Cairo 1999; Ibn Khurdādhbih, *al-Masālik wa-l-mamālik*, ed. M. J. de Goeje, Leiden 1889; Ibn Qutayba, *al-Maʿārif*, ed. Tharwat ʿUkāsha, Cairo 1960; al-Ibshīhī, *al-Mustaṭraf*, ed. Darwīsh al-Juwaydī, Beirut 1996; Imrūʾ al-Qays, *Dīwān*, ed. Muḥammad Abū l-Faḍl Ibrāhīm, Cairo 1958, repr. 1990; al-Jawharī, *al-Ṣiḥāḥ*, ed. Aḥmad ʿAbd al-Ghaffūr ʿAṭṭār, 6 vols., Cairo 1956; Jubrān Khalīl Jubrān, Irām Dhāt al-ʿImād, *al-Badāʾiʿ wa-l-ṭarāʾif* (Cairo 1923, repr. 2013), 71–85; al-Khalīl b. Aḥmad, *al-ʿAyn*, ed. Mahdī al-Makhzūmī and Ibrāhīm al-Sāmarrāʾī, 8 vols., Baghdad 1980–5; Labīd, *Dīwān*, ed. Iḥsān ʿAbbās, Kuwait 1962; al-Masʿūdī, *Murūj al-dhahab*, ed. Charles Pellat, 7 vols., Beirut 1966–79; Muqātil b. Sulaymān, *Tafsīr*, ed. ʿAbdallāh Maḥmūd Shiḥāta, 5 vols., Cairo 1979–89; Nashwān al-Ḥimyarī, *Shams al-ʿulūm*, ed. Ḥusayn b. ʿAbdallāh al-ʿUmarī, 12 vols., Damascus 1999; al-Qaṭāmī, *Dīwān*, ed. Ibrāhīm al-Sāmarrāʾī and Aḥmad Maṭlūb, Beirut 1960; al-Qurṭubī, *Jāmiʿ aḥkām al-Qurʾān*, ed. Sālim Muṣṭafā al-Badrī, 21 vols., Beirut 2000; Sayyid Quṭub, *Fī ẓilāl al-Qurʾān*, 8 vols., Cairo 1968; al-Ṭabarī, *Jāmiʿ al-bayān*, ed. Ṣidqī Jamīl al-ʿAṭṭār, 30 vols., Beirut 1999; al-Ṭabarī, *Taʾrīkh al-rusul wa-l-mulūk*, ed. Muḥammad Abū l-Faḍl Ibrāhīm, 11 vols., Cairo 1960–77; al-Khaṭīb al-Tabrīzī, *Sharḥ al-qaṣāʾid al-ʿashr*, ed. Muḥammad Muḥyī l-Dīn ʿAbd al-Ḥamīd, Cairo, n.d.; ʿUbayd b. Sharya, *Akhbār al-Yaman*, ed. ʿAbd al-ʿAzīz al-Maqāliḥ, Cairo 1996; Wahb b. Munabbih, *al-Tījān*, ed. ʿAbd al-ʿAzīz al-Maqāliḥ, Cairo 1996; Yāqūt, *Muʿjam al-buldān*, 7 vols., Beirut 1957; al-Zamakhsharī, *al-Khashshāf*, ed. Muḥammad ʿAbd al-Salām Shāhīn, 4 vols., Beirut 1995.

STUDIES

Nicholas Clapp, *The road to Ubar*, Boston 1999; Paul M. Cobb, Iram, *EQ*; Charles Doughty, *Arabia deserta*, 2 vols., new ed., London 1936; Ranulph Fiennes, *Atlantis of the sands*, London 1992; H. St J. Philby, Rubʿ Al Khali, *Journal of the Royal Central Asian Society* 19 (1932) 569–86; Robert Hoyland, Mount Nebo, Jabal Ramm, and the status of Christian Palestinian Aramaic and Old Arabic in Late Roman Palestine and Arabia, in Michael Macdonald (ed.), *The development of Arabic as a written language* (Oxford 2010), 29–46; Washington Irving, *The Alhambra*, ed. William T. Lenehan and Andrew B. Myers, Boston 1983; ʿAbd al-Laṭīf al-Khaṭīb, *Muʿjam al-qirāʾāt*, Damascus 2000; M. C. A. Macdondald, *Literacy and identity in pre-Islamic Arabia*, Farnham UK and Burlington VT 2009; ʿAbd al-Salām Ṣaḥrāwī, al-Riḥla ilā Iram Dhāt al-ʿImād, *Alif* 32 (2009), 155–70; M. Raphael Savignac, Notes de voyage. Le sanctuaire d'Allat à Iram, *Revue Biblique* 41 (1932), 581–97; Aloys Sprenger, *Die alte Geographie Arabiens*, Bern 1875; Bertram Thomas, Ūbār. The Atlantis of the Sands of Rubʿ al Khali, *Journal of the Royal Central Asian Society* 20/2 (1933), 259–65; Peter Webb, Yemeni Arab identity in Abbasid Iraq. From the sublime to the ridiculous, in Walter Pohl and Rutger Kramer (ed.), *Empires and communities in the post-Roman and Islamic world*, Oxford 2019; Fawzi Zayadine and Saba Farès-Drappeau, Two North-Arabian inscriptions from the temple of Lāt at Wādī Iram, *Annual of the Department of Antiquities of Jordan* 42 (1998), 255–8.

PETER WEBB

ʿĪsā al-Kurdī

ʿĪsā al-Kurdī (1831–1912) was the *shaykh* of the Naqshbandiyya-Khālidiyya Ṣūfī brotherhood in late Ottoman Damascus.

ʿĪsā al-Kurdī was born in the village of Talḥa in the province of Diyarbakır to a family that was related to the Buhtān

(Bohtan) Kurdish *amīrs*, ruling family of the Kurdish principality of Buhtān, and claimed descent from the Prophet. At age twenty, he went on the *ḥajj* and visited, on his way back, al-Azhar mosque in Cairo and Shaykh Khālid's (d. 1827) mausoleum in Damascus. Upon his return, he followed the Naqshbandī-Khālidī path under several masters in Kurdistan, completing it, along with his religious studies, in 1871 under the guidance of Shaykh Qāsim al-Hādī.

ʿĪsā al-Kurdī emigrated to Damascus following the Russian-Ottoman war of 1877–8. Settling in the mostly poor-Kurdish Ṣālihiyya quarter, he associated with fellow Naqshbandīs, as well as with the Ṣūfī circle of the exiled *amīr* ʿAbd al-Qādir al-Jazāʾirī (d. 1883). He travelled twice to Istanbul, where he is said to have been a guest of the sultan Abdülḥamīd II (r. 1876–1909), and more than once to Beirut, Syria's gate to the West. For the rest of his life, he dedicated himself to religious education, preaching, and guidance, acquiring many disciples in both the Naqshbandī path and the scholarly sciences.

As a Naqshbandī-Khālidī, ʿĪsā al-Kurdī stressed the obligations of the *murīd* (disciple) to adhere to the Prophet's Sunna and the *sharīʿa* and to love his spiritual master. He preferred the silent *dhikr* and insisted on the performance of *rābiṭa*, a constant concentration on the *murshid*'s image, regardless of whether he was present or absent (*dhikr*, lit., remembrance, is the central Ṣūfī devotional exercise, in which participants recite a name or series of names of God, or a litany; it may be performed alone or communally and may involve chanting, movements, and music). He was critical of mystical practices that contravened *sharīʿa* and opposed the habit of evaluating Ṣūfī masters by their lineage rather than their spiritual excellence.

Like prominent masters before him, ʿĪsā al-Kurdī combined his mysticism with religious erudition. Recognised as an expert in Qurʾānic and *ḥadīth* exegesis, theology, and Shāfiʿī jurisprudence, he stressed man's responsibility for his deeds and favoured leniency concerning the adoption of rulings of other legal schools. Accordingly he sanctioned a shortened form of Friday prayer in his only epistle (unpublished but mentioned by Abū l-Khayr al-Maydānī d. 1961) and refused to prohibit smoking categorically.

Alarmed at growing Western and Salafī influences in society, ʿĪsā al-Kurdī supported Abdülḥamīd's Islamic policies and opposed nationalism and constitutionalism. He rejected rationalism, approved of visiting saints' tombs, and described *ijtihād* as nothing but the recollection of God's names. To protect Ṣūfism he advised concealment and re-emphasised the practice of *ṣuḥba* (companionship) amongst his deputies. Favouring collective leadership, he refrained from appointing anyone of them as his successor. He encouraged promising students to concentrate on their studies, even at the expense of their mystical training, and renounced the Naqshbandī injunction to seek influence with rulers. Directing much of his effort to the lower classes, he stressed instead the *shaykh*'s duties towards the poor and urged his disciples not to abandon their livelihoods, even for the sake of their commitment to the Ṣūfī path.

ʿĪsā al-Kurdī ordained numerous deputies, most of them immigrants like himself or from amongst the lower social strata. Prominent amongst them were ʿAṭāʾallāh al-Kasam (d. 1938), Syria's Ḥanafī *muftī* during the French Mandate, Abū l-Khayr al-Maydānī, head of the League of ʿUlamāʾ following independence, and Amīn al-Zamalkānī (d. 1927) and Ibrāhīm al-Ghalāyinī (d. 1958), who spread the Naqshbandī path in the poor neighbourhoods and the countryside. Aḥmad Kuftārū (Ahmed Kuftaro, d. 2004), Syria's grand *muftī* under the ruling Baʿth party, was the son of one of ʿĪsā's last deputies, Amīn Kuftārū.

Bibliography

Muḥammad Muṭīʿ al-Ḥāfiẓ and Nizār Abāẓa, *Taʾrīkh ʿulamāʾ Dimashq fī l-qarn al-rābiʿ ʿashar al-hijrī*, Damascus 1986–91; Abū l-Khayr al-Maydānī, *Qabasāt min anwār tarjamat mawlānā ʿĪsā al-Kurdī*, Leiden University Libraries, MS 680A; Itzchak Weismann, The forgotten shaykh. ʿĪsā al-Kurdī and the transformation of the Naqshbandī-Khālidī order in twentieth century Syria, *WI* 43 (2003), 273–93.

Itzchak Weismann

J

Jakarta Charter

The **Jakarta Charter** (Indon., Piagam Jakarta) is the common name for a text that emerged from debates over the formulation of Sukarno's Pancasila (five pillars) ideology in 1945, in which the fifth of its pillars (in Sukarno's original iteration), asserting Belief in God (Ke-Tuhan-an), was further qualified with the addition of a controversial clause that stipulated that Muslims in the new nation would be obliged to observe Islamic law *(dengan kewadjiban mendjalankan sjariʿat Islam bagi pemeluk-pemeluknja).* This formulation (which came to be know as the Seven Words) came to be included in a draft preamble to the national constitution in the months preceding Indonesia's declaration of independence in 1945. In a last-minute reversal, however, the Seven Words on the obligation of Muslims to observe Islamic law were struck from the preamble, reportedly as a concession to the Christian population of the eastern Indonesian archipelago.

This unexpected turn of events came to be viewed by some Muslim Indonesians as a betrayal of their aspirations for independence and an ungracious recompense for their participation in the struggles that led to it. Some segments of the Muslim community were reluctant to relinquish completely the idea of a constitutional provision for the state implementation of Islamic law. The idea of defining the Indonesian nation as an Islamic state was brought to the table again through the vigorous constitutional debates of the 1950s, which were eventually quashed under Sukarno's system of Guided Democracy (Demokrasi Terpimpin). Others took the struggle outside the official arena of politics to pursue armed struggles for the establishment of an Islamic State (Darul Islam) in several areas of the country, including West Java, South Sulawesi, South Kalimantan, and Aceh, the last of which was not fully suppressed until 1962. While Islamic political activism was also severely curtailed under President Suharto (in office 1967–98), with the collapse of his New Order regime in 1998 new attempts to reassert the Seven Words of the Jakarta Charter in projects for constitutional reform were launched by some re-emerging Islamist factions but failed to pass when put to a vote before the

People's Consultative Assembly (Majelis Permusyawaratan Rakyat) in 2002.

Bibliography

Endang Saifuddin Anshari, The Jakarta Charter of June 1945. A history of the gentlemen's agreement between the Islamic and the secular nationalists in modern Indonesia, M.A. thesis, McGill University 1976; B. J. Boland, *The struggle of Islam in modern Indonesia*, The Hague 1971; R. Michael Feener, *Muslim legal thought in modern Indonesia*, Cambridge 2007; Thoralf Hanstein, *Islamisches Recht und nationales Recht*, Frankfurt am Main 2002; Tim Lindsey, *Indonesia. Law and society*, Annandale, New South Wales 2008[2]; Muhammad Yamin, *Naskah persiapan undang-undang dasar 1945*, Jakarta 1959.

R. Michael Feener

Jān-i Jānān, Maẓhar

Maẓhar Jān-i Jānān (1111–95/1699–1781), a leading Naqshbandī-Mujaddidī Ṣūfī *shaykh* in Mughal Delhi, was born into a noble family of Afghan extraction that served in the Mughal administration. He received military as well as religious education, especially in *ḥadīth* studies, but decided at the age of eighteen to give up that official vocation in favour of the Ṣūfī quest. Moving to Delhi, he followed the path under a succession of masters of the Muajaddidī offshoot of the Naqshbandiyya (whose eponymous founder, Bahāʾ al-Dīn Naqshband, died in Bukhara in 791/1389), thereby uniting in his spiritual genealogy different lines of descent deriving from the founder, Aḥmad Sirhindī (d. 1034/1624), known posthumously as the "renovator" *(mujaddid)* of Islam in the second millenium. These were Nūr Muḥammad Badāʾūnī (d. 1134/1722), Ḥāfiẓ Saʿdallāh (d. 1153/1740), and Muḥammad ʿĀbid Sunnāmi (d. 1160/1747), with whom he completed the path.

Maẓhar Jān-i Jānān became head of the central Mujaddidī lodge in Delhi around the mid-twelfth/eighteenth century. Although strict in his rules of conduct, many sought his initiation, normally into the Naqshbandiyya but occasionally also into the Qādiriyya, Chishtiyya, or Suhrawardiyya brotherhoods. He wrote little but ordained numerous deputies—many of them, like himself, of Afghan extraction—from the Panjāb in the northwest to the Deccan in the south. He regularly corresponded with them and undertook frequent journeys to visit and guide them. Maẓhar was assassinated in 1195/1781 by Shīʿī zealots after allegedly making derogatory remarks against the *taʿziya* procession (which commemorates Imām Ḥusayn's death at the battle of Karbalāʾ, 61/680; in South Asia, *taʿziyas* are imitations of the mausoleums of Karbalāʾ, generally made of coloured paper and bamboo).

As heir to the Naqshbandī-Mujaddidī tradition, Maẓhar Jān-i Jānān followed strictly the precepts of *sharīʿa*, alongside his adherence to the *ṭarīqa* (lit., way, hence Ṣūfī brotherhood), and was particularly attached to the prophet Muḥammad. Appalled by the rapid disintegration of the Mughal Empire and the mounting disorder in Delhi at this time, however, he introduced several innovations in the path, for which reason his spiritual line is sometimes referred to as Shamsiyya-Maẓhariyya (as Mazhar Jān-i Jānān's *laqab* (honorific name) was Shams al-Dīn Ḥabīballāh ("Sun of the Religion, God's beloved"). In contrast to Sirhindī's injunction to approach the rulers in order to guide them on the path of *sharīʿa*, Maẓhar focused on the integrity of the Muslim community. Seeking common ground with the other Ṣūfī brotherhoods, he stressed that both Sirhindī's *waḥdat al-shuhūd* (unity of witness) and the commonly accepted *waḥdat al-wujūd* (unity of being), going back to the teachings of the famous *shaykh* of Andalusian origin Muḥyī al-Dīn Ibn al-ʿArabī (d. 637/1240), were integral parts of Ṣūfī teaching. He was also prepared to accept the performance of music in *dhikr* ceremonies (as long as the *dhikr* conformed to *sharīʿa*) although not the *ʿurs* (lit., wedding, with God) celebrations commemorating a Saint's death, which, in his view, contravened it (*dhikr*, lit., remembrance, is the central Ṣūfī devotional exercise in which participants recite a name or series of names of God, or a litany; it may be performed alone or communally and may involve chanting, movements, and music). Perhaps under the influence of the earlier reformist scholar Shāh Walī Allāh (d. 1176/1762–3), Maẓhar strove to reduce disagreements amongst the legal schools by referring them to reliable *ḥadīth*s. He also endeavoured to improve relations between Sunnīs and Shīʿīs, claiming that respect for the Ṣaḥāba (the Prophet's Companions, whom the Shīʿa reject) was not an essential of faith. Attaching great importance to the education of women, Maẓhar authorised his wife to guide female adherents.

The greatest departure of Maẓhar Jān-i Jānān from the Naqshbandī-Mujaddidī tradition was his lenient attitude towards Hindus. He postulated that they too professed the unity of the One and should therefore be exonerated from the charge of *shirk* (polytheism). He even recognised Krishna and Rama as prophets and the Vedas as of divine origin and described Hindu idol-worship as resembling the Ṣūfī *rābiṭa* (concentration on the *murshid*'s image (lit., binding)). Maẓhar nevertheless described the Hindus as *kuffār* (unbelievers), as distinct from polytheists, because they did not follow the divine laws delivered by Muḥammad. He admitted Hindu disciples into his circle, although mostly on the basis of a shared interest in Persian and Urdu poetry.

Maẓhar Jān-i Jānān's deputies included some prominent Ṣūfī *shaykh*s and scholars of late twelfth/eighteenth- and early nineteenth-century India. Foremost amongst them were Shāh Ghulām ʿAlī (ʿAbdallāh Dihlawī, d. 1824), his successor as leader of the Delhi Mujaddidiyya, who was responsible for the spread of the brotherhood outside the Subcontinent, and Naʿīmallāh Bahrāʾichī (d. 1803), who moved to Lucknow and inspired the formation of a syncretic Hindu offshoot of the Naqshbandī that still exists. Also important were some of Maẓhar's more scholarly disciples, who helped formulate his teachings. These included the purist Qāḍī Thanāʾallāh Pānīpatī (d. 1810), who devoted many works to the defence of the Mujaddidiyya, and Ghulām Yaḥyā ʿAẓīmābādī of Lucknow (d. 1186/1772), who clarified his master's position regarding the controversy over Aḥmad Sirhindī's concept of *waḥdat al-shuhūd*.

Bibliography

Thomas Dahnhardt, *Change and continuity in Indian Ṣūfism. A Naqshbandi-Mujaddidi branch in the Hindu environment*, New Delhi 2002; Warren Fusfeld, *The shaping of Sufi leadership in Delhi. The Naqshbandiyya Mujaddidiyya, 1750 to 1920* (Ph.D. diss., University of Pennsylvania 1981), 116–53; Saiyid Athar Abbas Rizvi, *Shāh Walī-Allāh and his times*, Canberra 1980; Muhammad Umar, Mirza Mazhar Jan-i Janan. A religious reformer of the eighteenth century, *Studies in Islam* 6 (1969), 118–54; Itzchak Weismann, *The Naqshbandiyya. Orthodoxy and activism in a worldwide Sufi tradition*, London and New York 2007.

Itzchak Weismann

Jassy, Treaty of

The **Treaty of Jassy**, signed at Jassy (Iaşi, in today's eastern Romania), the capital of Moldavia (Boğdan), on 15 Cemaziülevvel (Jumādā I) 1206/9 January 1792, with the mediation of Britain and Prussia, ended the Russo-Ottoman War of 1201–7/1787–92 in Russia's favour. Though usually viewed in Ottoman history as an indicator of the Empire's decline, it inspired comprehensive reforms, and Britain ultimately intervened to check growing Russian power in the Balkans and Black Sea.

Neither side achieved its chief goal in the war: the resurrection of Byzantium and the kingdom of Dacia under Russia's protection was doomed, and the Ottomans abandoned their hope of recovering the Crimea. Austria joined with Russia in the conflict, and the Sublime Porte was aligned with Sweden, while the Porte's Prussian ally did not declare war on Russia. The Treaty of Sistova (4 Zilhicce (Dhū l-Ḥijjah) 1205/4 August 1791) ended the struggle with Austria, which made no gains because of the French Revolution and domestic turmoil. Moreover, revolutionary wars and problems in Poland distracted Russia during the conflict. Prompted by military defeats, the commanders of the Ottoman forces compelled Selim (Selīm) III (r. 1203–22/1789–1807) to open negotiations for peace.

The preliminary treaty signed at Kalas (today's Galaţi, in Romania), on 11 Zilhicce 1205/11 August 1791, guided the subsequent peace congress (13 Rebiülevvel (Rabīʿ I) 1206—15 Cemaziülevvel 1206/10 November 1791–9 January 1792). Under the terms of the final treaty, the Porte reconfirmed its past recognition of the Crimea and the Taman peninsula as Russian territory and the Kuban River as its border with Russia in the Caucasus (Article 1). The Russians returned Ismail, in the Danubian estuary, and Anapa, on the north coast of the Black Sea, to the Ottomans. The treaty provisions also included the release of all captives without ransom, except for converts, though identification of actual Russian subjects caused complications (Articles 1 and 8).

The plenipotentiaries, Count Aleksandr A. Bezborodko (d. 1799) and Abdullah (ʿAbdullāh) Birrī Efendi (d. 1212/1797–8), negotiated vigorously about war indemnities, Kuban autonomy, and North African piracy. Russia renounced its demand for reparations, despite Ottoman readiness to compromise, and also relinquished its claim for an autonomous Kuban in return for an Ottoman guarantee of remuneration in case of incursions by marauding tribes across the border (Article 6). In accordance with the terms of the Treaty of Sistova, The Ottomans accepted financial responsibility for any future pillaging of Russian merchants by Muslim corsairs (Article 7). A new dictate was the appointment of hospodars (princes) of Wallachia-Moldavia for seven years, with Russian approval (Article 4). Russian territorial gains were limited to the region of Ochakov (Özi) and Yedisan, between the Dniester and Bug rivers (Article 3). Finally, Russia became the protector of the eastern Georgian kingdom of Kartli-Kakheti (Article 5).

Bibliography

Kemal Beydilli, *1790 Osmanlı-Prusya ittifakı. Meydana gelişi-tahlili-tatbiki* (Istanbul 1984), 57–60; Kemal Beydilli, Sekbanbaşı risalesi'nin müellifi hakkında, *Türk Kültürü İncelemeleri Dergisi* 12 (2005), 221–4; Sadık Müfit Bilge, *Osmanlı çağı'nda Kafkasya, 1454–1829* (Istanbul 2015), 304; Alan G.

Cunningham, The Ochakov debate, in E. Ingram (ed.), *Anglo-Ottoman encounters in the age of revolution* (London 1993), 1–31; Ali Osman Çınar, *Mehmed Emin Edib Efendi'nin hayatı ve tarihi*, Ph.D. diss., Marmara Üniversitesi (Istanbul 1999), 263–79; Christopher Duffy, *Russia's military way to the West. Origins and nature of Russian military power, 1700–1800*, London 1981; Cengiz Fedakar, *Kafkasya'da imparatorluklar savaşı* (Istanbul 2014), 84–7, 216–22; Alan W. Fisher, *The Russian annexation of the Crimea, 1772–1773*, Cambridge 1970; *Muahedat-ı umumiye mecmuası* (Istanbul 1877, repr. Ankara 2008), 4:4–14; Gabriel Noradounghian, *Recueil d'actes internationaux de l'Empire ottoman* (Paris 1900), 2:16–21; Hugh Ragsdale, Russian foreign policy, 1725–1815, in Dominic Lieven (ed.), *The Cambridge history of Russia*, vol. 2 (Cambridge 2006), 512–5; Will Smiley, Let *whose* people go? Subjecthood, sovereignty, liberation, and legalism in eighteenth-century Russo-Ottoman relations, *Turkish Historical Review* 3 (2012), 196–228; Johann Wilhelm Zinkeisen, *Geschichte des osmanischen Reiches in Europa* (Gotha 1859), 6:841–3.

Kahraman Şakul

al-Jazarī, Badīʿ al-Zamān

Badīʿ al-Zamān Abū l-ʿIzz Ismāʿīl b. al-Razzāz **al-Jazarī** (b. c.530/1136, d. 602/1206) was an outstanding scholar, engineer, and inventor. The only information about his life is found in the introduction to his richly illustrated manuscript containing a collection of fifty mechanical devices and inventions, with their detailed construction plans. His family originated in al-Jazīra (Upper Mesopotamia, between the Tigris and the Euphrates). Badīʿ al-Zamān (prodigy of the age) was an honorary title used also for various important men, as was the honorific Abū l-ʿIzz (father of the well respected).

Most of his life, al-Jazarī served the Turkmen Artuqid dynasty (c.494–812/1101–1409), kings of Diyār Bakr (Diyarbakır) in al-Jazīra. In 602/1206, shortly before he died, he finished the manuscript that shows him to have been an outstanding engineer and inventor. His work marks the climax of the Muslim art of engineering in his era. He states that he had had twenty-five years' experience when he began the book and needed seven years to complete it. Contemporary appreciation of his endeavour is reflected in the number of copies of the manuscript that were produced for centuries afterward. The book was also translated into Persian and Turkish. Today, copies of the book are held in European and American museums and libraries. The earliest was finished, as stated in the manuscript, at the end of Shaʿbān 602/mid-April 1206, when al-Jazarī was already dead. This earliest extant manuscript is held in Istanbul in the Topkapi Palace Museum Library (MS 3472). It is titled *al-Jāmiʿ bayn al-ʿilm wa-l-ʿamal al-nāfiʿ fī ṣināʿat al-ḥiyal (Olağanüstü mekanik araçların bilgisi hakkında kitap)* ("A compendium on the theory and useful practice of the mechanical arts") and was used by Ahmad Y. al-Hassan for the Arabic edition of the text. The English translation by Donald R. Hill is based mainly on a manuscript titled *Kitāb fī maʿrifat al-ḥiyal al-handasiyya* ("The book of knowledge of ingenious mechanical devices"), written in 891/1486 and held in the Bodleian Library, Oxford.

The book deals with six categories of mechanical devices with detailed and accurate instructions for their construction. Each object is accompanied by an explanatory drawing. There are the following categories: clocks, "vessels and figures suitable for drinking sessions," pitchers and basins, "fountains and perpetual flutes," "machines for raising water," and miscellaneous pieces, such as doors locks and a protractor. Al-Jazarī states that he describes only devices that he has built himself. To some extent, his constructions were influenced by the devices of earlier "engineers," as were his fountains by the three Banū Mūsā brothers (fl. third/ninth-century) in Baghdad. He describes the improvements he made in the constructions of his predecessors. Many other devices are original inventions. Some of his machine designs were certainly of practical use, while others were meant to provide amusement, as, for instance, various curiosity automata and robots such as a boat with automaton musicians to entertain guests at royal parties or joke devices such as trick drinking vessels (one of the vessels appears to contain water but is empty, another one appears empty but produces water). Of particular interest are the constructions of various clocks: the monumental castle water-clock with twelve sets of doors, five musicians playing on the sixth, ninth, and twelfth hours of daylight, and many other interconnected animations; the water-clock of the drummers; the water-clock of the boat; the beaker water-clock; the water-clock of the peacocks; the candle-clock of the swordsman; the candle-clock of the scribe; the monkey candle-clock; and the candle-clock of the doors. The most spectacular of his clock constructions is the weight-powered three-metre-high elephant water-clock [Illustration 1]. In it, al-Jazarī connected Indian and African culture (the elephant) with Chinese (dragons), Persian (the phoenix), Greek (waterworks), and Islamic culture (the turban). The description of this spectacular clock led to several modern attempts to reconstruct it, the best known being in a Dubai shopping mall.

Many of al-Jazarī's ideas and machines (re-)appeared in Europe only centuries later. This is particularly true for the system combining a crank with a connecting rod in water-raising machines that can be found in Europe only from the beginning of the ninth/fifteenth century but that was already described in al-Jazarī's manuscript of 602/1206. It is possible that the knowledge and descriptions of his mechanical devices were transmitted to Europe via Spain, although other transmission channels can be imagined, particularly during the Crusades and via later travellers.

Bibliography

Works of al-Jazarī

The book of knowledge of ingenious mechanical devices (2016) https://www.ebuliz.com; Olağanüstü mekanik araçların bilgisi hakkında kitap = *The book of knowledge of ingenious mechanical devices*, Ankara 1990 (facs. ed.); *The treatise of al-Jazarī on automata. Leaves from a manuscript of the Kitāb fī maʿ arifat al-ḥiyal al handasiya in the Museum of Fine Arts, Boston, and elsewhere*, ed. Ananda K. Coomaraswamy, Boston 1924; *al-Jāmiʿ bayn al-ʿilm wa-l-ʿamal al-nāfiʿ fī ṣināʿat al-ḥiyal*, ed. Aḥmad Yūsuf al-Ḥasan, Aleppo 1979; *The book of knowledge of ingenious mechanical devices (Kitāb fī maʿrifat al-ḥiyal al-handasiyya) by Ibn al-Razzaz al-Jazari*, trans. Donald R. Hill, Dordrecht and Boston 1974; *el-Câmiʿ beyne'l-ʿilm ve'l-ʿamel en-nâfiʿ fī eṣ-ṣinaâʿti'l-ḥiyel (al-Jāmiʿ bayna al-ʿilm wa-l-ʿamal al-nāfiʿ fī al-ṣināʿat al-ḥiyal)*, Turk. trans. Sevim Tekeli, Melek Dosay, and Yavuz Unat, Ankara 2002.

Studies

Jane A. Aiken, Truth in images. From the technical drawings of Ibn al-Razzaz al-Jazari, Campanus of Novara, and Giovanni de'Dondi to the perspective projection of Leon Battista Alberti, *Viator* 25 (1994), 325–60; Ulrich Alertz, The horologium of Hārūn al-Rashīd presented to Charlemagne. An attempt to identify and reconstruct the clock using the instructions given by al-Jazarī, in Siegfried Zielinski and Eckhard Fürlus (eds.), *Variantology*, vol. 4, *On deep time relations of arts, sciences and technologies in the Arabic-Islamic world and beyond* (Cologne 2010), 19–42; Ahmad Y.

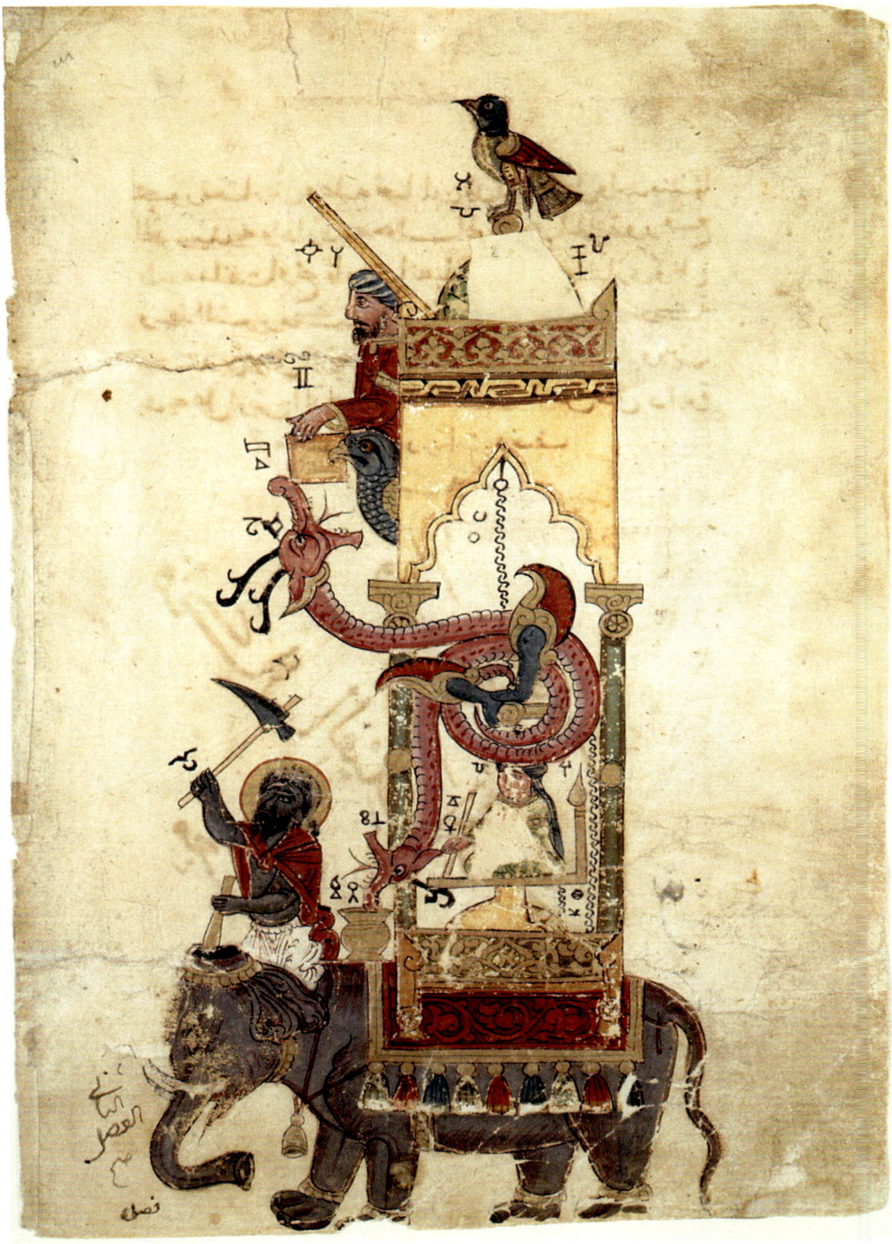

Illustration 1 Al-Jazarī's elephant water-clock from a manuscript dated 715/1315. Ink, opaque watercolor, and gold on paper. Bequest of Cora Timken Burnett, 1956, the Metropolitan Museum of Art, New York (57.51.23).

al-Hassan and Donald R. Hill, *Islamic technology. An illustrated history*, Cambridge 1986; Donald R. Hill, al-Djazarī, *EI2*; Donald R. Hill, *Studies in medieval Islamic technology. From Philo to al-Jazari, from Alexandria to Diyār Bakr*, ed. David A. King, Aldershot UK and Brookfiled VT 1998; Francis Maddison, Al-Jazari's combination lock. Two contemporary examples, in Julian Raby (ed.), *The art of Syria and the Jazira 1100–1250* (Oxford 1985), 141–57; *Gunalan* Nadarajan, Islamic automation. A reading of al-Jazari's *The book of knowledge of ingenious mechanical devices*, in Oliver Grau (ed.), *MediaArtHistories* (Cambridge MA and London 2006), 163–78; Lotfi Romdhane and Saïd Zeghloul, Al-Jazari (1136–1206), in Marco Ceccarelli (ed.), *Distinguished figures in mechanism and machine science. Their contributions and legacies*, pt. 2 (Dordrecht 2010), 1–21; George Saliba, The function of mechanical devices in medieval Islamic society, in Pamela O. Long (ed.), *Science and technology in medieval society* (New York 1985), 141–51; Fuat Sezgin et al. (eds.), *Badi'azzaman Ibn ar-Razzaz al-Jazari (d. after 602/1206). Texts and studies*, Frankfurt am Main 2001; Abdullah Uzun and Fahri Vatansever, Ismail al Jazari machines and new technologies, *Acta Mechanica et Automatica* 2 (2008), 91–4.

Several recent shorter but richly illustrated articles on al-Jazarī and his mechanical devices and inventions, mainly by Salim al-Hassani, can be found at http://www.muslimheritage.com.

Gerhard Jaritz

al-Jinān

Al-Jinān ("The gardens") was an influential Arabic journal (*majalla*) of the late nineteenth century, the formative period of the private Arabic press. It was founded by the prominent Lebanese scholar Buṭrus al-Bustānī (1819–83) and edited mainly by his son Salīm (1848–84). Appearing fortnightly in Ottoman Beirut from 1870 to 1886, finally edited by Najīb (1862–1919), *al-Jinān* both mirrored and fostered the Arab cultural and literary awakening *(al-nahḍa)* of that time. It came to be the prototype of modern secular Arabic magazines such as Yaʿqūb Ṣarrūf's *al-Muqtaṭaf* (1876–1952) and Jurjī Zaydān's *al-Hilāl* (1892, still being published as of this writing).

According to the opening note published in the first issue, *al-Jinān*'s purpose was to "spread and strengthen universal knowledge" among Arabs and "to revive and improve the Arabic language." Excluding religious matters, the journal featured a wide range of other subjects: current political affairs in the Ottoman Empire, Egypt, and Europe; the Arab encounter with Western modernity; chapters from European and Eastern history; new scientific achievements; anecdotes of various sorts *(mulaḥ)*; and women's issues. Numerous editorials *(jumal siyāsiyya)* by Salīm al-Bustānī and other contributions conveyed the notions of Arab (Syrian) patriotism, unity, civilisation *(tamaddun)*, and social reform. The journal's patriotic mission found its most striking expression in the motto *Ḥubb al-waṭan min al-īmān* ("Love of the homeland is part of faith"), which appeared on the cover of the first issue of 1870.

Al-Jinān is also notable for its major impact on the genesis of modern Arabic fiction. Above all, this is a result of Salīm al-Bustānī's literary output. His fictional narratives, among them nine historical and social novels *(riwāyāt)*, including *al-Huyām fī jinān al-Shām* ("Passionate love in the gardens of the Syrian lands," 1870), *Zanūbiyā* (1871), *Asmāʾ* (1873), *Salmā* (1878–9), and *Sāmiya* (1882–3), were serialised in the journal's literary section, *fukāhāt* (amusements). Recent scholarship has re-evaluated them as "trailblazers of their genre" (Sheehi, 79).

However, unlike other early Arabic periodicals, *al-Jinān* was not a one-man-project, but had a transregional authorship. Female writers also wrote for it, among them Maryānā Marrāsh (1849–1919), from Aleppo, the first prominent Syrian Arab female journalist who contributed to the periodical Arabic press.

From the start, *al-Jinān*'s production followed modern Western publishing standards. It was printed in the al-Bustānī family-owned printing office *(Maṭbaʿat al-Maʿārif)*, using the popular American Arabic typeface procured from the Beirut American missionary press. Each issue *(juzʾ)* contained 32 to 36 pages, made up of texts and occasionally also illustrations. At the end of each year of publication, an index *(fihris)* was produced.

According to a missionary report of 1873, *al-Jinān* was published in a run of about 1,500 copies. The standard way to obtain a copy was through subscription and mail deliveries. The publishers arranged for local agents *(wukalāʾ)* to promote the journal's distribution. The great majority of the subscribers *(mushtarikūn)* came from Beirut, other Lebanese towns, and Egypt, with smaller numbers from other urban locations in the Arab East and the Maghrib. The journalistic texts targeted the intellectual elite and the common people alike *(al-khāṣṣa wa-l-ʿāmma)*, but *al-Jinān*'s readers—men and women, Christians and Muslims—usually belonged to the social circles of the Arab middle class educated at the first modern schools in the Arab world.

Bibliography

Sources

al-Jinān, 1/1870–14/1883, 15/1884–5, 16/1885–6, Beirut; Mīshāl Jiḥā (ed.), *Salīm al-Bustānī*, London 1989; Salīm al-Bustānī, *Iftitāḥiyyāt majallat al-Jinān al-Bayrūtiyya 1870–1884*, ed. Yūsuf Quzmā Khūrī, 2 vols., Beirut 1990; Yūsuf Quzmā Khūrī (ed.), *al-Mulaḥ fī majallat "al-Jinān" al-Bayrūtiyya. Nawādir wa-fukāhāt*, 2 vols., Beirut 1993.

Studies

Ami Ayalon, *The press in the Arab Middle East. A history*, New York and Oxford 1995; Ami Ayalon, Modern texts and their readers in late Ottoman Palestine, *MES* 38 (2002) 17–40; Ashraf A. Eissa, *Majallat al-Jinān* Arabic narrative discourse in the making, *QSA* 18 (2000), 41–9; Dagmar Glaß, *Der Muqtaṭaf und seine Öffentlichkeit. Aufklärung, Räsonnement und Meinungsstreit in der frühen arabischen Zeitschriftenkommunikation*, 2 vols. Würzburg 2004; Constantin Iulian Georgescu, *A forgotten pioneer of the Lebanese nahḍah. Salīm al-Bustānī (1848–1884)*, Ph.D. diss., New York University 1978; Sharon Halevi and Fruma Zachs, "Asma'' (1873) The early Arabic novel as social compass, *Studies in the Novel* 39 (2007), 416–30; Elizabeth M. Holt, Narrative and the reading public in 1870s Beirut, *JAL* 40 (2009), 37–70; Elizabeth M. Holt, From gardens of knowledge to Ezbekiyya after midnight. The novel and the Arabic press from Beirut to Cairo, 1870–1892, *MEL* 16 (2013), 232–48; Yūsuf Quzmā Khūrī, *Rajul sābiq li-ʿaṣrihi. Al-muʿallim Buṭrus al-Bustānī, 1819–1883*, Beirut 1994; Stephen Sheehi, *Foundations of modern Arab identity*, Gainsville FL 2004; Suhayl Zakī Sulaymān, *Taṭawwur al-thaqāfa al-ʿilmiyya fī Lubnān wa-Miṣr fī ʿaṣr al-nahḍa (1905–1950)*, Beirut 1987; Fīlīb Dī Ṭarrāzī, *Taʾrīkh al-ṣiḥāfa al-ʿArabiyya*, 2 vols., Beirut 1913–4, reprint 1967; Fārūq Ṣāliḥ al-ʿUmar, *al-Jinān 1870–1886. Min majallat al-ʿArabiyya fī marḥalat al-taʾsīs*, Baghdad 1990; Itzchak Weismann and Fruma Zachs (eds.), *Ottoman reform and Muslim regeneration* (London 2005), 111–26, 127–48; Fruma Zachs, *The making of a Syrian identity. Intellectuals and merchants in nineteenth century Beirut*, Leiden 2005; Fruma Zachs, "Under Eastern eyes." East on West in the Arabic press of the *nahḍa* period, *SI* 1 (2011), 124–43; Fruma Zachs and Sharon Halevi, From *difāʿ al-nisāʾ* to *masʾalat al-nisāʾ* in Greater Syria. Readers and writers debate women and their rights, 1858–1900, *IJMES* 41 (2009), 615–33.

Dagmar Glaß

al-Jīzī

Abū Muḥammad al-Rabīʿ b. Sulaymān b. Dāʾūd al-Azdī **al-Jīzī** (d. 256/870) was a student of the famous jurist Muḥammad b. Idrīs al-Shāfiʿī (d. 204/820). He studied under al-Shāfiʿī in al-Fusṭāṭ and died and was buried in Giza (hence his *nisba* al-Jīzī). He related the legal opinions of al-Shāfiʿī as well as those of the jurist ʿAbdallāh b. ʿAbd al-Ḥakam (d. 214/829), a student of Mālik b. Anas (d. 179/795) and associate of al-Shāfiʿī. Al-Jīzī was better known as a *ḥadīth* transmitter, however, and narrated *ḥadīth* on the authority of al-Shāfiʿī and others, such as ʿAbdallāh b. Wahb (d. 197/813), a companion of Mālik b. Anas who helped spread Mālikī doctrine in Egypt, the Basran *ḥadīth* transmitter Isḥāq b. Wahb (d. 204/819–20), and the Egyptian transmitter ʿAbdallāh b. Yūsuf al-Tinnīsī (d. c. third/ninth century). Al-Jīzī was considered a reliable transmitter; Abū Dāʾūd (d. 275/889) and al-Nasāʾī (d. 303/915), compilers of two of the six canonical books of the Sunnī tradition, narrated *ḥadīth* on his authority, as did others, such as Abū Bakr b. Abī Dāʾūd (d. 316/928), the son of the Abū Dāʾūd al-Sijistānī (d. 275/889), another compiler of a canonical book of Sunnī tradition, and the Egyptian Shāfiʿī jurist Abū Jaʿfar al-Ṭaḥāwī (d. 321/933).

In spite of his pre-eminence and learning, al-Jīzī wrote nothing, and biographical information about him is scant. It was only in about the seventh/thirteenth century that his reputation as a legal scholar and transmitter of al-Shāfiʿī's doctrine became a point of interest for Shāfiʿī jurists. Mamlūk-era Shāfiʿī scholars, including al-Nawawī (d. 676/1277), al-Rāfiʿī (d. 623/1226), Ibn Khallikān (d. 681/1282), and al-Isnawī (d. 772/1370), all took an interest in al-Jīzī. They were concerned in particular with two points of legal doctrine that he may have transmitted. First, he reported, on the authority of al-Shāfiʿī, that reciting the Qurʾān with voice modulation *(bi-l-alḥān)* is disapproved. Second, he said that after the death of an animal, its pelt must be purified through tanning. He based this decision on analogy with how animals are conceived of when they are alive, no distinction being made between the purity of the pelt and the animal itself. There is some confusion in the Mamlūk sources about various reports of al-Shāfiʿī's doctrine attributed to our al-Jīzī but which were actually narrated by al-Rabīʿ b. Sulaymān al-Murādī (d. 270/883), also a student of al-Shāfiʿī, who transmitted all of the latter's writings.

Bibliography

al-Isnawī, *Ṭabaqāt al-shāfiʿiyya*, ed. Kamāl Yūsuf al-Ḥūt (Beirut 1407/1987), 1:26–7; Jonathan E. Brockopp, *Early Mālikī law. Ibn ʿAbd al-Ḥakam and his major compendium of jurisprudence* (Leiden 2000), index; al-Dhahabī, *Siyar aʿlām al-nubalāʾ*, ed. Shuʿayb al-Arnāʾūṭ et al. (Beirut 1417/1996[11]), 12:591–2; Ibn Khallikān, *Wafayāt al-aʿyān*, ed. Iḥsān ʿAbbās (Beirut 1398/1978), 2:292–94; Ibn Qāḍī Shuhba, *Ṭabaqāt al-shāfiʿiyya*, ed. al-Ḥāfiẓ ʿAbd al-ʿAlīm Khān (Hyderabad 1399/1979), 1:64–5; Christopher Melchert, *The formation of the Sunni schools of law, 9th–10th centuries C.E.* (Leiden 1997), index; Tāj al-Dīn al-Subkī, *Ṭabaqāt al-shāfiʿiyya al-kubrā*, ed. Maḥmūd Muḥammad al-Ṭanāḥī and ʿAbd al-Fattāḥ Muḥammad al-Ḥilw (Cairo 1383/1964), 2:132; al-Nawawī, *Tahdhīb al-asmāʾ wa-l-lughāt*, ed. Muḥammad Munīr Dimashqī et. al. (Beirut n.d.), 1:187–8.

Elias Saba

K

Karachay-Cherkessia

Karachay-Cherkessia (Karaçay-Cerkesiya, Karacay-Cerkesiya) is a republic in the western Caucasus, a part of the Russian Federation. It is bordered by the Kabardino-Balkar Republic to the east, Georgia and Abkhazia to the south, Stavropol Krai to the north, and Krasondar Krai to the west.

Karachay-Cherkessia lies on the northern slopes of the Greater Caucasus, and the highest point of Europe, the inactive volcano Elbrus (5,642 metres), is located in the republic. The main rivers are the Kuban and its tributaries, the Teberda, Bolshoy Zelenchuk, Urup, and Bolshaya Laba.

The population of Karachay-Cherkessia was 466,432 on 1 January 2017. Karachays and Russians prevail in the republic, constituting, according to the 2010 census, 41 percent and 31.6 percent of population, respectively. They are followed by Cherkess (11.9 percent), Abazins (7.8 percent), Nogays (3.3 percent), and others. One-quarter of the population lives in the republic's capital Cherkessk, the former Cossack village of Batalpashinskaya.

The official languages of the Karachay-Cherkess Republic are Russian, Karachay-Balkar, East Circassian, Abaza, and Nogay. In 2012, 48 percent of the population was Muslim (34 percent of them regarding themselves as neither Sunnī nor Shīʿī), 14 percent Orthodox Christian, and 12.2 percent animists. The Spiritual Board of the Muslims of Karachay-Cherkessia and Stavropol was founded in 1990 and comprises one hundred ten official and nineteen unregistered Muslim communities.

The territory of Karachay-Cherkessia has been inhabited since the Middle Palaeolithic. At the turn of the first millennium C.E. Alans began to settle in the lowlands. At the end of the fourth century C.E. they were pushed by the Huns back into the highlands, thereby making Karachay-Cherkessia a western part of Alania. One of the routes of the Silk Road led through Karachay-Cherkessia for centuries.

At the end of the first/seventh century, Turks (Bulgars, Khazars, and others) began to penetrate the territory of Karachay-Cherkessia and Turkisize the local population. Most influential was the wave of Kipchaks, who arrived in the fifth/eleventh century. As a result of this mixture in the seventh-eighth/thirteenth-fourteenth century, the Karachay-Balkar people was engendered, to be divided into the Karachay and Balkar branches, not later than the eleventh/seventeenth century. When, in the seventh/thirteenth century, Kipchaks and Alans were forced by the Mongols to leave the lowlands, this area was occupied by the Adyghs (i.e., Circassians). Abazins had been settling in Karachay-Cherkessia since the eighth/fourteenth century, and they were joined by the Nogays in the eleventh/seventeenth century.

In 1829, under the terms of the Treaty of Edirne (Adrianople), the Ottoman Empire recognised Russian possession of the territory, which had been conquered the previous year by the Russian Empire. From 1918 to 1921 Karachay-Cherkessia was part of various political units. In 1922 it became the Karachay-Cherkess Autonomous District of the Soviet Union and in 1926 was divided into Karachay, Circassian, and Russian areas.

In 1942–3 Karachay-Cherkessia was occupied by German troops, and in 1944 the Karachays were accused of collaborating with the Nazis and deported to Central Asia. The Karaçay District was abolished, but, after the rehabilitation of the Karachays in 1957, it was re-established as the united Karachay-Cherkess District. The second attempt to divide it up—into Karachay, Circassian, Abazin, and Cossak areas—was made in 1989–91 but failed due to the results of the referendum on the national structure of the republic, held in Karachay-Cherkessia on 28 March 1992. The Karaçay-Cerkes Republic was proclaimed the same year.

Bibliography

E. P. Alekseeva, *Drevniaia i srednevekovaia istoriia Karachaevo-Cherkesii*, Moscow 1971; Z. B. Kipkeeva, *Narody Severo-Zapadnogo i Tsentral'nogo Kavkaza. Migratsii i rasseleniye (60e gody XVIII–60e gody XIX veka)*, Moscow 2006; E. V. Kratov and N. V. Kratova, *Islam v Karachaevo-Cherkesskoĭ Respublike*, Cherkessk 2007; V. P. Nevskaia (ed.), *Ocherki istorii Karachaevo-Cherkesii*, Cherkessk 1967 (vol. 1) and Stavropol (vol. 2) 197272; B. B. Piotrovskiĭ (ed.), *Istoriia narodov Severnogo Kavkaza*, Moscow 1988.

Veronika Tsibenko

Kisve bahası

Kisve bahası (Ott. Turk., or *baha-i kisve*, cash value of clothing) is an Ottoman administrative/chancery term used for cash disbursements to new Muslims who converted to Islam in the presence of the sultan or other Ottoman dignitaries. The practice is of historiographical significance, as it marks the last stage of the process of conversion to Islam in the Balkans and reflects changing mechanisms for social mobility in Ottoman society.

Rewarding new Muslims financially or with the gift of new clothes, the most visible attribute of conversion, was part of the Islamic tradition long before the Ottomans and was justified with reference to the Qurʾān (28:52–4). Until the middle of the eleventh/seventeenth century, however, rewards were given on an ad hoc basis or on special occasions. It was only after the practice of conversion in the palace (or other places in the presence of the sultan) became widespread under Mehmed (Meḥmed) IV (r. 1058–99/1648–87) (Baer, 190–7) that the term *kisve bahası* entered Ottoman administrative practice to describe treasury disbursements to converts. According to a register of new Muslims from 1090–1/1679–80, conversions in the royal quarters took place daily (Minkov, 223). Most of these new Muslims were from the Balkans. In addition to receiving *kisve bahası*, they were considered clients of the royal family and, in many cases, enjoyed other privileges, such as appointments to the janissary corps or other posts. These appointments can be linked to *walāʾ al-muwālāt*, the Islamic tradition of contractual relationship between a convert and his patron (Minkov, 215).

The procedure for paying out *kisve bahasi* was set in motion by the potential convert submitting a petition *(arzuhal)* to the sultan to allow him to accept Islam in his presence. This document was considered a contract between the convert and the sultan (Minkov, 163). Once the conversion ceremony was finished, the petition was delivered to the office of the grand vizier, who confirmed the conversion and ordered the *başdefterdar* (chief treasurer) to pay the cash equivalent of Muslim attire, depending on the social status and sex of the converts. The *başdefterdar* authorised the issuance of a treasury bill *(tezkere-i hazine)*, which was produced by the *başmuhasebe* (central accounting department). All these steps were recorded in the margins of the petition. In most cases, the converts received their money in two or three days. The actual monetary value varied according to the sex of the converts and their social standing. According to the 1679–80 register, boys received 700 *akçe*s, girls 1000, men 1200, and women 2170. The difference might be explained by the women's more elaborate clothing or as a compensation for lost dowry. People of higher social status received the value of a luxury set of clothes *(mükemmel kisve)*, which could be as high as 6000 *akçes*. These amounts were substantial; a boy's *kisve bahası* was equal to the annual salary of an *acemi oğlan* (janissary cadet), while the combined amount for a family was sufficient to buy a house (Minkov, 186).

Although records of *kisve bahası* disbursements and petitions can be found also in the nineteenth century, the practice constituted a significant social phenomenon only from 1080/1670 to 1143/1730, the last stage of the conversion process in the Balkans (Minkov, 63). There are several hundred extant petitions from this period, suggesting that thousands converted through the institution of *kisve bahası*, which was probably institutionalised because of changes to social mobility in Ottoman society. The political and military elite no longer relied on the regular levies *(devşirme)* from the non-elite class *(reaya)* for filling its ranks, depending instead on the promotion of family members and protégés. By having converts-cum-protégés considered clients of the royal family and rewarded with public funds and appointments, the elite essentially transformed a social-religious custom into an instrument of the renewal of their ranks. For example, in 1073–4/1663, 252 vacant Janissary positions in the *cebeci* (armourer's) corps were filled by palace servants *(emekdar)*, sons of Janissaries *(kuloğlu)*, and new Muslims (Uzunçarşılı, 2:6). Non-Muslim *reaya* also seized the opportunity for social advancement through the *kisve bahası* practice, because it, unlike the *devşirme*, was voluntary.

Bibliography

Sources

Sofia, National Library of Bulgaria: NBKM 1, NBKM 1A, NBKM 112, NBKM 119, NBKM 145, CG, NPTA XVIII, NPTA XX, OAK, SL; Istanbul, Başbakanlık Osmanlı

Arşivi, Ali Emiri (Mehmed IV), Bab-ı Defter Baş Muhasebe.

STUDIES

Nikolay Antov, Kisve Bahası arzuhalleri. Osmanlı döneminde Balkanlarda İslamlaşma sürecine dair bir kaynak, *Kebikeç* 5/10 (2000), 89–105; Marc David Baer, *Honored by the glory of Islam. Conversion and conquest in Ottoman Europe*, Oxford 2008; M. Kalitzin, A. Velkov, and E. Radushev (eds.), *Osmanski izvori za islamizatsionnite protsesi na Balkanite (XVI–XIX v.)*, Sofia 1990; Anton Minkov, *Conversion to Islam in the Balkans. Kisve Bahası petitions and Ottoman social life, 1670–1730*, Leiden 2004; İsmail Hakkı Uzunçarşılı, *Osmanli devleti teşkilatindan. Kapikulu ocaklari*, Ankara 1944.

ANTON MINKOV

Kumyks

Kumyk (Qumuq) is the original name of the largest Turkic-speaking group in the North Caucasus.

1. Population and origins

According to the 2010 Russian census, Kumyks number 503,060. They are commonly known in historical sources also as Caucasian or Dagestan Tatars. Most Kumyks live in Dagestan (Daghestan, 431,736 or 14.8% of the republic's population), the rest in Chechnya (Gudermessky District), North Ossetia (Mozdoksky District), Tyumen Oblast, Stavropol Krai, and Moscow. Thousands of Kumyks live in other post-Soviet states (Ukraine, Kazakhstan, Turkmenistan, Azerbaijan, Belarus, and Latvia) and in the Middle East (Turkey, Jordan, Iran, and Syria).

Kumyks traditionally do not live in the highlands, dominating the Kumyk plateau in northern Dagestan and the bordering lands between the Terek river in the north and the Bashlychay and Ulluchay rivers in the south and the lands of northern Ossetia and Chechnya along the Terek river. Pliny the Elder (d. 79 C.E.) and Dionysius Periegetes (fl. second century C.E.) mentioned an ancient people called Kom or Kamak inhabiting the plateau; they were perhaps the ancestors of the Kumyks.

Contemporary Kumyk researchers using linguistic and genetic data claim that Kumyks and other Tukic peoples trace their origins back to the ancient Middle East. They consider Kumyks the direct descendants of the Turkic-speaking Bulgars, Khazars, and Kipchaks, although this thesis contradicts the generally accepted version of the slow formation of the Kumyk people as a mixture of the local non-Turkic population with Turkic peoples—the Sabir, Barsil, Bulgar, Khazar, Kipchak, Oghuz, Akkoyunlu (Āq Qoyūnlū) and many others—who migrated to the North Caucasus from the fourth/tenth century to the tenth/sixteenth.

2. Early history and Russian imperial rule

Kumyks had, throughout the centuries, played the leading role in the lowlands of Dagestan. The *shamkhālate* of Tarkī, the *khānate* of Mekhtuli, and the principalities of Endirey, Aksay, Koste, Utamysh, and Bragun are considered Kumyk states (*shamkhāl* was the title of the Kumyk rulers). While the Ṣafavid and Ottoman empires competed in the tenth/sixteenth century for control of the Caucasus, establishing vassalage relationships with local governors—from 986/1578 to 998/1590 the *shamkhālate* of Tarkī was included in the Ottoman Empire—Kumyk *shamkhāls* and princes sought support from the Russian tsars, becoming their vassals. The Russians had strengthened their influence by building fortresses in strategic locations.

In the tenth/sixteenth century Cossacks began to settle in Kumyk territory.

The Russian advance in the North Caucasus resulted in the incorporation of the Kumyk lands into the Russian Empire. By the Treaty of Gulistan concluded between Russia and Persia in 1813, the territory became, de jure, part of Russia. Nevertheless, the *shamkhālate* of Tarkī and the *khānate* of Mekhtuli existed officially under Russian protection until 1867, when they were reorganised into the Temir Khan Shura District of the Dagestan Oblast.

In the nineteenth century, especially after the Crimean War (1853–6), thousands of religiously motivated Kumyks migrated to the Ottoman Empire, even though freedom of religion was not limited by the Russian government and Islamic law *(sharīʿa)* was used in the Dagestan courts under Russian rule.

Kumyks in the Russian Empire were able to preserve and develop their culture. Noble Kumyks were educated in the best educational institutions in Stavropol, Tiflis, Moscow, and Saint Petersburg and continued their studies in Europe. Some of these well educated Kumyks had close ties to ideologues of Turanism and socialism and the Ottoman opposition group known as the Young Turks.

For example, the Kumyk émigré to the Ottoman Empire Ahmed Saib Kaplan (d. 1918) was one of the Young Turks and a founder of the Society for the Defence of the Rights of Turko-Tatar Muslims in Russia, along with the Tatar leader of the pan-Turkic movement Yusuf Akçurin (d. 1935). Kaplan and Akchurin were delegates from the Caucasus to the Third Congress of the Oppressed Peoples, held in Lausanne in 1916 under the auspices of the Union of Nationalities, and in the socialist 1917 Stockholm Peace Conference.

3. Soviet rule

Jelal-ad-Din Korkmasov (d. 1937) another prominent Kumyk socialist leader and one of the founders of the first Turkish socialist party, was also in close contact with Yusuf Akçurin. After the Russian revolution of February 1918 he headed the Military Revolution Committee of Dagestan and the government of Dagestan Oblast, which became, in 1921 the Dagestan Autonomous Soviet Socialist Republic. His Kumyk companions in the socialist movement of Dagestan were Ullubiy Buinaksky (d. 1919), the founder of the Communist Party of Dagestan, and Soltan-Said Kazbekov (d. 1920), the head of the Dagestan Defence Council.

Although Kumyks were seen as the main supporters of socialism in Dagestan, many of them (primarily officers in the Russian army) took part in the anti-communist movement. Amongst them were the *shamkhāl* Nuh-Bek Tarkovsky (d. 1951)—the commander of the Dagestan Cavalry Regiment of the Caucasian Native Cavalry Division of the Imperial Russian army (the so-called Savage Division), the Dagestan chief of the Union of Mountaineers, and the temporary "dictator" of the Dagestan *shamkhāl*—and his close friend Rasul-Bek Kaitbekov (d. 1921), the chief of staff of the Dagestan army, both of whom collaborated with the anti-Bolshevik volunteer army of Anton Denikin (d. 1947). Nuh-Bek was also minister of war of the Mountainous Republic of the Northern Caucasus (1917–20), in which Kumyks played a prominent role: the chairmen of the parliament were Zubair Temirhanov (d. 1952) and Daniyal Apashev (d. 1920), the minister of foreign affairs was Gaydar Bammatov (d. 1965), the minister of the interior was Rashid-Han Kaplanov (d. 1937), and the minister of justice was Tajutdin Penzullaev (d. after 1921).

4. Post-Soviet period

Kumyks next entered the political life of the Dagestan in the late 1980s, when numerous ethnic mobilisations took place in the USSR. In 1989 the Kumyk national movement Tenglik (Equality) was founded. Its activists demanded the creation of the Kumyk Republic, under the principle of self-determination.

The key issue provoking this activity was rights over the "historical Kumyk lands," which were occupied by "mountaineers" (Avars, Dargins, and Laks). Kumyks consider the lowland region of the Dagestan—with its main cities, including the capital Makhachkala—their national territory. Mass migration of the mountaineers to the lowlands during the Soviet period, which was caused by economic conditions and encouraged by the authorities during sovietisation, led to the loss of Kumyk dominance in the region. In addition, the Kumyks of the capital's suburbs was forced to resettle in Chechen villages in 1944 after the deportation of the Chechens to Central Asia. When the Chechens returned in 1957, the Kumyks remained without land because it had been given to the Avars.

An additional impetus to Kumyk protest activity was the decision of the Dagestan authorities to create near Makhachkala (i.e., on Kumyk lands) the Novolakskiĭ district for the Laks, who had a destiny similar to that of the Kumyks—they were resettled in 1944 in Chechen villages in the Aukhovskiĭ District and had to share their land with Chechens after their return. To protect their lands from the "foreigners," Kumyks organised strikes, sit-ins, and demonstrations, including blocking roads and railroads. In 1991 the special National Council (Milli Majlis) was elected and began to act as the alternative government of the Kumyks in the Dagestan.

This lasted until 1993, when the situation in Dagestan was stabilised with the support of the federal authorities. Since 2012, however, the Kumyk protests have been regaining momentum. Together with Nogays (another Turkic people), Kumyks are demanding the federalisation of Dagestan and the return of their lands. This hurts interethnic relations in Dagestan, especially between Kumyks, Avars, Chechens, and Laks.

5. The Kumyk language

The Kumyk language belongs to the Kipchak branch of the Turkic language family. For centuries it was used as a lingua franca by the North Caucasian peoples. Beginning in the nighteenth century Kumyk was taught at universities and schools in the Russian Empire. It was studied by the famous Russian writers Mikhail Lermontov (d. 1841) and Leo Tolstoy (d. 1910) and was used in classic Russian literature. Diplomatic correspondence with Russians beginning in the tenth/sixteenth century were written in Kumyk. In 1923 Kumyk was chosen as the official language of Dagestan. In the 1930s Russian began to prevail in Dagestan, but Kumyk retains its official status, along with the languages of other peoples of the republic. In 1929 the Arabic script of the Kumyk language was replaced by the Latin and, in 1938, the Latin by the Cyrillic.

6. Kumyk religion and society

Kumyks are predominately Sunnī Muslims of the Shāfiʿī school of law *(madhhab)*, along with some Ḥanafīs, although there are some Shīʿī Muslims amongst them. Kumyks adopted Islam under the influence of the Saljūks and Laks, from the sixth/twelfth century to the ninth/fifteenth. The centuries-long coexistence of local customary law *(ʿādāt)* with *sharīʿa* led to the formation of what is called "traditional Islam." Islamic modernism also gained popularity amongst the Kumyks through the adoption of ideas of the Jadid reformist movement at the end of the nineteenth century.

In the nineteenth century, Kumyks retained a social hierarchy that consisted of princes *(bey/bek)*, nobles (*uzden* of different kinds), free villagers *(azat)*, servants *(chagar)*, and slaves *(kul)*, but the patrilineal clans *(tukhum)*, were rarely seen by that time. Kumyks practised the common Caucasian traditions, highly valuing hospitality, pursuing blood vengeance, and raising a child in a vassal family *(atalikat)*. Kumyk livelihood is traditionally in agriculture, fishing, animal husbandry, and trade.

Bibliography

A. S. Akbiev, *Kumyki. Vtoraya polovina 17–pervaya polovina 18 veka*, Makhachkala 1998; Manaĭ Alibekov, *Adaty Kumykov*, Makhachkala 1927; K. M. Aaliev, *Kumyki v voennoĭ istorii Rossii*, Makhachkala 2010; G. S. Fëdorov-Guseĭnov, *Istoriia proiskhozhdeniya kumykov*, Makhachkala 1996; Ė. N. Gadzhiev, Kumykskaya diaspora v Turtsii. Istoriia i sovremennost, *Obshchestvennye nauki* 6/1 (2015), 30–4; S. Sh. Gadzhieva, *Kumyki. Istoriko-ètnograficheskoe issledovanie*, Moscow 1961; M.-R. A. Ibragimov and A. M. Adzhiev, Kumyki, *Narody Dagestana* (2002), 472–92; Ömer Karataş and Mehmed Said Arbatlı, Kumuk Türklerin Kafkasya'dan Anadolu'ya göçü, *Tarih İncelemeleri Dergisi* 30/1 (2015), 101–20; Yu. Kul'chik (ed.), *Dagestan. Kumykskiĭ ètnos*, Moscow 1993; *Kumykskiĭ entsiklopedicheskiĭ slovar'*, Makhachkala 2012; M. B. Lobanov-Rostovskiĭ, Kumyki. Ikh nravy, obychai i zakony, special issue, *Kavkaz* 37–8 (1846); A. I. Osmanov, *Agrarnye preobrazovaniia v Dagestane i pereselenie gortsev na ravninu (20–70e gody 20 veka)*, Makhachkala 2000; I. Pantiukhov, *O Kumykah. Antropologicheskiĭ ocherk*, Tiflis 1895; D.-M. Shikhaliev, Rasskaz Kumyka o Kumykah, special issue, *Kavkaz* 37–44 (1848)

Veronika Tsibenko

L

Laks

The **Laks** are an indigenous people of the mountainous part of Daghestan, in the Northern Caucasus. Ancient Greek authors (Herodotus 7.72, Strabo 11.5.1, Plutarch, *Pompey*, 35) mentioned the Ligyes (Λίγυες), Legaes (Λήγας), and Leges (Λήγες), who are supposed to be the ancestors of Laks as well as of the Lezgis and some other peoples of Daghestan. The capital of Lakia, the historical land of the Laks, is Kumukh (Ar. Ghumīk), so the Laks are known also as Kazi-Kumukhs.

In the sixth century C.E., Kumukh was incorporated into the Sāsānid empire. The ruling dynasty became related by marriage to the Sāsānids (r. 224–651 C.E.) and fought alongside them against the Khazars. Kumukh was invaded by the Arabs in the first/seventh century, leading to the early penetration of Islam there. The first stone Friday-prayer mosque was built as early as 161–2/777–9, but the governors *(shamkhāl)* of Kumukh—being of either Arab or Turkic origins, according to various sources—became Muslims only in seventh/thirteenth century. In 637/1240 Kumukh was occupied by the Mongols for no more than a few years. At the end of the eighth/fourteenth century, the capital of the Laks was named Ghāzī-Kumukh (Kazi-Kumukh), reflecting the striving of its inhabitants for Islam and the prominent role of the city in the dissemination of Islam across Daghestan.

The Kazikumukh *shamkhālate* dominated Daghestan until 1052/1642, when it broke into several units, including the Laks' Kazikumukh khānate. In the twelve/eighteenth century the khānate seized control of the Shīrvān region, in the eastern Caucasus, which led to a confrontation with the Ṣafavids (r. 907–1135/1501–1722) and to temporary alliances between the Laks and the Ottomans. At the end of the same century, armed conflicts with Russian forces occurred, resulting in the capture of Kumukh by the Russian Empire in 1820. Laks began to serve in the Russian army and to develop secular education and Lak culture.

Despite this, many Laks joined the holy war *(ghazawāt)* against the Russians, amongst whom were several deputies (*naibs*) of the North Caucasian leader

Imām Shāmil (r. 1834–59). Shāmil's spiritual leader was Jamāl al-Dīn al-Kazikumukhi (d. 1866), a Lak *shaykh* of the Naqshbandī Ṣūfī order. Shāmil tried three times to incorporate Kumukh into his imāmate, but each time Russian troops repelled his attacks.

In 1860 the khānate was replaced by the Kazikumukh District, headed by a Russian staff officer. With the beginning of the Russo-Ottoman war of 1877–8, the Laks rebelled and attempted to restore the khānate. After the uprising was crushed, its leaders, including the last *khān*, Jafar Ibn Aglar (r. 1877), and the scholar Hasan al-Alqadari (d. 1910) were executed or exiled. Some Laks emigrated to the Ottoman Empire, Iran, and Britain.

In 1921 the Kazikumukh District was made part of the Daghestan Autonomous Soviet Socialist Republic and in 1922 was renamed the Lakskiĭ District. In 1935 the Kulinskiĭ District was added to Dagestan. The Laks of the Russian Federation live predominantly in those two districts, where they constitute the majority of the population. After the deportation of the Chechens in 1944, the Laks were forced to move from the mountains to the plains, to settle in the Chechens' Aukhovskiĭ District, known thereafter as Novolakskiĭ (New Lakskiĭ). The Laks form the largest ethnic group in the district, despite the return of the Chechens. In the early 1990s the local government suggested the revival of the Aukhovskiĭ District and the resettlement of the Laks in lands near Daghestan's capital, Makhachkala. This project was not realised, because it provoked resistance amongst the Laks themselves, as well amongst the Khumukhs on whose historical lands it was intended to establish the Novolakskiĭ District.

The total number of Laks in Russia (2010 census) is 178,630, and nearly fifteen thousand Laks live in other post-Soviet states. Laks are Muslims of the Shāfiʿī school of Sunnī Islam. The Lak language belongs to the Nakh-Dagestanian language group and comprises five dialects. The alphabet has been officially Cyrillic only since 1938, although it was used in secular education from the 1860s to the 1910s, along with the Arabic alphabet, which had been in use since the ninth/fifteenth century but was replaced by the Latin in 1928. Contemporary Laks also speak Russian.

Terrace farming and animal husbandry provide the traditional livelihoods for Laks, along with leather- and copper-working, goldsmithing, jewelery, and pottery. Laks are also known for making unique weapons, decorated in gold, silver, enamel, and ivory. On account of the difficult geographical conditions in their homeland the Laks have been accustomed to travel as seasonal workers to Central Asia, the Near East, and, later, Russia.

Bibliography

B. B. Bulatov and S. A. Luguev, *Dukhovnaya kul'tura narodov Dagestana v XVIII–XIX veka (Avartsy, dargintsy, laktsy)*, Makhachkala 1999; A. G. Bulatova, *Laktsy. Istoriko-ètnograficheskoe issledovanie (XIX–nachalo XX v.)*, Makhachkala 2000; S. I. Gabiev, *Laki, ikh proshloe i byt'*, Makhachkala 2002; Laktsy. Ekonomika, istoriya, kultura, nauka, traditsii, *Vozrozhdenie* 7 (Makhachkala 2001), 1–184; L. I. Lavrov, *Ėtnografiya Kavkaza*, Leningrad 1982; S. A. Luguev, *Obshchestvennyĭ byt' Laktsev vo vtoroĭ polovine 19–nachale 20 veka*, Makhachkala 1981; R. Marshaev and B. Butaev, *Istoriya Laktsev*, Makhachkala 1991; P. K. Uslar, *Lakskiĭ yazik*, Tiflis 1890.

Veronika Tsibenko

Lembaga Dakwah Islam Indonesia

Lembaga Dakwah Islam Indonesia (LDII, the Indonesian Islamic Proselytisation Institute) is a controversial and, in the eyes of its opponents, an extremist and deviant Islamic organisation. It has changed its name several times after being banned under previous names and was known serially as Darul Hadis, Islam Jamaah, Yayasan Karyawan Islam (YAKARI), and Lembaga Karyawan Islam (LEMKARI) before adopting the name Lembaga Dakwah Islam Indonesia in 1990.

After living for ten years in Mecca, H. Nurhasan Ubaidah Lubis (d. 1982), the founder of this organisation, returned to Indonesia in 1952 and established a religious boarding school *(pesantren)* at Kediri (East Java). He asserted that he had a uniquely correct understanding of Islam and the only valid means to teach it—his *manhaj* (method, way of knowing)—which would transmit Islam as found in Mecca and Medina directly from him to following generations of teachers and students. This *manhaj* rested on the Qurʾān and *ḥadīth* alone and was to be studied in word-for-word interlinear translations from Arabic into *pegon* (Javanese written in Arabic script) or other Indonesian languages. All other sources were considered invalid and ignored or condemned.

With no room for traditionalist, modernist, or liberal thought, or Ṣūfism, all other Muslims and their associations were, in Nurhasan's eyes, deviant because they did not share his *manhaj*. His followers therefore should not pray with others who did not adhere to his *manhaj*.

Interestingly, modern management techniques are also taught at LDII's central *pesantren*, in Kediri. LDII's leaders say that this reflects the historic connection between Islam and commerce. The *pesantren* itself is managed like a modern school and, given the narrow focus of the *manhaj*, its course of study is rather brief (no more than 1.5 years, according to its 2003 manager, H. Kuncoro). LDII has produced many graduates since its foundation, and its prayer halls and mosques are widely distributed in Java and in all other provinces of Indonesia.

In 2017, some internet sources claimed that LDII had more than 25 million adherents, but this seems unlikely. There is, however, no doubt that LDII is a significant presence, whose followers probably do number in the millions.

Because of LDII's uncompromising rigidity in rejecting all other understandings of Islam, it has generated opposition throughout its history. In 1971, the Indonesian attorney general declared it illegal to spread its teachings, but the organisation resurfaced in 1972 with a new name and an affiliation with Golkar, the government party under the Suharto regime (1968–98). Despite this political protection, the ministries of religion and the interior, the Majelis Ulama Indonesia (Indonesian Religious Scholars' Council, a quasi-official body), a provincial attorney general's office, the local government of Kediri, and the police investigated the organisation in 1988. Even the head of Golkar in East Java, a stronghold of the traditionalist organisation Nahdlatul Ulama, agreed that it should be disbanded, but the central government in Jakarta allowed it to carry on under its new name, as the LDII. While these conflicts continued at various governmental levels, social conflict broke out occasionally. After the fall of the Suharto regime in 1998, when Golkar was no longer able to protect it, LDII prayer halls were subject to physical attacks.

LDII has not always been on the defensive but has denounced and threatened its critics. In the early 2000s, H. Hartono Ahmad Jaiz (b. 1953), one of the foremost LDII critics, was threatened at public meetings. As an example, in 2006 he was speaking in Surakarta, a major base for extremist Islamist movements, at a meeting organised by a network of Islamist radicals led by Mohammad Kalono. LDII supporters attacked the venue, reportedly arriving in seventy vehicles. Hartono was rescued by the police, whose station was then besieged by the LDII until both sides agreed to end the standoff.

Yet LDII carried on, with a notable presence in Kediri, where it was founded and where its headquarters boasts a ninety-nine-metre minaret that is the tallest in East Java, called the Menara Asmaul Husna (the minaret of the ninety-nine Beautiful Names of God). From 1998 onwards there were some rare signs that the LDII wished to build bridges to other Islamic associations, but the deeply rooted animosities remained and not infrequently led to physical confrontations and violence. The organisation had become too large to be easily destroyed, as some of its enemies might have wished.

Bibliography

M. C. Ricklefs, *Islamisation and its opponents in Java. A political, social, cultural and religious history, c. 1930 to the present*, Singapore and Honolulu 2012. Most publications in Indonesian about LDII are produced by its enemies; see e.g., the Salafī journal *Sabili* 13/21 (1427/2006) and two publications by Hartono Ahmad Jaiz, titled *Aliran dan paham sesat di Indonesia* (Deviant schools of thought and understanding in Indonesia), Jakarta 2002, and *Bahaya Islam Jama'ah-LEMKARI-LDII* (The danger of Islam Jama'ah-LEMKARI-LDII), Jakarta 1419/1998. The organisation has its own website http://www.ldii.or.id/.

M. C. Ricklefs

M

Mangkunagara I

Prince **Mangkunagara I** (1726–95), known also as Raden Mas Said, as Suryakusuma and, posthumously, as Pangeran Samber Nyawa ("soul catcher"), was one of the most flamboyant figures of eighteenth-century Java. He was born in the court of Kartasura on 7 April 1726. His father was exiled in 1728, and his mother died before he was two, leaving him orphaned in the court at an early age. Much was expected of him because of his ancestry, and there were prophecies of his future greatness. He proved to be popular and able to gather many followers.

In 1740, when Mangkunagara was just fourteen, he left the court and joined the rebels in what is known as the Chinese War (1740–3) and began to develop into one of the most formidable warriors of the eighteenth century. In 1746, when the Third Javanese War of Succession (1746–57) broke out upon the rebellion of his uncle Prince Mangkubumi (later Sultan Hamengkubuwana I of Yogyakarta, r. 1749–92), Mangkunagara joined Mangkubumi as his commander-in-chief *(senapati)*. With this rebellion, the Dutch East India Company (Vereenigde Oost-Indische Compagnie, VOC, est. 1602, bankrupt 1799) faced the most formidable threat to itself in Java since Sultan Agung's sieges of Batavia in 1628–9. In 1749, Mangkubumi was declared the monarch of the rebel side. His alliance with Mangkunagara fell apart in 1752–3, however, leading to internecine warfare. When the VOC gave in to Mangkubumi's demands in 1755 and recognised him as the first sultan of Yogyakarta, Mangkunagara was left to fight on alone.

In February 1757, Mangkunagara was reconciled with Susuhunan Pakubuwana III of Surakarta (r. 1749–88); this reconciliation was recognised by the VOC in March 1757. At the age of thirty-one, Mangkunagara thus became a semi-independent senior prince under the Surakarta kingdom. He was the founder of the Mangkunagaran principality and is known as Prince Mangkunagara I (r. 1757–95). His later years were full of piety and artistic activity, but for this man, who was a warrior through and through, a life of peace at court was often frustrating.

To deal with the marginalisation that he experienced in later years, he formed an alliance with his erstwhile most bitter enemy, the VOC. For the Company, he represented a welcome makeweight in dealing with the Javanese courts, as the VOC itself declined towards its bankruptcy at the end of the century. This alliance was carried forward by Mangkunagara's descendants into colonial times.

Throughout his years of war and peace, Mangkunagara showed concern for the welfare and morale of his followers. He was a pious Muslim of what may be called Java's mystic synthesis, which had, by his time, become the dominant form of Islam in Java. This was Ṣūfism marked by three notable characteristics exemplified in Mangkunagara I's life: a strong commitment to Islamic identity; observation of the five pillars of Islam; and, despite the first two, an acceptance of the reality of local spiritual forces, from those that occupied caves, trees, road crossings, and other places to grand figures such the Goddess of the Southern Ocean (Ratu Kidul) and Sunan Lawu, the spirit of Mount Lawu, where Mangkunagara I fought many of his battles and where he was buried.

Mangkunagara I claimed to have copied out the Qurʾān at least six times in his life. He frequently gathered hundreds of religious students together for group recitations of the Qurʾān *(katam Qur'an)*. These occasions were often accompanied by grand displays of princely style, such as cannon salutes, *gamelan* performances, and dance parties. He composed several works in Javanese, the most remarkable, titled *Serat Babad Pakunegaran*, being his autobiography (the earliest known in Javanese), covering his years at war. Mangkunagara I's piety was, however, no barrier to heavy drinking, described in his autobiography and other sources; jenever (Dutch gin) was his favourite tipple.

He was of short stature, even by Javanese standards, and, as the years passed, he suffered increasingly from yaws (framboesia). After his death, as was customary in Java, he was given a posthumous appellation: he was fittingly dubbed Prince Samber Nyawa ("soul catcher"), the name of his battle standard.

Bibliography

M. C. Ricklefs, *Soul Catcher. Java's fiery prince Mangkunagara I, 1726–1795*, Singapore, Copenhagen, and Honolulu 2018.

M. C. Ricklefs

Mataram

Mataram is a district in south-central Java, bordered on the north by Mount Merapi and on the south by the Indian Ocean. It is a well-watered site with rich volcanic soils that can support heavy concentrations of population and has been the site of much of the imperial history of Java since pre-Islamic days. It is centred on the present-day city of Yogyakarta, located at approximately latitude S 7°47', longitude E 110°22'.

The pre-Islamic kingdom of Mataram is notable for many fine Hindu and Buddhist temples built in the eighth and ninth centuries, the most famous of which are Borobudur and Prambanan. In the early tenth century, the centre of gravity of Javanese history, including the main court and, apparently, much of the population, shifted to East Java, possibly because of a devastating volcanic eruption in the Mataram area.

Courts and population returned to Mataram from the late sixteenth century, when a new dynasty, referred to as the Mataram dynasty, established its court there. The Islamisation of south-central Java accompanied this political development. In 1680, in the wake of civil war, a new court was established at Kartasura, in the neighbouring Pajang district. In 1749, however, a rival court was again founded in Mataram. From that time to the present, there have been courts in both districts, based in Yogyakarta in Mataram and in Surakarta (or Solo) in Pajang.

Bibliography
M. C. Ricklefs, *A history of modern Indonesia since c.1200*, Basingstoke and Stanford 2008[4].

M. C. Ricklefs

Muḥammad al-Wālī

Muḥammad al-Wālī b. Sulaymān b. Abī Muḥammad al-Wālī al-Fulānī al-Baghirmāwī al-Barnāwī al-Ashʿarī al-Mālikī (fl. c.1099/1688) was a religious scholar (*ʿālim*) in Baghirmī, a vassal state of Bornu (Bornū), in central Sudanic Africa. He was born in the village of Abgar, in Baghirmī, where his family had settled one or two generations earlier. The family were members of the Fulbe (Ar., Fūlānī) ethnic/professional group, which played an important role in the propagation of Islam in Africa. According to oral tradition, Muḥammad al-Wālī studied in Birni Gazargamu, the capital of the ancient sultanate of Kanem-Bornu. On his way to Mecca, he studied with the Shāfiʿī jurist and *ḥadīth* scholar Muḥammad b. ʿAlā al-Dīn al-Bābilī (d. 1077/1666–7), who attracted students from various legal schools and countries. Al-Wālī is said to be buried in what is now Abgar Wali, a small village southeast of Ndjamena, the capital of Chad. The only certain date in his biography is found in one of his works (*Muʿīn al-ṭālib wa-l-rāghib*, "Instrument for the student and instruction for the amateur," about Arabic grammar), which was completed in1099/1688.

Al-Wālī saw himself as a *mutakallim*, a scholar in the field of rational or philosophical thinking (*kalām*). His ten or eleven works—all in Arabic but not all attributable to him with certainty—cover the fundamental fields of Muslim learning. One concerns jurisprudence (*al-Adilla al-ḥisān fī taḥrīm shurb al-dukhān*, "Valid proof for the prohibition of smoking"). It is a strongly worded refutation of a treatise by the Mālikī *shaykh* al-Azhar Nūr al-Dīn al-Ujhūrī (born in Ujhur, north of Cairo, d. 1066/1656), who had declared that smoking was permitted. Two of the works teach the Arabic language, and the others concern *tawḥīd* (theology, lit., unicity (of God)). Usuman dan Fodio (ʿUthmān b. Muḥammad Fūdī, d. 1817), the founder of the Sokoto sultanate in 1806, considered al-Wālī and his father—no work by the latter has been preserved—as the pre-eminent scholars of Baghirmi. Al-Wālī's short poem *ʾAwṣikum yā maʿshar al-ikhwān* ("I urge you, O brothers"), in which he urges young believers not to waste their time in idleness, was published in print in Kano in 1965. His *Urjūza fī ḥudūth al-ʿālam* ("A poem on the creation of the world"), an arrangement (*naẓm*) of a text about the creation of the world, was commented upon up to the twentieth century.

Al-Wālī's most copied text is *al-Manhaj al-farīd fī maʿrifat ʿilm al-tawḥīd* ("The peerless method for understanding the science of *tawḥīd*"). It is a commentary on the *ʿAqīda al-ṣughra* ("Smaller creed") by al-Sanūsī (d. 895/1490), which treats the Ashʿarī doctrine of God's attributes. In his introduction, al-Wālī writes that he only translated the work (in Fulfulde) of Fulbe scholars before him. Indeed, the commentary is clearly rooted in the tradition of the *kabbe*, a Fulbe method of teaching *tawḥīd* that is marked on the one hand by the oral transmission of knowledge and on the other by the combination with Ṣūfism. He clearly made some additions too, but the significance of his translation and the basis of his reputation lies in his timing. In the eleventh/seventeenth century, Muslim society in central Sudanic Africa saw important changes: Islam spread outside of towns and royal courts to new groups of believers. It entailed two issues that al-Wālī's translation addressed. First, the identity of the "true" Muslim, and second, the status of the "true" expert in Islam, at a time when the increasing demand for Muslim specialists was met not only by *ʿulamāʾ* (scholars) but also by storytellers, diviners, and magico-religious practitioners. *Al-manhaj al-farīd* transmitted the uncompromising message that those who could not reproduce the explanations of God's attributes were considered unbelievers. And, by translating the popular Fulfulde oral "text" into Arabic and therefore into writing, al-Wālī claimed it as the property of classically trained *ʿulamāʾ* and so strengthened their position.

Bibliography

Unpublished manuscripts of Muḥammad al-Wālī

al-Adilla al-ḥisān fī bayān taḥrīm shurb al-dukhān, Leiden University Libraries, Or. 8362; *ʿAwṣikum ya maʿshar al-ikhwān*, Evanston IL Northwestern University, John Melville Herskovits Library, Falke 1687, Falke 862 Falke 1850, Hunwick 174.2; *Manhal māʾ ʿadhb li-ʿilm asrār ṣifāt al-rabb*, Evanston IL Northwestern University, John Melville Herskovits Library, Hunwick 196; *Muʿīn al-ṭālib wa-mufīd al-rāghib*, Kaduna, Nigeria, National Archive, D/AR7/4 and P/AR2/62 *Tadrīb al-ṭullāb ʿalā ṣināʿat al-iʿrāb*, Kaduna Nigeria, National Archive, N/AR2/27; *Urjūza fī ḥudūth al-ʿālam*, Evanston IL Northwestern University, John Melville Herskovits Library, Falke 2414.

Other unpublished manuscripts

Muḥamad Bello, *Infāq al-maysūr fī taʾrīkh bilād al-Takrūr*, Leiden University Libraries, Or 14063; Ibrahīm Ṣāliḥ, *Kitāb al-istidhkār li-ʿulamāʾ Kānim Burnū min al-akhbār wa-l-athār* (uncatalogued), Evanston IL, Northwestern University, John Melville Herskovits Library.

Other source

Dorrit van Dalen, *Doubt, scholarship and society in 17th-century central Sudanic Africa*, Leiden 2016 (includes the Arabic text and an English translation of *al-Adilla al-ḥisān fī bayān taḥrīm shurb al-dukhān*).

Studies

Hamid Bobboyi, Relations of the Bornu *ʿulamāʾ* with the Sayfawa rulers. The role of the *maḥrams*, *Sudanic Africa* 4 (1993), 175–204; Louis Brenner, Three Fulbe scholars in Bornu, *The Maghreb Review* 10/4–6 (1985), 107–13; John O. Hunwick and Razaq Abubakre (compilers), *The Arabic literature of Africa*, vol. 2, *The writings of central Sudanic Africa*, Leiden 1995.

Dorrit van Dalen

N

al-Naḥḥās, Abū Jaʿfar

Abū Jaʿfar Aḥmad b. Muḥammad b. Ismāʿīl **al-Naḥḥās** (d. 338/950) was an Egyptian philologist with expertise in the fields of Qurʾānic philology, grammar, and pre-Islamic Arabic poetry.

From Egypt, al-Naḥḥās, who is also called Ibn al-Naḥḥās or al-Ṣaffār by some biographers, travelled to Baghdad, where he studied philology under al-Zajjāj (d. 311/923), who familiarised him with the *Kitāb* by the famed grammarian Sībawayh (d. c.180/796). He also studied philology with ʿAlī b. Sulaymān al-Akhfash al-Aṣghar (d. 315/927), Nifṭawayh (d. 323/935), and Abū Bakr Ibn al-Anbārī (d. 328/940), and *ḥadīth* with Abū ʿAbd al-Raḥmān al-Nasāʾī (d. 303/915) and others (for a long list of his teachers see item no. 4 below, ed. al-Lāḥim, Beirut 1412/1991, 1:42–77). After finishing his studies he returned to Egypt, where he became a famous teacher of philology himself.

The Arab biographers do not give any significant details about his life. The only story that was often retold is the extraordinary event that caused his death. As the account goes, he was reciting some verses aloud, sitting on the steps of the Nilometer, a stone structure on the river's edge used to measure water levels. A passerby heard him and, thinking that he was a sorcerer casting a spell on the Nile, gave him a hard kick. Al-Naḥḥās fell into the river and drowned on the spot.

The biographical sources agree that al-Naḥḥās was a diligent author, who wrote about fifty books, among them masterpieces, such as his voluminous books on Qurʾānic grammar and recitation (items 1, 3–5 below) and commentaries on pre-Islamic Arabic poetry (items 7–9), which were all transmitted by his disciple Abū Bakr Muḥammad b. ʿAlī b. Aḥmad al-Udfuwī (d. 388/998). For a list of his disciples, see item no. 4 below, ed. al-Lāḥim, Beirut 1412/1991, 1:77–81). The following works are edited:

1. *Iʿrāb al-Qurʾān* ("The desinential inflection of the Qurʾān"), ed. Zuhayr Ghāzī Zāhid, 3 vols., Baghdad 1977–80; 5 vols., Beirut 1985[2].

2. *al-Kalām ʿalā tafṣīl iʿrāb qawl Sībawayh fī awwal al-Kitāb*, on the desinential inflection in the beginning of Sībawayh's *Kitāb*, ed. Ḥātim Ṣāliḥ al-Ḍāmin, in *Kitābān fī l-naḥw li-Abī Jaʿfar al-Naḥḥās wa-li-bn al-Ḥanbalī*, Damascus 1425/2004, 7–27.

3. *Maʿānī l-Qurʾān* ("The meanings of the Qurʾān"), ed. Muḥammad ʿAlī al-Ṣābūnī, 6 vols., Mecca 1408–10/1988–9. The incomplete work ends with Sūra 48 (al-Fatḥ).

4. *al-Nāsikh wa-l-mansūkh fī l-Qurʾān al-karīm. Riwāyat Abī Bakr Muḥammad b. ʿAlī b. Aḥmad al-Udfuwī al-naḥwī*, on abrogating and abrogated verses in the Qurʾān, ed. Shaʿbān Muḥammad Ismāʿīl, Cairo 1407/1986; ed. Muḥammad ʿAbd al-Salām Muḥammad, Kuwait 1408/1988; with the title *al-Nāsikh wa-l-mansūkh fī kitāb Allāh ʿazza wa-jalla wa-khtilāf al-ʿulamāʾ fī dhālika* ed. Sulaymān b. Ibrāhīm b. ʿAbdallāh al-Lāḥim, 3 vols., Beirut 1412/1991, reprint Riyadh 1430/2009.

5. *al-Qaṭʿ wa-l-iʾtināf* ("On pause and starting again in Qurʾānic reading"), ed. Aḥmad Khaṭṭāb al-ʿUmar, Baghdad 1398/1978; ed. ʿAbd al-Raḥmān b. Ibrāhīm b. ʿAbd al-Raḥmān al-Maṭrūdī, 2 vols., Riyadh 1413/1992; with the title *al-Qaṭʿ wa-l-iʾtināf aw al-waqf wa-l-ibtidāʾ*, ed. Aḥmad Farīd al-Mazīdī, Beirut 1434/2013.

6. *Risāla fī l-lāmāt* ("On the syntax of the preposition *li-* and the particle *la-*), ed. Ṭāhā Muḥsin, *al-Mawrid* 1/1–2 (Baghdad 1391/1971), 143–50.

7. *Sharḥ abyāt Sībawayh*, a commentary on the verses quoted by Sībawayh in his *Kitāb*, ed. Zuhayr Ghāzī Zāhid, Najaf 1974; ed. Aḥmad Khaṭṭāb, Aleppo 1394/1974; ed. Wahba Mutawallī ʿUmar Sālima, Cairo 1405/1985.

8. *Sharḥ dīwān Imriʾ al-Qays*, ed. [Abū Ḥafṣ] ʿUmar [b. ʿAbdallāh] al-Fajjāwī, Amman 2002.

9. *Sharḥ al-qaṣāʾid al-tisʿ al-mashhūrāt*, a commentary on nine celebrated pre-Islamic *Muʿallaqāt* odes, ed. Aḥmad Khaṭṭāb, 2 vols., Baghdad 1393/1973.

10. *Ṣināʿat al-kuttāb*, a compendium of grammar and general knowledge for secretaries, ed. Badr Aḥmad Ḍayf, Beirut 1410/1990; additional remarks on this edition by Nūrī Ḥammūdī al-Qaysī, *Majallat Majmaʿ al-Lugha al-ʿArabiyya al-Urdunnī* 53 (Amman 1997), 231–6; with the title *ʿUmdat al-kuttāb* ed. Bassām ʿAbd al-Wahhāb al-Jābī, Beirut 1425/2004.

11. *al-Tuffāḥa fī l-naḥw*, a short treatise on grammar, ed. Kūrkīs ʿAwwād Baghdad 1385/1965; ed. Māhir ʿAbd al-Ghanī Karīm, Cairo 1412/1991.

Bibliography

Sources

al-Zubaydī, *Ṭabaqāt al-naḥwiyyīn*, ed. Muḥammad Abū l-Faḍl Ibrāhīm (Cairo 1392/1973) 220–1; al-Tanūkhī, *Taʾrīkh al-ʿulamāʾ al-naḥwiyyīn* ed. ʿAbd al-Fattāḥ Muḥammad al-Ḥulw (Riyadh 1401/1981), 33–5; Ibn al-Anbārī *Nuzhat al-alibbāʾ*, ed. Ibrāhīm al-Sāmarrāʾī (Baghdad 1970[2]), 217–8; Yāqūt, *Muʿjam al-udabāʾ*, ed. Iḥsān ʿAbbās (Beirut 1993) 1:468–70; al-Qifṭī, *Inbāh al-ruwāt*, ed Muḥammad Abū l-Faḍl Ibrāhīm (Cairo 1369–93/1950–73), 1:101–4; Ibn Khallikān *Wafayāt al-aʿyān*, ed. Iḥsān ʿAbbās (Beirut 1968), 1:99–100; al-Dhahabī, *al-ʿIqd al-thamīn fī tarājim al-naḥwiyyīn*, ed. Yaḥyā Murād (Cairo 1425/2004), 66–7; al-Dhahabī, *Siyar aʿlām al-nubalāʾ*, ed. Shuʿayb al-Arnaʾūṭ et al (Beirut 1406/1986[4]), 15:401–2; al-Dhahabī, *Taʾrīkh al-Islām*, ed. ʿAbd al-Salām Tadmurī (Beirut 1413/1993), 25:155–6; al-Ṣafadī, *al-Wāfī bi-l-wafayāt*, ed. Iḥsān ʿAbbās (Wiesbaden 1389/1969), 7:362–4; al-Fīrūzābādī, *al-Bulgha fī tarājim aʾimmat al-naḥw wa-l-lugha*, ed. Muḥammad al-Miṣrī (Kuwait 1407/1987), 62; al-Suyūṭī, *Bughyat al-wuʿāt*, ed. Muḥammad Abū l-Faḍl Ibrāhīm (Cairo 1384/1964), 1:362; al-Suyūṭī, *Tuḥfat al-adīb fī nuḥāt Mughnī l-labīb*, ed. Ḥasan al-Malkh and Suhā Naʿja (Irbid 1426/2005), 2:768–9.

Studies

ʿAlī b. Muḥammad al-ʿImrān, *al-Imām Abū Jaʿfar Ibn al-Naḥḥās wa-atharuhu fī l-ḥadīth wa-ʿulūmihi*, Mecca 1429; Aḥmad Jamāl al-ʿUmarī, *Manhaj Abī Jaʿfar al-Naḥḥās fī sharḥ al-shiʿr*, Cairo 1983; Aḥmad Khaṭṭāb al-ʿUmar, *Abū Jaʿfar al-Naḥḥās*, Baghdad 1988; J. C. Vadet, Ibn al-Naḥḥās, *EI2*; *GAL* 1:132; *GALS* 1:201; *GAS* 8:242–3; 9:207–9.

Reinhard Weipert

S

Ṣabrī, Ismāʿīl

Ismāʿīl Ṣabrī (d. 1923) is generally considered the most important Egyptian poet of Madrasat al-Iḥyāʾ (the Revivalist School) after Maḥmūd Sāmī al-Bārūdī (d. 1904), Aḥmad Shawqī (d. 1932), Ḥāfiẓ Ibrāhīm (d. 1932), and Khalīl Muṭrān (d. 1949). In a famous formulation, his poetry, composed mostly in the early twentieth century, has been described as concerned primarily with love, death, and nationalism (Tawfīq, 64; see also Jayyusi, 1:40).

Ṣabrī was born in Cairo in 1854 to a middle-class mercantile family of Ḥijāzī origin. In 1866 he was enrolled in the government central primary school, the Amīriyya. In 1870, he was admitted to the prestigious Madrasat al-Idāra wa-l-Alsun (School of Administration and Languages), where he studied bureaucratic procedures and subjects related to government administration. He also studied the early Arab poets, developing a particular fondness for al-Buḥturī (d. 284/897), whose influence can be discerned in his mature poetry, and he became proficient in Arabic, Turkish, and French. His exemplary work attracted the attention of the minister of education, ʿAlī Mubārak (d. 1893), who arranged a fellowship for Ismāʿīl to pursue legal studies in France (Tawfīq, 44–5), but not before Ṣabrī had published several poems in praise of Khedive Ismāʿīl (r. 1863–79) in early issues of *Rawḍat al-madāris* ("Garden of the schools"), a periodical published by the Ministry of Education for distribution to government schools nationwide (Tawfīq, 68–9; Brugman, 34).

In 1873, Ṣabrī enrolled at the University of Aix-Marseille, where he obtained a *licence* in law in 1878. During his legal studies, he also read widely in French literature, including the works of Alphonse de Lamartine (d. 1869). Critical opinion remains divided about the extent to which Ṣabrī's poetry was influenced by this experience (al-ʿAqqād, 34; Brugman, 34; Tawfīq, 60–2; M. Ṣabrī, 34–46; Jayyusi, 1:40). It is probably safe to follow critics like Jayyusi (1:41) and Muḥammad Ṣabrī (29) in their celebration of Ismāʿīl's use of *wijdān* (personal emotion) or "wistfulness" in his poetry, without drawing too specific a parallel with the techniques characteristic of French romanticism, like the use of apostrophe, extensive adjectival qualification, and pathetic fallacy.

After his return to Egypt in 1878, Ṣabrī held a succession of supervisory positions in the Egyptian government and legal system, culminating in his appointment as governor of Alexandria, 1896–9 (Tawfīq, 47). He retired early, in 1908, which freed him to write more political poetry (Tawfīq, 49), including famous poems celebrating the deposition of the Ottoman sultan ʿAbd al-Ḥamīd II in 1908 (Tawfīq, 82–4), denouncing the Italian invasion of Libya in 1911 (Tawfīq, 85–6), and condemning (belatedly) the 1906 Dinshaway incident (Tawfīq, 113–8; Brugman, 35), a dispute between British officers and residents of the eponymous village that resulted in some villagers being executed and which stirred nationalist opinion. Probably his most notable poem of the period was a glorification of Egyptian civilisation (1909), put in the mouth of an ancient Egyptian pharaoh (Tawfīq, 87–90; M. Ṣabrī, 55–7; Brugman 35). Ṣabrī, a follower and supporter of the Egyptian nationalist leader Muṣṭafā Kāmil (d. 1908), was appointed chair of the commission charged with erecting a statue in Kāmil's honour; the statue was erected in 1921 (Tawfīq, 102–10). Ṣabrī passed away two years later. At his funeral, his legacy was lavishly commemorated by his contemporaries (Tawfīq, 52–9).

Bibliography

ʿAbbās Maḥmūd al-ʿAqqād, *Shuʿarāʾ Miṣr wa-bīʾātuhum fī l-jīl al-māḍī*, Cairo 1937; J. Brugman, *An introduction to the history of modern Arabic literature in Egypt* (Leiden 1984), 33–5; Salma Khadra Jayyusi, *Trends and movements in modern Arabic poetry* (Leiden 1977), 1:39–42; Ismāʿīl Ṣabrī, *Dīwān Ismāʿīl Ṣabrī Bāshā*, comp. Ḥasan Rifʿat, ed. Aḥmad al-Zayn, Cairo 1938; Muḥammad Ṣabrī, *Ismāʿīl Ṣabrī. Ḥayātuhu wa-shiʿruhu*, Cairo 1923; Najīb Tawfīq, *Ismāʿīl Ṣabrī Bāshā. Shaykh al-shuʿarāʾ, ḥayātuhu wa-atharuhu fī l-adab wa-fī ʿaṣrihi*, Cairo 1985.

Terri DeYoung

CUMULATIVE LIST OF ENTRIES 2019–4

Aaron 2007-2 : 1
Aaron ben Elija of Nicomedia 2008-1 : 1
ʿAbābda 2008-2 : 1
Abagirskiy 2017-1 : 1
Abān b. ʿUthmān b. ʿAffān 2007-3 : 1
Abān al-Lāḥiqī 2007-2 : 2
Abangan 2007-2 : 3
Abāqā 2010-2 : 1
Abarqubādh 2009-1 : 1
Abarqūh 2009-3 : 1
Abarshahr 2011-2 : 1
ʿAbāṭa Muḥammad Ḥasan 2010-2 : 9
Abay Qunanbayulı 2007-2 : 6
ʿAbbād b. Salmān 2009-3 : 2
ʿAbbād b. Ziyād b. Abī Sufyān 2009-2 : 1
ʿAbbādān (Ābādān) 2010-1 : 1
al-ʿAbbādī 2014-1 : 1
ʿAbbādids 2011-4 : 1
ʿAbbās I 2016-1 : 1
ʿAbbās II 2008-2 : 2
ʿAbbās III 2009-3 : 3
al-ʿAbbās b. ʿAbd al-Muṭṭalib 2009-2 : 2
ʿAbbās b. Abī l-Futūḥ 2007-2 : 7
al-ʿAbbās b. al-Aḥnaf 2009-1 : 2
al-ʿAbbās b. ʿAmr al-Ghanawī 2011-1 : 1
ʿAbbās b. al-Ḥusayn al-Shīrāzī 2014-2 : 1
al-ʿAbbās b. al-Maʾmūn 2013-4 : 1
al-ʿAbbās b. Mirdās 2008-1 : 2
al-ʿAbbās b. Muḥammad b. ʿAlī 2013-3 : 1
al-ʿAbbās b. al-Walīd b. ʿAbd al-Malik 2008-1 : 3
ʿAbbās Efendī 2008-2 : 5
ʿAbbās Ḥilmī I 2014-2 : 2
ʿAbbās Ḥilmī II 2007-1 : 1
ʿAbbās, Iḥsān 2010-2 : 10
ʿAbbās Mīrzā 2012-1 : 1
ʿAbbās Sarwānī 2007-2 : 9
ʿAbbāsa bt al-Mahdī 2008-1 : 4
ʿAbbāsī 2009-3 : 4
al-ʿAbbāsī 2008-1 : 6
ʿAbbāsī, Shaykh 2011-4 : 5
ʿAbbāsid art and architecture 2012-1 : 4
ʿAbbāsid music 2019-4 : 1
ʿAbbāsid Revolution 2007-1 : 2
Abbasquluağa Bakıxanov 2015-1 : 1
ʿAbbūd, Mārūn 2007-2 : 10
ʿAbd al-Aḥad Nūrī Sīvāsī 2009-3 : 6
ʿAbd al-ʿAzīz al-Amawī 2007-2 : 10
ʿAbd al-ʿAzīz b. al-Ḥajjāj b. ʿAbd al-Malik 2008-1 : 6
ʿAbd al-ʿAzīz b. Marwān 2009-2 : 3
ʿAbd al-ʿAzīz b. Mūsā b. Nuṣayr 2013-4 : 2
ʿAbd al-ʿAzīz b. al-Walīd b. ʿAbd al-Malik 2008-1 : 7
ʿAbd al-ʿAzīz Dihlawī 2010-1 : 3
ʿAbd al-ʿAzīz al-Mahdawī 2016-2 : 1

ʿAbd al-Bāqī, Shaykh 2011-1 : 2
ʿAbd al-Bārī 2007-2 : 11
ʿAbd al-Bāsiṭ ʿAbd al-Ṣamad 2018-6 : 1
ʿAbd al-Ghaffār Khān 2015-1 : 2
ʿAbd al-Ghafūr of Swāt 2015-1 : 4
ʿAbd al-Ghanī al-Nābulusī 2012-1 : 20
ʿAbd al-Hādī, ʿAwnī 2009-1 : 4
ʿAbd al-Hādī Shīrāzī 2015-4 : 1
ʿAbd al-Ḥafīẓ b. al-Ḥasan 2016-3 : 1
ʿAbd al-Ḥakīm 2013-3 : 2
ʿAbd al-Ḥakīm, Khalīfa 2008-1 : 8
ʿAbd al-Ḥamīd b. Yaḥyā al-Kātib 2009-1 : 4
ʿAbd al-Ḥamīd-i Lāhawrī 2012-3 : 1
ʿAbd al-Ḥaqq Bāba-yi Urdū 2009-1 : 8
ʿAbd al-Ḥaqq Dihlavī 2016-2 : 3
ʿAbd al-Ḥayy Ḥasanī 2012-3 : 2
ʿAbd al-Ḥayy al-Laknawī 2011-1 : 3
ʿAbd al-Ḥayy, Ṣāliḥ 2007-2 : 12
ʿAbd al-Ḥusayn Mūnis ʿAlī Shāh 2015-4 : 2
ʿAbd al-Ilāh 2007-2 : 13
ʿAbd al-Jabbār b. ʿAbd al-Qādir al-Jīlānī 2009-1 : 9
ʿAbd al-Jabbār b. ʿAbd al-Raḥmān 2009-4 : 1
ʿAbd al-Jabbār b. Aḥmad al-Hamadhānī 2007-3 : 9
ʿAbd al-Karīm 2012-1 : 28
ʿAbd al-Karīm Kashmīrī 2015-3 : 1
ʿAbd al-Karīm Wāʿiẓ Emīr Efendī 2013-4 : 3
ʿAbd al-Khāliq al-Ghijduwānī 2010-1 : 9
ʿAbd al-Laṭīf 2013-4 : 4
ʿAbd al-Laṭīf al-Baghdādī 2018-6 : 2
ʿAbd al-Laṭīf, Bahādur 2016-2 : 7
ʿAbd al-Majīd al-Khānī 2011-1 : 4
ʿAbd al-Malik b. Ḥabīb 2009-4 : 2
ʿAbd al-Malik b. Qaṭan al-Fihrī 2009-1 : 10
ʿAbd al-Malik b. Ṣāliḥ 2007-3 : 18
ʿAbd al-Malik al-Muẓaffar 2009-2 : 4
ʿAbd al-Muʾmin al-Dimyāṭī 2013-4 : 8
ʿAbd al-Muqtadir 2010-1 : 12
ʿAbd al-Muṭṭalib b. Hāshim 2007-2 : 13
ʿAbd al-Nabī 2012-3 : 3
ʿAbd al-Nabī Qazvīnī 2014-2 : 3
ʿAbd al-Qādir, Amīr 2014-2 : 5
ʿAbd al-Qādir b. ʿAlī b. Yūsuf al-Fāsī 2009-2 : 6
ʿAbd al-Qādir al-Baghdādī 2007-3 : 19
ʿAbd al-Qādir Dihlawī 2011-2 : 2
ʿAbd al-Qādir al-Jīlānī 2009-1 : 11
ʿAbd al-Qādir al-Marāghī, b. Ghaybī 2007-3 : 21
ʿAbd al-Quddūs Gangohī 2012-2 : 1
ʿAbd al-Quddūs, Iḥsān 2007-2 : 15
ʿAbd al-Raḥīm Dihlawī 2016-3 : 3
ʿAbd al-Raḥīm Khān 2009-3 : 7
ʿAbd al-Raḥīm al-Qināʾī 2012-3 : 3
ʿAbd al-Raḥmān (Sanchuelo) 2010-1 : 13
ʿAbd al-Raḥmān, ʿĀʾisha 2007-2 : 16
ʿAbd al-Raḥmān b. ʿAbdallāh al-Ghāfiqī 2010-2 : 12
ʿAbd al-Raḥmān b. ʿAwf 2015-3 : 2
ʿAbd al-Raḥmān b. Ḥabīb al-Fihrī 2016-4 : 1
ʿAbd al-Raḥmān b. Khālid b. al-Walīd 201[illegible]-1 : 1
ʿAbd al-Raḥmān b. Muʿāwiya 2009-2 : 7
ʿAbd al-Raḥmān b. Rustam 201[illegible]-3 : 1
ʿAbd al-Raḥmān b. Samura 2017-4 : 1
ʿAbd al-Raḥmān al-Ifrīqī 200[illegible]-3 : 9
ʿAbd al-Raḥmān Katkhudā 201[illegible]-1 : 1
ʿAbd al-Raḥmān Khān 201[illegible]-2 : 13
ʿAbd al-Raḥmān Sirrī 200[illegible]-2 : 10
ʿAbd al-Raḥmān al-Ṣūfī 200[illegible]-1 : 9
ʿAbd al-Raḥmān al-Thughūrī 201[illegible]-1 : 6
ʿAbd al-Raḥmān al-Zaylaʿī 201[illegible]-4 : 9
ʿAbd al-Rashīd b. ʿAbd al-Ghafūr 201[illegible]-1 : 14
ʿAbd al-Rashīd Jawnpūrī 201[illegible]-4 : 6
ʿAbd al-Rashīd al-Tattawī 2007-2 : 18

ʿAbd al-Rāziq, ʿAlī 2009-1 : 14
ʿAbd al-Rāziq, Muṣṭafā 2008-1 : 12
ʿAbd al-Razzāq b. ʿAbd al-Qādir al-Jīlānī 2010-2 : 13
ʿAbd al-Razzāq Beg Dunbulī 2008-2 : 6
ʿAbd al-Razzāq al-Kāshānī 2009-3 : 10
ʿAbd al-Razzāq al-Samarqandī 2014-1 : 2
ʿAbd al-Razzāq al-Ṣanānī 2007-1 : 7
ʿAbd al-Riḍā Khān Ibrāhīmī 2013-3 : 3
ʿAbd al-Ṣabūr, Ṣalāḥ 2007-2 : 20
ʿAbd al-Salām b. Muḥammad 2010-1 : 16
ʿAbd al-Ṣamad Hamadhānī 2012-3 : 8
ʿAbd al-Ṣamad al-Falimbānī 2007-2 : 25
ʿAbd al-Sattār Lāhawrī 2015-1 : 6
ʿAbd al-Wādids 2009-2 : 11
ʿAbd al-Wahhāb Ilhāmī 2010-2 : 15
ʿAbd al-Wahhāb, Muḥammad 2009-4 : 4
ʿAbd al-Wāḥid b. Zayd 2011-2 : 3
ʿAbd al-Wāḥid Bilgrāmī 2014-3 : 1
ʿAbd al-Wāḥid al-Marrākushī 2009-2 : 14
ʿAbd al-Waḥīd Turkistānī 2013-4 : 11
Abdalan-ı Rum, historical 2012-4 : 1
Abdalan-ı Rum, literature 2015-3 : 4
ʿAbdalī 2008-1 : 14
ʿAbdallāh b. ʿAbbās 2012-1 : 30
ʿAbdallāh b. ʿAbd al-Malik b. Marwān 2013-4 : 13
ʿAbdallāh b. ʿAbd al-Muṭṭalib 2010-2 : 16
ʿAbdallāh b. ʿAlawī al-Ḥaddād 2012-1 : 43
ʿAbdallāh b. ʿAlī 2010-1 : 17
ʿAbdallāh b. ʿĀmir 2008-1 : 15
ʿAbdallāh b. ʿAwn 2008-1 : 16
ʿAbdallāh b. Ḥanẓala 2008-2 : 7
ʿAbdallāh b. al-Ḥasan 2009-2 : 15
ʿAbdallāh b. al-Ḥusayn 2007-2 : 21
ʿAbdallāh b. Jaʿfar b. Abī Ṭālib 2010-2 : 18
ʿAbdallāh b. Jaḥsh 2011-2 : 5
ʿAbdallāh b. Judʿān 2010-1 : 18
ʿAbdallāh b. Khāzim 2015-2 : 1
ʿAbdallāh b. Maymūn 2013-3 : 4
ʿAbdallāh b. Muʿāwiya 2013-4 : 14
ʿAbdallāh b. Muḥammad b. ʿAbd al-Raḥmān 2011-2 : 5
ʿAbdallāh b. Mūsā b. Nuṣayr 2014-1 : 3
ʿAbdallāh b. Muṭīʿ 2009-2 : 16
ʿAbdallāh b. Rawāḥa 2009-2 : 17
ʿAbdallāh b. Sabaʾ 2016-1 : 6
ʿAbdallāh b. Salām 2013-4 : 16
ʿAbdallāh b. Ṭāhir 2007-3 : 21
ʿAbdallāh b. Ubayy 2009-2 : 18
ʿAbdallāh b. ʿUmar b. ʿAbd al-ʿAzīz 2009-2 : 19
ʿAbdallāh b. ʿUmar b. al-Khaṭṭāb 2009-2 : 20
ʿAbdallāh b. Wahb 2016-1 : 8
ʿAbdallāh b. al-Zubayr 2009-2 : 22
ʿAbdallāh Bihbihānī 2011-1 : 8
ʿAbdallāh, Mirzā 2007-3 : 23
ʿAbdallāh, Muḥammad ʿAbd al-Ḥalīm 2008-1 : 17
ʿAbdallāh Pasha 2007-2 : 22
ʿAbdallāh Shaṭṭār 2013-4 : 17
ʿAbdallāh Ṣūfī Shaṭṭārī 2010-2 : 19
ʿAbdallāh al-Taʿīshī 2009-1 : 17
ʿAbdallāh al-Tulanbi 2007-3 : 23
ʿAbdallāh, Yaḥyā l-Ṭāhir 2010-2 : 20
ʿAbdān, Abū Muḥammad 2007-2 : 23
ʿAbdī 2012-1 : 47
ʿAbdī Bābā 2011-3 : 2
ʿAbdī Bukhārī 2007-3 : 24
ʿAbdī Shīrāzī 2008-2 : 8
ʿAbdorauf Fitrat 2007-2 : 19
Abduction 2011-4 : 8
ʿAbduh, Muḥammad 2007-3 : 25
Abdul Kadir Semarang 2008-1 : 18
Abdul Karim Amrullah (Haji Rasul) 2007-1 : 9
Abdul Rahman, Tunku 2007-1 : 10
Abdülhalim Memduh 2014-2 : 8
Abdülhamid I 2010-1 : 7
Abdülhamid II 2007-3 : 4
Abdulla Şaiq (Talıbzadə) 2015-1 : 8
Abdullah b. Abdul Kadir Munsyi 2007-2 : 26
Abdullah Cevdet 2017-1 : 2
ʿAbdullāh Frères 2007-1 : 11
Abdullah Kaşgari 2014-4 : 1
Abdullah Paşa Kölemen 2014-1 : 4
Abdülmecid Firişteoğlu 2018-6 : 8

Abdülmecid I 2017-5 : 1
Abdulmuhyi 2007-3 : 32
Abdurrahman Hibri 2017-4 : 2
Abdürrahman Nureddin Paşa 2008-1 : 9
Abdurrahman Şeref 2014-2 : 9
Abdurrahman Wahid 2013-1 : 4
Abdurrauf Singkili 2007-2 : 27
Abdürreşid İbrahim Efendi 2018-5 : 1
Abhā 2008-2 : 11
al-Abharī, Athīr al-Dīn 2008-2 : 11
ʿĀbid 2015-1 : 9
ʿAbīd b. al-Abraṣ 2007-3 : 32
Abid Husain 2007-3 : 34
Abidjan 2009-3 : 14
Abikoesno Tjokrosoejoso 2007-2 : 30
al-Abīwardī 2007-2 : 31
Abkhaz 2013-4 : 19
Ablution 2007-2 : 32
Abnāʾ 2009-2 : 26
Abortion 2007-3 : 35
Abraha 2009-2 : 27
Abraham 2008-1 : 18
Abraham b. Dāwūd 2012-2 : 3
Abraham bar Ḥiyya 2007-3 : 38
Abraham de Balmes 2009-1 : 19
Abraham Ibn Ezra 2019-2 : 1
Abrek 2008-1 : 29
Abrogation 2007-3 : 40
Absence and presence 2009-3 : 16
Abū ʿAbdallāh al-Baṣrī 2011-3 : 3
Abū ʿAbdallāh al-Shīʿī 2008-1 : 30
Abū ʿAbdallāh Yaʿqūb b. Dāʾūd 2016-3 : 4
Abū l-ʿĀliya al-Riyāḥī 2007-1 : 12
Abū ʿAlqama al-Naḥwī 2007-2 : 38
Abū l-ʿAmaythal 2007-2 : 39
Abū ʿAmmār ʿAbd al-Kāfī b. Abī Yaʿqūb 2008-1 : 34
Abū ʿAmr b. al-ʿAlāʾ 2009-1 : 20
Abū ʿAmr al-Shaybānī 2015-4 : 5
Abū ʿAmr al-Ṭabarī 2008-2 : 13
Abū l-Aswad al-Duʾalī 2012-3 : 9
Abū ʿAṭāʾ al-Sindī 2008-2 : 14
Abū l-ʿAtāhiya 2009-1 : 23
Abū l-Aʿwar al-Sulamī 2009-4 : 5
Abū ʿAwn Abd al-Malik b. Yazīd 2010-1 : 19
Abū Ayyūb al-Anṣārī 2013-3 : 7
Abū l-ʿAẓm, Maḥmūd 2008-2 : 15
Abū Bakr 2015-2 : 2
Abū Bakr al-ʿAtīq 2014-1 : 6
Abū Bakr b. Sālim 2010-1 : 25
Abū Bakr Bā Kathīr 2013-3 : 8
Abū l-Barakāt Munīr Lāhawrī 2009-4 : 6
Abū Bayhas 2008-1 : 36
Abū Bishr Ḥawshab al-Thaqafī 2007-3 : 48
Abū Dahbal al-Jumaḥī 2015-2 : 7
Abū l-Dardāʾ 2009-1 : 26
Abū Dāwūd al-Sijistānī 2007-3 : 49
Abu Dhabi 2013-4 : 22
Abū l-Dhahab, Muḥammad Bey 2008-1 : 37
Abū Dharr al-Ghifārī 2016-1 : 9
Abū Dhuʾayb 2007-1 : 13
Abū Duʾād al-Iyādī 2007-2 : 40
Abū Dulāma 2007-2 : 40
Abū l-Faḍl-i ʿAllāmī 2009-1 : 26
Abū l-Faraj al-Iṣfahānī 2007-3 : 51
Abū l-Fatḥ b. ʿAbd al-Ḥayy b. ʿAbd al-Muqtadir 2009-1 : 30
Abū l-Fatḥ Khān Zand 2011-2 : 6
Abū l-Fatḥ Mirzā, Sālār al-Dawla 2008-2 : 16
Abū l-Fidāʾ 2008-1 : 39
Abū Fudayk 2007-2 : 41
Abū l-Futūḥ al-Rāzī 2007-3 : 55
Abū Ghānim Bishr b. Ghānim al-Khurāsānī 2007-1 : 14
Abū l-Ghayth b. Jāmil 2008-2 : 17
Abū Ḥafṣ al-Ballūṭī 2015-4 : 7
Abū Ḥafṣ al-Ḥaddād 2009-3 : 18
Abū Ḥafṣ al-Miṣrī 2007-2 : 42
Abū Ḥafṣ al-Shiṭranjī 2007-2 : 43
Abū Ḥafṣ Sughdī 2009-1 : 31
Abū Ḥafṣ ʿUmar b. Jamīʿ 2007-3 : 57
Abū Ḥafṣ ʿUmar al-Hintātī 2009-2 : 32
Abū l-Ḥajjāj Yūsuf al-Uqṣurī 2012-3 : 11
Abū Ḥāmid al-Qudsī 2013-4 : 25
Abū Ḥanīfa 2007-2 : 43
Abū l-Ḥasan Gulistāna 2009-4 : 7
Abū l-Ḥasan Khān Ghaffārī 2009-4 : 8
Abū l-Ḥasan Zayd Fārūqī 2014-1 : 8

Abū Hāshim 2009-2 : 33
Abū Hāshim al-Ṣūfī 2011-2 : 8
Abū Ḥātim al-Malzūzī 2011-3 : 5
Abū Ḥātim al-Rāzī 2011-3 : 7
Abū Ḥātim al-Sijistānī 2007-2 : 52
Abū l-Haytham al-Jurjānī 2014-3 : 3
Abū Ḥayya al-Numayrī 2007-3 : 58
Abū Ḥayyān al-Gharnāṭī 2008-1 : 40
Abū l-Hindī 2008-1 : 41
Abū l-Hudā al-Ṣayyādī 2007-3 : 58
Abū l-Hudhayl 2008-1 : 43
Abū Hurayra 2007-2 : 53
Abū l-Ḥusayn al-Baṣrī 2007-1 : 16
Abū Ḥuzāba 2008-2 : 19
Abū l-ʿIbar 2007-2 : 55
Abū ʿĪsā al-Iṣfahānī 2009-2 : 35
Abū ʿĪsā al-Warrāq 2008-1 : 45
Abū Isḥāq al-Ilbīrī 2007-2 : 56
Abū Isḥāq al-Isfarāyīnī 2008-2 : 19
Abū Jahl 2007-3 : 59
Abū Kāmil Shujāʿ b. Aslam al-Miṣrī 2007-3 : 62
Abū l-Khaṭṭār al-Husām b. Ḍirār al-Kalbī 2009-1 : 32
Abū l-Khayr al-Ishbīlī 2008-2 : 21
Abū Māḍī, Īliyā 2007-3 : 63
Abū Madyan 2016-1 : 10
Abū Maḥallī 2015-2 : 8
Abū Manṣūr Ilyās al-Nafūsī 2012-2 : 4
Abū Manṣūr al-Iṣfahānī 2008-1 : 47
Abū Maʿshar 2007-3 : 64
Abū Maʿshar al-Sindī 2015-2 : 10
Abū l-Mawāhib al-Shādhilī 2009-2 : 37
Abū Mikhnaf 2009-3 : 20
Abū Misḥal 2007-2 : 57
Abū Muḥammad Ṣāliḥ 2013-3 : 9
Abū Muslim al-Khurāsāni 2015-4 : 9
Abū l-Muʾthir al-Bahlawī 2017-2 : 1
Abū l-Najm al-ʿIjlī 2007-2 : 58
Abū Naṣr al-ʿIyāḍī 2009-3 : 25
Abū Nuʿaym al-Iṣfahānī 2011-1 : 10
Abū Nukhayla 2008-2 : 21
Abū Nuwās 2007-1 : 19
Abū l-Qāsim Khān Kirmānī Ibrāhīmī 2009-4 : 10
Abū l-Qāsim Lāhutī 2018-5 : 4
Abū Qubays 2008-1 : 50
Abū Rīda, Muḥammad ʿAbd al-Hādī 2007-3 : 67
Abū Righāl 2007-2 : 59
Abū Riyāsh 2008-1 : 52
Abū Saʿd al-Makhzūmī 2008-2 : 22
Abū Safyān 2009-3 : 25
Abū Saʿīd b. Abī l-Khayr 2009-3 : 26
Abū Saʿīd b. Sulṭān Muḥammad 2013-2 : 1
Abū Saʿīd Bahādur Khān 2018-3 : 1
Abū Saʿīd Shāh 2009-3 : 30
Abū l-Sāj 2009-1 : 33
Abū Salama Ḥafṣ b. Sulaymān al-Khallāl 2009-2 : 38
Abū Salama al-Samarqandī 2008-1 : 53
Abū l-Ṣalt al-Harawī 2009-3 : 31
Abū l-Ṣalt Umayya b. ʿAbd al-ʿAzīz 2009-1 : 35
Abū l-Sarāyā al-Shaybānī 2011-4 : 10
Abū Shabaka, Ilyās 2008-1 : 54
Abū Shādī, Aḥmad Zakī 2007-1 : 23
Abū Shakūr al-Sālimī 2009-3 : 32
Abū Shāma Shihāb al-Dīn al-Maqdisī 2009-2 : 40
Abū Shujāʿ 2016-2 : 9
Abū Sufyān 2009-2 : 41
Abū l-Suʿūd 2009-3 : 33
Abū Ṭāhir Ṭarsūsī 2007-3 : 68
Abū Ṭālib 2009-2 : 42
Abū Ṭālib al-Makkī 2010-1 : 27
Abū Ṭālib Tabrīzī 2009-4 : 12
Abū l-Ṭamaḥān al-Qaynī 2009-1 : 38
Abū Tammām 2007-3 : 70
Abū Tāshufīn I 2011-1 : 14
Abū Tāshufīn II 2011-1 : 14
Abū l-Ṭayyib al-Lughawī 2007-2 : 60
Abū Thawr 2012-1 : 49
Abū Turāb 2008-1 : 55
Abū Turāb al-Nakhshabī 2009-4 : 12
Abū ʿUbayd al-Qāsim b. Sallām 2008-1 : 55
Abū ʿUbayda 2007-1 : 24
Abū ʿUbayda b. al-Jarrāḥ 2007-3 : 75
Abū ʿUthmān al-Dimashqī 2008-1 : 58
Abū l-Wafāʾ al-Būzjānī 2008-2 : 22
Abū l-Walīd al-Ḥimyarī 2007-3 : 77
Abū Yaʿqūb al-Khuraymī 2008-1 : 60
Abū Yaʿqūb al-Sijistānī 2007-1 : 25

Abū Yaʿqūb Yūsuf b. ʿAbd al-Muʾmin 2008-2 : 25
Abū Yaʿqūb Yūsuf al-Hamadānī 2010-1 : 30
Abū Yaʿzā 2016-3 : 5
Abū Yazīd al-Nukkārī 2013-1 : 9
Abū Yūsuf 2011-4 : 11
Abū Yūsuf Yaʿqūb al-Manṣūr 2007-2 : 61
Abū Zahra, Muḥammad 2008-2 : 28
Abū Zakariyyāʾ al-Warjlānī 2012-2 : 5
Abū Zayd al-Anṣārī 2010-2 : 21
Abū Zayd, Naṣr Ḥāmid 2012-4 : 4
Abū Zayd al-Qurashī 2007-2 : 63
Abū Ziyād al-Kilābī 2007-2 : 64
Abū Zurʿa al-Dimashqī 2007-2 : 65
Abū Zurʿa al-Rāzī 2010-1 : 33
Abubakar Gumi 2014-1 : 10
Abūqīr 2009-1 : 39
Abyaḍ, Jūrj 2008-2 : 30
Abyan 2007-3 : 78
Aceh 2007-1 : 26
Acknowledgement 2008-1 : 61
Acquisition 2008-2 : 30
Acre 2007-2 : 66
Action in Ṣūfism 2009-2 : 44
ʿĀd 2008-2 : 33
al-Ādāb 2007-1 : 32
Adab a) Arabic, early developments 2014-3 : 4
Adab b) and Islamic scholarship in the ʿAbbāsid period 2013-4 : 34
Adab c) and Islamic scholarship after the "Sunnī revival" 2013-4 : 38
Adab d) in Ṣūfism 2009-1 : 40
Adab e) modern usage 2014-2 : 10
Adab al-muftī 2008-2 : 33
Adab al-qāḍī 2007-3 : 79
Adabiyah school 2007-2 : 68
Adakale 2009-3 : 37
Adalet Partisi 2017-4 : 3
Adam 2008-1 : 64
Adana 2012-4 : 7
Adapazarı 2010-1 : 35
Adarrāq 2011-3 : 8
Aḍḍāḍ 2012-4 : 10
Adelard of Bath 2008-2 : 37
Aden 2007-2 : 69
Ādhar, Ḥājjī Luṭf ʿAlī Beg 2011-3 : 10
Adhruḥ 2013-4 : 43
ʿAdī b. Ḥātim 2007-3 : 83
ʿAdī b. Musāfir 2011-1 : 15
ʿAdī b. al-Riqāʿ 2009-1 : 43
ʿAdī b. Zayd 2009-2 : 46
Adīb Naṭanzī 2010-1 : 37
Adīb Nīshāpūrī 2016-3 : 9
al-ʿĀḍid li-Dīn Allāh 2009-1 : 44
al-ʿĀdil b. al-Sallār 2015-2 : 14
ʿĀdil Shāh 2009-4 : 14
ʿĀdil Shāhīs 2010-2 : 23
Adile Sultan 2008-1 : 68
Adıvar, Abdülhak Adnan 2008-1 : 70
Adıyaman 2008-1 : 71
ʿAdliyya courts 2007-2 : 70
Administrative law 2008-2 : 38
ʿAdnān 2016-3 : 10
Adni, Recep Dede 2017-5 : 3
Adoption 2008-1 : 72
Adrār of Ifoghas 2011-2 : 10
Adrar of Mauritania 2008-1 : 76
ʿAḍud al-Dawla 2009-3 : 138
ʿAḍud al-Dawla 2011-2 : 12
ʿAḍud al-Dīn Muḥammad b. ʿAbdallāh 2009-2 : 47
ʿAḍud al-Mulk, ʿAlī Riḍā Qājār 2008-1 : 78
Advice and advice literature 2007-1 : 34
Aesthetics 2010-2 : 25
Aetius 2008-1 : 80
Āfāq, Khwāja and the Āfāqiyya 2011-3 : 11
ʿAfar 2017-5 : 5
ʿAfār and Issa 2008-2 : 43
al-Afḍal b. Badr al-Jamālī 2007-2 : 73
Afḍal al-Dīn Turka 2008-1 : 80
Afḍal al-Ḥusaynī 2014-2 : 14
al-Afḍal, Kutayfāt 2015-2 : 16
Afdeeling B 2007-2 : 75
Afghanistan, art and architecture 2007-3 : 85
Afghāns in India 2007-1 : 59
Aflaḥ b. ʿAbd al-Wahhāb 2014-1 : 11
Aflākī ʿĀrifī 2017-1 : 4
ʿAflaq, Michel 2009-1 : 46
Afrāsiyābids 2015-2 : 18
Africa Muslims Agency 2013-3 : 15
Afshār 2010-1 : 38
Afshārids 2012-1 : 50
Afshīn 2011-3 : 14
Afṭasids 2011-2 : 15
Afterlife 2009-3 : 39
al-Afwah al-Awdī 2007-2 : 76
Afyonkarahisar 2011-1 : 16
Agadez 2018-2 : 1
Agadir 2007-2 : 77
Āgahī (Muḥammad Riḍā) 2015-1 : 9
Aganafat 2008-2 : 45
Ağaoğlu, Samet 2016-2 : 11
Agathodaimon 2008-1 : 82
Agehi 2014-1 : 13
Ageng Tirtayasa, Sultan 2007-1 : 62

Āghā Muḥammad Qājār 2012-1 : 53
al-Aghlab al-ʿIjlī 2009-3 : 46
Ağıt 2014-1 : 14
Agnosticism 2009-2 : 47
Agolli, Vehbi 2008-1 : 82
Agop, Güllü 2007-1 : 64
Agra 2011-3 : 15
Ağrı 2010-1 : 42
Agung, Sultan 2007-2 : 78
Agus Salim 2007-2 : 80
al-Aharī, ʿAbd al-Qādir 2009-3 : 46
al-Aḥbāsh 2010-2 : 35
Aḥbāsh movement in Subsaharan Africa 2014-2 : 15
al-Ahdal, ʿAbd al-Raḥmān b. Sulaymān 2007-1 : 64
al-Ahdal family 2010-1 : 43
Aḥdāth 2010-2 : 37
Ahdi 2017-5 : 7
Ahi 2013-2 : 4
Aḥidus 2009-1 : 47
Ahl-i Ḥadīth 2007-3 : 92
Ahl al-ḥall wa-l-ʿaqd 2007-1 : 65
Ahl-i Ḥaqq 2009-2 : 51
Ahl al-Kisāʾ 2008-1 : 83
Ahl al-raʾy 2009-2 : 50
Ahl al-Ṣuffa 2009-1 : 48
Ahl Sunna in Niger 2018-1 : 1
Ahlī-yi Shīrāzī 2008-2 : 45
Aḥmad, name of the Prophet 2007-3 : 97
Aḥmad b. Abī Duʾād 2007-1 : 68
Aḥmad b. Abī l-Ḥawārī 2010-1 : 45
Aḥmad b. ʿAlī Manṣab 2013-3 : 17
Aḥmad b. ʿAliwa 2011-2 : 18
Aḥmad b. ʿAlwān 2008-2 : 47
Aḥmad b. ʿĀṣim al-Anṭākī 2010-1 : 47
Aḥmad b. Ḥābiṭ 2009-2 : 58
Aḥmad b. Ḥanbal 2009-4 : 15
Aḥmad b. Idrīs 2012-2 : 7
Aḥmad b. Muḥammad b. ʿAbd al-Ṣamad 2009-2 : 60
Aḥmad b. Muḥammad b. Sālim 2008-1 : 84
Aḥmad b. Sahl 2009-2 : 60
Aḥmad b. Sumayṭ 2009-2 : 61
Aḥmad b. Ṭūlūn 2011-1 : 18
Aḥmad b. Yaḥyā, Hamīd al-Dīn 2008-1 : 85
Aḥmad Bābā al-Tinbuktī 2011-3 : 39
Aḥmad Bey 2007-3 : 98
Aḥmad-i Bukhārī 2013-1 : 23
Aḥmad Grāñ 2011-3 : 42
Aḥmad-i Jām 2009-1 : 51
Aḥmad al-Kabīr 2010-1 : 48
Aḥmad Khān, Sayyid 2010-1 : 50
Aḥmad Khaṭīb of Minangkabau 2007-3 : 102
Aḥmad Khaṭīb Sambas 2007-1 : 69
Aḥmad Lamīn al-Shinqīṭī 2009-1 : 50
Aḥmad Lobbo 2017-5 : 9
Aḥmad al-Nāṣirī al-Salāwī 2008-1 : 86
Aḥmad Rifaʾi (or Ripangi) 2007-2 : 81
Aḥmad Rizā Khān Barelwī 2007-1 : 71
Ahmad Sanusi bin Abdurrahim of Sukabumi 2007-2 : 83
Aḥmad Shāh Durrānī 2015-2 : 21
Ahmad Siddiq 2007-1 : 75
Aḥmad al-Ṭayyib b. al-Bashīr 2010-2 : 40
Aḥmad Yār 2007-3 : 104
Aḥmad, Zakariyyā 2007-1 : 76
Aḥmadābād 2007-1 : 76
Aḥmadī 2015-1 : 10
al-Aḥmadī 2007-1 : 79
al-Yāfiʿī, Ṣalāḥ
Aḥmadīlīs 2011-4 : 13
Aḥmadiyya 2007-1 : 80
Aḥmadiyya (Badawiyya) 2016-1 : 26
Aḥmadiyya-Idrīsiyya 2010-2 : 42
Aḥmadiyya-Rashīdiyya 2013-3 : 19
Aḥmadnagar 2017-5 : 10
Aḥmadpūrī, Gul Muḥammad 2015-2 : 23
al-Aḥmar, Abū l-Ḥasan 2008-1 : 87
Aḥmed I 2009-3 : 47
Aḥmed II 2009-4 : 23
Aḥmed III 2012-1 : 55
Ahmed Arifi Paşa 2008-1 : 87
Ahmed Azmi Efendi 2007-1 : 86
Ahmed Cevad Paşa, Kabaağaçzade 2008-2 : 49
Ahmed Cevdet Paşa 2009-2 : 62
Ahmed Esad Paşa 2008-2 : 49
Ahmed Hamdi Paşa 2008-2 : 50
Ahmed Haşim 2017-5 : 17
Ahmed İzzet Bey 2016-2 : 12
Ahmed Lütfü Efendi 2007-1 : 87
Ahmed Midhat Efendi 2012-2 : 10
Ahmed Midhat Şefik Paşa 2008-1 : 88
Ahmed Muhtar Paşa, Katırcıoğlu Gazi 2008-2 : 50
Ahmed Paşa 2014-1 : 15
Ahmed Paşa, Bonneval 2012-2 : 11
Ahmed Paşa, Bursalı 2007-1 : 87

Ahmed Paşa, Gedik 2009-3 : 49
Ahmed Paşa, Hersekzade 2011-2 : 20
Ahmed Paşa, Melek 2008-2 : 51
Ahmed Paşa, Şehla 2010-1 : 55
Aḥmed Pasha, al-Khāʾin 2010-1 : 54
Ahmed Rasim 2013-1 : 24
Ahmed Resmi 2009-2 : 64
Ahmed Rıza 2009-4 : 25
Ahmed Şemseddin Marmaravi 2013-4 : 43
Ahmed Şuayb 2010-1 : 56
Ahmed Tevfik Paşa, Okday 2008-1 : 89
Ahmed Vefik Paşa 2009-1 : 54
Aḥmedī 2012-3 : 18
al-Ahrām 2007-1 : 88
Aḥrār Movement 2009-4 : 27
Aḥrār, ʿUbaydallāh 2015-1 : 11
al-Aḥsāʾ 2008-1 : 89
al-Aḥsāʾī, Aḥmad 2008-1 : 90
al-Aḥwal 2019-4 : 8
al-Ahwānī, Aḥmad Fuʾād 2008-2 : 51
Aḥwash 2009-1 : 54
al-Ahwāz 2009-2 : 65
ʿĀʾisha al-Bāʿūniyya 2007-1 : 89
ʿĀʾisha bt. Abī Bakr 2011-2 : 22
ʿĀʾisha bt. Aḥmad al-Qurṭubiyya 2009-3 : 50
ʿĀʾisha bt. Ṭalḥa 2010-1 : 57
ʿĀʾisha Qandīsha 2007-2 : 85
Aïssaouas (ʿĪsāwa) 2009-2 : 67
Ajal 2008-2 : 52
ʿAjārida 2007-3 : 106
Ajem-Turkic 2014-1 : 15
al-ʿAjjāj 2007-1 : 89
ʿAjlūn 2007-1 : 90
Ajmal Khān, Ḥakīm 2009-1 : 56
ʿAjmān 2007-2 : 85
Ajmer 2009-3 : 51
Ajnādayn 2014-1 : 16
Ajūdānbāshī 2009-3 : 54
Ajvatovica 2012-4 : 12
Ak Kirman 2010-2 : 72
Aka Gündüz 2015-3 : 6
al-ʿAkawwak, ʿAlī b. Jabala 2008-1 : 92
Akbar 2011-2 : 27
Akçe 2007-1 : 91
Akhavān Thālith, Mahdī 2015-1 : 16
Akhbāriyya and Uṣūliyya 2007-1 : 92
al-Akhḍarī, ʿAbd al-Raḥmān 2019-2 : 5
al-Akhfash 2009-2 : 68
Akhījūq 2009-3 : 56
Akhī-Qādiriyya 2011-4 : 21
Akhisar 2010-1 : 58
Akhlāṭ 2011-4 : 22
Akhmīm 2009-1 : 56
Akhsīkath 2009-2 : 70
al-Akhṭal 2007-2 : 86
al-Akhṭal al-Ṣaghīr 2009-1 : 58
Akhteri 2018-1 : 3
Ākhūnd al-Khurāsānī 2010-2 : 45
Akif Mehmed Paşa 2011-2 : 36
Akıncı 2014-3 : 14
ʿAkkāsbāshī, Ibrāhīm 2009-3 : 57
Aksaray 2011-1 : 20
Akşehir 2011-1 : 21
Aksel, Malik 2014-2 : 16
Aktham b. Ṣayfī 2014-4 : 2
al-Akwaʿ, Muḥammad 2007-2 : 87
Āl-i Aḥmad, Jalāl 2013-2 : 7
Āl al-Shaykh 2009-1 : 58
ʿAlāʾ al-Dawla, Aḥmad Khān 2009-3 : 59
ʿAlāʾ al-Dīn al-Samarqandī 2008-2 : 54
ʿAlāʾ al-Mulk, Maḥmūd Khān 2009-3 : 60
Alaca Ḥiṣār (Kruševac) 2010-1 : 59
Alagözoghlu, Savvas S. 2014-2 : 18
ʿAlāʾī, Shaykh 2009-1 : 60
ʿĀlam ārā-yi ʿAbbāsī 2008-2 : 56
ʿĀlam-i Nisvān 2010-1 : 60
ʿAlamī family 2008-2 : 58
Alamūt 2007-2 : 88
Alāns 2009-2 : 71
Alanya 2009-4 : 29
Ālāol 2013-3 : 22
Alaşehir 2010-1 : 61
Alauddin Riayat Syah al-Kahar (of Aceh) 2007-2 : 90
Alauddin Tumenanga ri Gaukanna, Sultan 2007-2 : 91
ʿAlawī dynasty 2007-1 : 96
al-ʿAlawī, Jamāl al-Dīn 2009-2 : 73
ʿAlawī, Muḥammad b. ʿAlī 2007-1 : 99
ʿAlawī, Wajīh al-Dīn 2010-1 : 62
ʿAlawīs, classical doctrines 2010-1 : 64
ʿAlawīs, contemporary developments 2010-1 : 69
ʿAlawiyya (in Ḥaḍramawt) 2010-2 : 47
ʿAlawiyya (in Syria and Palestine) 2009-2 : 75
ʿAlawiyya (in the Maghrib) 2009-3 : 62
ʿAlawiyya in East Africa 2013-3 : 24
Alay 2016-1 : 27
Albania 2010-1 : 72
Alborz College 2010-1 : 76
Album 2015-4 : 17
Alchemy 2016-2 : 15
Alembic 2007-2 : 92
Aleppo (pre-Ottoman) 2013-4 : 45

Aleppo, architecture	2011-2 : 37
Aleppo, Ottoman	2014-1 : 18
Alevi music	2013-3 : 25
Alevīs	2008-1 : 93
Alexandria (early period)	2011-4 : 23
Alexandria (modern period)	2011-4 : 36
Alexandria, School of	2016-4 : 2
Alexandropol, Treaty of	2015-1 : 18
Alfā	2008-2 : 59
Alfā Hāshim	2010-1 : 77
Alfonso the Wise	2008-2 : 60
Algebra	2007-1 : 101
Algerian Literature	2007-2 : 93
Algiers	2007-1 : 104
Algorithm	2007-2 : 96
Alhambra	2008-1 : 121
Ali Aziz Efendi	2009-4 : 89
ʿAlī b. al-ʿAbbās al-Majūsī	2009-2 : 76
ʿAlī b. ʿAbdallāh b. ʿAbbās	2009-2 : 77
ʿAlī b. Abī Ṭālib	2008-2 : 62
ʿAlī b. Ḥanẓala b. Abī Sālim	2008-1 : 135
ʿAlī b. al-Ḥusayn	2013-3 : 26
ʿAlī b. al-Ḥusayn b. al-Ḥusayn b. ʿAlī al-Qurashī	2008-2 : 71
ʿAlī b. Ḥusayn Wāʿiẓ Kāshifī	2009-1 : 60
ʿAlī b. Ibrāhīm al-Qummī	2008-1 : 136
ʿAlī b. ʿĪsā	2009-3 : 64
ʿAlī b. ʿĪsā b. Dāʾūd b. al-Jarrāḥ	2013-2 : 10
ʿAlī b. Khalaf al-Kātib	2007-2 : 97
ʿAlī b. Muḥammad al-Wafāʾ	2007-2 : 98
ʿAlī b. Muḥammad al-Zanjī	2010-1 : 79
ʿAlī b. Sulaymān al-Muqaddasī	2012-3 : 19
ʿAlī b. ʿUbayda al-Rayḥānī	2009-1 : 61
ʿAlī b. al-Walīd	2009-3 : 66
ʿAlī Bey al-Kabīr	2007-2 : 100
ʿAlī Dede al-Sigetvārī	2011-4 : 40
ʿAlī Dīnār	2015-1 : 19
Ali Ekber Hıtai	2013-3 : 26
Ali Ekrem Bolayir	2014-1 : 24
ʿAlī Emīrī	2010-2 : 50
ʿAlī l-Hādī	2017-2 : 2
Ali Haji, Raja	2007-2 : 102
Ali Hasjmy	2016-3 : 12
ʿAlī Ḥaydar	2007-2 : 105
ʿAlī Hormova	2009-4 : 33
Ali İhsan Sabis	2015-2 : 24
ʿAlī Kurdī Maqtūl	2011-2 : 46
ʿAlī Mardān Khān Bakhtiyārī	2008-2 : 72
ʿAlī Mubārak	2007-3 : 108
ʿAlī Murād Khān Zand	2012-1 : 58
ʿAlī Muttaqī	2009-1 : 63
Ali Paşa Çorlulu	2009-3 : 65
Ali Paşa, Damat (Şehit)	2012-2 : 14
Ali Paşa, Hadım	2010-2 : 51
Ali Paşa Hekimoğlu	2008-1 : 138
Ali Paşa, Mehmed Emin	2008-2 : 73
Ali Paşa, Sürmeli	2009-3 : 66
Ali Paşa Tepedelenli	2014-3 : 16
ʿĀlī Qāpū	2008-2 : 74
ʿAlī al-Qārī	2014-3 : 18
ʿAlī Qulī Jadīd al-Islām	2009-3 : 68
ʿAlī Qulī Khān	2007-2 : 106
ʿAlī al-Riḍā	2009-3 : 69
Ali Rıza Paşa	2016-3 : 12
ʿAlī Shīr Navāʾī	2011-1 : 22
ʿAlī Suʿāvī	2012-1 : 59
ʿAlī al-Zaybaq, Romance of	2007-2 : 107
ʿAlids	2008-2 : 78
Alimuddin, Sultan (of Sulu)	2007-1 : 107
Aliran	2007-2 : 109
ʿAlizāda, Ghazāla	2013-2 : 14
Allāh Virdī Khān	2015-1 : 20
Allāh Virdī Khān	2009-4 : 36
Allāh-Naẓar	2012-1 : 61
Allahu akbar	2007-3 : 110
Allāhumma	2009-3 : 74
Allusion (in Ṣūfism)	2012-2 : 15
ʿAllūya	2019-4 : 9
ʿAlma	2014-3 : 21
al-Almālī, Maḥmūd	2011-1 : 29
Almāmī	2008-2 : 81
Almamy ʿAbd al-Qādir	2012-1 : 62
Almaty	2010-1 : 81
Almaz	2013-3 : 28
Almohads	2014-1 : 25
Almoravids	2009-3 : 75
Almucantar	2009-1 : 66
Alp Arslan	2013-2 : 15
Alpago, Andrea	2008-2 : 82
Alptekin	2011-2 : 47
ʿAlqama	2009-1 : 66
Alqās Mīrzā	2015-4 : 21
Altai	2010-2 : 52
Altai, region, culture and language	2010-2 : 54
Altaians	2010-2 : 55
Altınay, Ahmed Refik	2014-4 : 3
Altruism	2010-2 : 56
Altūntāsh al-Ḥājib	2016-1 : 29
Aludel	2011-2 : 48
Alus, Sermet Muhtar	2016-3 : 14
al-Ālūsī family	2009-1 : 68
al-Aʿmā al-Tuṭīlī	2009-1 : 72
Amal	2008-2 : 83
ʿAmal (judicial practice)	2007-2 : 112
ʿAmālīq	2009-2 : 81
Amān	2007-3 : 111
Amānallāh Pānīpatī	2011-2 : 49

Amānallāh Shāh 2010-1 : 82
Amangkurat I, Susunan 2007-2 : 117
al-ʿAmāra 2007-2 : 119
al-Aʿmash 2009-1 : 73
Amasya 2012-2 : 16
Amasya, Treaty of 2015-4 : 23
Amber 2007-2 : 119
Ambiguity 2013-4 : 50
Ambon 2007-1 : 109
Amen 2009-3 : 80
Amghar 2007-3 : 113
ʿAmīd 2009-4 : 37
al-Āmidī, Abū l-Qāsim 2010-1 : 84
al-ʿAmīdī, Abū Saʿīd 2008-1 : 138
al-ʿAmīdī, Rukn al-Dīn 2008-2 : 84
al-Āmidī, Sayf al-Dīn 2012-3 : 20
ʿĀmil, Jabal 2009-3 : 81
ʿĀmila 2010-1 : 87
al-ʿĀmilī Iṣfahānī, Abū l-Ḥasan 2009-1 : 78
Amīn, Aḥmad 2008-2 : 85
Amīn al-Ḍarb 2010-2 : 59
Amīn al-Ḍarb II 2008-2 : 86
Amīn al-Dawla 2008-1 : 139
Amīn al-Dīn Abū l-Qāsim Ḥājjī Bula 2011-1 : 31
al-Amīn, Muḥammad 2010-2 : 61
al-Amīn, Muḥsin 2008-2 : 87
Amīn, Qāsim 2007-2 : 120
Amīn, ʿUthmān 2008-2 : 88
Āmina 2007-3 : 114
Amīna 2010-2 : 64
Amīna-yi Aqdas 2010-2 : 65
Amīnjī b. Jalāl b. Ḥasan 2009-1 : 80
Aminu Kano 2013-2 : 18
ʿĀmir I and II 2007-1 : 110
Amīr-ākhūr-bāshī 2010-2 : 67
Amīr ʿAlī, Sayyid 2009-2 : 81
al-Āmir bi-Aḥkām Allāh 2011-2 : 51
Amīr al-ḥājj 2015-1 : 22
Amīr Kabīr 2015-4 : 24
Amīr Khurd 2015-2 : 27
Amīr Khusraw Dihlavī 2017-3 : 1
Amīr-i Lashkar 2011-1 : 35
Amīr majlis 2009-3 : 84
al-Amīr, Muḥammad b. Ismāʿīl 2007-1 : 111
Amīr Niẓām Garrūsī, Ḥasan ʿAlī Khān 2008-2 : 89
Amīr Silāḥ 2009-4 : 38
Amīr al-umarāʾ 2011-1 : 33
ʿĀmirids 2013-4 : 54
Amjad Ḥaydarābādī 2019-3 : 1
al-ʿĀmm wa-l-khāṣṣ 2007-3 : 115
Amma Aççıgıya 2018-1 : 4
Amman 2007-2 : 122
Amman, Mīr 2014-1 : 32
ʿAmmār b. ʿAlī al-Mawṣilī 2008-2 : 92
ʿAmmār b. Yāsir 2011-2 : 53
ʿAmmār, Banū (Libya) 2015-3 : 8
ʿAmmār, Banū (Syria) 2014-3 : 24
ʿAmmār al-Baṣrī 2009-4 : 39
Ammonius (Ps.) son of Hermias 2007-1 : 111
ʿAmmūriyya 2007-1 : 112
Ampel, Sunan 2007-2 : 122
Amputation 2010-1 : 89
Amr (theology) 2011-3 : 45
ʿAmr b. ʿAdī 2010-1 : 90
ʿAmr b. al-ʿĀṣ 2010-2 : 68
ʿAmr b. Dīnār 2009-3 : 84
ʿAmr b. Hind 2010-2 : 69
ʿAmr b. Kirkira 2009-3 : 86
ʿAmr b. Kulthūm 2008-2 : 93
ʿAmr b. al-Layth 2010-1 : 91
ʿAmr b. Luḥayy 2008-1 : 141
ʿAmr b. Maʿdīkarib 2009-2 : 83
ʿAmr b. Masʿada 2010-1 : 92
ʿAmr b. Qamīʾa 2007-2 : 123
ʿAmr b. ʿUbayd 2008-2 : 94
Amrī Shīrāzī 2008-2 : 96
Āmū Daryā 2018-3 : 3
Amulet 2007-2 : 124
ʿAmwās, plague of 2016-2 : 28
Ana Bacı 2016-1 : 30
Anabolu 2008-1 : 142
Anadolu Ḥisārı 2008-2 : 97
Analogy 2013-1 : 25
Anamur 2008-2 : 97
ʿĀnāniyya 2011-3 : 48
ʿAnāq 2009-1 : 81
Anarchism 2012-2 : 19
Anas b. Mālik 2011-4 : 41
Anastasiades, Leontinos 2013-3 : 28
Anatomy 2007-2 : 126
ʿAnaza 2012-1 : 63
ʿAnbar Ānā 2010-1 : 93
al-Anbārī, Abū Bakr 2009-1 : 82
al-Anbārī, Abū Muḥammad 2009-1 : 83
al-ʿAnbarī, ʿUbaydallāh b. al-Ḥasan 2015-3 : 9
Anbiya, Sĕrat 2007-1 : 113
Ancients and Moderns 2007-1 : 113
ʿAndalīb, Khvāja Muḥammad 2014-1 : 33
al-Andalus, etymology and name 2017-5 : 18
al-Andalus, political history 2017-5 : 25
Andalusian art and architecture 2007-3 : 118
Andalusian music 2009-2 : 84
Andelib, Mehmet Esat 2016-3 : 15
Andijān uprising 2012-2 : 20
Angāre 2009-1 : 84
Angels 2009-3 : 86
Angels in art and architecture 2007-1 : 114

Angkatan Belia Islam Malaysia 2007-1 : 11
Anglo-Muhammadan law 2009-1 : 84
Animals 2014-3 : 25
Animals, in law 2008-1 : 144
Animism 2007-1 : 116
Anīs 2017-2 : 3
Anīs al-Dawla 2009-1 : 91
Anjuman-i Khuddām-i Kaʿba 2008-2 : 98
Anjuman-i Khuddām-i al-Ṣūfiyya 2013-3 : 29
Anjuman-i Maʿārif 2010-1 : 95
Ankara, Treaty of 2015-2 : 29
ʿAnnāzids 2014-3 : 32
Annihilation and abiding in God 2008-1 : 148
Anniyya 2009-2 : 92
al-ʿAnqāʾ, Muḥammad 2014-2 : 20
Anqaravī, Ismāʿīl 2009-3 : 99
al-Anṣār (Sudan) 2009-3 : 101
ʿAnṣara 2015-4 : 28
al-Anṣārī, ʿAbdallāh 2019-3 : 4
al-Anṣārī, Abū l-Ḥasan 2009-1 : 92
al-Anṣārī, Abū l-Qāsim 2009-2 : 94
Anṣārī Mukhtār Aḥmad 2007-3 : 133
al-Anṣārī, Murtaḍā b. Muḥammad 2008-2 : 100
al-Anṣārī, Zakariyyāʾ 2012-2 : 24
Ansor 2007-2 : 131
Antakya 2019-1 : 1
Antalya 2007-1 : 117
al-Antāqī, Yaḥyā b. Saʿīd 2009-3 : 103
ʿAntar Sīrat 2007-2 : 133
ʿAntara 2008-2 : 101
Antemoro 2013-2 : 19
Anthologies, Arabic literature (pre-Mongol period) 2007-1 : 118
Anthologies, Arabic Literature (post-Mongol period) 2007-1 : 124
Anthologies, Ottoman 2014-3 : 35
Anthropology of Islam 2016-3 : 16
Anthropomorphism 2011-4 : 46
Antimony 2014-2 : 21
Antinomianism 2014-2 : 22
Anti-Ṣūfī polemics 2012-2 : 26
Anṭūn, Faraḥ 2010-2 : 70
Anūshirwān b. Khālid 2009-2 : 96
Anvarī, Awḥad al-Dīn 2017-5 : 35
Anwāʾ 2007-2 : 137
Apendi 2013-4 : 55
Aphorism 2009-1 : 93
Apocalypse 2007-1 : 128
Apollo Group 2007-3 : 135
Apollonius of Perge 2011-1 : 35
Apollonius of Tyana 2009-4 : 39
Apology 2007-2 : 138
Apostasy 2007-1 : 131
Apostle 2009-3 : 104
Appeal 2007-2 : 139
Aq Shams al-Dīn 2013-1 : 29
Āq-Sunqur al-Bursuqī 2010-1 : 96
Āqā Najafī Iṣfahānī 2011-3 : 49
Āqā Najafī Qūchānī 2010-2 : 72
al-ʿAqaba 2007-2 : 143
ʿAqīl b. Abī Ṭālib 2009-3 : 105
ʿAqīl Khān Rāzī 2013-4 : 55
ʿĀqila 2008-2 : 102
Aqın 2013-2 : 23
ʿAqīqa 2007-3 : 136
ʿAql, Saʿīd 2017-5 : 39
al-ʿAqqād, ʿAbbās Maḥmūd 2007-1 : 134
Aqrābādhīn 2009-1 : 97
al-Aqṣā mosque 2009-1 : 97
al-Aqṣā mosque, art and architecture 2007-1 : 136
al-Aqsarāyī, Karīm al-Dīn 2008-2 : 104
Aqueduct 2007-2 : 144
Arab Higher Committee 2018-4 : 1
Arab League 2011-2 : 55
Arab Revolt 2016-1 : 32
ʿAraba, Wādī 2010-1 : 97
Arabacı Ali Paşa 2017-1 : 6
Arabesk 2013-3 : 31
Arabesque 2010-1 : 97
al-Aʿrābī, Abū Saʿīd 2010-1 : 100
al-ʿArabī, Muḥammad Nūr al-Dīn 2015-3 : 11
Arabian Nights 2007-1 : 137
Arabian Peninsula 2008-2 : 105
Arabian Peninsula, art and architecture 2009-1 : 102
Arabic language: pre-classical 2016-5 : 1
Arabic language: the dialects 2008-2 : 118
Arabic literature 2007-1 : 145
Arabism, Arabists 2008-2 : 125
Arabs (anthropology) 2013-3 : 32
Arabs (historical) 2010-2 : 73
al-ʿArabshāhī, Mīr Abū l-Fatḥ 2019-1 : 3
Arad 2008-1 : 150
al-Aʿrāf 2017-4 : 4
ʿArafāt 2009-3 : 107
ʿArafāt, Yāsir 2008-1 : 151
Arakan 2009-4 : 42
Aral (sea) 2014-4 : 5
Arapkir 2009-1 : 114
Ararat 2012-4 : 14

Arawān 2011-4 : 55
Araz, Nezihe 2016-3 : 23
Arbitration 2014-3 : 37
Archaeology 2009-4 : 47
Archery 2007-1 : 155
Archimedes 2007-3 : 137
Architecture 2007-3 : 139
Archives and chanceries: Ethiopia 2019-2 : 7
Archives and chanceries: Arab world 2012-4 : 17
Archives and chanceries: Ottoman Empire and Turkey 2012-3 : 23
Archives and chanceries: pre-1500, in Arabic 2013-2 : 24
Archives: Central Asia 2016-5 : 6
Arcot 2010-2 : 78
Ardabīl 2007-2 : 146
Ardahan 2011-1 : 37
Arghūn b. Abāqā 2009-3 : 109
Argot, Turkish 2013-2 : 32
Argots 2007-2 : 150
ʿArīb 2013-3 : 35
ʿArīb b. Saʿīd al-Qurṭūbī 2007-1 : 160
ʿArīḍa, Nasīb 2008-2 : 125
ʿArīf 2007-1 : 161
Arif Çelebi 2018-2 : 3
ʿArīf Chelebī 2007-3 : 170
ʿĀrif Qazvīnī 2014-2 : 27
ʿĀrifī Harawī, Mawlānā Maḥmūd 2009-1 : 114
Aristotle and Aristotelianism 2008-1 : 153
Arithmetic 2009-2 : 96
al-ʿArjī 2009-2 : 101
Arkoun, Mohammed 2015-1 : 24
Arkush 2010-1 : 101
Armenia (topography) 2014-1 : 36
Armenia, Armenians: 1100-1 :895 2016-3 : 24
Arms and armour 2007-2 : 151
Army, India (c. 1200-1 :947) 2015-1 : 27
Army of Iran, since 1800 2015-1 : 32
Army, Ottoman (1300-1 :700) 2016-1 : 33
Army, Ottoman (1700-1 :923) 2018-6 : 10
al-Arnāʾūṭ, Maʿrūf Aḥmad 2008-2 : 126
Arpalık 2010-1 : 103
al-Arrajānī 2007-2 : 158
al-ʿArrāqiyya 2016-2 : 29
Arrogance 2008-2 : 127
Arşi Tireli 2016-4 : 6
Arşi Yenipazarlı 2017-1 : 8
Arslān Arghun 2014-4 : 5
Arslān al-Dimashqī 2009-4 : 66
Arslan, Shakīb 2007-3 : 171
Arslān-bāb 2014-4 : 6
Arsūf, battle of 2007-3 : 172
al-Arsūzī, Zakī 2009-1 : 115
Artemidorus of Ephesus 2007-1 : 162
Artificial insemination 2007-2 : 158
Artisans, Iran 2011-3 : 56
Artisans, Ottoman and post-Ottoman 2011-3 : 65
Artisans (pre-1500) 2012-2 : 29
Artist, status of 2009-2 : 102
Artvin 2011-1 : 38
ʿArūbī 2018-6 : 18
Arung Palakka 2007-2 : 160
Arūr 2009-3 : 111
Arzan 2019-4 : 10
Arzew 2009-2 : 110
Ārzū 2019-2 : 10
ʿAṣabiyya 2016-3 : 31
Asad b. ʿAbdallāh 2009-3 : 112
Asad b. al-Furāt 2008-1 : 169
Asad Beg Qazvīnī 2015-2 : 29
al-Asad, Ḥāfiẓ 2013-2 : 34
Asad, Muḥammad 2009-1 : 116
Asadābādh 2014-3 : 41
Asadī Ṭūsī 2015-3 : 12
Āṣaf b. Barakhyā 2009-2 : 110
Āṣaf al-Dawla 2007-3 : 173
Āṣaf Jāh 2009-2 : 111
Āṣaf Khān 2008-2 : 135
Āṣaf al-lughāt 2010-1 : 104
Āṣafī Harawī 2009-2 : 115
al-Aṣamm 2011-3 : 71
al-Aṣamm, Sufyān b. Abrad al-Kalbī 2014-4 : 7
Aṣbagh b. al-Faraj 2009-1 : 117
Asceticism 2007-1 : 163
Asclepius 2011-1 : 38
al-Aṣfar 2007-1 : 170
Asfār b. Shīrawayhī 2019-3 : 7
al-Aʿshā 2010-1 : 106
Aʿshā Bāhila 2009-2 : 115
Aʿshā Hamdān 2007-2 : 162
Ashanti 2007-3 : 174
al-Ashʿarī, Abū Burda 2010-2 : 81
al-Ashʿarī, Abū Mūsā 2016-2 : 31
al-Ashʿath b. Qays 2009-3 : 113
Ashgabat 2010-1 : 108
Ashhab 2009-3 : 115
ʿĀshiq Iṣfahānī 2014-3 : 43
Ashīr 2009-4 : 67
Ashjaʿ al-Sulamī 2009-3 : 117
Ashkivarī, Quṭb al-Dīn 2011-1 : 39
Ashraf ʿAlī Thānavī 2015-3 : 14
Ashraf Ghilzay 2009-4 : 68
Ashraf Jahāngīr al-Simnānī 2012-2 : 36
Ashraf Māzandarānī 2011-1 : 41
Ashrafī 2013-2 : 35
al-Ashtar, Mālik b. al-Ḥārith 2014-3 : 44

al-Āshtiyānī, Ḥasan 2008-2 : 136
Ashugh 2015-2 : 31
ʿĀshūr Nuʿmān 2009-2 : 116
ʿĀshūrāʾ (Shīʿism) 2013-3 : 36
ʿĀshūrāʾ (Sunnism) 2011-1 : 43
Âşık 2007-1 : 170
Âşık Çelebi 2017-2 : 5
Aşık Mehmed 2014-2 : 28
Âşık Ömer 2016-2 : 33
Aşık Veysel 2007-3 : 177
Aṣīla 2010-1 : 108
ʿĀṣim 2013-1 : 30
Aşıq Pəri 2016-1 : 44
ʿĀşıqpaşazāde 2012-1 : 67
Asīr-i Iṣfahānī 2009-4 : 69
Āsiya 2009-2 : 117
ʿAskar Mukram 2015-3 : 17
al-ʿAskarī, Abū Aḥmad 2009-1 : 118
al-ʿAskarī, Abū Hilāl 2007-2 : 162
Aşki İlyas 2018-3 : 5
Askiya Muḥammad 2018-2 : 6
Asmāʾ bt. Abī Bakr 2009-3 : 118
Asmahān 2017-5 : 41
al-Aṣmaʿī 2009-3 : 119
al-Asmar al-Faytūrī 2011-4 : 56
ʿAsqalān 2009-3 : 122
Assassins 2007-3 : 178
Association Musulmane des Etudiants d'Afrique Noire 2015-4 : 30
Assyrian Christians 2013-1 : 31
Astana 2008-1 : 171
Astarābādh 2017-4 : 5
Astarābādī, Faḍlallāh 2015-1 : 35
al-Astarābādhī, Raḍī al-Dīn 2009-2 : 118
Astrakhan 2010-1 : 109
Astrolabes, quadrants, and calculating devices 2007-1 : 171
Astrology 2007-2 : 165
Astronomy 2009-1 : 120
al-Aswad b. Yaʿfur 2009-2 : 118
Aswan 2007-1 : 175
Asyūṭ 2009-1 : 150
ʿAṭāʾ b. Abī Rabāḥ 2009-1 : 153
Ata, Üsküplü 2018-3 : 6
ʿAtābā 2014-4 : 9
Atābak (Atabeg) 2010-2 : 84
Atai 2013-2 : 36
Ātashī, Manūchihr 2016-2 : 34
Atatürk, Mustafa Kemal 2010-1 : 112
Aṭfayyash, Muḥammad b. Yūsuf 2016-3 : 35
Athanasius of Balad 2009-1 : 155
al-Ātharī 2009-2 : 119
Atheism (premodern) 2009-4 : 70
Atheism (modern) 2015-3 : 17
Athens 2008-2 : 138
Athīr al-Dīn Ākhsīkatī 2016-4 : 7
Athos 2009-3 : 124
Atıf Efendi 2007-3 : 180
ʿĀtika bint Shuhda 2013-2 : 39
Atil 2009-2 : 120
ʿAtīra 2010-1 : 116
Ātish, Ḥaydar ʿAlī 2015-4 : 32
Atomism 2013-1 : 32
al-Aṭrash, Farīd 2008-2 : 141
al-Aṭrash, Sulṭān 2008-1 : 172
Atsız b. Muḥammad 2015-1 : 43
al-ʿAttābī 2009-3 : 127
ʿAṭṭār, ʿAlāʾ al-Dīn-i 2011-3 : 74
ʿAṭṭār, Farīd al-Dīn 2016-2 : 36
al-ʿAṭṭās, Aḥmad b. Ḥasan 2007-2 : 176
al-Aṭṭās family 2010-1 : 117
Attorney 2009-2 : 121
Attributes of God 2007-2 : 176
Australia 2007-1 : 176
Authority, judicial 2018-3 : 7
Authority, religious 2011-2 : 57
Autobiography in Arabic literature (since 1900) 2010-1 : 121
Autobiography, Urdu 2015-1 : 45
Automata 2009-4 : 74
Avarice, in premodern Arabic literature 2016-1 : 44
Avarız 2009-3 : 135
Avars 2009-3 : 129
Āvāz 2007-2 : 182
Averroism 2011-1 : 48
Avlonya 2013-4 : 56
Avni (Mehmed II) 2017-1 : 9
ʿAwaḍ, Luwīs 2011-3 : 75
Awadh 2008-2 : 143
Awāʾil 2014-2 : 29
ʿAwāna b. al-Ḥakam al-Kalbī 2015-4 : 33
al-ʿAwāzim 2007-2 : 183
Awdaghost 2009-4 : 80
ʿAwfī, Sadīd al-Dīn 2015-3 : 20
Awḥad al-Dīn al-Rāzī 2009-2 : 122
Awḥadī Marāghaʾī 2011-1 : 59
Awlād al-Nās 2007-2 : 184
Awlād al-Shaykh 2012-4 : 22
ʿAwlaqī 2007-2 : 185
Awrangzīb 2011-1 : 64
al-Aws 2014-4 : 10
Aws b. Ḥajar 2007-2 : 187
ʿAwwād, Tawfīq Yūsuf 2009-2 : 123
al-Awzāʿī 2009-3 : 136
Axundzadə, Mirzə Fətəli 2015-2 : 32
Āya 2008-1 : 172
Aya Mavra (Lefkas) 2012-4 : 24
Aya Stefanos, Treaty of 2017-5 : 42
Ayas Mehmed Paşa 2017-1 : 10
Ayaşlı, Münevver 2014-2 : 35
Aybak, al-Muʿizz ʿIzz al-Dīn 2009-4 : 82

al-ʿAydarūs 2011-1 : 76
Aydede 2013-1 : 39
ʿAydhāb 2015-3 : 22
ʿAydīd, ʿAbdallāh b. Abī Bakr 2007-1 : 178
Aydın 2009-4 : 85
Ayin 2009-4 : 86
Ayisyiyah 2007-2 : 188
Ayla 2015-4 : 35
ʿAyn Jālūt 2007-1 : 178
ʿAyn Mūsā 2007-3 : 181
ʿAyn al-Quḍāt al-Hamadhānī (life and work) 2008-2 : 145
ʿAyn al-Quḍāt al-Hamadhānī (intellectual legacy) 2008-2 : 149
Aynabakhtı 2009-4 : 87
al-ʿAynī, Badr al-Dīn 2014-3 : 45
ʿAynī, Ṣadr al-Dīn 2014-4 : 14
ʿĀyşe Ṣıddīqa 2009-4 : 88
Ayvalık 2010-1 : 124
Ayvaz Dede 2011-3 : 76
Ayverdi, Samiha 2016-3 : 37
Ayyām al-ʿArab 2007-3 : 182
ʿAyyār 2014-1 : 38
Ayyūb, Dhū l-Nūn 2007-2 : 189
Ayyūb, Rashīd 2007-2 : 190
Ayyūbid art and architecture 2007-1 : 179
Ayyūbids 2007-2 : 191
ʿAyyūqī 2015-4 : 37
Āzād, Abū l-Kalām 2009-2 : 124
Āzād Bilgrāmī, Ghulām ʿAlī 2013-2 : 40
Āzād Khān Afghān 2012-1 : 68
Azalay 2011-2 : 62
Āzar 2009-1 : 155
Azāriqa 2008-1 : 174
al-Azdī, Abū l-Muṭahhar 2011-4 : 60
al-Azdī, Abū l-Walīd 2009-1 : 156

al-Azdī, Abū Zakariyyāʾ 2010-1 : 125
Azep 2013-1 : 41
Azerbaijani literature 2015-2 : 34
al-Azhar, modern period 2007-3 : 185
al-Azharī, Abū Manṣūr 2007-3 : 188
al-Azharī, Khālid b. ʿAbdallāh 2008-1 : 176
ʿAzīma and rukhsa 2007-3 : 188
Azimuth 2009-1 : 157
al-ʿAzīz bi'llāh 2009-1 : 158
ʿAzīz al-Dīn al-Nasafī 2012-1 : 69
ʿAzīz Koka 2008-2 : 151
ʿAzīz Maḥmūd, Shaykh of Urūmiyya 2012-4 : 27
ʿAzīz Miṣr 2009-4 : 90
al-ʿAẓm family 2007-3 : 190
Azov (Azak) 2010-1 : 128
Āzurda 2013-4 : 59
ʿAzza al-Maylāʾ 2013-2 : 41
ʿAzzām, ʿAbdallāh 2009-3 : 138
ʿAzzām, Samīra 2007-3 : 191
Bā ʿAbbād 2014-1 : 41
Bā ʿAlawī 2011-1 : 80
Bā Kathīr, ʿAlī Aḥmad 2011-1 : 81
Bā Makhrama, ʿUmar 2010-2 : 88
Ba, Tijani 2014-1 : 43
Bā Wazīr 2014-1 : 44
Baabullah 2009-3 : 141
Baal 2013-3 : 40
Bāb (in Shīʿism) 2010-2 : 90
Baba 2014-3 : 48
Baba Faraj 2013-3 : 41
Baba İlyas-i Horasani 2015-1 : 48
Bābā Sammāsī 2015-3 : 25
Bābā Ṭāhir (ʿUryān) 2009-4 : 92
Babaeski 2013-1 : 43
Babai 2015-1 : 51

Bābak 2011-1 : 82
Bābur 2008-2 : 153
Bachetarzi, Mahieddine 2018-2 : 9
Badāʾ 2015-4 : 39
Badajoz 2018-3 : 14
Badakhshī, Nūr al-Dīn Jaʿfar 2016-3 : 39
Badar ud-Din 2009-3 : 141
Badawī al-Jabal 2010-1 : 130
al-Badawī, al-Sayyid 2016-1 : 47
Bādghīs 2010-1 : 132
Badīʿ 2009-3 : 142
al-Badīʿ al-Asṭurlābī 2009-2 : 128
Badīʿ al-Dīn 2009-3 : 144
Badía y Leblich, Domingo 201[illegible]-1 : 12
al-Badīʿī, Yūsuf 2009-3 : 147
Badīʿiyya 2009-4 : 94
Badr 201[illegible]-3 : 78
Badr al-Dīn al-Ḥasanī 201[illegible]-1 : 44
Badr al-Dīn Ibn Mālik 2009-1 : 161
Badr al-Dīn Tabrīzī 2016-4 : 9
al-Badr al-Ḥabashī 201[illegible]-1 : 84
Badr al-Jamālī 201[illegible]-1 : 133
Badr Shīrvānī 2009-4 : 96
al-Badrī, Abū l-Tuqā 2009-3 : 147
Badrī Kashmīrī 2009-4 : 97
Bādūsbānids 2013-5 : 5
Baeza 201[illegible]-2 : 38
Bağçasaray 201[illegible]-1 : 55
Baggara 2013-3 : 43
al-Baghawī Abū Muḥammad 201[illegible]-1 : 86
Baghdad, 1500-1 :932 2015-3 : 41
Bāghnawī, Ḥabīballāh 2012-3 : 28
Bagirmi 201[illegible]-4 : 62
Bahāʾ al-Dawla 2015-1 : 55
Bahāʾ al-Dīn Zuhayr 2010-1 : 134

Bahā Tevfīq 2012-1 : 72
Bahaeddin Şakir 2014-2 : 37
Bahāʾī Meḥmed Efendi 2016-1 : 48
Bahari 2017-2 : 7
Bahāwalpūr 2017-1 : 13
Bahcat Muṣṭafā Efendi 2009-3 : 148
al-Bāhilī, ʿAbd al-Raḥmān b. Rabīʿa 2014-3 : 49
Baḥīrā 2011-3 : 82
Bahmanī dynasty 2016-5 : 8
Bahmanyār b. al-Marzubān 2009-1 : 163
Baḥr al-ʿUlūm, ʿAbd al-ʿĀlī 2015-2 : 40
Baḥr al-ʿUlūm, Muḥammad Mahdī 2009-3 : 149
Bahrain 2017-5 : 44
Bahrām 2011-4 : 63
Bahrām Mīrzā 2012-1 : 73
Bahrām Shāh 2010-1 : 135
Bahrām Shāh b. Ṭughril Shāh 2011-1 : 88
al-Baḥrānī, Aḥmad b. Muḥammad 2009-3 : 150
al-Baḥrānī, ʿAlī b. Sulaymān 2009-3 : 151
al-Baḥrānī, Yūsuf b. Aḥmad 2012-1 : 75
Baḥya b. Paqūda 2012-3 : 30
Bai Shouyi 2015-4 : 41
Baikal 2012-1 : 76
Bāj 2011-3 : 83
Bāja 2012-4 : 30
al-Bajalī 2014-2 : 38
al-Bājī, Abū l-Walīd 2011-1 : 89
Bajkam, Abū l-Ḥusayn 2014-4 : 16
al-Bājūrī, Ibrāhīm b. Muḥammad 2009-2 : 130
Bākharzī, Yaḥyā 2014-1 : 47
Bakhīt al-Muṭīʿī, Muḥammad 2010-2 : 92
Bakhshī (Central Asia) 2018-4 : 3
Bakhshī (Mughal) 2014-4 : 17
Bakht Khān 2009-3 : 152
Bakhtāvar Khān 2015-3 : 26
Bakhtiyār-nāma 2010-1 : 137
Baki 2013-2 : 41
al-Bakkāʾī, Aḥmad 2013-3 : 44
Bakr al-Mawṣilī 2010-2 : 92
al-Bakrī, Abū l-Ḥasan 2019-4 : 12
al-Bakrī, Abū ʿUbayd 2011-4 : 64
al-Bakrī, Muḥammad b. Abī l-Ḥasan 2019-4 : 14
al-Bakrī, Muṣṭafā Kamāl al-Dīn 2014-2 : 39
Bakriyya 2015-3 : 29
Baku architecture 2014-3 : 50
Balaban, Ghiyāth al-Dīn 2011-3 : 84
al-Balafīqī 2010-2 : 93
Balāghī, Muḥammad Jawād 2013-1 : 45
Balambangan 2009-3 : 153
al-Balʿamī 2016-2 : 41
Balāsāghūn 2010-2 : 95
al-Balawī 2015-3 : 31
Baldırzade Mehmed Efendi 2015-1 : 57
Bale 2013-3 : 46
Balıkesir 2015-2 : 41
Bālis 2010-2 : 96
Balj b. Bishr 2011-2 : 63
Balkan Wars 2018-1 : 5
Balkans 2015-3 : 32
Balkar 2013-1 : 46
Balkh 2010-1 : 138
Balkhash 2012-1 : 77
al-Balkhī, Abū Muṭīʿ 2009-3 : 154
al-Balkhī, Abū Zayd 2009-4 : 32
al-Ballanūbī 2019-4 : 16
Balta Limanı Commercial Treaty 2018-1 : 8
Baltacıoğlu, İsmail Hakkı 2013-2 : 45
Baluchistan and the Baluch people 2019-3 : 10
Balyan, family of architects 2014-3 : 52
al-Balyānī, Amīn al-Dīn 2018-6 : 25
Bamba, Ahmadu 2013-4 : 63
Bāmiyān 2012-2 : 39
Bānat Suʿād 2016-1 : 49
al-Bandanījī 2019-1 : 6
Bandar ʿAbbās 2012-1 : 78
Bangladesh Awami League 2015-4 : 45
Bāniyās (Buluniyas) 2010-1 : 141
Bāniyās (Paneas) 2010-1 : 142
Banja Luka 2014-1 : 48
al-Banjārī, Muḥammad Arshad 2012-1 : 81
Banjarmasin 2009-3 : 156
Banks and banking, historical 2015-1 : 58
Banks and banking, modern 2015-1 : 62
al-Bannānī family 2009-3 : 158
Banquet 2011-1 : 92
Banten 2010-1 : 143
Banūrī, Muʿizz al-Dīn 2015-3 : 41
Baqī b. Makhlad 2013-4 : 66
Baqīʿ al-Gharqad 2010-1 : 146
Baqliyya 2011-2 : 64
Baqqāl-bāzī 2013-2 : 46
Baqṭ 2010-1 : 147
al-Barāʾ b. ʿĀzib 2011-1 : 93
al-Barāʾ b. Maʿrūr 2010-2 : 97
Barābra 2012-4 : 32
Barāhima 2009-1 : 165
al-Barānis 2016-2 : 48

Baraq Baba 2013-1 : 49
Barāq Ḥājib 2017-3 : 6
Barāq Khān Chaghatay 2015-2 : 42
al-Barbahārī 2009-3 : 160
Barbaros Hayreddin 2011-2 : 65
Barbaṭ 2010-1 : 149
al-Barbīr, Aḥmad 2009-3 : 162
Barcelona 2014-1 : 50
Barelwī, Sayyid Aḥmad 2013-1 : 50
Barelwīs 2011-1 : 94
Barghash 2009-4 : 99
Barhebraeus 2014-2 : 40
Bari, Seh 2008-2 : 160
Barīd 2010-1 : 151
al-Barīdī 2010-1 : 153
Barīra 2010-2 : 98
Barjawān 2009-4 : 100
Barlaam and Josaphat 2012-1 : 83
Barmakids 2012-3 : 32
Barnāvī ʿAlāʾ al-Dīn Chishtī 2019-4 : 18
Barqūq, al-Malik al-Ẓāhir 2011-4 : 67
al-Barrādī, Abū l-Qāsim 2015-3 : 43
Barrī Imām 2012-1 : 86
Barsbāy, al-Malik al-Ashraf 2013-4 : 67
Barṣīṣā 2013-3 : 47
al-Bārūdī, Maḥmūd Sāmī 2009-1 : 168
Barus 2011-2 : 67
Barzakh 2011-2 : 67
Barzakh, Ṣūfī understanding 2012-1 : 88
Barzinjīs 2012-2 : 41
Barzū-nāma 2010-1 : 155
Başgil, Ali Fuat 2011-4 : 69
Bashīr b. Saʿd 2011-3 : 87
Bashīr, Munīr 2018-1 : 9
Bashīr Shihāb II 2016-4 : 10
Bashīr, Vaikam Muḥammad 2013-2 : 47
Bashkir 2012-4 : 33
al-Baṣīr, Abū ʿAlī 2009-3 : 162
Basiret 2013-3 : 48
Basīsū, Muʿīn 2009-3 : 163
Basmala 2010-1 : 156
Basra until the Mongol conquest 2015-1 : 67
Basra since the Mongol conquest 2015-1 : 68
Baṭāʾiḥī, Abū ʿAbdallāh 2014-3 : 53
Batak 2010-1 : 161
Batal Hajji Belkhoroev 2010-1 : 164
Baʿth Party 2011-2 : 71
Baths, art and architecture 2012-3 : 38
Bāṭiniyya 2009-1 : 170
Batriyya 2014-2 : 44
al-Baṭsh, ʿUmar 2018-3 : 15
al-Baṭṭāl, ʿAbdallāh 2011-3 : 89
Bātū b. Jochī 2015-4 : 47
Batu, Selahattin 2016-1 : 50
Batuah, Datuk 2009-4 : 102
Bāul 2018-2 : 11
al-Bāʿūnī 2014-3 : 55
Bayʿa 2014-4 : 18
Bayān b. Samʿān 2011-2 : 74
Bayān in Persian 2015-4 : 49
Bayana 2017-5 : 47
Bayansirullah 2009-3 : 164
Bayar, Mahmut Celal 2011-1 : 99
Bayat, Sunan 2009-3 : 165
al-Bayātī, ʿAbd al-Wahhāb 2007-3 : 192
Baybars I, al-Malik al-Ẓāhir 2010-2 : 98
Baybars II, al-Malik al-Muẓaffar 2012-4 : 34
Baybars al-Manṣūrī 2011-3 : 91
Baybarsiyya 2015-3 : 44
Baydas, Khalīl 2009-3 : 166
al-Bayḍāwī 2017-5 : 53
Bāydū 2015-4 : 52
Baye Fall movement 2014-2 : 46
Bayezid I 2015-1 : 70
Bayezid Paşa 2015-1 : 73
al-Bayhaqī, Abū Bakr 2011-1 : 100
al-Bayhaqī, Ibrāhīm b. Muḥammad 2009-2 : 132
Bayrām Khān 2012-3 : 44
Bayram Paşa 2013-1 : 55
Bayramiyye 2016-3 : 46
Bāysunghur, Ghiyāth al-Dīn 2011-4 : 70
Bayt al-Ḥikma 2009-2 : 133
Bayt al-ṭāʿa 2009-3 : 166
Bayur, Yusuf Hikmet 2012-3 : 46
al-Bayyumī, ʿAlī b. Ḥijāzī b. Muḥammad 2012-3 : 46
al-Bayyūmiyya 2012-4 : 35
Bazaar, Arab lands 2011-3 : 92
Bazaar, Anatolia and the Balkans 2011-3 : 96
Bazaar, Indian subcontinent 2013-2 : 49
Bazaar, Iran and Central Asia 2011-3 : 98
Bāzargān, Mahdī 2011-2 : 75
Bazīgh b. Mūsā 2013-1 : 56
Beautiful names of God 2015-4 : 54
Bedil, Qādir Bakhsh 2013-1 : 58
Bedreddin Simavnalı 2013-4 : 61
Behazin 2017-5 : 57
Beirut 2019-4 : 19
Beja (in Portugal) 2012-3 : 47
Béjaïa 2011-4 : 71
Bektaş, Ḥacı 2012-4 : 36
Bektaşiyye 2014-4 : 21
Belgium, Islam in 2017-1 : 16
Belgrade 2012-3 : 49

Belief and unbelief in classical Sunnī theology 2010-2 : 101
Belief and unbelief in Shīʿī thought 2017-2 : 8
Bello, Ahmadu 2011-3 : 104
Ben Achour, Abderrahmane 2018-5 : 9
Ben Bādīs 2016-1 : 51
Ben Barka, Mehdi 2018-5 : 10
Benavert 2014-3 : 56
Bengal architecture 2011-1 : 101
Bengali literature 2011-1 : 118
Benin 2014-2 : 49
Benjamin 2013-3 : 49
Bennabi, Malek 2018-6 : 27
Bequest 2009-1 : 174
Berat 2016-2 : 50
Beratlı 2009-1 : 178
Berberā 2011-4 : 73
Berkand, Muazzez Tahsin 2016-3 : 48
Berke b. Jochi Khān 2015-2 : 44
Berkyaruq 2013-4 : 69
Besermyans 2011-3 : 107
Beşir Çelebi 2014-1 : 51
Beşīr Fuʾād 2012-4 : 39
Beste 2013-2 : 52
Beta Israel 2015-3 : 45
Beyani 2017-1 : 21
Beyatlı, Yahya Kemal 2013-1 : 59
Beyoğlu 2012-2 : 45
Beyşehir 2013-2 : 53
Bezm-i Alem 2015-2 : 47
Bhadreshwar 2015-4 : 57
al-Bharūchī, Ḥasan b. Nūḥ 2013-4 : 71
Bhopā 2011-1 : 123
Bībī Jamāl Khātūn 2010-1 : 165
Bibliographies, Arabic 2015-2 : 48
Bīdil, ʿAbd al-Qādir 2015-4 : 59
Bidlīsī, ʿAmmār 2011-1 : 132
Bihāfarīd b. Farwardīn 2010-2 : 111
al-Bihbahānī, Āyatallāh Muḥammad 2009-3 : 170
al-Bihbahānī, Muḥammad ʿAlī 2009-3 : 169
al-Bihbahānī, Muḥammad Bāqir 2009-3 : 172
Bījāpūr 2012-1 : 91
Bilāl b. Jarīr al-Muḥammadī 2017-4 : 7
Bilbaşar, Kemal 2016-3 : 49
al-Bilbaysī 2010-1 : 165
Bilecik 2019-1 : 8
Bilgrāmī brothers 2019-1 : 10
Bilma 2013-4 : 72
Bilqīs 2011-2 : 77
Bin Bāz 2011-2 : 79
Bin Laden, Usama 2017-4 : 8
Bioethics 2009-4 : 102
Biography of the Prophet 2011-3 : 108
al-Biqāʿī 2010-2 : 113
Biʾr Maʿūna 2011-4 : 75
Birecik 2012-2 : 47
Birgi 2013-2 : 55
Birgivī Meḥmed 2017-3 : 7
Birth control 2009-4 : 108
Birthday of the Prophet 2017-5 : 58
al-Bīrūnī 2013-3 : 50
Birzāl, Banū 2013-1 : 60
al-Birzālī, ʿAlam al-Dīn 2011-1 : 133
al-Bishr 2011-1 : 134
Bishr b. al-Barāʾ 2011-2 : 83
Bishr b. al-Muʿtamir 2018-1 : 10
Bishr b. al-Walīd 2011-1 : 136
Bishr al-Ḥāfī 2011-2 : 83
Bisṭāmī, Abd al-Raḥmān 2010-2 : 115
Bisṭāmī Bāyazīd 2012-3 : 51
Bisṭāmī Shihāb al-Dīn 2013-3 : 56
al-Bīṭār, ʿAbd al-Razzāq 2010-1 : 167
al-Bīṭār, Ṣalāḥ al-Dīn 2017-5 : 62
Bitlis 2014-1 : 52
Bitola 2014-1 : 54
al-Biṭrūjī 2009-3 : 173
Bıyıklı Mehmed Paşa 2019-3 : 16
Bizerta 2011-4 : 77
Black Death 2014-3 : 57
Black Sea 2013-4 : 73
Bloodletting and cupping 2019-2 : 13
Boabdil 2013-4 : 81
Body, in law 2012-2 : 48
Bohras 2013-2 : 56
Bonang, Sunan 2009-3 : 175
Bonjol, Imam 2011-3 : 116
Book 2013-2 : 66
Bookbinding 2009-2 : 137
Boon companion 2011-1 : 137
Booty 2015-4 : 62
Boran, Behice 2013-4 : 83
Boratav, Pertev Naili 2016-4 : 12
Börekçi, Mehmed Rifat 2015-2 : 52
Bornu 2015-4 : 65
Bosnia and Herzegovina 2013-2 : 73
Bostancıbaşı 2018-5 : 12
Botany 2012-1 : 98
Bouaké 2014-2 : 51
Boumedienne, Houari 2013-2 : 81
Bourguiba 2011-2 : 85
Boy Scouts 2019-4 : 25
Boyaciyan, Arşag Agop 2013-1 : 61
Boz Ulus 2012-2 : 51
Bozcaada 2012-2 : 53
Bozkurt, Mahmut Esat 2016-1 : 54
Brakna 2014-2 : 52
Breath and breathing 2011-3 : 118
Brethren of Purity 2013-4 : 84
Bridge 2011-3 : 120

Brunei 2009-4 : 113
Bryson 2015-3 : 47
Buʿāth 2011-4 : 77
Bucharest 2018-6 : 30
Bucharest, Treaty of 2019-1 : 15
Buda 2014-2 : 53
Budayl b. Warqāʾ 2010-1 : 169
Bughā al-Kabīr 2010-2 : 117
Bughā al-Saghīr 2010-2 : 118
al-Bughṭūrī, Maqrīn 2013-3 : 57
Bugis 2009-4 : 117
Buhlūl 2009-4 : 120
Built environment, in law 2009-3 : 176
Buisan of Maguindanao 2009-4 : 121
Bukayr b. Māhān 2011-2 : 88
Bukayr b. Wishāḥ 2011-2 : 90
Bukhara art and architecture 2019-4 : 27
al-Bukhārī 2012-2 : 54
al-Bukhārī, ʿAlāʾ al-Dīn 2013-1 : 63
Bukhārlıq 2011-3 : 130
Bukovina 2013-1 : 64
Būlāq 2014-3 : 60
al-Bulaydī, Muḥammad al-Ḥasanī 2013-1 : 65
Bulgaria 2012-2 : 58
Bulghārs 2011-2 : 92
Bullhe Shāh 2009-3 : 179
al-Bulqīnī family 2013-4 : 90
Buluggīn b. Zīrī 2011-4 : 79
Bumiputera 2009-4 : 122
al-Būnasī, Abū Isḥāq 2016-2 : 51
Bundār 2015-3 : 49
al-Bundārī, al-Fatḥ b. ʿAlī 2013-4 : 91
Bundu 2014-2 : 55
Bungsu, Raja 2009-4 : 122
al-Būnī 2011-1 : 140
Būrān 2010-2 : 118
al-Burāq 2012-4 : 40
Burayda b. al-Ḥuṣayb 2011-4 : 80
Burdur 2013-4 : 93
Burhān al-Amawī 2015-3 : 50
Burhān al-Mulk, Mīr Muḥammad 2011-1 : 143
Burhān-i qāṭiʿ 2015-1 : 75
Burhāniyya 2015-3 : 51
Būrids 2015-2 : 53
Burkina Faso 2012-3 : 54
Burma (Myanmar), Muslims in 2009-4 : 123
Bursa 2015-1 : 76
Bursa, art and architecture 2012-3 : 55
Bursalı Mehmed Tahir 2017-5 : 64
Burṭās 2011-2 : 98
al-Burzulī 2010-2 : 119
Busḥāq Aṭʿima 2014-4 : 30
Bushire 2017-1 : 23
al-Būṣīrī 2010-1 : 171
Busr b. Abī Arṭāt 2011-4 : 81
Bust 2017-2 : 16
al-Bustānī family 2018-6 : 30
al-Bustī, Abū l-Qāsim 2014-3 : 61
al-Būṭī, Muḥammad Saʿīd Ramaḍān 2015-3 : 54
al-Butr 2016-3 : 50
Būyid art and architecture 2009-4 : 132
Buzurg-Ummīd, Kiyā 2016-2 : 52
Byzantium 2010-2 : 122
Cabolek 2009-4 : 139
Cadiz 2013-2 : 85
Caesarea 2011-4 : 83
Cafer Çelebi, Tacizade 2016-4 : 14
Cafer Efendi 2016-3 : 52
Cain and Abel 2011-4 : 87
Cairo, modern period 2017-2 : 22
Cairo, Ottoman 2018-2 : 14
Çaka Bey 2013-4 : 94
Çakeri 2017-4 : 13
Çakmak, Fevzi 2013-4 : 95
Calatayud 2011-2 : 102
Calatrava 2011-4 : 90
Calendar of Córdoba 2011-1 : 145
Caliph and caliphate up to 1517 2016-5 : 17
Call to prayer 2015-2 : 56
Camel, Battle of the 2014-2 : 57
Cameroon 2018-1 : 13
Çamlıbel, Faruk Nafiz 2015-1 : 80
Çandarlı family 2015-1 : 81
Çandarlızade Ali Paşa 2018-1 : 15
Caniklizade family 2016-5 : 32
Çankırı 2013-1 : 67
Canon and canonisation, in classical Arabic literature 2011-1 : 146
Canon and canonisation of ḥadīth 2017-4 : 14
Canon and canonisation of the Qurʾān 2013-3 : 59
Cantemir, Dimitrie 2012-4 : 47
Capacity, legal 2011-4 : 92
Çapanoğulları 2013-1 : 68
Cape Town 2014-2 : 58
Capital punishment 2011-2 : 104
Capitalism, Islam and 2015-1 : 82
Caravanserai, Iranian 2012-3 : 62
Çar-ender-çar 2018-2 : 20
Carita Sultan Iskandar, Carita Nabi Yusuf, and Kitab Usulbiyah 2017-5 : 66
Carpets 2011-4 : 95

Cartography 2016-4 : 15
Caspian Sea 2018-4 : 5
Castille 2012-4 : 56
Cat 2015-2 : 58
Caucasus, post-1500 2016-4 : 29
Caucasus, pre-1500 2014-4 : 32
Cautery 2019-2 : 17
Cavid Bey, Mehmed 2017-5 : 68
Cavid Paşa 2018-1 : 17
Cek Ko-po 2009-4 : 140
Celal Sahir Erozan 2016-4 : 33
Celalzade Mustafa Çelebi 2018-1 : 18
Çelebizade İsmail Asım 2018-1 : 19
Celibacy 2013-3 : 68
Cem 2011-2 : 111
Cem Sadisi 2016-3 : 53
Cemal Paşa 2016-4 : 33
Cemal Süreya 2017-5 : 69
Cemaleddin Aksarayi 2014-2 : 61
Cenap Şahabettin 2014-2 : 64
Cenotaph 2010-2 : 129
Centhini, Serat 2011-1 : 149
Cerrahi-Halveti order 2019-2 : 19
Çeşme 2012-2 : 70
Cetinje 2013-3 : 69
Cevri 2019-1 : 17
Chad 2011-2 : 113
Chaghatay Khān 2015-3 : 58
Chaghatay literature 2018-5 : 13
Chaldean Christians 2016-4 : 37
Chams 2010-1 : 173
Chanak Crisis 2015-2 : 60
Chancery manuals 2014-3 : 63
Chanceri 2011-2 : 117
Chāndnī Chawk 2011-3 : 132
Chapar b. Qaidu 2016-3 : 54
Charity since 1900 2016-3 : 56
Charkhī, Yaʿqūb-i 2019-1 : 18
Chechnya 2012-2 : 73
Chen Keli 2011-2 : 119
Chihil Sutūn 2011-2 : 122
Children of Israel 2011-2 : 124
China, Islam in, contemporary period 2012-2 : 84
China, Islamic architecture in 2015-4 : 69
Chinese Muslim literature 2014-2 : 65
Chinggis Khān 2017-4 : 24
Chinggisids 2015-3 : 60
Chios 2015-2 : 60
Chirāgh ʿAlī Khān, Maulvī 2011-2 : 128
Chishtī Muʿīn al-Dīn 2015-2 : 61
Chishtiyya 2016-1 : 56
Chittor 2011-3 : 133
Christian religion (premodern Muslim positions) 2017-2 : 26
Christian-Muslim relations in modern sub-Saharan Africa 2017-2 : 32
Christian-Muslim relations in the Indian subcontinent 2017-2 : 34
Chronogram, Muslim Southeast Asia 2016-5 : 34
Chronogram, Ottoman 2016-1 : 61
Chronogram, Persian 2015-1 : 88
Chūbak, Ṣādiq 2018-1 : 21
Chūbānids 2016-3 : 59
Churās, Shāh Maḥmūd 2017-5 : 70
Chuvash 2013-1 : 69
Chyhyryn campaign 2016-4 : 40
Cigalazade Sinan Paşa 2018-5 : 15
Cik di Tiro 2011-4 : 109
Çırāghān 2011-3 : 135
Circassians, Mamlūk 2012-3 : 69
Circassians, modern 2016-4 : 43
Circle of Justice 2012-1 : 104
Circumambulation 2011-4 : 110
Cirebon 2009-4 : 140
City panegyric, in classical Arabic 2011-2 : 130
Çivizade 2018-6 : 36
Claims of God and claims of men 2011-3 : 136
Client 2017-2 : 37
Codicology 2017-1 : 26
Coffee and coffeehouses, Iran 2015-4 : 95
Coffee and coffeehouses, Ottoman 2012-1 : 110
Command, in Islamic law 2015-3 : 65
Commander of the Faithful 2011-4 : 112
Commitment, in modern Arabic literature 2010-2 : 140
Committee of Union and Progress 2015-1 : 90
Communauté Musulmane du Burkina Faso 2014-3 : 66
Communism 2014-4 : 38
Communism in Indonesia 2018-1 : 22
Comoros 2012-2 : 90
Companionship 2016-3 : 62
Compass 2015-3 : 67
Concubinage, in Islamic law 2014-4 : 42
Confession 2017-2 : 40
Congratulations, Arabic 2014-2 : 73
Congress of Arab Music 1932 2018-3 : 17

Constantinus Africanus 2011-2 : 131
Constitution of Medina 2012-2 : 100
Constitutional Revolution in Iran 2016-1 : 61
Consul 2011-2 : 133
Contagion 2010-1 : 180
Contract law 2013-3 : 70
Cordoba 2014-1 : 58
Córdoba, architecture 2019-2 : 20
Correspondence, philosophical 2015-2 : 63
Corruption 2014-1 : 60
Çorum 2013-4 : 96
Cossack Brigade 2016-4 : 46
Costume albums 2018-1 : 25
Côte d'Ivoire 2018-4 : 8
Cotonou 2019-2 : 28
Courts of law, historical 2017-1 : 39
Courts of law, Ottoman 2016-2 : 54
Covenant (religious) pre-eternal 2014-2 : 74
Createdness of the Qurʾān 2015-3 : 70
Creed 2014-3 : 67
Crescent (symbol of Islam) 2014-4 : 47
Crete 2014-2 : 78
Crimea 2012-1 : 113
Crown 2011-4 : 114
Crusades 2014-4 : 49
Çukurova 2013-1 : 70
Cumalı, Necati 2014-2 : 81
Cumhuriyet 2011-2 : 135
Cursing, ritual 2018-3 : 22
Custody, child 2014-3 : 73
Custom as a source of law 2014-3 : 76
Customs dues, historical 2015-3 : 72
Cyprus 2011-4 : 118
al-Dabbāgh, ʿAbd al-ʿAzīz 2011-3 : 141
al-Ḍabbī, Abū Jaʿfar 2016-2 : 58
Dabīr, Mirzā Salāmat ʿAlī 2011-3 : 143
Dabistān-i madhāhib 2013-1 : 72
al-Dabūsī, Abū Zayd 2014-1 : 64
Dadanitic 2019-3 : 18
Dāgh Dihlavī 2014-1 : 66
Daghestan 2013-1 : 73
Dahbīdiyya 2016-2 : 59
Dahira 2017-5 : 73
Dahiratoul Moustarchidina wal Moustarchidaty 2014-1 : 70
Dahlak Islands 2015-1 : 92
Daḥlān, Aḥmad b. Zaynī 2016-5 : 36
Dahlan, Haji Ahmad 2014-1 : 73
Daḥlān, Iḥsān Jampes 2019-4 : 43
Dahrīs 2012-4 : 59
Dāʿī (in Ismāʿīlī Islam) 2012-4 : 66
Dajjāl 2012-2 : 105
Dakar 2014-3 : 82
Dakhinī Urdū 2015-2 : 71
al-Dakhwār 2019-1 : 21
Dāmād 2013-1 : 90
Damad İbrahim Paşa 2016-1 : 65
al-Dāmaghānī, Abū ʿAbdallāh 2017-1 : 48
Damanhūrī, Aḥmad 2013-4 : 98
Damascus, Ottoman 2014-1 : 75
Damietta 2018-3 : 25
Damirdāshiyya 2016-1 : 67
Danākil 2014-4 : 65
Dandanakan, Battle of 2013-3 : 81
Dandarāwiyya 2013-4 : 100
al-Dānī 2014-1 : 89
Daniel 2012-3 : 72
Daniel al-Qūmisī 2013-2 : 87
Danişmendname 2015-4 : 102
Danubian Principalities 2014-3 : 85
Daqāyiqī Marvazī 2014-3 : 89
al-Daqqāq, Abū ʿAbdallāh 2018-5 : 18
al-Daqqāq, Abū ʿAlī 2016-1 : 69
Dār al-ʿadl (premodern) 2012-4 : 70
Dār ʿadl (modern) 2012-2 : 106
Dār al-Funūn, Iranian 2013-2 : 90
Dār al-Ḥikma 2014-3 : 91
Dār al-Islām and dār al-ḥarb 2016-5 : 37
Dār al-Nadwa 2016-3 : 65
Dār al-ʿUlūm 2012-2 : 109
Dārā Shikūh 2018-1 : 28
al-Dārānī, Abū Sulaymān 2013-2 : 91
al-Dāraquṭnī 2012-3 : 74
Darb al-Arbaʿīn 2015-3 : 74
Dardanelles 2013-1 : 91
Dardic and Nuristani languages 2013-4 : 101
al-Dardīr, Aḥmad, and Dardīriyya 2011-4 : 125
al-Dārimī 2012-4 : 74
al-Dārimī, Abū Saʿīd 2015-3 : 74
al-Darjīnī, Aḥmad 2012-4 : 75
Darphane 2019-4 : 45
Darqāwa 2018-1 : 30
Dars-i Niẓāmī 2015-2 : 74
Darul Arqam 2017-2 : 45
Darü'l-Hikmeti'l İslamiye 2016-1 : 70
Darul Islam 2014-2 : 82
Darülfünun, Ottoman 2013-1 : 92
Darüşşafaka 2015-2 : 77
Darzī, Muḥammad b. Ismāʿīl 2012-3 : 77

Dātā Ganj Bakhsh, shrine of 2014-4 : 66
Dā'ūd al-Anṭākī 2010-1 : 183
Daud Beureu'eh 2016-5 : 48
Daura 2014-3 : 92
David 2012-3 : 78
Daʿwa modern practices 2017-1 : 50
Dawlat Khān Lodī 2015-1 : 93
Dawlatshāh Samarqandī 2017-2 : 46
Dawlatshāh Samarqandī 2015-4 : 103
Dāwūd b. Jirjīs 2012-2 : 112
Dāwūd b. Khalaf 2011-4 : 127
Dāwūd al-Faṭṭānī 2016-1 : 72
Dāwūd al-Qayṣarī 2015-1 : 94
Dāwūd al-Ṭā'ī 2012-2 : 113
Dāya Rāzī 2012-3 : 81
al-Daybulī, Abū Mūsā 2014-4 : 68
Ḍayf, Shawqī 2012-2 : 115
Dayı 2015-2 : 78
al-Daylamī, Muḥammad b. al-Hasan 2013-2 : 92
Dayṣanīs 2012-2 : 116
Death in Islamic law 2014-1 : 91
Dede 2012-1 : 119
Dede Korkut 2014-4 : 69
Deedat, Ahmed 2018-2 : 23
Definition 2014-2 : 85
Dehhani 2016-3 : 66
Delhi, architecture 2014-3 : 93
Deli Birader, Gazali 2014-2 : 89
Deli Orman 2014-4 : 72
Demak 2011-2 : 136
Demir Baba Tekke 2015-1 : 96
Democritus 2015-2 : 79
Demokrat Parti 2016-2 : 67
Denmark, Muslims in 2014-2 : 91
Deobandīs in Africa 2015-4 : 104
Deposit 2013-4 : 103
Dermagandhul, Serat 2013-1 : 94
Dervish 2011-4 : 129
Devil (Satan) 2018-5 : 19
Dewan Dakwah Islamiyah Indonesia 2017-2 : 48
al-Dhahabī 2016-1 : 73
Dhahabiyya 2012-2 : 118
Dhawq 2015-1 : 97
Dhawq, Ibrāhīm 2011-3 : 145
Dhimma 2012-3 : 87
Dhow 2016-5 : 50
Dhū l-Faqār 2012-4 : 77
Dhū l-Kifl 2012-2 : 121
Dhū l-Nūn al-Miṣrī 2012-4 : 79
Dhū l-Rumma 2011-3 : 147
Didactic poetry, Arabic 2011-4 : 135
Dietary law 2012-1 : 121
Dihkhudā, ʿAlī-Akbar 2018-6 : 38
al-Dihlawī, Shāh Walī Allāh 2015-4 : 106
Dihqān 2015-1 : 104
Dīk al-Jinn 2011-4 : 137
Dilā' 2019-4 : 46
Dilmaçoğulları beyliği 2014-3 : 101
al-Dimyāṭī, Nūr al-Dīn 2015-2 : 80
Dīn-i ilāhī 2015-2 : 81
al-Dīnawarī, Abū Saʿd 2016-2 : 68
Diogenes 2012-2 : 123
Dioscorides 2014-4 : 73
Dipanagara 2012-2 : 126
Dire Dawa 2014-1 : 94
Ḍirghām b. ʿĀmir 2014-4 : 75
Disciple in Ṣūfism 2018-2 : 24
Dīwān Group 2012-4 : 81
Ḍiyā' al-Dīn al-Makkī 2016-2 : 69
Diyāb, Maḥmūd 2012-1 : 126
al-Diyārbakrī, al-Ḥusayn 2015-3 : 75
Diyarbekri, Abdussamed 2013-2 : 93
Djambek, Djamil 2014-3 : 102
Djenné 2015-3 : 78
Djibouti 2017-1 : 54
Djula 2016-2 : 70
Dobhāshī 2014-4 : 77
Döger (Ghuzz) 2018-1 : 33
Dogon 2018-4 : 13
Dome 2017-5 : 74
Dome of the Rock 2014-4 : 78
Dongola 2015-3 : 80
Donkey (eschatological aspects) 2013-3 : 82
Dönme 2012-3 : 92
Doughty, Charles Montagu 2018-1 : 34
Doxography 2015-2 : 83
Drama, Urdu 2014-1 : 95
Dreams 2012-3 : 96
Druzes 2013-4 : 104
al-Duʿājī, ʿAlī 2012-1 : 126
Dualism 2012-1 : 127
Dūbayt in Arabic 2014-1 : 96
al-Dukālī,ʿAbd al-Wāḥid 2018-5 : 27
Dukayn al-Rājiz 2011-4 : 138
Dulkadir 2017-2 : 49
Dunqul, Amal 2012-2 : 129
al-Duwayhī, Ibrāhīm al-Rashīd 2011-4 : 139
East Africa 2016-2 : 74
Əbdürrəhim bəy Haqverdiyev 2015-1 : 109
Ebubekir Ratib Efendi 2016-4 : 50
Ebüziyya Mehmed Tevfik 2015-3 : 83
Edebiyat-ı Cedide 2017-5 : 82
Edhem Paşa 2016-3 : 70
Edirne 2018-3 : 28
Edirne, Treaty of 2016-2 : 79
Education, early-Ottoman 2016-2 : 80
Education, general (up to 1500) 2017-4 : 29

Education in Muslim Southeast Asia 2017-1 : 58
Education in the Indian subcontinent 2017-4 : 48
Education, later Ottoman 2018-3 : 35
Efendi 2017-5 : 84
Eger 2016-4 : 52
Egypt, art and architecture 2018-1 : 36
Egypt until 1517 2016-3 : 72
Əhməd Cavad Axundzadə 2015-2 : 88
Elements 2014-2 : 93
Əli bəy Hüseynzadə 2015-2 : 89
Elias of Nisibis 2014-4 : 85
Elijah 2012-2 : 131
Elisha 2012-4 : 84
Elixir 2013-4 : 109
Elvān Çelebi 2019-4 : 48
Emanation 2016-1 : 81
Emin Nihad 2017-1 : 62
Empedocles 2011-4 : 142
Emrullah Efendi 2018-1 : 41
Encümen-i şuara 2017-1 : 63
Encyclopaedias, Arabic 2015-2 : 90
Enderun Mektebi 2017-1 : 64
Enderuni Fazıl 2015-2 : 94
Entente Liberale 2017-3 : 12
Epicureanism 2013-4 : 112
Epigram, classical Arabic 2012-1 : 131
Epigram, Persian 2016-2 : 83
Epistemology in philosophy 2018-4 : 17
Equator 2016-4 : 53
Erbakan, Necmettin 2016-3 : 78
Erbervelt, Pieter 2012-2 : 132
Eritrea 2015-4 : 112
Erotica, Ottoman 2018-4 : 28
Erucakra 2015-4 : 117
Erzincan 2018-5 : 32
Erzurum 2016-2 : 85
Esendal, Memduh Şevket 2018-2 : 27
Esotericism and exotericism 2015-2 : 96
Eşrefoğlu Rumi 2016-4 : 55
Essence and existence 2015-4 : 118
Esztergom 2016-1 : 90
Eternity 2014-3 : 104
Ethics in philosophy 2015-1 : 110
Ethics in Sufism 2016-1 : 92
Ethiopia, Islam and Muslims in 2014-4 : 88
Euboea 2015-4 : 124
Euclid 2013-4 : 114
Eunuchs 2015-3 : 84
Euthanasia 2015-1 : 117
Eutychius of Alexandria 2013-3 : 83
Eve 2018-1 : 42
Evidence 2016-2 : 87
Evliya Celebi 2016-1 : 95
Evren, Kenan 2018-1 : 44
Existence in philosophy and theology 2017-4 : 52
Exorcism 2014-4 : 93
Expiation 2011-2 : 138
Eyüp 2016-3 : 79
Ezekiel 2012-4 : 85
Fable 2016-1 : 100
Fable, animal, in Muslim Southeast Asia 2019-4 : 50
Faculties of the soul 2018-6 : 41
Faḍāʾil 2018-3 : 40
Fadak 2018-3 : 45
Faḍal Shāh 2012-2 : 134
al-Fāḍil al-Hindī 2013-1 : 97
al-Faḍl b. al-Ḥubāb 2015-3 : 93
al-Faḍl b. Marwān 2013-1 : 98
al-Faḍl b. al-Rabīʿ 2016-3 : 84
al-Faḍl b. Sahl 2013-1 : 99
al-Faḍl b. Shādhān 2012-3 : 104
Faḍl-i Ḥaqq Khayrābādī 2015-2 : 104
Faḍl-i Imām Khayrābādī 2015-2 : 106
Faḍl al-Shāʿira 2012-4 : 88
Faḍlallāh al-Burhānpūrī 2012-3 : 106
Faḍlī Namangānī 2017-1 : 66
Fahri 2014-4 : 96
Fahri of Bursa 2013-4 : 121
Fakhkh 2016-3 : 85
Fakhr al-Dīn Dihlavī 2018-6 : 48
Fakhr al-Din Maʿn 2015-4 : 127
Fakhr-i Mudabbir 2012-4 : 89
Fakhruddin, H. A. R. 2014-4 : 97
al-Fākhūrī, Arsānyūs 2016-4 : 56
Fākhūrī, ʿUmar 2012-3 : 108
Fakih Usman, Kyai Haji 2013-2 : 95
Fakiri (Kalkandelenli) 2013-4 : 122
Fallata 2016-2 : 94
Fānī Badāyūnī 2017-3 : 14
Fānī Kashmīrī 2012-3 : 109
Fansuri, Hamzah 2016-1 : 106
Faqīh, Bā 2012-4 : 91
Faqīr, Faqīr Muḥammad 2012-3 : 111
al-Fārābī 2015-2 : 108
al-Fārābī, music 2015-4 : 129
Farāhānī, Adīb al-Mamālik 2013-4 : 123
Farāhī, Ḥamīd al-Dīn 2019-3 : 20
Faraj, Alfrīd 2012-4 : 93
Faraj, al-Malik al-Nāṣir b. Barqūq 2015-3 : 94
Farangī Maḥall 2013-1 : 102
Farāz, Aḥmad 2012-2 : 135
al-Farazdaq 2012-4 : 94
Farghana Valley 2014-2 : 96
al-Farghānī 2013-1 : 107
al-Farghānī, Saʿīd al-Dīn 2016-2 : 96

Farḥāt, Ilyās 2012-4 : 98
Farīd 2012-2 : 137
Farīd al-Dīn Masʿūd 2018-1 : 46
Farīdī, Shahīdallāh 2017-4 : 62
Farīghūnids 2015-4 : 132
Fāris, Bishr 2013-1 : 109
al-Fārisī, Abū ʿAlī 2012-3 : 113
al-Fārisī, Kamāl al-Dīn 2014-3 : 114
Farmān, Ghāʾib Ṭuʿma 2012-4 : 100
Farqad al-Sabakhī 2012-1 : 134
al-Farrāʾ 2012-3 : 115
Farrukh Ḥusayn 2017-1 : 67
Farrūkh, ʿUmar 2013-1 : 110
Farrukhābād 2015-3 : 97
Farrukhī Sīstānī 2012-3 : 118
al-Fārūq 2012-4 : 101
al-Fārūqī, ʿAbd al-Bāqī 2016-5 : 53
Fārūqīs 2016-2 : 98
al-Fārūthī, ʿIzz al-Dīn 2012-1 : 135
Fasānjus, Banū 2016-5 : 55
al-Fasawī, Yaʿqūb 2016-2 : 102
al-Fāshir 2019-2 : 32
Fashoda incident 2013-1 : 111
al-Fāsī family 2018-5 : 35
al-Fāsī, Taqī l-Dīn 2015-2 : 127
al-Fāsiyya 2015-4 : 134
Faskyu (Ithaca) 2017-1 : 78
Fatahillah 2012-2 : 138
al-Faṭānī, Aḥmad b. Muḥammad Zayn 2016-5 : 56
al-Fatāt 2012-2 : 139
al-Fatāwā l-ʿĀlamgīriyya 2012-3 : 120
Fatayat Nahdlatul Ulama 2018-5 : 39
Fatehpur Sikri 2018-4 : 39
al-Fatḥ 2015-4 : 136
al-Fatḥ b. Khāqān 2013-1 : 112
al-Fatḥ al-Mawṣilī 2013-3 : 85
Fatḥallāh Shīrāzī 2015-2 : 128
Fatḥī, Ḥasan 2015-2 : 129
al-Fātiḥa 2013-2 : 96
Fatiḥpurī, Niyāz 2012-2 : 140
Fāṭima bt. Muḥammad 2014-2 : 100
Fāṭimid art and architecture 2012-3 : 123
Fatimids 2014-1 : 98
Fatma Aliye 2018-1 : 50
Fatwā, premodern 2017-4 : 63
Fatwā, modern 2017-4 : 69
Fatwa, modern media 2017-4 : 74
Favour (divine) 2013-2 : 100
Fawwāz, Zaynab 2012-3 : 132
Fayʾ 2013-2 : 102
Fayḍ, Fayḍ Aḥmad 2012-3 : 133
Fayḍī, Abū l-Fayḍ 2016-3 : 86
Fayḍiyya 2016-4 : 57
Fayṣal b. ʿAbd al-ʿAzīz 2016-3 : 89
al-Faytūrī, Muḥammad 2017-2 : 65
Fayyāḍ, Ilyās 2013-1 : 113
al-Fazārī 2016-3 : 91
al-Fazārī, ʿAbdallāh b. Yazīd 2016-5 : 57
Fazli 2015-1 : 119
Fazzān 2019-2 : 33
Fear of God and hope (in Ṣūfism) 2012-4 : 102
Federation of Arab Republics 2012-1 : 136
Fehim Süleyman 2016-3 : 93
Fenarizade 2014-1 : 110
Fener 2013-1 : 114
Feraizcizade Mehmet Şakir 2015-1 : 120
Ferhad Paşa 2017-5 : 85
Ferhad u Şirin (in Turkic literatures) 2016-1 : 109
Feridun Bey 2014-2 : 108
Ferman 2016-2 : 103
Ferraguto, Pietro 2014-3 : 115
Fetihname 2014-3 : 116
Feyzullah Efendi 2018-4 : 45
Fez 2013-2 : 104
Fibonacci, Leonardo 2016-4 : 58
Fiction, Arabic, modern 2014-4 : 98
Fiction, Persian 2013-1 : 115
Fiction, Urdu 2012-3 : 137
Fidāʾīyyān-i Islām 2013-1 : 119
Figani 2014-4 : 103
Fighānī Shīrāzī, Bābā 2012-3 : 141
Fijār 2012-4 : 104
Fikrī, ʿAbdallāh 2013-4 : 125
Finance 2014-4 : 104
Fındıkoğlu, Ziyaeddin Fahri 2015-4 : 140
Fines 2013-1 : 120
Fiqh, faqīh, fuqahāʾ 2015-2 : 130
Firdawsī, Abū l-Qāsim, and the Shāhnāma 2017-2 : 66
Firdawsiyya 2012-4 : 105
Firdevsi-yi Rumi 2016-4 : 61
Fīrūz Shāh Tughluq 2017-5 : 87
Fitna in early Islamic history 2012-4 : 107
Fiṭra 2016-2 : 104
Flagellation 2015-2 : 133
Flags 2014-3 : 119
Flood 2013-3 : 86
Flores 2013-2 : 110
Fodi Kabba Dumbuya 2013-2 : 112
Fondaco 2013-2 : 113
Forgery in ḥadīth 2018-5 : 41
Fort William College 2013-1 : 122
Fortress, in the Middle East 2015-2 : 134
Forty Traditions 2016-2 : 107
Foundling 2013-1 : 124
Fountain 2013-4 : 126
Franks 2013-2 : 114
Free verse, Arabic 2013-3 : 89
Freemasonry 2014-4 : 112
Friday prayer 2016-5 : 60
Friend of God 2013-3 : 90

al-Fuḍayl b. ʿIyāḍ 2013-3 : 92
Fūdī, ʿAbdallāh 2016-2 : 111
Fūdī, ʿUthmān 2016-2 : 112
Fūmanī, ʿAbd al-Fattāḥ 2018-2 : 29
Funerary practices 2013-2 : 116
Funj 2015-4 : 141
al-Fūrakī, Abū Bakr 2013-4 : 128
Furāt b. Furāt al-Kūfī 2012-4 : 108
Futa Toro 2015-2 : 139
Futūḥ 2012-2 : 141
Futuwwa (in Ṣūfism) 2012-3 : 143
Fuuta Jalon 2017-4 : 76
al-Fuwaṭī, Hishām b. ʿAmr 2016-1 : 110
Fuzuli, Mehmed b. Süleyman 2014-3 : 124
Gabriel 2014-3 : 126
Gagauz (language and literature) 2013-3 : 95
Gagauz people 2015-1 : 122
Galatasarayı 2015-2 : 141
Galen 2013-4 : 130
Ganizade Nadiri 2016-5 : 64
Garami 2018-6 : 51
Gardens 2014-2 : 112
Gardizi 2013-2 : 127
Gasprinski, İsmail 2015-3 : 101
Gatholoco, Suluk 2013-1 : 127
Gaur 2014-2 : 122
Gaza 2014-4 : 116
Gaza, art and architecture 2014-4 : 120
Gazel (Qəzəl) in Azerbaijani literature 2016-4 : 64
Gazi Hüsrev Bey 2018-1 : 52
Gecekondu 2013-4 : 134
Gedik 2014-4 : 126
Gelenbevi, İsmail 2015-1 : 123
Gelibolulu Mustafa Ali 2015-1 : 125
Genç Kalemler 2013-4 : 137
Gender and law 2017-1 : 81
General average 2014-3 : 129
Generation and corruption 2016-2 : 114
Genetic testing 2013-3 : 96
Geomancy 2013-3 : 98
Georgius de Hungaria 2017-5 : 92
Gerakan Aceh Merdeka 2017-3 : 16
Gerard of Cremona 2014-1 : 112
Germany, Islam in 2014-3 : 138
Geuffroy, Antoine 2013-3 : 101
Ghadīr Khumm 2014-2 : 123
al-Ghāfiqī, Abū Jaʿfar 2016-2 : 119
al-Ghāfiqī, Muḥammad 2013-3 : 102
Ghamkolvi, Sufi Sahib 2013-3 : 103
Ghana, Muslims in contemporary 2013-1 : 128
Ghanī Kashmīrī 2014-3 : 138
Ghānim, Fatḥī 2013-3 : 105
Ghawwāṣī 2014-2 : 128
Ghaylān al-Dimashqī 2013-4 : 139
Ghazal in Persian 2016-2 : 121
Ghazālī Mashhadī 2014-3 : 140
al-Ghazālī, Muḥammad 2015-1 : 127
Ghāzān Khān Maḥmūd 2019-2 : 37
Ghāzī al-Dīn Ḥaydar 2013-3 : 106
al-Ghāzī Ghumūqī 2018-2 : 31
Ghāzī Miyāṇ, Sālār Masʿūd 2013-4 : 141
Ghaznavid art and architecture 2015-3 : 103
Ghaznavids 2016-3 : 95
Ghazw 2013-4 : 143
Ghiyāth al-Dīn Tughluq Shāh I 2018-2 : 34
Ghiyāth al-Dīn Tughluq Shāh II 2016-4 : 65
al-Ghubrīnī, Abū l-ʿAbbās 2016-2 : 127
al-Ghubrīnī, Abū Mahdī 2016-2 : 128
Ghūl 2013-4 : 144
Ghulām Aḥmad, Mīrzā 2013-3 : 107
Ghulām ʿAlī Shāh 2013-3 : 110
Ghulām Farīd 2015-1 : 132
Ghulām Khalīl 2015-4 : 145
Ghulām Rasūl 2015-1 : 135
Ghulāt (extremist Shīʿīs) 2018-2 : 37
al-Ghumārī, ʿAlī b. Maymūn 2015-2 : 128
Ghurāb, Banū 2017-4 : 79
Ghurābiyya 2015-1 : 137
Ghūrid art and architecture 2014-2 : 129
Ghūrids 2015-3 : 109
al-Ghuzūlī 2016-3 : 105
Gifts 2015-3 : 111
Girāy Khāns 2012-1 : 138
Giri, Sunan/Panĕmbahan 2012-4 : 111
Girona 2014-1 : 113
Gīsū Darāz, Bandanavāz 2014-2 : 132
Gıyaseddin Keyhüsrev I 2018-1 : 53
Glass 2018-5 : 44
Globalisation and Muslim societies 2014-3 : 141
Globes (celestial and terrestrial) 2016-2 : 129
Gnāwa 2019-1 : 23
Gnosticism 2017-4 : 82
Gobind Singh 2014-1 : 114
Goddess of the Southern Ocean (Ratu Kidul) 2015-1 : 138
Gog and Magog 2015-3 : 113
Golconda art and architecture 2014-2 : 133
Golconda, history 2016-2 : 132
Gold 2014-3 : 145
Golden Horde 2016-3 : 106
Goliath 2014-1 : 115

Gondwāna 2013-3 : 114
Gontor, Pondok Modern 2014-4 : 129
Gospel, Muslim conception of 2014-4 : 130
Gospel of Barnabas 2014-1 : 116
Goyā, Faqīr Muḥammad Khān 2013-1 : 139
Grammar and law 2015-3 : 129
Granada 2014-4 : 135
Granada art and architecture 2013-3 : 116
Grand National Assembly (Turkey) 2018-2 : 47
Grand vizier 2019-4 : 53
Gratitude and ingratitude 2014-1 : 121
Grave visitation/worship 2016-1 : 112
Greece, Muslims in 2014-1 : 124
Greek fire 2013-4 : 146
Greek into Arabic 2016-1 : 116
Gregory Thaumaturgus 2013-3 : 127
Gresik 2013-2 : 130
Gritti, Alvise 2016-4 : 66
Guarantee 2013-3 : 128
Guild 2015-1 : 130
Gūjars 2015-2 : 143
Gulbadan Begam 2010-1 : 185
Gulbarga art and architecture 2014-2 : 138
Gülhane, Edict of 2015-3 : 133
Gulkhanī Muḥammad Sharīf 2015-3 : 135
Gulshaniyya 2018-6 : 52
Gulshīrī, Hūshang 2013-2 : 131
Gümülcineli Ahmed Asım Efendi 2014-4 : 141
Gümüşhanevi, Ahmed Ziyaeddin 2016-1 : 134
Gunābādiyya 2013-4 : 148
Günaltay, Mehmet Şemsettin 2015-1 : 134
Gunung Jati, Sunan 2014-3 : 148
Gürsel, Cemal 2016-2 : 137
Gürses, Müslüm 2016-4 : 67
Guruş 2019-4 : 55
Güzelce Ali Paşa 2014-1 : 129
Gwalior 2018-3 : 49
Gwalior Fort, art and architecture 2015-1 : 136
Ḥabāʾib Southeast Asia 2018-1 : 56
Ḥabash al-Ḥāsib al-Marwazī 2017-4 : 87
Ḥabīb b. Maslama al-Fihrī 2016-4 : 70
Ḥabīballāh Khān 2017-2 : 87
Habsi 2017-4 : 90
Ḥaddād, Fuʾād 2016-2 : 139
Hadice Turhan Sultan 2017-3 : 19
Hadım Süleyman Paşa 2019-2 : 40
Ḥadīth 2018-4 : 48
Ḥadīth commentary 2018-4 : 61
Ḥadīth, Ibāḍism 2016-2 : 140
Ḥadīth qudsī 2017-4 : 91
Hadiyya (Ethiopia) 2016-3 : 113
Ḥaḍra in Ṣūfism 2016-4 : 72
Ḥaḍramī diaspora Southeast Asia 2018-3 : 51
Ḥāfiẓ 2018-5 : 52
Hafiz İsmail Paşa 2018-6 : 63
al-Ḥāfiẓ li-Dīn Allāh 2017-2 : 89
Hafiz Post 2016-5 : 66
Ḥafṣ al-Fard 2017-1 : 95
Hafsa Sultan 2017-5 : 94
Hagar 2017-3 : 21
Hagiography, Persian and Turkish 2018-6 : 65
Hagiography in South Asia 2019-4 : 57
Haji, Sultan 2017-4 : 97
Ḥājib 2018-1 : 59
al-Ḥājj, Unsī 2016-4 : 74
al-Ḥajjāj b. Yūsuf b. Maṭar 2016-4 : 75
Ḥājjī l-Dabīr 2016-4 : 77
Ḥājjī Pasha 2017-3 : 22
al-Ḥakam b. ʿAbdal 2016-4 : 78
al-Ḥakam b. Qanbar 2016-4 : 79
al-Ḥākim bi Amr Allāh 2017-3 : 24
al-Ḥakīm, Tawfīq 2016-1 : 137
al-Ḥakīm al-Tirmidhī 2018-5 : 58
Ḥākimiyya 2017-3 : 30
Ḥāl (theory of “states” in theology) 2016-5 : 67
Halay 2018-6 : 69
Halevi, Judah 2018-1 : 63
al-Ḥalīmī, Abū ʿAbdallāh 2010-1 : 189
Halkevleri 2018-1 : 68
Ham 2017-4 : 99
Ḥamā 2017-2 : 91
Ḥamā, art and architecture 2017-2 : 93
Hamadānī, ʿAlī 2015-2 : 147
al-Hamadhānī, Badīʿ al-Zamān 2019-2 : 41
Ḥamādisha 2011-4 : 145
Ḥamallāh 2017-3 : 32
Hāmān 2017-4 : 100
Ḥamās 2017-1 : 97
al-Ḥamawī, ʿAlwān 2016-5 : 71
Ḥamdān b. Abān al-Lāḥiqī 2019-3 : 25
Ḥamdān Qarmaṭ 2016-5 : 73
Hamdullah Efendi 2017-1 : 99
Hamengkubuwana I, Sultan 2016-4 : 80
Ḥamīd al-Dīn Qāḍī Nāgawrī 2016-5 : 74
Ḥamīd al-Dīn Ṣūfī Nāgawrī 2016-5 : 76
Ḥamīd Qalandar 2017-3 : 35
Hamidullah, Muhammad 2017-2 : 96

Hamka (Haji Abdul Malik Karim Amrullah) 2017-2 : 98
al-Ḥammāmī 2016-2 : 144
Hamon, Moses 2016-4 : 81
Hampī 2018-6 : 70
al-Ḥāmūlī, ʿAbduh 2018-2 : 49
Ḥamza b. ʿAbd al-Muṭṭalib 2016-3 : 114
Ḥamza b. ʿAlī 2017-2 : 102
Ḥamza b. Bīḍ 2016-2 : 145
Ḥamza Makhdūm 2017-4 : 101
Ḥamza, Romance of 2018-1 : 70
Ḥamzat-Bek al-Dāghistānī 2017-2 : 104
al-Ḥanafī, Aḥmad b. Abī Bakr 2016-4 : 82
Hang Tuah, Hikayat 2016-4 : 83
Hānsavī, Jamāl al-Dīn 2018-6 : 73
Ḥanẓala b. Ṣafwān (prophet) 2016-4 : 86
Ḥaqqānī, ʿAbd al-Ḥaqq 2018-2 : 50
Ḥaqqī, Yaḥyā 2017-3 : 36
Ḥarāfīsh 2017-4 : 103
Harakada al-Islah 2019-1 : 28
Harakada Mujahidinta al-Shabab 2019-1 : 30
Harar 2016-5 : 77
al-Hararī, ʿAbdallāh 2013-2 : 133
Ḥaraṭīn in Mauretania 2017-2 : 105
Haravī, Amīr Ḥusaynī 2011-4 : 147
Hareket Ordusu 2017-4 : 104
Harem, in the Middle East 2018-6 : 74
al-Ḥarīrī 2016-5 : 80
al-Ḥārith b. Ḥilliza 2017-3 : 39
al-Ḥārith b. Kalada 2017-2 : 109
Ḥāritha b. Badr al-Ghudānī 2017-4 : 105
Haron, Abdullah 2017-1 : 102
Harthama b. Aʿyan 2018-3 : 53
Hārūt and Mārūt 2017-5 : 95
Hasaitic 2016-4 : 88
Ḥasan b. ʿĀmir 2016-5 : 85
al-Ḥasan b. Ṣāliḥ 2016-4 : 90
al-Ḥasan al-Baṣrī 2017-1 : 103
Hasan Beyzade 2018-2 : 53
Ḥasan Ghaznavī 2012-3 : 149
Ḥasan II 2017-3 : 40
Hasan Mustapa 2017-3 : 42
Ḥasan Niẓāmī 2017-1 : 107
Ḥasan-i Ṣabbāḥ 2016-4 : 91
Hasankeyf 2018-6 : 80
Hasbi Ash Shiddieqy 2017-5 : 97
Ḥasdāy b. Shaprūṭ 2019-3 : 26
Ḥashwiyya 2016-5 : 86
Ḥasrat Mohānī 2016-4 : 97
Hassan, A. 2017-3 : 44
Hasyim Asy’ari 2017-5 : 98
Hātif Iṣfahānī 2018-1 : 72
Ḥātim al-Aṣamm 2019-4 : 59
Hatt-ı Hümayun 2018-6 : 82
Hatta, Mohammad 2016-4 : 99
Ḥaṭṭīn 2017-3 : 45
Hausaland 2017-3 : 47
Ḥawāla, money transfer 2016-5 : 87
Hawāwīr 2018-6 : 83
Ḥawḍ 2016-4 : 101
Ḥāwī, Khalīl 2017-3 : 49
al-Ḥawrānī, Akram 2019-2 : 44
Ḥayāt al-Dīn b. Saʿīd 2016-4 : 102
Ḥayāt Maḥmūd 2015-1 : 140
Ḥaydar ʿAlī 2017-1 : 109
Ḥaydar Ḥasan Mirzā, Āghā 2019-1 : 32
Ḥaydar, Qurrat al-ʿAyn 2017-3 : 50
Ḥayṣa Bayṣa 2017-1 : 111
Ḥayy b. Yaqẓān 2018-1 : 74
Hazairin 2016-5 : 91
Hazāras 2017-4 : 106
Heart in Ṣūfism 2018-1 : 76
Hekimbaşı 2016-4 : 104
Hell 2010-2 : 143
Henna 2016-4 : 105
Heraklion 2017-5 : 100
Hermann of Carinthia 2018-1 : 79
Hermes and Hermetica 2009-3 : 182
Hero of Alexandria 2017-2 : 111
Hibatallāh b. Muḥammad 2018-3 : 54
Hidāyat, Riḍā Qulī Khān 2018-3 : 56
Hidāyat, Sādiq 2016-3 : 116
Ḥifnī al-Mahdī 2018-5 : 71
Highway robbery 2016-5 : 92
Hijāʾ 2017-3 : 52
Hijar 2017-4 : 112
Ḥijāz Railway 2017-5 : 102
Hijra 2018-2 : 54
Hilāl al-Ṣābiʾ 2017-4 : 113
al-Hilālī, Taqī al-Dīn 2018-4 : 68
Ḥilm 2017-3 : 55
Hind bt. al-Khuss 2016-4 : 107
Hind bt. ʿUtba 2018-5 : 72
Hindi 2018-5 : 74
Hippocrates 2017-3 : 59
al-Ḥīra 2016-5 : 94
al-Ḥīrī, Abū ʿUthmān 2018-4 : 69
Ḥiṣār-ī Fīrūza 2016-5 : 95
Ḥisba (modern times) 2017-3 : 63
Ḥiṣn al-Akrād 2017-3 : 65
Historiography, Ottoman 2018-2 : 58
Ḥizb al-Daʿwa al-Islāmiyya 2016-4 : 107
Hizbullah, Barisan 2018-3 : 58
Homicide and murder 2016-5 : 98
Homs 2017-2 : 112
Homs, art and architecture 2017-2 : 114
Hotin 2015-1 : 144
Ḥourī 2016-4 : 109
Household 2016-4 : 111

Ḥubaysh b. al-Hasan al-Dimashqī 2017-4 : 115
Hūd 2017-3 : 70
Hudhayl, Banū 2017-3 : 73
Hudood Ordinances 2017-1 : 112
Ḥujr b. ʿAdī l-Kindī 2016-4 : 113
Hülegü b. Toluy b. Chinggis Khān 2018-3 : 59
Ḥulmāniyya 2018-2 : 73
Humā 2018-4 : 71
Humām al-Dīn al-Tabrīzī 2016-3 : 119
Ḥumayd al-Arqaṭ 2018-2 : 74
Ḥumayd b. Thawr al-Hilālī 2016-3 : 121
Ḥumaynī 2017-3 : 75
Humāyūn, Nāṣir al-Dīn 2017-4 : 117
Ḥums 2017-5 : 103
Ḥunayn b. Isḥāq 2017-3 : 76
Hünkar İskelesi, Treaty of 2017-4 : 119
Hürrem Sultan 2017-3 : 83
Ḥurūfiyya 2016-1 : 139
al-Ḥuṣarī, Maḥmūd Khalīl 2018-6 : 84
Ḥusayn, Aḥmad 2016-3 : 123
al-Ḥusayn b. ʿAlī b. Abī Ṭālib 2016-3 : 124
Husayn, Muhammad Kamil 2019-4 : 61
Ḥusayn, Shaykh 2016-5 : 102
Ḥusayn, Ṭāhā 2017-3 : 84
Ḥusayn Vāʿiẓ Kāshifī 2017-3 : 88
al-Ḥusaynī, Ṣadr al-Dīn 2017-2 : 117
Hüseyin Hilmi Paşa 2016-5 : 105
Ḥusnī, Dāwūd 2017-5 : 104
al-Ḥuṣrī, Abū Isḥāq 2017-4 : 121
al-Ḥuṣrī al-Ḍardīr 2018-2 : 75
al-Ḥuṭayʾa 2016-2 : 146
Iamblichus 2017-2 : 120
ʿIbādat-khāna 2017-3 : 97
Ibdāl 2016-5 : 106
Ibn al-Abbār, Abū Jaʿfar 2018-1 : 81
Ibn al-Abbār, al-Quḍāʿī 2016-4 : 116
Ibn ʿAbd al-Barr 2019-3 : 27
Ibn ʿAbd al-Ḥakam, ʿAbdallāh 2019-1 : 34
Ibn ʿAbd al-Ḥakam family 2017-4 : 125
Ibn ʿAbd al-Malik al-Marrākushī 2018-5 : 83
Ibn ʿAbd Rabbih 2017-2 : 121
Ibn ʿAbd Rabbihi, Abū ʿUthmān 2018-1 : 82
Ibn ʿAbd al-Ṣamad 2016-5 : 107
Ibn ʿAbd al-Ẓāhir 2017-4 : 125
Ibn ʿAbdūn 2017-1 : 116
Ibn ʿAbdūn al-Jabalī 2018-3 : 62
Ibn Abī l-Ashʿath 2017-4 : 128
Ibn Abī l-Bayān 2018-1 : 83
Ibn Abī l-Dunyā 2018-5 : 85
Ibn Abī l-Ḥadīd 2018-2 : 78
Ibn Abī l-Iṣbaʿ 2017-3 : 100
Ibn Abī l-Rijāl, ʿAlī 2018-4 : 74
Ibn Abī Ṭayyiʾ 2017-4 : 130
Ibn Abī Uṣaybiʿa 2019-2 : 47
Ibn Abī Zamanīn 2016-4 : 118
Ibn Abī Zarʿ 2017-1 : 118
Ibn Abī Zayd al-Qayrawānī 2017-3 : 101
Ibn Abī l-Zinād 2019-1 : 36
Ibn al-ʿAdīm 2017-5 : 106
Ibn ʿAjība 2016-4 : 119
Ibn ʿAmīra al-Makhzūmī 2017-3 : 104
Ibn ʿAmmār, Abū Bakr 2016-5 : 108
Ibn ʿAqīl, Abū l-Wafāʾ 2017-3 : 105
Ibn al-Aʿrābī, Abū ʿAbdallāh 2016-5 : 111
Ibn al-ʿArabī, Abū Bakr 2018-3 : 63
Ibn ʿArūs 2018-4 : 76
Ibn ʿAsākir family 2017-3 : 108
Ibn al-Ashtarkūnī 2018-1 : 84
Ibn ʿĀṣim al-Gharnāṭī 2018-2 : 82
Ibn ʿAskar 2018-4 : 79
Ibn ʿAṭāʾ Aḥmad 2017-3 : 111
Ibn ʿAṭāʾallāh al-Iskandarī 2019-4 : 64
Ibn Aʿtham al-Kūfī 2019-1 : 36
Ibn al-Athīr, Majd al-Dīn 2017-1 : 119
Ibn ʿAṭṭāsh, ʿAbd al-Malik 2017-4 : 132
Ibn ʿAṭṭāsh, Aḥmad 2017-4 : 133
Ibn al-Baladī 2017-2 : 123
Ibn Bāna, ʿAmr 2019-4 : 72
Ibn al-Bannāʾ, Abū ʿAlī 2017-4 : 133
Ibn al-Bannāʾ al-Marrākushī 2018-1 : 85
Ibn Baqī 2017-3 : 113
Ibn Baraka al-Bahlawī 2016-2 : 148
Ibn Barrajān 2017-3 : 115
Ibn Bashkuwāl 2018-1 : 87
Ibn Bassām al-ʿAbartāʾī 2018-1 : 90
Ibn Bassām al-Shantarīnī 2018-2 : 85
Ibn Baṭṭūṭa 2016-5 : 112
Ibn al-Bazzāz al-Ardabīlī 2018-6 : 86
Ibn al-Buhlūl 2018-3 : 65
Ibn Daftarkhwān 2017-5 : 109
Ibn Dāniyāl 2016-3 : 131
Ibn Darrāj al-Qasṭallī 2016-5 : 117
Ibn al-Dawādārī 2016-4 : 122
Ibn Dāwūd al-Iṣfahānī 2017-2 : 124
Ibn Dhakwān, Aḥmad 2018-3 : 66
Ibn al-Dubaythī 2017-2 : 126

Ibn al-Dumayna 2019-1 : 38
Ibn Duqmāq 2017-1 : 121
Ibn Durayd 2018-1 : 92
Ibn Faḍlān 2017-3 : 121
Ibn Fahd 2017-2 : 127
Ibn al-Faḥḥām 2018-5 : 87
Ibn al-Faraḍī 2016-5 : 118
Ibn Farḥūn 2018-2 : 88
Ibn al-Fāriḍ 2016-5 : 121
Ibn Farīghūn 2017-1 : 123
Ibn Fūrak 2017-2 : 130
Ibn Gabirol 2016-4 : 123
Ibn Ghālib al-Gharnāṭī 2017-2 : 132
Ibn Habal 2016-5 : 124
Ibn al-Habbāriyya 2015-3 : 137
Ibn Ḥamdīn 2019-4 : 73
Ibn Ḥamdīs 2019-4 : 75
Ibn Ḥamdūn 2018-1 : 94
Ibn Ḥāmid 2016-4 : 125
Ibn al-Ḥannāṭ 2017-5 : 110
Ibn Harma 2018-1 : 95
Ibn Ḥasday, Abraham 2019-2 : 50
Ibn Ḥasdāy, Abū l-Faḍl 2018-2 : 90
Ibn Ḥasdāy, Abū Jaʿfar 2018-2 : 91
Ibn Ḥawqal 2017-1 : 125
Ibn al-Ḥawwās 2018-2 : 92
Ibn al-Haytham, ʿAbd al-Raḥmān 2019-2 : 52
Ibn Ḥayyūs 2016-4 : 129
Ibn Ḥibbān al-Bustī 2018-3 : 68
Ibn Ḥijjī 2016-4 : 127
Ibn Hindū 2016-5 : 125
Ibn Hubayra 2018-3 : 69
Ibn Hūd, Badr al-Dīn 2017-5 : 111
Ibn Hūd al-Muʾtaman 2018-4 : 81
Ibn Hudhayl al-Fazārī 2018-1 : 97
Ibn ʿIdhārī al-Marrākushī 2016-4 : 128
Ibn al-Imām al-Shilbī 2017-3 : 128
Ibn ʿInaba 2017-4 : 135
Ibn Isḥāq 2019-4 : 76
Ibn Isrāʾīl al-Dimashqī 2017-5 : 114
Ibn Jaʿfar 2017-4 : 137
Ibn Jāmiʿ 2019-4 : 79
Ibn al-Jazarī 2018-5 : 89
Ibn al-Jillīqī 2016-5 : 127
Ibn Jubayr 2017-3 : 129
Ibn Jumayʿ 2017-4 : 138
Ibn Jurayj 2016-2 : 149
Ibn Kabar 2017-5 : 116
Ibn Kammūna 2016-4 : 130
Ibn Kathīr, ʿImād al-Dīn 2016-5 : 128
Ibn Khafīf 2016-5 : 137
Ibn Khaldūn, ʿAbd al-Raḥmān 2018-4 : 83
Ibn Khaldūn, Yaḥyā 2016-4 : 134
Ibn al-Khallāl al-Baṣrī 2018-3 : 70
Ibn Khallikān 2018-5 : 91
Ibn al-Khammār 2018-6 : 88
Ibn al-Khashshāb 2017-4 : 139
Ibn al-Khaṣīb, Abū ʿAlī 2017-2 : 134
Ibn al-Khaṭīb, Lisān al-Dīn 2017-5 : 116
Ibn Khurdādhbih 2018-6 : 92
Ibn Khuzayma 2018-3 : 71
Ibn Killis 2017-4 : 140
Ibn Kunāsa 2017-2 : 135
Ibn al-Labbāna 2018-1 : 100
Ibn Lajaʾ 2017-5 : 123
Ibn Luyūn 2017-3 : 133
Ibn al-Maḥrūma 2016-4 : 136
Ibn Māja 2016-3 : 134
Ibn Makkī 2017-1 : 128
Ibn Manẓūr 2016-3 : 135
Ibn Mardanīsh 2017-3 : 135
Ibn Marzūq 2016-4 : 136
Ibn Maṣāl 2018-5 : 100
Ibn Masarra 2016-5 : 143
Ibn Mashīsh, ʿAbd al-Salām 2016-5 : 145
Ibn al-Māshiṭa 2019-4 : 80
Ibn Masʿūd, ʿAbdallāh 2018-3 : 73
Ibn Maʿṣūm 2018-1 : 102
Ibn Maṭrūḥ 2017-2 : 136
Ibn Mattawayh 2012-1 : 147
Ibn Mawlāhum Khayālī 2018-1 : 104
Ibn Maymūn 2017-1 : 129
Ibn Mayyāda 2018-1 : 105
Ibn Misjaḥ 2018-1 : 106
Ibn Mītham 2019-2 : 53
Ibn Muʿādh al-Jayyānī 2017-3 : 137
Ibn Mufliḥ 2017-3 : 139
Ibn Muḥriz 2018-2 : 93
Ibn Mujāhid 2017-5 : 124
Ibn al-Mulaqqin 2018-2 : 93
Ibn Muljam 2016-2 : 151
Ibn al-Mundhir al-Naysābūrī 2018-2 : 96
Ibn Munīr al-Ṭarābulusī 2019-2 : 54
Ibn Muqbil 2018-1 : 107
Ibn al-Murābiʿ 2018-2 : 98
Ibn Muyassar 2017-5 : 125
Ibn al-Muzawwiq 2018-3 : 77
Ibn al-Nabīh 2017-2 : 137
Ibn Nāʿima al-Ḥimṣī 2018-1 : 109
Ibn al-Najjār, Muḥibb al-Dīn 2017-3 : 140
Ibn Nawbakht, Mūsā 2019-1 : 39
Ibn Nujayd 2018-4 : 101
Ibn Nujaym 2018-2 : 99
Ibn Nuṣayr 2010-1 : 192
Ibn al-Qalānisī 2019-1 : 40
Ibn Qalāqis 2018-1 : 110
Ibn Qasī family 2018-4 : 102
Ibn al-Qaṭṭāʿ, al-Yaḥṣubī 2018-5 : 101
Ibn al-Qaysarānī, Abū ʿAbdallāh 2017-2 : 139

Ibn Qiba 2019-2 : 56
Ibn Qunfudh 2019-2 : 58
Ibn al-Qūṭiyya 2018-6 : 97
Ibn Quzmān 2019-2 : 60
Ibn al-Rāhib 2019-1 : 41
Ibn al-Raqqām 2019-1 : 44
Ibn Rashīq 2018-2 : 101
Ibn Riḍwān al-Mālaqī 2018-6 : 99
Ibn Rushayd 2019-1 : 46
Ibn Rushd, Abū Muḥammad 2009-1 : 181
Ibn al-Sāʿātī, Bahāʾ al-Dīn 2018-1 : 113
Ibn al-Sāʿātī, Fakhr al-Dīn 2019-2 : 63
Ibn Saddiq 2017-4 : 142
Ibn al-Ṣaffār 2019-1 : 49
Ibn al-Ṣaghīr 2018-4 : 103
Ibn al-Ṣāʾigh al-ʿAntarī 2018-1 : 114
Ibn al-Samḥ, Abū ʿAlī 2019-2 : 64
Ibn Saʿūd, ʿAbd al-ʿAzīz 2018-4 : 105
Ibn Sawdakīn 2017-5 : 127
Ibn al-Ṣayrafī, Tāj al-Riʾāsa 2018-5 : 102
Ibn Shaddād, Bahāʾ al-Dīn 2019-1 : 51
Ibn Shaddād, ʿIzz al-Dīn 2018-5 : 104
Ibn Shāhīn al-Ẓāhirī 2019-3 : 29
Ibn Shahrāshūb 2019-1 : 53
Ibn Sharaf al-Qayrawānī 2019-2 : 66
Ibn al-Shāṭir 2019-2 : 67
Ibn al-Sulaym al-Aswānī 2018-1 : 116
Ibn Surayj, ʿUbayd 2018-5 : 105
Ibn al-Ṣūrī 2019-1 : 55
Ibn Tafrājīn 2014-1 : 132
Ibn al-Thumna 2018-2 : 103
Ibn Ṭufayl 2018-1 : 116
Ibn Ṭūmlūs 2018-1 : 122
Ibn al-Ukhuwwa 2019-3 : 31
Ibn Uṣfūr 2019-1 : 56
Ibn Wāfid al-Lakhmī 2019-1 : 58
Ibn Wahb, Isḥāq b. Ibrāhīm 2018-1 : 124
Ibn Wahbūn al-Mursī 2018-2 : 103
Ibn Waḥshiyya 2019-1 : 61
Ibn Wakīʿ al-Tinnīsī 2018-3 : 78
Ibn al-Walīd, al-Ḥusayn b. ʿAlī 2018-3 : 79
Ibn Wallād 2019-2 : 72
Ibn Wāṣil 2016-4 : 139
Ibn al-Zarqālluh 2018-3 : 80
Ibn al-Zayyāt al-Tādilī 2019-1 : 65
Ibn al-Zubayr al-Gharnāṭī 2019-1 : 69
Ibrāhīm ʿĀdil Shāh II 2018-4 : 106
Ibrāhīm b. al-Ashtar 2018-3 : 84
Ibrāhīm b. Isḥāq al-Ḥarbī 2018-3 : 87
Ibrāhīm b. al-Mahdī 2018-3 : 88
Ibrāhīm b. al-Mahdī (music) 2018-3 : 90
Ibrāhīm b. Shīrkūh 2019-1 : 72
Ibrāhīm b. al-Walīd 2019-3 : 33
Ibrāhīm Bey 2018-5 : 106
Ibrāhīm Bey Abū Shanab 2018-5 : 108
İbrahim Edhem Paşa 2018-1 : 125
Ibrāhīm, Ḥāfiẓ 2017-4 : 143
İbrahim Hakkı Paşa 2018-1 : 126
Ibrahim (Mansur Syah) 2018-4 : 107
Ibrāhīm al-Mawṣilī 2018-6 : 100
İbrahim Müteferrika 2016-5 : 147
Ibrāhīm Sulṭān b. Shāh Rukh 2018-5 : 109
Ibrail 2018-4 : 108
al-Ibshīhī, Bahāʾ al-Dīn 2018-2 : 105
Iconoclasm 2019-3 : 34
al-Idkāwī al-Muʾadhdhin 2019-2 : 74
Idrīs ʿImād al-Dīn 2018-4 : 111
Idrīs, Suhayl 2019-3 : 40
Idrīs, Yūsuf 2014-1 : 137
al-Idrīsī, Abū ʿAbdallāh 2018-3 : 91
Idrīsids 2018-5 : 110
Idrīsiyya, in Indonesia 2018-2 : 107
ʿIfrīt 2018-3 : 99
Ikhwān, Saudi Arabia 2018-4 : 114
İlhan, Attila 2019-3 : 42
Īlkhānids 2019-4 : 81
Iltutmish 2018-2 : 109
ʿImād al-Mulk 2018-3 : 100
Imagination in philosophy 2018-3 : 103
al-Imām 2017-2 : 141
İmam Hatip schools 2018-1 : 127
Imāmate in Khārijism and Ibāḍism 2017-4 : 145
Imāmbāra 2018-2 : 112
İmamzade Mehmed Esad 2016-3 : 138
Immolation 2017-4 : 149
Imperial Arsenal 2015-1 : 142
Impetus, in philosophy 2019-1 : 74
Īnāl al-Ajrūd, al-Malik al-Ashraf 2018-1 : 129
Īnālids 2018-1 : 133
ʿInāyat Khān 2018-5 : 118
Independence Courts 2018-3 : 105
India (Hind) 2007-1 : 185
Indian diaspora in Africa 2018-2 : 115
Indian Ocean early-modern 2019-3 : 44

Indonesia: Java from the coming of Islam to 1942 2019-4 : 97
Indonesia: Islam and politics since 1942 2019-4 : 106
Indonesia: social ecology and ethno-cultural diversity 2019-2 : 75
Initiation in Ṣūfism 2018-6 : 101
Inshāʾ Allāh Khān 2019-1 : 77
Institut Agama Islam Negeri 2017-3 : 142
İntizami 2018-6 : 105
Intoxication in Ṣūfism 2019-1 : 80
Iqrītish dynasty 2016-3 : 140
Iqtibās 2019-1 : 83
Īraj Mīrzā 2018-2 : 120
Iram 2019-4 : 117
al-Īrānshahrī, Abū l-ʿAbbās 2019-1 : 85
ʿIrāqī, Fakr al-Dīn 2017-5 : 129
al-Irjānī, Abū Yaḥyā Zakariyyāʾ 2018-4 : 115
al-Irsyad 2018-6 : 106
ʿĪsā al-Kurdī 2019-4 : 121
Isaac 2018-1 : 135
al-Isfarāyīnī, Abū Ḥāmid 2009-4 : 34
al-Isfarāyīnī, ʿIṣām al-Dīn 2018-6 : 108
İsfendiyaroğulları (Candaroğulları) 2019-2 : 79
al-Isfizārī, Abū Ḥāmid 2018-4 : 116
Isḥāq b. Ibrāhīm al-Mawṣilī 2018-6 : 109
Isḥāq Efendi, Başhoca 2009-1 : 182
Ishmael 2018-1 : 137
Iskandar Beg Munshī 2018-4 : 118
Islamic Foundation 2017-5 : 132
Islamic Movement in Nigeria 2019-2 : 83
İsmail Beliğ 2014-1 : 140
Ismāʿīl Bey 2018-5 : 119
İsmail Dede Efendi 2018-2 : 121
İsmail Ferruh Efendi 2018-1 : 140
Ismāʿīl Minangkabau 2019-3 : 48
Ismāʿīl, Muṣṭafā 2018-6 : 110
İsmeti 2018-6 : 111
Isnād 2018-5 : 120
Isrāfīl 2018-3 : 106
Isrāʾīliyyāt 2019-3 : 49
Istanbul, Treaty of 2018-5 : 124
Istiqlāl Party 2018-6 : 113
al-Itihad al-Islamiya 2019-1 : 87
Iʿtiṣām al-Dīn 2017-5 : 133
Iʿtiṣāmī, Parvīn 2017-5 : 135
Izetbegović, Alija 2018-6 : 114
Izmir 2017-2 : 142
ʿIzrāʾīl (ʿAzrāʾīl) 2018-3 : 108
ʿIzz al-Dawla 2019-1 : 88
ʿIzz al-Dīn Kāshānī 2018-2 : 123
ʿIzz al-Dīn al-Mawṣilī 2018-3 : 110
İzzet Mehmed Paşa, Safranbolulu 2018-3 : 111
Jabarti 2015-1 : 146
Jābir b. Ḥayyān 2019-1 : 91
Jābir b. Zayd 2019-1 : 97
al-Jābirī, Muḥammad Ṣāliḥ 2018-3 : 113
Jabrā, Jabrā Ibrāhīm 2014-1 : 141
Jacob bar Shakkō 2019-2 : 86
Jacob of Edessa 2019-1 : 98
Jaʿd b. Dirham 2016-5 : 150
Jadidism 2018-5 : 126
Jahān Sūz 2018-5 : 129
Jahāngīr 2011-2 : 144
Jaipur 2019-3 : 54
Jakarta Charter 2019-4 : 124
Jakhanke 2016-1 : 145
Jalāl al-Dīn Aḥsan 2018-2 : 126
Jalāl al-Dīn Mangburnī 2018-1 : 142
Jalāl al-Dīn Yazdī 2018-6 : 115
Jālib, Ḥabīb 2018-3 : 114
Jamāhīriyya 2019-1 : 99
Jamāl al-Dīn Iṣfahānī 2018-3 : 116
Jamālzada, Muḥammad ʿAlī 2018-2 : 128
Jān-i Jānān, Maẓhar 2019-4 : 125
al-Janbīhī, Muḥammad 2018-4 : 124
Janissaries 2017-2 : 146
Janjīrā 2018-2 : 131
al-Jannābī, Abū Saʿīd 2018-3 : 117
al-Jannābī, Abū Ṭāhir 2018-3 : 119
al-Jannāwunī, Abū Zakariyyāʾ 2008-2 : 161
Jassin, Hans Bague 2018-4 : 125
Jassy, treaty of 2019-4 : 127
Javanese Wars of Succession 2017-5 : 137
al-Jawharī, Ismāʿīl b. Ḥammād 2018-2 : 133
al-Jawnpūrī, Maḥmūd 2012-4 : 113
al-Jawwānī 2019-1 : 101
al-Jazarī, Badīʿ al-Zamān 2019-4 : 128
al-Jazarī, Shams al-Dīn 2018-5 : 130
al-Jazūlī, Abū Mūsā 2019-3 : 59
al-Jazzār, Abū l-Ḥusayn 2016-4 : 141
Jerusalem since 922/1516 2018-4 : 127
Jidda 2018-6 : 118
Jigar Murādābādī 2018-2 : 136
Jimma 2018-2 : 138
al-Jinān al-Jinān 2019-4 : 131
Jinnah, Mohammad Ali 2019-1 : 103

al-Jisr family 2019-1 : 105
al-Jisrī, ʿAlī b. ʿĪsā 2009-1 : 184
Jīvan, Aḥmad 2018-5 : 132
al-Jīzī 2019-4 : 133
Jochi b. Chinggis Khān 2018-5 : 134
John of Damascus 2018-3 : 120
Jubrān, Jubrān Khalīl 2014-2 : 142
Juḥā 2017-5 : 139
Jumadil Kubra 2018-2 : 139
al-Jundulānī, Abū Muḥammad 2008-2 : 162
al-Jundī, Anwar 2018-4 : 140
Jundīshāpur 2015-3 : 139
al-Jurāwī 2018-1 : 146
Jurayj 2019-1 : 108
Jurayrī, ʿAbdallāh 2019-2 : 87
Jurna 2017-5 : 141
Kaarta 2019-3 : 62
Kabābīsh 2018-3 : 123
Kachchh 2019-3 : 63
Kadın 2018-3 : 124
Kadınlar Dünyası 2018-5 : 137
Kāfūr, Malik 2019-3 : 67
Kāhī 2019-1 : 110
Kajoran, Raden 2017-5 : 143
Kākatīya dynasty 2018-2 : 142
al-Kalābādhī 2018-3 : 125
Kalāt, khānate of 2019-3 : 69
Kalaidha, Serat 2018-4 : 142
Kalijaga, Sunan 2018-6 : 125
Kalīm Kāshānī 2019-2 : 89
Kalīmallāh Shāhjahānābādī 2018-3 : 127
al-Kalwadhānī, Abū l-Khaṭṭāb 2019-2 : 91
Kalyana 2019-2 : 92
Kamāl al-Dīn Iṣfahānī 2018-3 : 129
Kamālī, Ḥaydar ʿAlī 2018-3 : 132
Kamaniçe 2013-1 : 141
Kanafānī, Ghassān 2018-1 : 148
al-Kānimī 2018-3 : 133
Kano 2018-6 : 126
Karabakh, Nagorno 2018-6 : 128
al-Karābīsī, Aḥmad 2019-2 : 95
Karachay-Cherkessia 2019-4 : 134
Karachi 2019-1 : 111
Karaferye (Veroia) 2019-1 : 115
Karaim (language) 2017-5 : 144
Karak 2018-5 : 138
Karakol Cemiyeti 2018-4 : 143
Karamani Mehmed Paşa 2018-1 : 150
Karaosmanoğlu, Yakup Kadri 2018-4 : 143
Karaosmanoğulları 2018-4 : 145
Kārkhāna 2018-5 : 143
al-Karkhī, Maʿrūf 2019-3 : 73
Karlowitz (Karlofça) 2018-5 : 146
Kars, Treaty of 2018-2 : 144
Kartid dynasty 2017-5 : 146
Kartini, Raden Ajeng 2018-2 : 145
Kartosuwiryo, Sekarmaji Marjan 2018-4 : 147
Kasravī, Aḥmad 2018-5 : 149
Kasrāyī, Siyāvash 2018-6 : 131
Katanov Nikolay 2018-6 : 133
al-Kātibī al-Qazwīnī 2019-1 : 117
Katsina 2019-1 : 122
Kauman 2018-4 : 148
Kawāhla 2018-3 : 134
Kawār 2018-2 : 147
Kay Kāʾūs b. Iskandar 2018-2 : 148
Kayalpatnam 2018-3 : 135
al-Kayyāl 2018-3 : 143
Kazakhstan 2018-6 : 133
Kedhiri, Babad 2013-1 : 142
Kemal Ümmi 2019-2 : 97
Kemankeş Ali Paşa 2014-4 : 143
al-Khabbāz, Yaḥyā 2019-3 : 75
Khālid b. Ṣafwān 2019-2 : 98
Khalwatiyya in Indonesia 2019-3 : 76
Khambāyat 2019-3 : 78
Khandesh 2019-3 : 79
Khārṣīnī 2019-2 : 100
al-Khaṣībī, Abū ʿAbbās 2016-3 : 144
al-Khaṣībī, Abū ʿAbdallāh 2016-5 : 152
Khatʾak 2019-2 : 101
Khāyrbak 2018-6 : 142
Khilāfat movement 2019-2 : 103
Khiṭaṭ 2019-3 : 81
Khoqand 2018-6 : 143
al-Khuldī, Jaʿfar 2019-3 : 84
al-Khūnajī, Afḍal al-Dīn 2010-2 : 149
Khvāja-yi Jahān 2019-3 : 87
Khvājū Kirmānī 2019-1 : 124
Khwushḥāl Khān Khatʾak 2019-2 : 105
Kıbrıslı Mehmed Emin Paşa 2019-1 : 128
Kılıç Ali Paşa 2014-4 : 145
Kilwa 2019-2 : 108
Kimeks 2019-3 : 88
Kipchak 2019-3 : 89
al-Kirmānī, Ḥamīd al-Dīn 2017-1 : 131
Kisve bahası 2019-4 : 135
Kizimkazi 2019-2 : 113
Kızlar Ağası 2019-2 : 114
Koca Mustafa Paşa 2019-3 : 93
Kochi 2019-2 : 116
Kong 2019-3 : 94
Köprülü, Mehmed Fuad 2019-1 : 129
Korkud (şehzade) 2019-1 : 131
Köse Dağı, battle of 2019-2 : 122
Kösem Sultan 2019-3 : 96
Kosovo Polje, First Battle of 2019-2 : 124
Kozhikode 2019-1 : 132
Kritoboulos of Imbros 2019-2 : 125
Kubrā, Najm al-Dīn 2019-3 : 97
Kubraviyya 2019-3 : 101
Küçük Hüseyin Paşa 2017-5 : 149
Küçük Kaynarca 2019-3 : 108

Kūh-i Nūr 2018-4 : 149
Kuloğlu 2018-4 : 151
Kumasi 2019-1 : 138
Kumyks 2019-4 : 137
Laks 2019-4 : 141
Lala Mustafa Paşa 2018-6 : 148
Lala Şahin Paşa 2019-3 : 110
al-Lamkī Aḥmad 2015-4 : 150
Lawu, Sunan 2018-6 : 149
Laz 2018-3 : 145
Lembaga Dakwah Islam Indonesia 2019-4 : 143
Lembaga Kajian Islam dan Sosial 2018-6 : 150
Leo Africanus 2019-3 : 111
Leran 2019-2 : 127
Levant Company 2019-1 : 140
Lexicography, Persian 2019-3 : 114
Lidj Iyasu 2019-3 : 120
Liyāqat ʿAlī Khān 2019-2 : 127
Lū<u>dh</u>iāńā 2019-2 : 131
Luqmānjī b. Ḥabīballāh 2019-2 : 132
Luṭfallāh, Muḥammad 2019-2 : 134
Lütfi Paşa 2019-3 : 122
Maʿbad b. ʿAbdallāh al-Juhanī 2019-3 : 124
Madagascar 2019-3 : 125
Madanī, Ḥusayn Aḥmad 2019-1 : 143
Madrasa in South Asia 2019-3 : 131
Madura 2019-2 : 136
Madurai 2019-3 : 138
Maḥbūb b. al-Raḥīl, Abū Sufyān 2019-1 : 145
Maḥfūẓ, Najīb 2008-2 : 164
Maḥmūd, ʿAbd al-Ḥalīm 2014-4 : 148
Maḥmūd Gāvān 2015-3 : 142
al-Majdhūb, ʿAbd al-Raḥmān 2014-2 : 146
al-Mājishūn 2009-2 : 151
Makhdūm-i Aʿẓam, Aḥmad 2012-1 : 150
Makhlūf, Muḥammad Ḥasanayn 2013-3 : 130
Malay and other languages of insular Southeast Asia 2019-1 : 147
al-Malībārī, Zayn al-Dīn 2019-3 : 146
al-Mālikī, Abū Bakr 2017-5 : 152
Mangkunagara I 2019-4 : 145
al-Mannūbiyya, ʿĀʾisha 2013-4 : 153
Mardāvīj b. Ziyār 2018-6 : 152
Maşizade Fikri Çelebi 2014-3 : 151
Masʿūd-i Saʿd-i Salmān 2011-2 : 152
Maʿṣūm ʿAlī Shāh Dakanī 2019-2 : 138
Mataram 2019-4 : 146
Megiser, Hieronymus 2017-2 : 151
Mehdizadə (Abbas Səhhət) 2015-2 : 152
Mehmed Esad, Sahaflar Şeyhizade 2016-2 : 153
Mezzomorto Hüseyin Paşa 2017-1 : 136
Mīrak al-Bukhārī 2018-2 : 153
Muḥammad al-Wālī 2019-4 : 147
al-Munajjim, Banū 2019-3 : 148
al-Murādī, Muḥammad Khalīl 2015-3 : 147
Mushfiq-i Kāẓimī, Murtaḍā 2019-2 : 141
Muways b. ʿImrān 2016-1 : 152
Muzakkar, Abdul Kahar 2018-2 : 154
al-Naḥḥās, Abū Jaʿfar 2019-4 : 149
Naon, Avram 2013-4 : 155
Niẓām Shāhīs 2017-3 : 146
Novel, Arabic 2014-1 : 152
Oromo 2014-2 : 148
Paşa 2014-2 : 151
Persian grammar 2018-3 : 148
Pir Sultan Abdal 2013-2 : 135
Reşid Rahmeti Arat 2016-3 : 146
Ṣabrī, Ismāʿīl 2019-4 : 151
al-Ṣaffār al-Bukhārī 2012-2 : 144
al-Samarqandī, Abū Ṭāhir 2013-2 : 137
Sarāy Malik Khānum 2013-2 : 139
Sayyid Baraka 2017-1 : 138
Sayyid Sulṭān 2014-3 : 153
Shaqīq al-Balkhī 2016-2 : 155
Shawqī, Aḥmad 2015-3 : 150
Sri Lanka 2015-1 : 148
Sub-Saharan African literature, ʿAjamī 2012-2 : 145
Suhrāb 2019-1 : 152
Sulṭān Ḥusayn Bāyqarā 2017-1 : 143
Sylhet Nagari 2015-1 : 152
Ṭalḥa b. ʿUbaydallāh 2014-4 : 150
Tamīm b. al-Muʿizz 2012-4 : 116
Tayyarzade Ata Bey 2015-4 : 151
al-Thamīnī, ʿAbd al-ʿAzīz 2010-1 : 194
Tokgöz, Aḥmed İḥsān 2013-1 : 144
Tūrsūn-zāda, Mīrzā 2018-6 : 155
Uluboy, Abdülbaki Fevzi 2016-3 : 149
United Kingdom, Muslims in the 2017-1 : 146
Vasi Alisi 2016-3 : 151
Wahab Chasbullah 2017-5 : 155
Yusuf Amiri 2016-4 : 144
Zarrūq, Aḥmad 2013-3 : 132
Zuhr, Banū 2019-2 : 145

Printed in the United States
By Bookmasters